THINKING GOVERNMENT

to understand. Chapter 1 therefore offers a basic introduction to Canadian government: the paradox of public perception it faces; its scope and presence in the life of this country's citizens; and the range of issues, policies, programs, and problems that governments, public services, and public sector management must daily confront.

Regardless of its complexity, however, the role of the state has always been central to political debate in this country, and that debate continues to divide public opinion. Chapter 2 probes the various ideological positions that have had, and are having, a profound impact on the practical life of governments and their relationship to Canadians. While conservative, social democratic, and liberal approaches to politics and the role of the state have all been significant to the development of Canadian public sector management, the most influential stream of thought has been liberalism, the vision of the broad political centre. Most governments in this country, and especially those in Ottawa, have taken a moderate approach to socio-economic policy, attempting to balance fiscal prudence and concern for economic growth and stability with progressive policies on social welfare, human rights, regional and cultural development, and the environment. This text explores the ways in which federal governments have sought a liberal and pluralistic approach to public policy and administration through practical reasoning, adaptation, and response based on these principles; that is, how governments have developed the ability to synthesize practical knowledge with a theoretical understanding of how the world works and how governments should respond to the needs of citizens.

While Canadian governments have come and gone over the past half-century, they have tended to adopt a similar style of governance. We examine the evolution of this style and the tensions it attracts in a period of competing demands for a smaller, less costly government that provides greater services. The push–pull between economical and effective government is accentuated by rival demands for fiscal prudence, greater national security against international terrorism, and enhanced social and environmental programming.

As views of the state's role have waxed and waned, however, one core truth remains: the state will always have a major role to play in the lives of Canadians. Public administration and public sector management will therefore continue to be important subjects of study for those wishing to know how this country is governed, why government power is exercised in certain ways and for whose benefit, and how the exercise of such power can be improved.

Chapters 3 and 4 offer a close view of the keystone institutions of the federal government and an assessment of the power relations within it. Prime ministerial power, cabinet decision making, and ministerial responsibility are crucial topics here, as well as the complex relationship between elected politicians and unelected public servants. Chapter 4 looks particularly at the current nature of the federal cabinet and the increasing concentration of political and administrative power in the hands of the prime minister and his or her closest associates. While analysis of the federal level of government takes centre stage, much of the understanding gained in these chapters relates to provincial governments and their inner workings as well.

Chapter 5 introduces public sector management theory and summarizes ways of thinking about country's economy has grown significantly, which has afforded hundreds of billions of dollars in tax cuts to individuals and corporations since the late 1990s.

Over the past decade and a half, through Liberal and Conservative and now again Liberal governments, we have also lived through periods of major tax cutting. The federal government now has substantially less revenue to spend on social and economic programs such as a national day care system or pharmacare program. Is this desirable? Do such tax cuts strengthen the economy by putting more money in the hands of Canadians to spend according to their own wishes, not those of bureaucrats? Should the role of government in this society in fact be reduced further? Should we perhaps look more to the private sector for solutions to health care, environmental protection, national infrastructure, and economic development?

Or do we need the opposite—a stronger state presence to address these and other social and economic challenges? But if the state is to address these matters, are Canadians ready and willing to have their taxes raised to pay for increased public services? And is the public sector capable of playing a progressive role in our society? Is it accountable and professional in its behaviour, able to establish public policy goals and achieve them through the efforts of talented and well-trained staff? Does the federal government in particular possess the leadership and managerial skills to administer national social and economic programs economically, efficiently, and effectively, providing citizens with value for money?

Simply put, can our system of public sector management be trusted to achieve the goals that Canadians might want to set for it? Or do we need

and want a less obtrusive government, a smaller state presence in modern Canadian life?

DEFINING THE INQUIRY

The questions just posed are the starting point of this review and investigation of Canadian government (primarily the federal government and its institutions), public administration, and public sector management, and they will be returned to many times throughout the work. But first we need to define our terms. Just what are public administration and public sector management? While the two terms are often used synonymously, there is an important distinction. **Public administration** is the broader concept, encompassing the study and oversight of all structures, institutions, policies, and programs of the state. **Public sector management**, as its name suggests, refers to how and why policies get formed, how they are turned into programs, and how those programs are implemented and evaluated. The latter concept thus focuses attention on the managerial operations of governments and their public servants, including the management of financial and human resources, while the former addresses the broad nature and structure of government. Throughout the text, key terms such as these are highlighted in bold with definitions provided in the glossary. Relevant websites are also listed at the end of each chapter, and these tools will help us to define our inquiry.

On a conceptual level, this analysis of the nature and working of the Canadian state rests on certain assumptions. I believe that Canadians perceive the state as important, yet so complex that its operational dynamics are difficult for most citizens came to be seen as the one man who could oust Harper, and he rode that wave to victory on October 19, 2015.

And what now? Will Canadians get a better government? One that is more open and responsive to Canadians' wants and needs? Will the Trudeau government be more accountable? Will it be smarter? In the years leading up to the next election in 2019 will we see a stronger economy and better environmental policies? More jobs? Economic diversification? Better health care and educational funding? Greater action on reducing social inequality while addressing the many problems still faced by Indigenous Canadians, recent immigrants, and women? Will Canadian foreign policy be stronger and more effective, or not? The Trudeau government came into office with high expectations. But such expectations often plant the seeds of bitter disappointment, of hopes unfulfilled.

THE FUNDAMENTALS

This short review of recent political issues and opinions illustrates a basic truth: Canadian political debate tends to revolve around the role and function of government. And as recent years have shown, this discussion can get emotional.

Despite modern consensus that governments will respect and nurture a mixed economy in which the private sector takes the lead in promoting growth, employment, and capital generation, the public sector is nevertheless accorded a strong role in social welfare and regulation of the private sector to ensure the maintenance of health and safety standards, labour and human rights, and environmental protection. The public sector also

engages in regional and economic development, sometimes through Crown corporations, and supports Canadian culture and identity by such means as the programming of the CBC, the broadcast regulations of the Canadian Radio-television and Telecommunications Commission (CRTC), and the work of the Commissioner of Official Languages.

But has this consensus been weakening in recent decades? Have we been witnessing a shift in federal politics from a liberal centre to a newly constructed conservative one? Did the Harper years truly change the way politics and government work in this country? Does the state, and especially for our purposes the federal government, still play a significant role in the life of this country? And should it? Beginning with the Mulroney government's privatization initiatives of the 1980s and the deficit cutting of the Chrétien government in the mid-1990s, the operational impact of the federal government has been steadily declining. For example, no new major federal social program has been launched in this country since the introduction of medicare through the Canada Health Act in the mid-1960s. The last social policy initiative of the federal and provincial governments on that scale was the creation of the Charter of Rights and Freedoms, which became law in 1982. Both these undertakings, now seen as cornerstones of the modern Canadian social welfare state, are decades old. And since the late 1980s, so-called conventional wisdom has suggested that we can no longer afford significant new social programs such as a national public child care system, the addition of pharmacare to the Canada Health Act, or publicly funded postsecondary institutions that eliminate tuition costs to students. But this government MPs were no longer free to speak their own minds. And many journalists found it increasingly difficult to get interviews with government ministers and backbench MPs. As the *Globe and Mail*'s Jeffrey Simpson repeatedly argued, all government communications seemed to flow through and be controlled by the Prime Minister's Office.

By the later years of his reign, critics were writing of Stephen Harper in increasingly bitter and despairing tones. Lawrence Martin complained of his increasingly despotic and Machiavellian form of leadership that was quickly turning Canada into "Harperland" (Martin 2010), while biographer Michael Harris referred to the prime minister as a "Party of One" (Harris 2014). And in 2015, in the months leading up to the fall election, Bob Rae, former NDP premier of Ontario and former interim leader of the federal Liberal Party, wrote of Stephen Harper's leadership style and substance as resulting in Canadians "now living in a democracy with dictatorial tendencies, and Canadians should not see their democratic institutions diluted and muzzled because of political timidity. Are Canadians ready to make a change?" (Rae 2015, 110).

All these criticisms were roundly rejected by the prime minister and his supporters as the ill-informed complaints of losers who were frustrated by the Conservatives' hold on power and ability to exercise the machinery of government far more efficiently and effectively than incompetent and corrupt Liberal administrations. Defenders of Stephen Harper's leadership style simply said that he displayed firm direction based upon a rock-solid moral compass, not unlike Winston Churchill or Ronald Reagan, and that most Canadians admired

his convictions and his ability to get things done. John Ibbitson, a sympathetic biographer, stressed in 2015 that Stephen Harper had fundamentally transformed Canada for the better. Core conservative values had become Canadian values. Tax rates had been reduced, likely permanently, the size and role of the federal government had been curtailed, the leading role of the private sector in generating economic growth had been reaffirmed, and Canadian diplomacy now resonated with moral clarity rooted to principle rather than vague "feel-good" sentimentality. The changes wrought by the Harper government had recast the nature of Canadian politics and government (Ibbitson 2015).

To the complaints that he was centralizing power in the hands of the Prime Minister's Office, more academic Conservative commentators claimed that prime ministers are always the key leaders of their governments and that such centralization of prime ministerial power had been a phenomenon in Canadian public sector management since the days of Pierre Trudeau. The Conservative majority win in the spring election of 2011 demonstrated that most of the electorate did not have deep qualms about the issue.

But times change. By the fall of 2015 a clear majority of Canadians were tired of the Harper government. While many continued to express support for free trade and lower taxes on the middle class, more and more Canadians were questioning Conservative policies on everything from environmental protection and global warming, to the wars in Iraq and Syria, to calling a national inquiry into missing and murdered Indigenous women. And, most palpably, a clear majority of Canadians were sick and tired of Stephen Harper's cold and divisive leadership style. Justin Trudeau could not win. He won minority governments in 2006 and 2008 and then won his first and only majority government in the election of 2011. It was following this election defeat that the Liberal Party opted for Justin Trudeau, the son of former Prime Minister Pierre Trudeau, as their new leader and would-be saviour.

While Conservatives hailed Stephen Harper as a great prime minister with towering political knowledge and tactical skill, his opponents damned him as narrow-minded and ideologically driven, excessively partisan and mean-spirited, a domineering and controlling leader with a limited vision for Canada and out of touch with broader social undercurrents. "I don't get into that second guessing of myself publicly," he once remarked, but some thought he *should* do a little more self-assessment. Those on the left disliked almost everything about Harper's government but were often divided on how far to push their opposition. Critics noted that cuts to the GST and corporate tax rates, by reducing the funding flowing to the federal government, also limited the social and economic policies it could promote.

Liberals criticized the Harper government for failing to provide a national, publicly funded system of child care and adequate funding for the Canadian Broadcasting Corporation (CBC). New Democrats attacked it for excessive spending on the military at the expense of social programs, for attacking unions and public sector employees, for bringing Canada deeper into the conflict in Afghanistan, and for abjectly supporting the US War on Terror with its concomitant problems of human rights abuses at home and abroad. Bloc Québécois antagonists challenged the Harper government on its failure to promote the Quebec economy, protect that province's forestry and agricultural sectors from American competition, or advance Québécois culture. And all the opposition parties found the Conservative government sorely lacking in its environmental policies, especially its position on global climate change. They stressed that Stephen Harper was a climate change denier prior to his entry into federal politics and that as prime minister he obstructed the development of an effective global treaty that would impose hard reductions on greenhouse gas emissions, help to develop carbon taxes, and promote green energy alternatives to carbon fuels.

Many critics also pointed at what they saw as an authoritarian and autocratic style of leadership. Liberals and New Democrats condemned the centralization of power in the Prime Minister's Office, whereby the prime minister and his key communications advisers tightly scripted all statements by ministers, their staffers, and senior public servants. Opposition party leaders complained that, far from opening up the process of government and making public sector management more transparent and accountable, the prime minister had stifled openness in government through his obsession with controlling the message and his obvious distaste for criticism. It came to be noted by journalists on the Ottawa beat that the Harper government came to view the opposition not as different political parties to be challenged in debate but as enemies to be ridiculed and denounced. Opposition MPs observed that public servants felt muzzled, that officers of parliament who challenged government policy assumptions risked punitive budget cutbacks, that the prime minister would even personally attack the Chief Justice of the Supreme Court of Canada, and that management. Taxes would be cut, starting with the goods and services tax (GST); needless regulation of the private sector would be eliminated; the role of the federal government in the economy would be trimmed; and free enterprise would be promoted. The Harper team also stressed that a new Conservative regime would promote a revised child care policy, eliminate the long-gun registry, refrain from legislating on abortion, and ensure a more harmonious relationship between the federal government and the provinces.

When you look at these campaign promises from 2006, the remarkable thing is not that Stephen Harper was able to orchestrate an electoral victory based on this platform, but that his government achieved most of these aims while operating from a minority position in parliament. A new Accountability Act was one of its first pieces of legislation. Tens of billions of dollars went to the military for new equipment and for waging wars in Afghanistan and eventually an air war over Libya in 2011 and over Iraq and Syria in 2014–15. The Criminal Code was amended to crack down on violent criminals and gang members, toughen rules for young offenders, and lengthen sentences served by convicts. Individual and corporate tax rates were reduced, and the GST was cut by two percentage points. The Harper government also introduced tax credits for private child care services. The Conservatives reduced regulation of the economy, especially in relation to environmental assessment plans, and promoted tighter economic links with the United States and free trade agreements with other countries, leading to tentative agreements with the European Union in 2014 and the Trans-Pacific Partnership in 2015. In international relations Canada became one of Israel's closest allies and supporters, sought closer trade relations with Asia (especially India and China), and advocated for global climate change agreements that would bind all countries equally while balancing greenhouse gas emission regulation against continued oil and natural gas development initiatives, such as the Alberta oil sands projects. Back on the domestic front, the Harper government abolished the long-gun registry and the long-form census, privatized the Canadian Wheat Board, stressed that most social policies were provincial responsibilities, recognized the Québécois as forming a nation within Canada, and kept its promise not to legislate on abortion.

This list of achievements is impressive and represents just some of the highlights from 2006 to 2015. Stephen Harper took pride in the fact that, on his watch, Canada weathered the 2008–09 global economic crisis, becoming the first state of the G8 to record positive growth and exit the recession in 2010. His government's Economic Action Plan of 2009–15 steered tens of billions of dollars into the Canadian economy to protect jobs, stimulate growth, and foster a stronger private sector. Between 2011 and 2015 his government also rebalanced the federal budget, at the expense of federal program cutbacks, service reductions, and the loss of some 19,000 public service jobs. And he managed these initiatives while showing firm, decisive leadership and crafty parliamentary tactics. He was truly the man at the centre, the leader of the country.

He also gave the opposition parties fits. He was able to humble previous Liberal leaders Stéphane Dion and Michael Ignatieff, forcing the Liberals on numerous occasions either to vote for Conservative bills or to refrain from voting on motions out of fear that they would precipitate an election they protection, of getting serious with climate change policy and reducing greenhouse gas emissions. He talked about the need to put more money into arts and culture and the CBC. And he affirmed that Canadian foreign policy had to change. It was time for Canada to be less bellicose on the world stage, to be more concerned about fighting the causes of conflicts rather than just simply bombing terrorists, and that humanitarian relief efforts, such as settling tens of thousands of Syrian refugees, had to become a major focus of Canada's role on the world stage.

But most importantly, Justin Trudeau simply told Canadians that he offered them a different style of leadership. Rather than the cold, authoritarian, hyper-partisan and divisive leadership of Stephen Harper, he promised them "sunny ways." In contrast to Harper's negativism and nasty closed-mindedness, Trudeau spoke in favour of openness, transparency, cooperation, and consultation. He would be a prime minister who would meet with and listen to Canadians, from premiers and mayors down to ordinary Canadians, and especially younger Canadians, those most susceptible to thinking that our system of government doesn't speak to or work for them. With such a message of hope and change, Justin Trudeau created a rising tide of Liberal red across the country on the evening of October 19, 2015. On that night, the Harper government and its decade in power came to a crashing end. The Conservatives were out; the New Democrats, the Greens, and the Bloc were down; and the Liberals were in. And as many Canadians noted over the following days and weeks, as the new Trudeau cabinet got down to governing, it felt like "we got our country back."

A PICTURE OF POLITICS

The 2015 election was, indeed, historic, highlighting that some elections do present Canadians with real alternatives and that electoral outcomes matter. It was also an emotional roller-coaster for Canadians of all political persuasions. For Conservatives and New Democrats, Greens and Blocistes, it brought bitter disappointment and some degree of anger; for Liberals it meant joy and vindication. And for many Canadians of a centre-left disposition, it promised relief from a tumultuous decade of Conservative rule, a decade marked by deep ideological debate regarding the nature of public policies, the role of the state in this society, and the type of leadership that Canadians need and deserve. To fully appreciate the magnitude of the change that occurred on election night 2015, you need to remember what the previous decade was like in the political life of Canada.

In the election that first brought them to power, Harper and his party promised that a new government would mean a new future for Canada. The scandals and corruption of the old Liberal administrations of Jean Chrétien and Paul Martin would be swept away, and the new government would pledge itself to accountability, transparency, and openness in its operations. New and decisive leadership would put an end to the years of dithering and incompetent public policy making. The Conservatives assured Canadians that the military would be strengthened; that the country would be a firm ally of the United States, especially in its War on Terror and the conflict in Afghanistan; and that the new government would get tough on crime. And Stephen Harper repeatedly committed a Conservative government to sound economic

Introduction

"My friends," said a beaming Justin Trudeau to the Canadian people on the evening of October 19, 2015, election night in Canada, "we beat fear with hope. We beat cynicism with hard work. We beat negative, divisive politics with a positive vision that brings Canadians together. Most of all, we defeated the idea that Canadians should be satisfied with less…. In Canada, better is always possible."

The 2015 federal election was historic. It pitted a variety of opposition parties against the governing Conservatives led by Prime Minister Stephen Harper, a man and a leader who had utterly dominated Canadian politics since he first came to power in 2006. The election very much became a referendum on the Harper legacy, and the Conservative base—32 per cent of the electorate—remained loyal to their leader and his vision of a Canada marked by low taxes, business-friendly economic policies, sensible environmental rules and regulations that do not harm Canada's role as an energy superpower, a small state that does not threaten the private sector, laws reflecting Canadians' desires to get tough on crime, and a principled foreign policy rooted to the muscular defence of our allies and opposition to our enemies. But after almost ten years in power, most Canadians were ready, more than ready, for a change.

The New Democrats, led by Thomas Mulcair, had served as the Official Opposition since 2011, and with strong public opinion polls leading into the election campaign, they were hoping to form the first-ever NDP federal government in Canadian history. To bolster their credibility as a government-in-waiting, the New Democrats promised that their traditionally progressive social and environmental policies would be married to economic policies of fiscal prudence, with the NDP assuring Canadians that a New Democratic government would always run balanced budgets. Meanwhile, both the Greens under Elizabeth May and the Bloc Québécois headed by Gilles Duceppe offered their respective and earnest approaches to sustainable environmental and socio-economic development and Quebec's special place in the country. But it was the Liberals under Justin Trudeau, running his first campaign as a party leader, who stole the show. With polls consistently showing that some 70 per cent of Canadians were opposed to Stephen Harper's leadership of the country, the question became which of the opposition parties might Canadians coalesce around as a viable alternative to the Harper Conservatives.

Day after day, Trudeau promised Canadians what many of them wanted to hear: that a Liberal government would cut taxes on the middle class while increasing them on the very rich; that a Liberal government would kick-start a sluggish national economy and generate jobs by investing in national infrastructure spending; and that to do so, a Liberal federal government would not be afraid to run modest deficits for three years before rebalancing the federal budget by 2019, just in time for the next general election. Trudeau also spoke in favour of stronger environmental

We cannot work or eat or drink; we cannot buy or sell or own anything; we cannot go to a ball game or a hockey game or watch TV without feeling the effects of government. We cannot marry or educate our children, cannot be sick, born or buried without the hand of government somewhere intervening. Government gives us railways, roads and airlines; sets the conditions that affect farms and industries; manages or mismanages the life and growth of the cities. Government is held responsible for social problems, and for pollution and sick environments. Government is our creature. We make it, we are ultimately responsible for it, and, taking the broad view, in Canada we have considerable reason to be proud of it. Pride, however, like patriotism, can never be a static thing; there are always new problems posing new challenges. The closer we are to government, and the more we know about it, the more we can do to help meet these challenges.

–Senator Eugene Forsey, *How Canadians Govern Themselves*, 1981, p. 1

PEMS	policy and expenditure management system
PM	prime minister
PMO	Prime Minister's Office
P&P	Priorities and Planning Committee
PPBS	planning-programming-budgeting system
PSC	Public Service Commission of Canada
PSIC	Public Service Integrity Commission
PSLRA	Public Service Labour Relations Act
PSLRB	Public Service Labour Relations Board
PSMA	Public Service Modernization Act
PSSRA	Public Service Staff Relations Act
RCMP	Royal Canadian Mounted Police
TB	Treasury Board of Canada
TBS	Treasury Board of Canada Secretariat
ZBB	zero-based budgeting system

Abbreviations

ACOA	Atlantic Canada Opportunities Agency
ADM	assistant/associate deputy minister
AECL	Atomic Energy of Canada Limited
BDBC	Business Development Bank of Canada
CBC	Canadian Broadcasting Corporation
CCF	Co-operative Commonwealth Federation
CCRA	Canada Customs and Revenue Agency
CHRO	(Office of the) Chief Human Resources Officer
CHST	Canada Health and Social Transfer
CRTC	Canadian Radio-television and Telecommunications Commission
CSIS	Canadian Security Intelligence Service
CSPS	Canada School of Public Service
DM	Deputy Minister
EMIS	expenditure management information system
FIRA	Foreign Investment Review Agency
FPRO	Federal–Provincial Relations Office
GST	goods and services tax
HRDC	Human Resources Development Canada
MBO	management by objectives
MFR	managing for results
MP	member of parliament
NAFTA	North American Free Trade Agreement
NCR	National Capital Region
NDP	New Democratic Party
NEB	National Energy Board
NEP	National Energy Policy
NFB	National Film Board
NPM	new public management
OPMS	operational performance measurement system
PAC	Public Accounts Committee
PBO	parliamentary budget officer
PCO	Privy Council Office

Acknowledgements

This fourth edition of *Thinking Government* is the result of years of thinking, writing, and teaching about public administration in Canada. Its genesis dates back over three decades, and countless students here at Cape Breton University have been the inspiration behind this book. My students over the years have been a very receptive audience and have helped to sharpen my thinking and teaching with respect to Canadian government and its myriad power relations. I wrote this book with students in mind. I have tried to produce a text that provides them with a solid foundation in Canadian public administration while also being readable, accessible, and interesting. I believe it is important for all Canadians to be knowledgeable about the nature and working of government and the exercise of power in this society. Such knowledge is vital to our democratic purpose, and I hope this work is a modest means to that end. Of course, it is the students now reading this book who can best judge whether or not I have succeeded.

I must also express my gratitude to two former Cape Breton University students who are now friends and colleagues. Alana Lawrence, a CBU MBA graduate, brought her expertise to bear in revising and updating the *Thinking Government* website, while also making it more engaging for students. Michelle Lahey, now a McGill Law School graduate, revised the special chapter on Canadian Administrative Law found on this website. Both of these young women are the epitome of the New Professional.

No book can exist without a publisher, and the leadership and staff at University of Toronto Press have been wonderful as they have supported the coming into being of this fourth edition. A big thank you is extended to Michael Harrison and Mark Thompson for their vision and encouragement. And a number of people at UTP have been pivotal in seeing this edition come together, notably Mat Buntin, Beate Schwirtlich, Ashley Rayner, Julia Cadney, Anna Del Col, and freelancers Eileen Eckert, Em Dash Design, proofreader Leanne Rancourt, and indexer François Trahan. Without their support this book would not exist.

I also thank the reviewers who read the earlier editions and whose constructive criticisms have made this a better book.

Finally, I embrace my dearest wife, Rosalie, who was always there to bounce ideas around, to think outside the box, and to insist that theory had to meet practice. When the task became a chore, Rosalie was always there to inspire, encourage, and enthuse. She is my Athena.

Contents

Thinking Government Website

This book has an associated website of additional information relevant to the issues addressed here, to help you deepen your knowledge of Canadian public administration. The website contains materials that correspond to the chapters of this book. For each chapter, you will find features such as

- a summary
- additional case studies and white papers not included in the text and extensions of text topics to provide more in-depth coverage or examples
- study questions
- a quiz
- downloadable extras: PDF files of tables and figures
- key terms
- web links

The website also provides you with a special bonus chapter on Canadian administrative law. This introduces the basic concepts of administrative law, the roles of quasi-judicial administrative tribunals, their relationship with the courts, and their relation to citizens. This is a side of government and government–citizen relations that few of us see or think about, but it is nonetheless important.

www.thinkinggovernment.com

Library and Archives Canada Cataloguing in Publication

Johnson, David, 1957–, author
    Thinking government : public administration and politics in Canada / David Johnson.—Fourth edition.

Title of second edition: Thinking government : public sector management in Canada, c2006.
Includes bibliographical references and index.
Issued in print and electronic formats.
ISBN 978-1-4426-3521-0 (paperback).—ISBN 978-1-4426-3522-7 (hardback).—ISBN 978-1-4426-3523-4 (html). —ISBN 978-1-4426-3524-1 (pdf)

    1. Public administration—Canada—Textbooks. 2. Canada—Politics and government—Textbooks. I. Johnson, David, 1957– . Thinking government II. Title.

JL108.J64 2016   351.71   C2016-903383-X
                                                        C2016-903384-8

We welcome comments and suggestions regarding any aspect of our publications—please feel free to contact us at news@utphighereducation.com or visit our Internet site at www.utppublishing.com.

North America
5201 Dufferin Street
North York, Ontario, Canada, M3H 5T8

2250 Military Road
Tonawanda, New York, USA, 14150
ORDERS PHONE: 1–800–565–9523
ORDERS FAX: 1–800–221–9985
orders e-mail: utpbooks@utpress.utoronto.ca

UK, Ireland, and continental Europe
NBN International
Estover Road, Plymouth, PL6 7PY, UK
ORDERS PHONE: 44 (0) 1752 202301
ORDERS FAX: 44 (0) 1752 202333
ORDERS E-MAIL: enquiries@nbninternational.com

Every effort has been made to contact copyright holders; in the event of an error or omission, please notify the publisher.

The University of Toronto Press acknowledges the financial support for its publishing activities of the Government of Canada through the Canada Book Fund.

Printed in the Canada.

THINKING
GOVERNMENT

PUBLIC ADMINISTRATION
AND POLITICS IN CANADA

DAVID JOHNSON

FOURTH EDITION

UNIVERSITY OF TORONTO PRESS

management, public sector organizational behaviour, and improving the quality of policy making and program delivery. This chapter devotes special attention to the distinguishing features of the public sector. It contrasts the long-standing ideals of rational management and decision making with the equally long-lasting notions of incrementalism, bounded rationalism, crisis management, and bureaucratic politics.

To understand power relationships and managerial thought, we need to make a close study of core aspects of public sector management. The managerial side of government is crucial to its effective functioning, yet it is precisely this feature of public administration that has been ignored in most previous studies and understood little by most Canadians. Chapter 5 therefore also analyzes the principal managerial components: financial management, human resources management, administrative law, service delivery, public sector ethics, accountability, and leadership. And again, although the main focus is federal, many of the organizational features, administrative dynamics, managerial issues, and basic power relations apply to provincial governments and their public services as well.

Chapter 6 narrows the focus to address the key issues of financial management: public sector budgeting; the nature of budget systems; deficit and debt control; fiscal restraint policy; and the choices that present themselves to governments as they struggle to enter today's world of balanced budgets, surplus revenues, and new policy and program options.

Chapter 7 then reviews the central issues in human resources policy: human resources management systems; the nature of patronage; the merit principle in hiring and promotion; the pros and cons of public service collective bargaining and public sector unions' right to strike; and the merits and demerits of affirmative action and employment equity policies.

Chapter 8 reviews contemporary public sector management reforms that are altering both the federal and provincial orders of government. I look at the concept of the reinvention of government, the theory of new public management, and the demonstrable impact that such initiatives have had on the practice of public administration. While these new approaches can be thought-provoking and influential as governments seek to "do more with less" in times of fiscal restraint, both their theoretical underpinnings and their practical usefulness have come in for severe criticism.

Although a fundamental transformation in the nature and role of government is both unlikely and undesirable, we have been witnessing a less dramatic yet significant reform, with much debate over the pluses and minuses. Governments are trying to deliver policies and programs to Canadians by more economical, efficient, effective, respectful, and accountable processes. Chapter 8 explores the nature of these actions and the policy and management directions that the federal government is carving out for itself. I devote specific attention to the issue of service delivery, a concern of growing importance to many government offices.

Chapter 9 studies the related concepts of accountability and public sector ethics. Accountability has always been a central concern of governments, public sector management, and indeed the public. Accountability is an amalgam of ministerial, legal, and social responsibility, as governments and their public services are called upon to respond effectively to all three of these duties. Crucial in this arena is the concept and practice of public sector ethics, which continue to have a vital role in effective government and public sector management. I stress the importance of ethics while highlighting the difficulties that governments have in putting codes of ethics into practice.

Finally, Chapter 10 assesses the future of public sector management, particularly with respect to the characteristics of both effective and failed leadership. One of the key arguments flowing through this work is that we can and should have the highest calibre of leadership within our governments. As students we need to study the nature and practice of government leadership, and as citizens we have a duty to insist upon it.

THE DUTIES OF THE STATE AND THE CITIZENRY

The paradox of perception versus reality regarding the state needs to be addressed on two fronts. The public requires a better understanding of the role, strengths, and limitations of public sector action. And governments—senior public service management in particular—must become better leaders within the state and within society. It isn't enough to provide effective and responsible administration of public services. Our leaders and managers ought to go beyond the normal routine of policy development and program implementation to become creative agents of governmental change and reform.

Canadian citizens still have very high expectations of their governments, but many feel apathy and cynicism over the way those expectations are met. Governments and public sector managers need to be more visionary and proactive if they are to combat those attitudes as they confront our current national challenges. They must also be more forthright and persuasive in defending the role of the state, even as that role is modified by the exigencies of an ever-changing socio-economic environment. The state will always be called upon to play a significant role in the life of this country; we need to ensure that the state leadership, and especially its permanent senior managerial ranks, are fully trained, capable, and knowledgeable.

And what about the job of citizens? Our officials undertake a complex and important mission on our behalf. We should appreciate this mission, understand the issues involved in the work of government, and develop good critical faculties to assess the merits and demerits of government leadership.

This book aims to be both informative and critical. We need to think about government, just as we need a government that can think and act strategically and effectively, responsibly, and responsively. All this is a civic duty.

REFERENCES AND SUGGESTED READINGS

Bricker, Darrell, and John Ibbitson. 2013. *The Big Shift: The Seismic Change in Canadian Politics, Business, and Culture and What It Means for Our Future*. Toronto: Harper Collins.

Finn, Ed. 2015. *Canada After Harper: His Ideology-Fuelled Attack on Canadian Society and Values, and How We Can Resist and Create the Country We Want*. Toronto: James Lorimer and Company.

Harris, Michael. 2014. *Party of One: Stephen Harper and Canada's Radical Makeover*. Toronto: Viking.

Ibbitson, John. 2015. *Stephen Harper*. Toronto: Signal/McClelland and Stewart.

Martin, Lawrence. 2010. *Harperland: The Politics of Control*. Toronto: Viking Canada.

Rae, Bob. 2015. *What's Happened to Politics?* Toronto: Simon and Schuster Canada.

CHAPTER 1

Thinking about Canadian Society and Government

What is the first part of politics? Education.

The second? Education.

And the third? Education.

–Jules Michelet, 1846

By the end of this chapter and having looked at its related web pages you'll be able to

- identify a paradox at the centre of how Canadians think about government and public service;
- explain the main differences between conservative and centre-left approaches to socio-economic policy;
- list and explain four uniquely Canadian policy areas that successive federal governments must confront; and
- identify the principal ideas of the new public management approach.

1 Thinking about Canadian Society and Government

The way most Canadians view their government, the **public service**, and **public sector management** is a puzzle—a paradox in that two contradictory positions are commonly held to be true.

On the one hand most Canadians, and probably many students who are beginning to read this book, have a jaundiced, even cynical attitude toward government. Governments tend to suffer from a terrible public image. They are seen as big, complex, unhelpful entities whose work is slow, inefficient, and wasteful. Government institutions—departments, agencies, offices—are likewise often viewed as confusing and bloated bureaucracies staffed by bureaucrats who are essentially overpaid, underworked incompetents, more concerned with self-interest than public interest. In this critical and bitter assessment, many Canadians think that their governments at best must be endured, like high taxes, and at worst constitute part of the problems facing the country rather than part of any solutions. The mention of concepts such as public administration and public service tends to be met with suspicious stares. Why would anyone be interested? Throughout the years of the Conservative government led by Prime Minister Stephen Harper, this way of thinking was simply accentuated, the basic policy message of his administration being that a smaller federal government was better, and that the leadership of the economy should be left to the private sector.

On the other hand most Canadians take great pride in this country and the quality of life to be found here. This feeling is periodically reinforced when Canada is ranked by the United Nations as having one of the highest living standards in the world. Most of us also take pride in the very favourable comparisons drawn between our quality of life and that of our southern neighbour. While we may have more in common with Americans than we usually like to admit, it's generally true that few of us actually want to live in the United States or believe that its living standard is superior to ours. When called upon to explain, we tend to point to government policies and programs and to public services as factors that elevate the quality of life in this country.

Most Canadians are proud of our health care system—a publicly administered and funded system guaranteeing a high calibre of medical care regardless of one's ability to pay. We are also proud of our education system, which provides all children with primary and secondary education administered through public schools financed jointly by provincial and federal governments. Our postsecondary system is also praised for offering all students who meet the admission standards a valuable, life-enhancing education, with the majority of the cost borne by the **state**. Many of us comment favourably on the state-established and -administered welfare system as well. The Canada Pension Plan and its Quebec counterpart offer retirement payments to all senior citizens, thereby providing them with a modicum of financial security. Federal employment insurance programs provide most Canadians facing unemployment with income support and job-related initiatives to help them return to the workforce. Provincial compensation systems guarantee to all workers hurt while on the job some recompense for income lost and injuries sustained. Provincial welfare systems ensure that all people who fall on hard times are guaranteed basic food, clothing, and shelter. To these policies and programs could be added others that Canadians often mention when reflecting on the building blocks of our quality of life: environmental regulation, human rights legislation, **multiculturalism** policy, health and safety laws, regional equalization, and support for arts and culture.

The intriguing point is that all these distinctive features of Canadian society are matters of public policy and public administration: they are the creations of governments and the subject of public sector management. And all these socially and economically important policies and programs have been developed, at different times in the past, in direct response to public pressure. Canadians have supported significant development and growth of the state to meet their needs and wants.

The irony is that while many Canadians hold high expectations of the role of the state in protecting and promoting their quality of life, these same citizens are critical of, and at times hostile to, the institutions of the state from which they receive these services. Why? Is government really so important to the lives of ordinary Canadians? If so, why the disconnection between perception and reality? Is it true that governments are inherently inefficient and ineffective? Are public servants essentially incompetent? Or are these viewpoints rooted in woeful ignorance of the nature of government, or wedded to ideological presupposition?

What is the true nature of the state in Canada?

This question poses an array of related ones. What do governments do? How have their roles evolved over the past century? What is the contemporary nature of government? How are public services organized, managed, and delivered? How do governments address such matters as financial management, human resources policy, administrative law, public service **ethics, accountability**, and leadership? Do Canadians receive the high quality of government services they expect? If not, what can be done to fix the problem? How have governments been coping with contemporary pressures for public sector reform, and what are we to make of recent changes in government operations? What choices do we have with respect to the role of the state? Can the nature and function of government be improved? Can the public sector be better managed?

In short, should we expect more of governments? And *can* we expect more?

THE STATE AND GOVERNANCE

We now confront important choices about the quality of our governance. The election of the Harper government in 2006 gave Canadians the most ideologically Conservative government in Canadian history. Stephen Harper came to power distrustful of the state, hostile to most of the socio-economic public policies established by a succession of both Liberal and Progressive Conservative federal governments since World War II, and wishing to see a dramatic reduction in the size and role of the federal government in the lives of ordinary Canadians. Over the following decade the Harper administration reconfigured the shape and tone of the federal government. It became smaller, less activist in the field of economic management, and less interested in concerns respecting social inequality, social justice, and fairness. As Prime Minister Harper said on more than one occasion, we should not "commit sociology" in looking at the root causes of problems in society. Rather, his government became much more hardline, focused on cutting taxes, cutting regulations on business, promoting the oil and gas industry, resisting national and international policies aimed at reducing greenhouse gas emissions, getting tough on crime, and being more concerned about enhancing the powers of police and security forces than guarding the rights and liberties enshrined in the Canadian Charter of Rights and Freedoms.

We also became more belligerent on the world stage. Gone were the days where Canada was known as an even-handed middle power and an international peacekeeper. Under the Harper government we became more a fighter than a peacemaker, fighting the Taliban in Afghanistan, fighting the Gaddafi regime in Libya, and fighting Jihadist terrorism and the Islamic State in Iraq and Syria. We also came to stand resolutely and without question behind the Israeli government of Benjamin Netanyahu in its dealings with the Palestinian question, just as we came to stand shoulder to shoulder with the Ukrainian government in its opposition to Vladimir Putin's Russia. While many Canadian supporters of Stephen Harper's brand of conservatism cheered on all these developments, many other Canadians of a centre-left perspective bemoaned these changes, wondering what was happening to the Canada they knew and loved.

The foregoing highlights why the federal election of 2015 was so significant. The Harper government was defeated and the Liberals returned to power after a bruising nine years in the opposition wilderness. And Justin Trudeau promised "sunny ways." He repeatedly assured Canadians that the state could and should play a leading role in the life of this country and that government action and intervention—with respect to economic growth, environmental protection and the reduction of greenhouse gas emissions; greater respect for the rights and interests of women, visible minorities, Indigenous Canadians, and the poor; and a more intelligent and multifaceted approach to foreign policy—was all possible and desirable. A Liberal government, he stressed, would be better and more responsive than the old Harper regime. It would be one marked by greater openness and accountability, with a desire to listen to the needs and concerns of all Canadians, not just those on the right-wing of the political spectrum, and it would be more representative of Canada in all its shades and hues of diversity. It would also be a government much more attuned to the broad centre of Canadian political and social life and its moderate, compassionate ideas.

The past two decades have revealed that Canadian politics are far from dull. We have witnessed great shifts in public opinion resulting in the election of different federal governments with sharply divided perspectives on how best to administer Canada, to run the economy, to manage social and environmental policies, and to project Canadian influence on the world stage. And all of these differences in policy approaches are contingent on how Canadians and their political leader view the role of the state in society.

It is actually quite easy to delineate the presence of the state in this society: it is all around us in a host of forms, institutions, and policies. Much more difficult—and much more likely to spark debate—is delineating the ways in which the Canadian state should apply the many powers it possesses. As we move from what is to what ought to be, the important issues of social action, managerial direction, and political vision emerge. As Richard Van Loon and Michael Whittington (1987, 1–18) have long argued, governing is all about making choices with regard to scarce resources in order to advance desired goals and to promote certain interests.

But what happens when goals are multiple and incompatible, when interests compete with one another? The result is acrimony and tension as citizens and their political parties and governments debate their future. These omnipresent debates, however, ultimately culminate in some form of government decision making. Policies and programs are chosen and designed to serve the interests deemed by the government of the day to be the most worthy of support. Such calculations will always be founded on a variety of professional, managerial, administrative, financial, ideological, and political considerations. But choices will be made. And through such choices there will always be policy and program winners and losers.

The complexity of governing Canada, especially from the perspective of the federal government, can be quickly appreciated through a review of just some of our major socio-economic, political, and cultural tensions. Governments confront issues that are important yet divisive, that generate not only great public interest and political controversy but also strong public expectation of some form of policy development or program enactment and administration.

SOCIO-ECONOMIC POLICY OPTIONS

THE CONSERVATIVE APPROACH

Consider first the differing expectations over the role of government with respect to **socio-economic policy**. Many conservatives criticize the idea that governments should play a large role in the everyday lives of citizens through social and economic planning. They lament the growth of the state since the end of World War II, the rise of government intervention in the economy through the means of **regulation**, the creation of **Crown corporations**, increased taxation, and the development of a wide variety of social welfare offerings to individuals as a matter of entitlement. These initiatives, it is argued, were not only poorly thought through but also put a great strain on the financial health of federal and provincial governments while promoting the growth of large, costly, and inefficient public sector bureaucracies that threaten the private sector principle of free enterprise (Campbell and Christian 1996, 48–61; Jackson and Jackson 2009, 397–402).

As the state grew, so the argument goes, governments became more and more removed from ordinary people and the "common sense" of market economics. Governments, often influenced or manipulated by the self-serving pleadings of special interest groups, seemed to believe that every perceived social or economic problem had a solution based on public sector intervention and the spending of public money. Of course, public servants themselves benefited from ideas that promoted the growth of the state, so they, too, became one of the forces pushing forward this **bureaucratization** of society. The result was a bloated public sector, runaway government **deficits** and debt, rising taxation, and the creation of an interventionist state that actually endangered the economic well-being of the country.

This view necessarily leads conservative critics to target the institutions and policies of governments themselves as the root of most of this country's problems over the past half-century and to focus accordingly on policy reforms. For those who believe that the growth of the state has been a problem, the solution is simple: cut government. We are all familiar with the basic policy prescriptions of this position: Crown corporations should be privatized, the economy should be deregulated, individual and corporate tax rates should be dramatically lowered, government bureaucracies should be substantially reduced, public sector deficit spending should be eliminated if not outlawed altogether, public debt should be paid down, public services should be "rationalized" (i.e., reduced), and free enterprise should be enthusiastically promoted. In short, governments should be given a much smaller role to play in the life of society, while the private sector should be encouraged to assume a leading position in providing the goods and services that people need and desire (Nelson 1995, 30–34; Johnston 1996, 103–4; Johnson 2005, 279–301).

Such conservative ideas have been very influential in this country over the past three decades, just as they have tended to dominate political and economic discourse and policy making throughout the Western world over this period. And in its decade of existence, the government of Stephen Harper engaged in some quite conservative policy making:

- Personal and corporate taxation rates were reduced.
- The goods and services tax (GST) was cut by two percentage points.
- Budgets became known for their sweeping omnibus bills, where hundreds of legislative changes were included with the budget, all designed to limit parliamentary oversight of such reforms.
- The policy-making role of the federal public service was reduced in favour of policy coming from the Prime Minister's Office and the Conservative Party; independent parliamentary watchdogs from the Parliamentary Budget Office, the Freedom of Information Commissioner, the Auditor General, and Elections Canada were all subject to partisan attack by the government for questioning government initiatives.
- Business regulation, including oversight of food production and rail safety, was reduced.
- Environmental assessment requirements were softened.
- The promotion of the oil and gas industry was made a national priority, as was the construction of pipelines to get its products to markets.
- Canada withdrew from the Kyoto Accord promoting the phased reduction of greenhouse gas emissions, and subsequently resisted newer and tougher measures to address climate change.
- The federal government rejected outright any form of carbon tax or any form of cap-and-trade system of emission credits as a threat to the health of the Canadian economy and a tax on ordinary Canadians.

- A national and public sector–led system of day care was rejected in favour of family tax credits.
- The Kelowna Accord, a national Indigenous socio-economic development initiative, was cancelled.
- Funding for the Canadian military was dramatically increased.
- Funding for social advocacy initiatives such as the Court Challenges Program of Canada and Status of Women Canada was reduced or cut altogether.
- The role of Crown corporations was questioned, and initiatives were taken to privatize some, such as the Canadian Wheat Board, Atomic Energy of Canada Limited (AECL), and Enterprise Cape Breton Corporation.
- Funding for the Canadian Broadcasting Corporation (CBC), Canada Post, and Via Rail was reduced.

THE LIBERAL AND SOCIAL DEMOCRATIC RESPONSE

These ideas of **government restraint** and a smaller, less active public service have not gone unchallenged. Liberal and social democratic criticism of reduced-state, free-enterprise approaches and support for progressive government leadership persist. Advocates of a continued or even enhanced state role in this society and its economy promote a wide range of arguments and alternatives. One criticism is that a curtailment of government necessarily means cutbacks to health, education, and social welfare, causing people in need of these services to suffer. Such cutbacks, it is argued, limit child care opportunities, harm the development of

First Nations, and weaken health care. Likewise, general policies of restraint mean fewer teachers in schools, fewer books in school libraries, fewer special and extracurricular programs, and indeed fewer schools. At the postsecondary level, the consequences of budget cuts are fewer professors and instructors; poorer, more rundown infrastructure; and, of course, ever-higher tuition fees. And for those concerned about welfare, government restraint policies simply result in fewer entitlements (welfare, employment insurance, worker compensation, pension benefits) payable to smaller numbers of claimants (Bell 2008; Anderson and Dyck 2016, 60–64).

Critics of restraint policies assert that, far from cutting such programs and others that address social and economic concerns, we should escalate their funding to meet growing needs, and that, if need be, taxes can and should be increased to provide the revenue for such initiatives. Those concerned with the rights of ethnic and racial minorities, mentally and physically disabled people, women, and others who have historically been marginalized by governments claim that state funding for human rights policies should be increased, with the expectation that federal and provincial human rights commissions would then be able to enforce and promote human rights law and policy more rigorously. Similarly, environmental advocates assert that existing environmental protection legislation should be more rigorously enforced, and that federal and provincial departments of environment and their regulatory agencies should be given greater powers and more funding to facilitate their work. To these critics, global climate change is real, and governments need to focus on it for environmental and

POLICY INSTRUMENTS

To address any issue, governments have at their disposal nine different policy instruments, ranging from benign neglect to substantial intervention. They will select one of the following levels of policy according to how serious they consider an issue to be and the degree to which the issue requires state attention.

1 **No action.** Leave the matter to the private sector.
2 **Symbolic state action.** Promote showpiece behaviour.
3 **Policy exhortation.** Use the power of persuasion.
4 **Spending via taxes.** Use the tax system to encourage desirable behaviour through tax credits, breaks, or incentives.
5 **Public spending.** Promote policy aims through programs directly funded by government.
6 **Regulation.** Promote policy aims by mandating and enforcing compliance with legally mandated regulatory frameworks.
7 **Taxation.** Promote policy aims by imposing tax burdens or penalties on those engaged in actions deemed luxurious, extravagant, unnecessary, or undesirable.
8 **Ownership.** Promote policy aims through direct state intervention, control, and ownership over particular fields of socio-economic activity.
9 **A state of emergency.** Assume full state control over the society and economy.

economic reasons. We need to save the environment, as well as the economy, from climate change. Green technologies, green energy, and green businesses are the way of the future, environmentalists stress, while industries reliant on the extraction and use of carbon fuels must and will be consigned to history. The sooner we begin to make the transition to a greener future through the development of non-carbon fuel sources, through greater energy efficiency, and with the institution of carbon taxes designed to encourage the promotion and use of green alternatives to carbon fuels, the quicker Canada will develop a sustainable economy for the twenty-first century. Likewise, promoters of labour reform stress that policy in this area needs to be improved, that the right to unionize and engage in free collective bargaining should be facilitated, that more public monies should be spent on federal and provincial labour relations and worker compensation boards, and that state enforcement of labour standards and occupational health and safety guarantees should be intensified (Ball et al. 2010, 67–72, 158–61).

A DIFFERENCE OF OPINION

Of course, conservative critics of increased state involvement in society contest all these propositions, asserting that such proposals would result, once again, in greater public spending, bigger bureaucracies, higher taxation, larger public deficits and debts, a weaker economy, and a more bothersome state. Advocates of smaller government and free enterprise propose that governments develop more effective ways to meet socio-economic needs by modelling their administration and management on proven and successful private sector approaches. Defenders of an ideologically progressive role for the state, on the other hand, contend that these ideas are predicated on a narrow, right-wing perspective, and that while the private sector may have a legitimate role to play in a modern, liberal democratic society, it should not be allowed to undermine and delegitimize the valuable function assumed by the public sector.

The complexities of socio-economic policy making were never more clearly observed than in the federal government's reaction to the global economic crisis that precipitated the recession of 2008–10. After initially claiming in a November 2008 update that the Canadian economy was sound and that the Conservative government would never support deficit spending, by February 2009 the Harper government had reversed course. It brought forward a budget designed to address the recession and stimulate the economy through an Economic Action Plan that launched infrastructure spending programs totalling $56 billion over two years. This program was paid for entirely through deficit spending, and the Conservatives now stressed that the federal government would be facing deficits until 2015. While Prime Minister Harper and his finance minister, Jim Flaherty, defended these actions as necessary to address a recession, Liberal and New Democratic critics were quick to point out the hypocrisy. They also noted that when Canada faced a major economic crisis brought on, in part, by questionable behaviour in the private sector in the United States, it was to governments that people turned, looking to

the public sector for help in alleviating the worst symptoms of the downturn and promoting long-term programs to ensure renewed growth and development. By 2015 the Conservative government had largely returned the federal government to a balanced budget through a combination of governmental spending restraint and increased tax revenues derived from a modestly growing economy. An emerging recession in that year, however, threw the government back into a deficit after it had already declared a budgetary surplus for 2015. At this time New Democrats and Liberals called for additional public spending on national infrastructure projects to help kick-start economic growth and create needed jobs, while the Harper government attacked these ideas, claiming that the last thing Canada needed was more government spending and higher deficits. In the fall election campaign of 2015 the federal Liberals affirmed that trying economic times called for the return to "modest" federal deficits, with this money being used to fund job-creating national infrastructure programs. Liberal plans for "modest" annual deficits in the $10 billion range, however, were blown away by a sharp decline in the international price of oil in the winter of 2015–16, with the first budget of the new Liberal government in 2016 forecasting a federal deficit of $30 billion.

All governments face sharp differences of opinion as they decide what courses of action, what policy and program options, are truly in the best interests of the people within their jurisdictions. They must govern complex societies and economies—replete with numerous and competing political parties, business interests, public interest groups, media voices, and concerned individuals, all of which will possess their own often entrenched and vocal expectations of right and wrong in public policy and management. And within this political environment, governments must often make hard choices in **public policy**, **program administration**, and public sector management. We will see in the next chapter that most Canadian governments, especially at the federal level, have taken a moderate, centrist approach to decision making, seeking to balance growth, stability, and governmental efficiency and economy with creative and relatively progressive policies on economic development, social and cultural issues, and environmental protection.

THE CANADIAN POLICY ENVIRONMENT

In hewing a path between competing ideologies, most governments simply reflect mainstream Canadian attitudes toward political moderation. Of course the devil is in the details, and so the debate continues over how successfully each government strikes that balance. The work of any Canadian government in broad matters of socio-economic policy development and program management is thus very complex, even before we consider the issues unique to our national government. Canadian federal governments face four ongoing challenges to public policy, public administration, and public sector management:

1 French–English relations and the issue of Quebec
2 Canadian regionalism, regional disparities, and regional policy
3 Canadian–American relations

4 Indigenous policy and relations with First Nations.

FRENCH-ENGLISH RELATIONS AND THE ISSUE OF QUEBEC

Constitutional Conundrums

How does a federal government serve the interests of the majority English-Canadian population while also promoting rival provincial interests, including those of Quebec? Quebec is distinct by virtue of the French influence on its history, demographics, culture, and politics. Roughly 80 per cent of the provincial population is French Canadian, and many of these people view themselves as Québécois, a linguistically, culturally, and ethnically distinctive nationality. Québécois do not see Quebec as a province *commes les autres* but as a nation within a nation, defined not only by its French characteristics but also by its politics of social and cultural survival in the face of English dominance both in Canada and throughout North America. Quebec, this viewpoint concludes, therefore needs and deserves special status in the form of state action and cultural protection. And most Québécois consider the provincial government best equipped to represent their aspirations and advance a Québécois policy agenda.

However, the federal government claims a role with respect to Quebec and the "French fact." Simply put, Quebec is part of the greater Canadian whole: the province sends 78 members to the federal parliament; the federal government is mandated to provide public policy and services for Quebec just as for any other province; and from the federal perspective, the French fact consists of more than Quebec, just as Quebec consists of more than the French fact since roughly 20 per cent of its population is either anglophone or **allophone**. Growing anxieties within Quebec over the future of French language and culture across the country and even the future constitutional status of the province have spurred the rise of separatist sentiment, and especially from the 1960s on, federal governments have devoted considerable time and effort to national unity.

The public policy efforts have been multifaceted and significant, though on either side of the issue are those who criticize not only the substance but the time, money, and procedural effort devoted to these initiatives at the expense of other priorities. Federal initiatives have extended from massive constitutional reform involving all the provincial governments to major new policies and programs, and even down to more mundane matters such as sponsoring sports and cultural events. The past five decades have witnessed a flurry of constitutional reform undertakings spearheaded by the federal government, but only one, in 1981, resulted in a major amendment of the constitution. The **Constitution Act, 1982** provides the federal and provincial governments with a domestic amending formula governing future constitutional change and establishes the **Charter of Rights and Freedoms** as the primary source of legal entitlements for everyone living in Canada.

In the 1990s, the Chrétien government stood back from proposing major constitutional amendments, preferring to address the Quebec issue through a so-called Plan A/Plan B approach to national unity (Archer et al. 1999, chap. 3; Gagnon 1999). Plan A calls for the federal government to provide sound social and economic policy throughout the country, with the aim of improving the quality of life for all people and thus undermining support for sovereignty in Quebec as Québécois come to realize they have more to gain by remaining a part of Canada than by separating from it. Plan B came on the heels of the excruciatingly close result of the 1995 Quebec referendum, when residents voted 49.4 per cent for provincial sovereignty and 50.6 per cent against. In light of that shock, Plan B calls upon the federal government to take a hard line with a separatist provincial government with respect to any future sovereignty referendum. As endorsed by a Supreme Court judgement in 1998, the approach stipulates that

- any such referendum must provide a clear question on separation;
- to be legitimate, any victory must be grounded in a clear majority and not a razor-thin margin; and
- the federal parliament will play a role in deciding whether the question is clear and the majority sufficient.

Finally, should these conditions be met, Plan B also stipulates that the federal government can and will enter into negotiations with a victorious separatist government but that all matters concerning a renewed relationship between Quebec and Canada will be subject to bargaining, including

- new international boundaries,
- the status of First Nations in Quebec,
- the possible partition of Quebec and retention within Canada of anglophone- and allophone-dominant regions, and

- all economic, financial, currency, and trade relations between a new Canada and a new Quebec.

The most recent major development on this constitutional front occurred in November 2006, when the government of Stephen Harper obtained parliamentary approval of a motion recognizing that "the Québécois form a nation within a united Canada." The wording was designed to recognize the sociological reality of the French fact within Canada while undermining Bloc Québécois criticism that the federal government and English Canada are incapable of embracing French Canada. To the Bloc, however, this recognition simply confirms claims that Quebec does constitute a nation and that at some point a majority of Québécois will want to see the province become a sovereign state. Both the Bloc Québécois and the Parti Québécois, moreover, continue to reject the logic of the federal government's Plan B, enshrined in the Clarity Act, which stipulates that a winning margin of victory in any future sovereignty referendum needs to reflect a clear majority of votes, not simply 50 per cent plus 1. Both these sovereigntist parties as well as the federal New Democratic Party support the idea that a simple majority in such a referendum, even if the margin of victory is just one vote, is enough for the sovereigntist side to declare victory, requiring the federal government to enter into negotiations with the government of Quebec respecting the establishment of a sovereign state of Quebec. This position of the federal NDP, while popular in Quebec, is very contentious in the rest of English Canada, with the federal Conservative and Liberal parties criticizing

the New Democrats for recklessly endangering Canadian national unity.

Linguistic and Cultural Policy

While such constitutional matters have been fundamentally important to the federal government and to the entire country, the federal relationship with Quebec extends far beyond them. The federal government has sought to provide good and effective governance of Quebec by recognizing through a variety of policy and administrative undertakings its obvious cultural distinctiveness and unique socio-economic needs (Dyck 2008, chap. 5). Foremost among these are the cultural and linguistic concerns of French Canadians throughout the country, which the federal government addressed through the Official Languages Act, 1969.

This Act establishes French and English as the official languages of Canada and mandates the federal government to support and promote them throughout the country through policies and programs of bilingualism and biculturalism. The government of Canada, as an institution, is officially bilingual, bearing a general duty to provide public services to any person, anywhere in the country, in the preferred official language. While both Liberal and Conservative federal governments have defended the policy as protecting the French language, it is hailed as being fair and even-handed in that it also specifically guards the interests of the English-Canadian and allophone minorities within the province of Quebec.

Through all its program activities, the federal government is keen to be, and to be seen to be, an active presence in the everyday life of the province. Those activities, after all, are the fundamental elements of Plan A and must be understood (and

THE CLARITY ACT

BACKGROUND

In 1995 Canadians witnessed a national near-death experience when the Quebec referendum on sovereignty resulted in a narrow 50.6 per cent to 49.4 per cent popular vote split in favour of Quebec remaining a part of Canada. Following this referendum the federal Liberal government of Jean Chrétien moved to clarify the rules regarding any such future vote. In 1998, in a reference to the Supreme Court of Canada respecting how Quebec could leave Canada, all nine judges affirmed that while Quebec does not have a constitutional right to unilaterally sever its relationship with the rest of the country, the rest of the country cannot keep Quebec in the federation against its will. If a majority of Quebeckers clearly wish to see their province/nation separate from Canada, then the federal and other provincial governments are obligated to negotiate the terms of separation with the government of Quebec.

THE DETAILS

While the Supreme Court said that Quebec has the right to leave Canada if it so wishes, the official expression of this interest to separate must be based on a "clear majority" in response to a "clear question." The judges themselves never defined just what a "clear majority" and a "clear question" would be, leaving these matters up to government leaders to decide, but they specifically said a mere majority of just one vote would be inadequate to trigger sovereignty renegotiations.

In 2000 the federal government passed the Clarity Act, with the following key provisions:

- That the federal House of Commons has the power to decide whether a proposed referendum question from the government of Quebec is clear.
- That any referendum question not solely referring to secession would be deemed "unclear."
- That the House of Commons would have the right, after a successful referendum vote to separate, to declare whether the margin of victory represented a clear majority of voters.
- That the House of Commons retained the right to override a referendum decision if it believed any of the provisions of the Clarity Act had been violated.

The basic logic of the Clarity Act is that a mere 50 per cent plus 1 of the vote is not sufficient for any future Parti Québécois government to declare victory in a future sovereignty referendum. Rather, a margin of victory significantly greater than 50 per cent plus 1 would be required to split up the country. But nowhere in the Clarity Act does the federal government list what a winning number would be. 55 per cent? 60 per cent? Two-thirds of the vote? Three-quarters? This lack of clarity in the Clarity Act has resulted in push-back from many in Quebec.

THE MAINSTREAM QUEBEC REACTION

Following the passage of the Clarity Act, the government of Quebec passed its own legislation, giving its National Assembly the sole right to determine any future sovereignty referendum question and whether such a referendum has been victorious. Even the Quebec provincial Liberal Party has endorsed this Act, affirming that it is up to the people of Quebec to determine their own constitutional future. This has also become the core position of the federal New Democratic Party. In 2005, in the Sherbrooke Declaration, the NDP affirmed that a simple majority of even a single vote in a sovereignty referendum would be sufficient to trigger constitutional negotiations between the government of Quebec and the federal and the other provincial governments.

WEIGHING THE CASE

Do you agree with the federal NDP and the other major parties in Quebec?

Is this a case of basic democracy where the majority should rule? But if so, are you prepared to see the onset of what would be very acrimonious and divisive negotiations harmful to Canadian unity and the national economy, just on the basis of the slimmest of votes?

If you disagree, if you believe the margin of victory in such a vote of such major consequences needs to be substantial in order to reopen the Canadian constitution, just what is the margin of victory the sovereignty side would need? What's the percentage? And is the federal government being disingenuous and Machiavellian in not providing a clear number in their Clarity Act?

will be understood by Quebec politicians) in light of the broader political and constitutional battle being waged by the federal government against the Québécois sovereignist movement (Gagnon 1999).

However well-intentioned Plan A might be to Canadian federalists, its implementation has been problematic, as the federal sponsorship scandal illustrated. Recognition of "the Québécois as a nation within a united Canada" also appears to have done little either to bolster federalist parties in Quebec or to weaken the popular appeal of the Bloc Québécois and its provincial counterpart, the Parti Québécois.

REGIONALISM, REGIONAL DISPARITIES, AND THE POLITICS OF ACCOMMODATION

To Have and Have Not

Just as French is a fact in Canada, so, too, is regionalism. The main regions—Atlantic Canada, Quebec, Ontario, the Prairies, British Columbia, and the Far North—are noteworthy not only for their historical sense of place and identity but also for their distinctive socio-economic and cultural composition. It is often said that Canada is a difficult country to govern, and a quick review of the regional nature of its territory and politics explains why. The economy of Atlantic Canada is vastly different from that of Ontario, just as the economic interests of British Columbia and the Prairies clash with those of Quebec. The regional economies compete directly with each other, causing people, industries, and provincial governments in each region to call on the federal government to develop economic policies beneficial to them. Thus, public opinion on the Prairies supports federal subsidies for grain producers, while farmers in Quebec want

funding to support the pork industry. Similarly, emerging high-tech and knowledge-based industries in Atlantic Canada want federal financial support for their activities, even though their success means additional competition for similar firms in Ontario and British Columbia. And naturally, public opinion in Ontario supports federal policies to bolster the economic strength and job-creation capacity of the province, deserving special consideration as the engine of the national economy.

The economic dominance of Ontario in the federation, on the other hand, provides a constant source of disgruntlement for those living elsewhere. Former Saskatchewan Premier Tommy Douglas once remarked, "Canada is like an old cow. The West feeds it. Ontario and Quebec milk it. And you can well imagine what it's doing in the Maritimes," and his sentiments have been widely shared. Many in the West argue that federal economic policy beneficial to Ontario's manufacturing interests has systematically discriminated against the economic development and industrial diversification of the Western provinces. In this respect, such historical federal economic policies as the **Crow's Nest Pass Agreement**, which established artificial rates for railway freight, and the oil and natural gas pricing arrangements that culminated in the **National Energy Policy** (NEP) of the early 1980s still rankle. Such feelings of alienation, moreover, are not simply a Western Canadian phenomenon. Many Atlantic Canadians view themselves and their economy as the forgotten members of the national family; while the rest of the country prospers, so the lament goes, unique Maritime economic problems receive haphazard and sporadic attention by the federal government, usually only in the lead-up to a federal election. And Atlantic provincial governments reflect public opinion in their region by pressing for federal commitment to policies that will address development in the economically disadvantaged periphery.

Other provincial governments, however, can be hostile to Atlantic Canadians' interpretation of their economic plight and critical of federal **equalization policy**. This policy, dating from the 1950s, channels federal funds to provinces that have total provincial revenues lower than the national provincial per capita average. The purpose is to ensure that the quality of public services in poorer provinces is roughly comparable to the national average. Ontario, Alberta, and British Columbia (the richest provinces) can claim that the economic difficulties faced by Atlantic Canada are inherent in that they derive from geographic isolation, historical reliance on natural resource industries now facing decline, and the rigidity of the regional labour market due to overly generous employment insurance and welfare payments. In fact, those payments are said to lead unemployed or underemployed Atlantic Canadians to remain in the region rather than migrate to where local economies are stronger and jobs more plentiful. From this perspective, federal regional development initiatives are part of the problem. They have been criticized historically as a response to the political-electoral aims of specific federal governments rather than the result of cogent thinking about sound national economic policy. This critique is often couched in terms of fiscal management. Those in the wealthier parts of the country complain that their tax dollars should not subsidize an approach to economic policy that is very expensive and has no clearly positive results.

In August 2015, for example, Brad Wall, the Conservative premier of Saskatchewan, called for a national dialogue on the reform of federal equalization policy, with Wall wanting to see at least half of the $17 billion then being sent to have-not provinces being earmarked instead for national infrastructure projects and tax cuts. Needless to say, Stephen McNeil, the Liberal premier of Nova Scotia, quickly attacked Wall's proposal, reminding the premier in Regina that Saskatchewan had once been a have-not province and it's important in a federation to have a financial structure in place to help provinces in need (*Chronicle Herald* 2015).

Federal governments seek equilibrium among these sharply divided perspectives, to soothe the interprovincial tensions they elicit. Note, though, that the Atlantic provinces are not alone in their continued support for a strong federal presence in equalization and regional development initiatives. Often, they are joined by the governments of Manitoba, Saskatchewan, and at times Quebec, provinces also frequently considered **have-not jurisdictions**. And the line between have and have-not moves with changing economic circumstances. By 2009–10 Newfoundland and Labrador had become a have province thanks to revenues from its offshore oil production, while Ontario had just slipped into have-not status due to recession. In that fiscal year, Ontario was eligible to receive $347 million in federal equalization funding. In 2015–16 Ontario received equalization payments totalling $2.4 billion. Given the volatility in the oil and gas sector, Newfoundland and Labrador's days as a have province will likely be quite limited.

The economic fault lines are very much between the richer parts of the country and the poorer, as the latter seek federal support for their economic and industrial advancement while the former complain that they must pay for programs of questionable use and in so doing subsidize their own economic competitors. The friction between the haves and have-nots is understandable, if not very pretty, and it demonstrates the difficult balancing act the federal government performs.

While mention of federal regional development policy can still elicit strong disagreement among citizens, it is necessary to recognize that all our federal and provincial governments are committed to the principle of equalization. A history of initiatives dates back to the 1950s, and the principle is enshrined in the Constitution Act, 1982. Despite interregional tensions, federal and provincial governments have shown that they can work together on certain joint policy undertakings, although usually with much bureaucratic haggling and infighting.

Demographics and Political Representation

Such interprovincial divisions are also found in other policy sectors. Linguistic rights and interest in policies of official bilingualism and biculturalism are of clear, if not uniform, importance in Quebec, New Brunswick, and the parts of Ontario and Manitoba that have large francophone populations, but less so elsewhere in Atlantic Canada, Ontario, and the West. Immigration, multiculturalism, and race-relations policy may be of great significance in Toronto, Montreal, Vancouver, and other large urban centres that attract substantial numbers of immigrants, but less so in rural and small-town Canada. Indeed, citizens who have little direct contact with recent immigrants and the new Canadian experience can be distinctly

hostile toward immigration, multiculturalism, and equality rights. Likewise, the policy concerns of rural and small-town Canada on issues as diverse as gun registration, regional development, and public sector job decentralization differ greatly from those found in the metropolitan centres.

Of course, the federal government is expected to govern in the best interests of all regions, and people, businesses, the media, and provincial governments will closely, if not jealously, review how well it is serving its mandate and how fairly it is distributing economic, financial, and social benefits across the country. An additional complication is population imbalance, as can be seen in Table 1.1. These figures highlight the vast demographic discrepancies between provinces and regions and the differing scope and magnitude of regional economies. The four Atlantic provinces combined, for example, have a smaller population than the city of Toronto. It is no wonder that Ontario is the economic powerhouse of the country, but it is equally noteworthy that Alberta and British Columbia are growing, both demographically and economically. The numbers also indicate the difficulties faced by Saskatchewan, Manitoba, and Atlantic Canada in promoting economic diversification through the development of secondary manufacturing and service industries when they have to compete against the established economic power and influence of much larger provinces and regions.

Just as the Canadian population is not evenly distributed geographically, so, too, electoral representation in the federal parliament varies considerably. As this country is a liberal democracy committed to the general principle of representation by population—one person, one vote—the

TABLE 1.1

Population Distribution and Parliamentary Representation, 2015

	POPULATION	% OF POPULATION	HOUSE OF COMMONS SEATS	% OF SEATS
Ontario	13,750,073	38.5	121	35.8
Quebec	8,245,470	23.1	78	23.1
British Columbia	4,666,892	13.1	42	12.4
Alberta	1,292,151	11.7	34	10.0
Manitoba	1,292,151	3.6	14	4.1
Saskatchewan	1,134,402	3.2	14	4.1
Nova Scotia	942,926	2.6	11	3.2
New Brunswick	753.319	2.1	10	2.9
Newfoundland and Labrador	525,756	1.5	7	2.1
Prince Edward Island	146,293	0.4	4	1.2
Northwest Territories	43,234	0.1	1	0.2
Nunavut	36,886	0.1	1	0.2
Yukon	36,789	0.1	1	0.2
Total	35,749,600	100	338	100

Source: Statistics Canada, Table 051-0005, Estimates of Population, 2015, Elections Canada, Electoral Districts by Province, 2015.

corresponding political reality is that Ontario, with over one-third of the total population, dominates representation in the federal House of Commons. As Table 1.1 shows, only Quebec comes anywhere close to Ontario's seat totals, with all other provinces and territories lagging far behind.

The political logic here is unmistakable. For a party to win federal power, it must do well in Ontario and either Quebec or the West. It is not necessary to win every region or province: regions or provinces with smaller populations and fewer parliamentary seats are expendable. Hence the long-noted and oft-lamented dominance of Ontario and Quebec over the political attention and agenda of the federal government. It's noteworthy that in the 2015 federal election the Liberals did extremely well in Ontario, especially in its vote-rich urban centres, while being quite competitive in Quebec. The party also made gains in the West, including Alberta and British Columbia. It also didn't hurt that the party swept every seat in Atlantic Canada.

MANAGING THE CANADIAN–AMERICAN RELATIONSHIP

Socio-Economic Policy

Canada has always possessed a multifaceted relationship with its American neighbour. While we have close economic ties with the United States, most Canadian leaders since Confederation have promoted policies designed to preserve a distinct national economy. Likewise, we have been greatly influenced by socio-cultural developments in the United States while attempting to maintain a society and culture separate from, and we hope better than, the American. As most Canadians show national pride—in characteristically reserved terms—they also demonstrate sympathy with policies designed to promote nationalism. In keeping with these sentiments, the federal government has been called upon to create policies, programs, and institutions to defend the uniqueness of Canada, promote a national identity, and protect national socio-economic interests. Initiatives ranging from the protectionist **National Policy** of John A. Macdonald's government in 1879 to the **Foreign Investment Review Agency** (FIRA) and National Energy Policy (NEP) of the Trudeau era—as well as the creation of such Crown corporations as Canadian National, Trans-Canada Airlines (later Air Canada), de Havilland, Canadair, Petro-Canada, and the Canada Development Corporation—can all be seen as federal undertakings to further the growth and development of the Canadian economy. But more than this, these initiatives and many others like them were promoted as ways of advancing distinctively Canadian approaches to building our economy so that substantial control over future growth and development would rest in Canadian, and not American, hands, for the benefit of Canadian citizens.

Similar dynamics can be observed in the history of Canadian social and cultural policy. In confronting the power and pervasive influence of American social and cultural ideas, institutions, and practices in this country—from dominance of television shows, movies, music, and publishing to the omnipresence of the American ideal of "life, liberty and the pursuit of happiness"—the federal government has defended uniquely Canadian social and cultural interests. Policies on such issues as gun control, universal public health care, state-subsidized postsecondary education, Canadian content rules and regulations in broadcasting—and the establishment of public cultural institutions such as the CBC, the NFB, the CRTC, and Telefilm Canada—have all served national demands. And they have all helped to distinguish Canadian society from that of the United States. Most Canadians, moreover, applaud such initiatives, recognizing that a key responsibility of the federal government is to defend our cultural identity, broadly defined, from being overwhelmed by American values and influences (Brooks 2014).

This policy area has become quite controversial over the past three decades as Canada entered into free trade agreements first with the United States in 1989 and then with the United States and Mexico in 1993 (NAFTA). These agreements are designed to reduce and eventually eliminate tariff and non-tariff barriers (subsidy and restrictive regulation) to trade between the signatory nations, to ease the free flow of goods and services, to enhance the ability of private firms in any one country to do business in the others, and to restrict the ability of governments from any signatory country to

FIGHTING JIHADI TERRORISM

Issue

What's the best way for Canada to confront the threat of Jihadi terrorism in other parts of the world as well as at home?

With the rise of the Islamic State in Iraq and Syria (ISIS) and its self-proclaimed declaration of war against Canada as well as a host of other Western nations such as the United States, Britain, France, Germany, and Australia, the Canadian government has been called upon to take action. This threat became all the more real when, in October 2014, Jihadi-inspired terrorist attacks occurred in St. Jean sur Richilieu, Quebec, and at the National War Memorial in Ottawa as well as within the Centre Block of Parliament itself.

The Response

Even before the attacks in Canada, the Harper government committed Canadian combat troops to the fight against ISIS. In the summer of 2014 Canada had joined a US-led coalition to combat ISIS in Iraq, with the Canadian military dispatching six CF-18s, two tanker aircraft, a surveillance plane, and a detachment of Canadian Special Forces troops to assist in the training of Kurdish forces fighting ISIS in northern Iraq. While Canada is also providing humanitarian relief to refugees who have fled from ISIS, Prime Minister Harper assured Canadians that there would be no major commitment of Canadian troops to a ground war in Iraq. Once in power, the Trudeau government altered the Canadian response. In early 2016, the CF-18s were withdrawn from this fight but the number of ground forces involved in training Kurdish troops was tripled, while commitments for humanitarian aid were increased.

Assessing the Response

Should Canadian troops be directly involved in the fight against Jihadi terrorism? If ISIS is the global threat Conservatives say it is, is Canada's response exceedingly minimal, more token than real? Should our actions be more robust? Should we be bombing ISIS? And should we be prepared to put "boots on the ground" and take the war to ISIS, "degrading and destroying" them, as US President Obama said was the original purpose of the mission? Or is this just what ISIS wants, a war between themselves and Western "infidels" invading a Muslim country, thereby justifying the *raison d'être* of ISIS? And would such a war be a disastrous quagmire for Canada, much like the American war in Iraq following its 2003 invasion of that country?

Or should Canadian policy be aimed more at providing humanitarian relief in areas suffering from such terrorism and in guarding Canada's borders from extremists trying to get into this land? Is ham-fisted Western intervention in the Middle East, like the 2001 intervention into Afghanistan and the 2003 US/British invasion of Iraq, actually a root cause of much of the instability and hatred within the region? Would the Middle East be better off with much less, rather than more, Western involvement in its affairs? Is the war against ISIS a fight for other Middle Eastern countries to take on? And should Canada be more concerned about addressing the radicalization of young Canadians here at home before they seek to become martyrs for their cause?

intervene in the free operation of the continental economy in order to provide specific benefits to specific national firms. One of the policy thrusts of the free trade undertaking was to entrench free enterprise and market approaches to economic development throughout the continent. As a consequence, Canada has drawn closer to the dominant American policy of supporting the private sector and more individualistic, business-oriented economic development, downplaying the role of the public sector in economic planning (Anderson and Sands 2007; Hale 2012).

The magnitude of this looming orientational shift in economic and government policy was sensed in 1988, during the so-called free trade election, when the campaign became a virtual referendum on the merits and demerits of free trade with the United States. The contest was one of the most bitter, passionate, and divisive elections in Canadian history. The Progressive Conservatives under the leadership of Brian Mulroney won, and the Canada–United States Free Trade Agreement was passed into law on January 1, 1989.

Although we have been living with free trade for approximately three decades, many Canadians remain very critical, or at least sceptical, of the policy, arguing that the supposed benefits of economic growth and job creation never materialized and that we, as a country, are slipping further and further into the American economic orbit while being subjected to a concomitant Americanization of Canadian society and social policy. These concerns are manifested now as Canadians consider the merits and demerits of the Trans Pacific Partnership (TPP) trade deal that would join most of the countries of the Pacific Rim into a free trade arrangement. Critics of the TPP in this country argue that Canada stands to lose its domestic dairy, chicken, and egg industries to foreign competition, while also having to give foreign corporations the right to sue federal and provincial governments should future Canadian laws and policies, such as those with respect to consumer and worker protection or environmental regulation, harm the profitability of those firms and the value of their capital investments in Canada.

Security Policy

Our interconnectedness with the United States is manifested not just through the trade relationship. Following the 9/11 terrorist attacks, the Canadian federal government worked strenuously to assure the United States that its northern border was secure. The government of Canada spent hundreds of millions of dollars in upgrading border security, increasing the number of border guards, developing high-tech security scanners at airports and harbours, and enhancing the role of the Canadian Security Intelligence Service (CSIS) and the Royal Canadian Mounted Police (RCMP) to track, investigate, and intercept possible security threats.

As Prime Minister Harper noted in defending such initiatives, they were justified in and of themselves not only to enhance Canadian security in a dangerous world but also to reassure Americans that they were secure from terrorist attacks via Canada. As such, Canada could maintain a relatively open border with the United States for purposes of trade and commerce without Americans feeling the need to stifle the border with overly restrictive security measures.

The so-called War on Terror has also led recent Liberal and Conservative governments to increase funding to the Canadian military and to deploy Canadian troops in combat missions in Afghanistan, with the Harper government extending this fight to Libya, Iraq, and Syria. The domestic terror attacks in St. Jean sur Richelieu and on Parliament Hill in October 2014, in turn, spurred the Harper government, with the support of the federal Liberals, to pass sweeping new anti-terrorism legislation known as Bill C-51. This act greatly expanded the powers of the RCMP and CSIS to engage in surveillance of suspected terrorists, to access and share information on such suspects, to detain them without charge, and to disrupt their activities, all with minimal judicial oversight and review, and with the application of the Charter of Rights and Freedoms being forestalled. The act of promoting terrorism, by deed or word, has also been criminalized, but with a definition of terrorism so broad that many journalists fear simply reporting on the activities or motivations of terrorist groups at home or abroad may result in charges being brought against journalists themselves. In coming to power in late 2015, the Trudeau government promised to amend this legislation, adding greater parliamentary oversight of security forces and reinstating the Charter protections.

Environmental Policy

Perhaps even more controversial than security policy has been the relationship between Canada and the United States on environmental policy. In 1997 the Liberal government of Jean Chrétien signed the Kyoto Accord, committing the country to significant reductions in greenhouse gas emissions. As with all signatory countries, Canada was committed to reducing total greenhouse gas emissions by 6 per cent by 2012 compared to 1990 levels. But Canada never lived up to these promises.

Between 1990 and 2008, rather than going down, total Canadian greenhouse gas emissions increased by 24.1 per cent. Meanwhile, the United States government under President George W. Bush rejected the Accord for imposing impossible burdens on the American economy while failing to effectively address the issue of environmental pollution emanating from developing countries.

While he was in opposition, Stephen Harper supported this Republican American position. Once he became prime minister in 2006, Harper continued to voice his opposition to the Kyoto Accord, stressing that any future global policy on climate change would have to involve both developed and developing countries. He also argued strongly in favour of intensity targets (which specify greenhouse gas emission reductions in terms of production and consumption such as GDP or energy use) instead of absolute targets (which specify reductions in total emissions). This approach allows for continued growth in the development and production of oil from the Alberta oil sands industries. The Harper government withdrew from the Kyoto Accord in 2011.

The federal government, however, does have a greenhouse gas emission reduction policy. In 2009, the government of Canada became a signatory to the Copenhagen Accord calling for a 17 per cent reduction in greenhouse gases by 2020 compared to 2005 levels. This reduction goal was much more modest than that set out in the Kyoto Accord, but even with this easier target, the Harper government failed to meet its international obligations. Between 2005 and 2014 Canada's greenhouse gas emissions were rising, not falling, with even Environment Canada predicting that by 2020 Canada would have reduced its emissions, at best, by only 1.5 per cent from 2005 levels, not the 17 per cent called for (Dronkers 2015). While the Harper government touted this reduction as a move in the right direction, environmentalists continued to assert that the federal government led by Stephen Harper showed no commitment to taking the greenhouse gas emission reduction policy seriously because to do so would threaten the economic growth potential of the Canadian oil and gas industry, especially in the Alberta oil sands.

In 2015, the Harper government announced new "ambitious" plans to cut Canadian greenhouse gas emissions by 30 per cent from 2005 levels by 2030. In 2005, such emissions accounted for 749 megatons of greenhouse gases. A 30 per cent reduction would mean a cut of almost 200 megatons. The CBC's Mark Gollum (2015) notes the obstacles to achieving such a goal. In 2013, emissions from all vehicles accounted for 88 megatons of pollution—not even half the 2030 objective. In 2013, total emissions from the Alberta oil sands totalled 62 megatons, meaning a complete shutdown of this industry would still be inadequate to meet the 2030 target. And no Canadian government of any political stripe wants to see that industry mothballed. If we are to meet this 2030 objective, most energy experts, including those from within the oil and gas industry itself, assert that a price must be put on greenhouse gas pollution, either through a carbon tax (the simplest method) or through the development of a cap-and-trade system of carbon credits for energy producers (the more complicated method) and through the tighter regulation of energy-producing technologies. All of these policy alternatives require leadership and action from Canadian governments and most especially from the federal government.

Over the past quarter-century such leadership has been woefully lacking. But the promises keep coming. At the G7 meeting in Bavaria, Germany, in the summer of 2015, the leaders of the industrialized world committed their countries to carbon-free economies—by 2100. And at the Paris Climate Change talks in Paris in December 2015, the new Trudeau government reaffirmed the Harper government's 30 per cent reduction in greenhouse gas emissions beneath 2005 levels by 2030 while also committing Canada to supporting the goal that global average temperatures should not rise more than 1.5 per cent above pre-industrial levels. Whether any of these commitments are achievable remains an open question (Ball et al. 2010, chap. 11).

ADDRESSING THE FIRST NATIONS

Relations between the Canadian government and the Indigenous peoples of this land have been historically characterized by a manipulative, abusive, and imbalanced power relationship. The revival of **First Nations** nationalism over the past 40 years has forced Canadian governments—especially the federal government—to acknowledge the injustices of the past and to redress them through better ways of managing Indigenous policy.

In promoting social and economic development for Indigenous peoples, the negotiation and renegotiation of **treaty rights** and **land claims** are of crucial importance. In many cases, British and Canadian governments entered treaties and then failed to comply with their obligations. In others, Indigenous leaders did not understand the language and therefore the terms of the treaties they signed, or were forced to sign them to get help for people ravaged by deprivation and disease. The fairness and legitimacy of many treaties are also

A FIRST NATIONS CHRONOLOGY

For much of Canadian history, the relationship between First Nations and French, British, and eventually Canadian authorities has been lamentable. First Nations were subject to colonization, appropriation of land, destruction of traditional economies, impoverishment, and systemic racial discrimination. In recent decades, however, First Nations have been undergoing a political renaissance as Indigenous Canadians reassert their cultural heritage and promote their social and economic development.

1700s–1800s First contact with Europeans

1763 Royal Proclamation recognizes Native nations

1800s–1900s Legal treaties developed between First Nations and European governments

1812–15 Indigenous nations ally themselves with Britain in the War of 1812

1867 British North America Act gives federal government constitutional responsibility for "Indians and lands reserved for the Indians"

1876 Parliament passes Indian Act, providing a legal framework for the reserve system

1880s–1920s Residential school system developed to assimilate Indigenous children into Canadian society

1960 Federal voting rights extended to treaty Indians living on reserves

1969 Federal White Paper on Indian policy promotes assimilation of Indigenous cultures into Canadian mainstream

1973 Supreme Court of Canada, in *Calder*, makes its first decision on Indigenous rights, referring to the Royal Proclamation of 1763 to affirm the existence of such rights at the time of first contact

1974–77 Berger Royal Commission on Mackenzie Valley Pipeline highlights plight of First Nations in Northwest Territories and spurs Native nationalism

1975 James Bay agreement between the government of Quebec and Cree and Inuit First Nations marks the birth of modern comprehensive land claim negotiations

1970s–90s Increased demand from First Nations for the negotiation/renegotiation of treaties and land claim settlements

1982 Constitution Act, 1982 recognizes rights of First Nations

Charter of Rights and Freedoms, s. 25, affirms constitutional status of the Royal Proclamation of 1763

1990s Supreme Court decisions in *Sparrow* (1990), *Delgamuukw* (1997), and *Marshall* (1999) affirm traditional Indigenous treaty rights and the validity of the Royal Proclamation of 1763

1992 **Charlottetown Accord**, part of which recognizes an inherent right of Indigenous self-government, is defeated

1996 Royal Commission on Aboriginal Peoples promotes Indigenous self-government

1999 Nunavut created

2000 The Nisga'a Final Agreement comes into effect, marking the first modern land claims agreement in British Columbia

2005 Martin Liberal government announces Kelowna Accord, with $5 billion earmarked for First Nations development

2006 Harper Conservative government cancels Kelowna Accord

2008 Prime Minister Harper officially apologizes on behalf of the people of Canada to Indigenous Canadians for historical abuses in the residential school system

2012 Crown–First Nations Gathering held in Ottawa between 170 chiefs and the governor general, the prime minister, and 12 cabinet ministers, to discuss improving relations between these governments

Idle No More movement arises as a grassroots initiative to promote Indigenous rights, Indigenous self-government, and ways and means of improving the quality of life for First Nations peoples

2015 Release of the Truth and Reconciliation Report into the history and legacy of the residential school system in Canada

Ongoing demands from Indigenous leaders for a national inquiry into murdered and missing Indigenous women

WHITE PAPER

questionable, due to differing cultural concepts of individual and collective rights, land ownership, private property entitlements, and **Aboriginal title**. In many places—most of British Columbia and the Far North, for example—treaties were never entered into at all, with the result that First Nations lands were simply occupied by white settlers in the absence of any formal legal process.

Given the questionable treaty process as well as the social and economic problems experienced by many First Nations, the federal government is now committed to renegotiate existing treaties and negotiate new ones where they are needed. Of course, such contemporary negotiation is fraught with controversy. Governments must ensure that First Nations have sufficient territory to be economically viable, balance ownership rights over hitherto Crown lands and natural resources, determine financial compensation for past injustices and lost entitlements, and provide current fiscal support for the operational management of First Nations. With respect to any one of these issues, governments are hard pressed to determine what is both just and constitutionally required for First Nations and also politically acceptable to the non-Indigenous majority. The debate over the Nisga'a Final Agreement, a land claims agreement within British Columbia that came into effect in 2000, highlights all of these problems. By 2011, growing anger amongst Indigenous peoples led to the convening of a Crown–First Nations Gathering in Ottawa in January 2012, where over 170 chiefs as well as the governor general, the prime minister, and cabinet ministers met to discuss ways to improve relationships between First Nations and the federal government, as well as enhancing the quality of life of Indigenous Canadians. By October

2012, however, anger at the slow pace of reform resulted in the rise of Idle No More, a grassroots First Nations movement seeking fairness and justice for Indigenous peoples, the promotion of self-government, and respect for Indigenous treaty rights. Idle No More also took the lead in demanding the federal government establish an independent royal commission to investigate the issues surrounding the problem of missing and murdered Indigenous women. Prime Minister Harper rejected calling such an investigation, stressing that the issue was one of law enforcement going forward, rather than the need to study a non-existent sociological phenomenon (Papillon 2014, chap. 6).

Despite such tensions in the relationships between Indigenous peoples, First Nations governments, and other Canadian governments, the federal government and most provincial governments are committed to the negotiation and creation of systems of Indigenous self-government. This commitment poses great challenges to Indigenous and non-Indigenous officials and citizens in terms of the meaning of self-government, the pros and cons of various models, and the nature of the political, economic, and legal relationships that such systems will create. These relationships will govern such matters as the equality rights of Indigenous men and women, the legal and political rights of non-Indigenous peoples residing on First Nations territory, the applicability of the Charter of Rights and Freedoms to First Nations, and the constitutionality of race-based approaches to rights entitlements.

Moreover, both the federal and First Nations governments need systems of public sector management that will further Indigenous self-government, stabilize the policy and administrative relationships between governments, and facilitate effective, responsible, and accountable public administration for First Nations people. After devolving or returning administrative authority to the leadership of First Nations, the federal government is expected to recognize the legitimacy of First Nations governments and to work cooperatively with them in the administration of government services, still largely funded by federal money. In turn, First Nations are called upon to develop the managerial expertise to administer their affairs in accordance with standard expectations of just and effective public administration. As with their federal and provincial counterparts, First Nations governments are expected to adhere to established concepts of administrative fairness and competence, with the same traits of economy, efficiency, and democratic accountability displayed in their governmental decision making. And just as federal and provincial governments have often struggled to live up to these standards, so First Nations governments have come in for criticism from citizens who demand greater accountability from their elected leaders.

GOVERNMENT CAPACITY, ACCOUNTABILITY, AND MANAGEMENT

It is not surprising that interest in governmental capability and accountability has increased in the past quarter-century, not only in the general public but also among political parties, interest groups, the media, and the public service itself. And as a result, Canadian governments have undertaken to improve their capacity to provide effective policy and program administration. Over the past three decades, for example, all governments in this country have been influenced by a new approach to thinking and doing public administration. Known as **new public management** (NPM), it adopts a rather conservative frame of reference that stipulates that governments need to be more businesslike in their undertakings, emulating the private sector in much of their work and even transferring to private hands responsibilities that have traditionally been considered essential duties of the public sector. As interest in NPM has grown, **privatization**, **deregulation**, contracting out, commercialization and user fees, decentralization, and the overall reduction of the public sector have intensified. All such policies are seen by advocates of NPM as a means not only of eliminating horrendous public sector deficits and controlling related debt but also of putting public sector management on a new, more creative footing.

All these claims, however, are highly contested. Critics contend that NPM presents a not-so-veiled threat to the integrity and role of the public sector by treating it as a poor imitation of the private sector rather than as a separate entity with distinct and valid forms of reasoning, problem solving, and decision making. Democratic, parliamentary government legitimizes and necessitates forms of management different from those in the competitive marketplace.

This issue has dominated Canadian political discourse for well over two decades and is likely to continue to preoccupy political thought and action. It poses questions about the type of government and public services that Canadians want, as reflected in such diverse issues as the modernization of health, educational, and social assistance policy; the maintenance and regulation of drinking water quality; the deterioration of public infrastructure; and environmental protection and quality. All these matters relate to the calibre of our governments and public services and thus of their accountability.

Accountability, then, becomes the one great theme flowing through all issues pertaining to government and through any analysis of governments and their management of public duties. All governments strive to be accountable to the needs and wishes of the public they serve, and all governments routinely claim that they are so accountable. Any study of government must therefore address the concept of accountability and the degree to which governments live up to expectations in this regard.

All democratic governments face the following demands:

- They must deliver excellent policies and services in the most economical and efficient manner possible.
- Their policies and programs must respond to general public needs as well as various special interests.
- Their role within the state must be intelligently designed and operated to strike a balance between public and private sector interests.
- Their actions and those of public servants must be consistent with the rules of administrative law, as well as with newly developing rules governing public sector ethics.
- Their decision making must be more open and transparent than ever before, subject to much more participation by interest groups and the general public than hitherto.

- They must exercise sound and prudent financial management of public money and their budgetary practices must be open, honest, and fiscally responsible.
- Their personnel management must reflect the legitimate promotion of a professional and competent public service, broadly representative of and sensitive to the community it serves. Nepotism, favouritism, and patronage must be disavowed and prohibited.
- They must establish administrative systems conducive to decision making that is wise, just, rational, and farsighted, and that advances the long-term interests of Canadians.
- They must possess strong leaders throughout the ranks of the public service capable of meeting these obligations.

Hence, the focus of this text is not only on the general nature of government and the role of the state in Canada but also on the nature and quality of its public sector management. How successfully are our governments living up to all these expectations? The next chapter turns to the political and ideological foundation of government in this country, assessing the competing schools of thought about the role of the state in society and thus the corresponding duties and responsibilities that should be borne by the public sector and its managers.

Two fundamental truths emerge in this chapter. The first is that the state plays a major role in the social and economic life of this country as well as in its environmental and foreign policy. The second is that Canadians are divided about the role of government. This leads to the paradox of power. Canadians can be very critical of their governments and bureaucracies, yet we also express great support for the social welfare system created by public policies. As we continue to explore the real world of public administration and public sector management, we will see that governments are constantly measured by how well they address the core issues of socio-economic policy, French–English relations, regionalism, Canadian–American relations, and Indigenous policy.

REFERENCES AND SUGGESTED READING

Albo, Gregory, David Langille, and Leo Panitch, eds. 1993. *A Different Kind of State? Popular Power and Democratic Administration*. Toronto: Oxford University Press.

Anderson, Christopher G., and Rand Dyck. 2016. *Studying Politics: An Introduction to Political Science*. 5th ed. Toronto: Nelson Education.

Anderson, Greg, and Christopher Sands. 2007. *Negotiating North America: The Security and Prosperity Partnership*. Washington, DC: Hudson Institute.

Archer, Keith, Roger Gibbins, Rainer Knopff, and Leslie A. Pal. 1999. *Parameters of Power: Canada's Political Institutions*. 2nd ed. Toronto: Nelson.

Asch, Michael, ed. 1997. *Aboriginal and Treaty Rights in Canada: Essays on Law, Equality and Respect for Difference*. Vancouver: UBC Press.

Ball, Terence, Richard Dagger, William Christian, and Colin Campbell. 2010. *Political Ideologies and the Democratic Ideal*, 2nd Canadian ed. Toronto: Pearson Canada.

Barker, Paul. 2008. *Public Administration in Canada*. Brief ed. Toronto: Nelson.

Bell, David V.J. 2008. "Political Culture in Canada." In *Canadian Politics in the 21st Century*, 7th ed., edited by Michael Whittington and Glen Williams, 228–59. Toronto: Nelson.

Bickerton, James, and Alain-G. Gagnon. 2014. *Canadian Politics*. 6th ed. Toronto: University of Toronto Press.

Bothwell, Robert. 1998. *Canada and Quebec: One Country, Two Histories*. Rev. ed. Vancouver: UBC Press.

Brooks, Stephen. 2014. "The Canada-United States Relationship." In *Canadian Politics*, 6th ed., edited by James Bickerton and Alain G. Gagnon, 437–58. Toronto: University of Toronto Press.

Campbell, Colin, and William Christian. 1996. *Parties, Leaders, and Ideologies in Canada*. Toronto: McGraw-Hill Ryerson.

Carroll, Barbara Wake, David Siegel, and Mark Sproule-Jones. 2005. *Classic Readings in Canadian Public Administration*. Toronto: Oxford University Press.

Chronicle Herald. 2015. "McNeil Slams Wall on Equalization Remarks." August 7, A7.

Doern, G. Bruce, and Christopher Stoney. 2010. *How Ottawa Spends 2010–2011: Recession, Realignment, and the New Deficit Era*. Montreal: McGill-Queen's University Press.

———, and Brian W. Tomlin. 1991. *Faith and Fear: The Free Trade Story*. Toronto: Stoddart.

Dronkers, Barend. 2015. "Top Stories from Canada's Latest Greenhouse Gas Emissions Inventory." Pembina Institute, April 23, 2015. www.pembina.org/blog/top-stories-from-canadas-latest-greenhouse-gas-emissions-inventory.

Dunn, Christopher. 2010. *The Handbook of Canadian Public Administration*. 2nd ed. Toronto: Oxford University Press.

Dyck, Rand. 2008. *Canadian Politics: Critical Approaches*. 5th ed. Toronto: Nelson.

Flanagan, Tom. 1995. *Waiting for the Wave: The Reform Party and Preston Manning*. Toronto: Stoddart.

———. 2009. *Harper's Team: Behind the Scenes in the Conservative Rise to Power*. 2nd ed. Montreal: McGill-Queen's University Press.

Gagnon, Alain-G. 1999. "Quebec's Constitutional Odyssey." In *Canadian Politics*, 3rd ed., edited by James Bickerton and Alain-G. Gagnon, 279–300. Toronto: University of Toronto Press.

Gollom, Mark. 2015. "Greenhouse Gas Emission: How Can Canada Cut 30%?" *CBC News*, May 25. www.cbc.ca/news/politics/greenhouse-gas-emissions-how-can-canada-cut-30-by-2030-1.3080447.

Hale, Geoffrey E. 2012. "Toward a Perimeter: Incremental Adaptation of a New Paradigm for Canada-US Security and Trade Relations." In *How Ottawa Spends, 2012–2013*, edited by G. Bruce Doern and Christopher Stoney, 106–26. Montreal: McGill-Queen's University Press.

Howlett, Michael, and M. Ramesh. 1995. *Studying Public Policy: Policy Cycles and Policy Subsystems*. Toronto: Oxford University Press.

Inwood, Gregory J. 2009. *Understanding Canadian Public Administration: An Introduction to Theory and Practice*. 3rd ed. Toronto: Pearson Prentice Hall.

Jackson, Robert J., and Doreen Jackson. 2009. *Politics in Canada: Culture, Institutions, Behaviour and Public Policy*. 7th ed. Toronto: Pearson Prentice Hall.

Johnson, William. 2005. *Stephen Harper and the Future of Canada*. Toronto: McClelland and Stewart.

Johnston, Larry. 1996. *Ideologies: An Analytical and Contextual Approach*. Toronto: University of Toronto Press.

Long, David, and Olive Dickason. 1996. *Visions of the Heart: Canadian Aboriginal Issues*. Toronto: Harcourt Brace.

Magnussen, Warren. 1999. "State Sovereignty, Localism, and Globalism." In *Canadian Politics*, 3rd ed., edited by James Bickerton and Alain-G. Gagnon, 57–78. Toronto: University of Toronto Press.

Martin, Lawrence. 2010. *Harperland: The Politics of Control*. Toronto: Viking Canada.

McCormack, Peter. 1996. "The Reform Party of Canada: New Beginning or Dead End?" In *Party Politics in Canada*, 7th ed., edited by Hugh G. Thorburn, 352–63. Scarborough, ON: Prentice Hall Canada.

McRoberts, Kenneth. 1993. *Quebec: Social Change and Political Crisis*. 3rd ed. Toronto: McClelland and Stewart.

Nelson, Ralph. 1995. "Ideologies." In *Introductory Readings in Canadian Government and Politics*, 2nd ed., edited by Robert M. Krause and R.H. Wagenberg, 25–40. Toronto: Copp Clark.

Papillon, Martin. 2014. "The Rise (and Fall?) of Aboriginal Self-Government." In *Canadian Politics*, 6th ed., edited by James Bickerton and Alain G. Gagnon, 113–31. Toronto: University of Toronto Press.

Phillips, Susan. 1999. "Social Movements in Canadian Politics: Past Their Apex?" In *Canadian Politics*, 3rd ed., edited by James Bickerton and Alain-G. Gagnon, 371–92. Toronto: University of Toronto Press.

Prince, Michael J. 1999. "From Health and Welfare to Stealth and Farewell: Federal Social Policy, 1980–2000." In *How Ottawa Spends 1999–2000: Shape Shifting: Canadian Governance toward the 21st Century*, edited by Leslie A. Pal, 151–98. Toronto: Oxford University Press.

Riggs, A.R., and Tom Velk. 1993. *Beyond NAFTA: An Economic, Political and Sociological Perspective*. Vancouver: The Fraser Institute.

Russell, Peter H. 1993. *Constitutional Odyssey: Can Canadians Become a Sovereign People?* 2nd ed. Toronto: University of Toronto Press.

Shields, John, and B. Mitchell Evans. 1998. *Shrinking the State: Globalization and Public Administration "Reform."* Halifax: Fernwood Publishing.

Simpson, Jeffrey. 2001. *The Friendly Dictatorship*. Toronto: McClelland and Stewart.

Van Loon, Richard J., and Michael S. Whittington, eds. 1987. *The Canadian Political System: Environment, Structure and Process*. 4th ed. Toronto: McGraw-Hill Ryerson.

Whittington, Michael, and Glen Williams, eds. 2008. *Canadian Politics in the 21st Century*. 7th ed. Toronto: Thomson Nelson.

RELATED WEBSITES

Canadian Social Research Links. www.canadiansocialresearch.net

Canoe. www.canoe.ca

Culture-Canada. www.culture-canada.ca

Government of Canada. www.canada.gc.ca

PoliticsWatch. www.politicswatch.com

CHAPTER 2

Ideologies of Government and Public Service

Ideology … is indispensable in any society if men are to be formed, transformed and equipped to respond to the demands of their conditions of existence.

–Louis Althusser, 1964

By the end of this chapter and its related web pages you'll be able to

- articulate the fundamental principles of conservatism, liberalism, and social democracy;
- identify how and why ideologies influence and interact with one another;
- relate political ideology to perceptions of the role of the state in modern Canadian society;
- describe the twentieth-century history of Canadian federal politics from an ideological perspective;
- explain how political parties interact with one another in ideological terms; and
- interpret the current Canadian political climate in relation to the role of the state.

2   Ideologies of Government and Public Service

What type of society do we want to live in? What is the right balance between individual and collective rights and duties? What is the appropriate role of the public sector? Individuals, corporations, interest groups, the media, political parties, and governments all wrestle with these fundamental political issues.

Governments and their administrative functions are omnipresent in the routine life of every Canadian, so such questions are crucial. They apply not only to the nature and working of government but also to how we think about politics and power. Politics and political ideas are at once the foundation of governments and the material from which public policy and public sector management approaches are fashioned. It is impossible to think about the work of governments without understanding the ideas, interests, and values that condition all governments.

This chapter examines the many links between politics, ideology, policy, and management. By probing the ideological foundations of Canadian politics and government we can discern the seeds of the paradox outlined in Chapter 1. Some ideas prevailing in Canadian political culture are very hostile to a large state presence in society, while others are hostile to a minimal one. In the interplay of these competing ideas, the politics of centrism defined the work of most governments in this country, especially at the federal level. At least this was the case until the election of the Conservative government led by Prime Minister Stephen Harper in 2006. Under his leadership Canadians were witnesses to the most ideologically conservative

government in Canadian history. And few Canadians were unmoved by this experience. Some loved it, others loathed it, and many wondered whether Canadian political culture was changing, and if it was, was it changing for the better?

THE PUBLIC-PRIVATE DIVIDE

In contrast to business enterprises and private sector management—where the prime focus is the continued viability, profitability, and rate of return of investment to owners and shareholders of the individual firm, as measured by the precise logic of the bottom line—government and public sector management are centred on the much more ambiguous world of party politics and "the public interest." Parties vie for government power on the grounds that they can provide—can promise—an approach to public policy and administration superior to that of other parties. This is the essence of party competition: parties compete for the favour of the voting public by advocating and packaging the messages and goals that each believes will garner maximum sympathy and support, or at least enough votes to win the next election. Such competition goes on year in and year out, though it reaches a climax during election campaigns, of course, when the electorate casts ballots to determine the composition of a new parliament or legislative assembly, either confirming the mandate of the previous government or electing a new one, with new goals.

Political belief and political action are vital to this cycle. Parties compete over policy ends and means, ideological beliefs, their own political and managerial records, and leadership style. Policy alternatives and assessments of the role of the state and of how government should advance its policy objectives become the staples of political and electoral debate. Unlike in the private sector, where debate tends to focus on strategic questions of private wealth generation, public sector deliberations address broad issues of public policy. Rather than dealing with matters of profit and loss, for which success and managerial competence are explicitly quantifiable and verifiable, governments must address socio-economic and cultural concerns that have no such clear and generally agreed-upon measures of success.

MEASURING GOVERNMENT SUCCESS

Common indications of success for a government are whether it promoted economic growth, strengthened social welfare and justice, and generally improved the quality of life of its citizens. Over the past 30 years Canadian governments became increasingly preoccupied with eliminating deficits and running balanced or even **surplus** budgets, while at the same time they faced public pressure to

- marry fiscal restraint with policies designed to help "ordinary Canadians" in the middle class;
- get tough on crime;
- strengthen health, education, and social services;
- promote environmental sustainability and address the reality of global climate change;
- advance Canadian interests and national security on the world stage; and
- elevate the quality of human rights and cultural and Indigenous policy, to name just a few major fields.

And, of course, following the terrorist attacks of 9/11, citizens wanted the federal government to enhance national defence, intelligence, air transportation safety, and border and other forms of security. This policy focus was only accentuated in the fall of 2014 with the terrorist attacks in St. Jean sur Richelieu in Quebec and at the National War Memorial and Parliament Hill in Ottawa, leading the Conservative government of Stephen Harper to pass Bill C-51, greatly strengthening the ability of Canadian police and national security agencies to track and disrupt suspected terrorist activities. This legislation was passed with the support of the federal Liberal Party, though the New Democrats opposed it on the grounds that it went disproportionately far in granting excessive and unnecessary powers to law enforcement authorities without these powers being subject to adequate judicial and parliamentary supervision. With respect to all these policy goals, however, terms such as *quality*, *promote*, *maintain*, *enhance*, *help*, *strengthen*, and *elevate* are subjective, open to political interpretation and judgement. They provoke disagreement because any assessment of what constitutes good government, good public policy, and good public sector management is influenced by political and philosophical viewpoint.

With the defeat of the Harper government in the fall of 2015 and the rise to power of the federal Liberals under Justin Trudeau, political debate in this country has changed once again. To liberals, this government is viewed as a saviour, having the inclination and the capacity to undo the damage of the Harper years and to return Canada to its centrist political roots. But to conservatives, Trudeau is seen as a political lightweight, a naïf with simplistic ideas that will harm the Canadian economy while weakening us on the world stage. And to **democratic socialists**, the new government is better than the old one, but is still a government lacking in progressive conviction and the ability to act on socialist ideals.

PHILOSOPHIES OF POLITICAL DISCOURSE

As parties compete for power in the political arena they must address the grand questions of public life. What is the ideal nature of government? What is the best relationship between the individual and the collectivity? Or the private and the public sector? How should the economy be organized and managed? Should free enterprise and a market economy be unfettered or controlled? Should individual liberty be privileged over social equality, or vice versa? Can some balance be struck between these two poles, and if so, how? Ultimately, these matters all rest on the role of the state and the policy directions it should follow.

All such questions, and many more like them, form the foundation of political life and public discourse as parties seek to distinguish themselves and their leadership as the ones that deserve to be entrusted by the electorate with the reins of government power. This quest is the essence of our political dynamic, centring on classic questions of political philosophy. And as we seek answers, various ideological strands emerge to define or sharpen differing viewpoints and bring philosophical coherence to an often raucous public forum. Although the ideological spectrum is wide, three schools of thought have dominated Canadian political discourse and government policy and

program development for well over a century: **conservatism, social democracy (Fabian socialism)**, and **liberalism** (Horowitz 1996; Bazowski 1999; Wiseman 2007; Bell 2008; Ball et al. 2010). The main concepts associated with each over the past 75 years can be described by a few core terms and phrases (see Table 2.1), though many books have been devoted to their intricacies.

THE CONSERVATIVE STATE

State Role
- The good government is the one that governs least.
- The public sector should support the private sector and ensure that it is economically healthy and socially viable.

Economic Policy
- Government regulation of the economy and of private firms should be as limited as possible.
- Government should support free enterprise and free trade.
- Government should look for solutions to social and economic problems first from the private sector—from private groups, charities, and religious institutions—and from individuals themselves.

Financial Policy
- Taxation should be as limited as possible, and tax policy should be designed to support, not hurt, the private sector.
- Governments should be fiscally prudent.
- Tax cuts are always preferable to new spending programs.

TABLE 2.1

Political Principles across the Spectrum

	CONSERVATISM	SOCIAL DEMOCRACY	LIBERALISM
Individualism vs. collectivism	Society is composed of individuals, each of whom bears responsibility for his or her own life.	Society is composed of groups and classes.	Society is composed of both individuals and groups.
Competition vs. communalism	Individuals are naturally competitive, trying to advance their self-interest.	People naturally form social units. The good of the many outweighs the self-interest of individuals.	Individuals are competitive but so too are they communal animals, caring about the public interest.
Rationalism	Individuals are capable of deciding independently how best to lead their lives. Individuals naturally look out for themselves and their families.	People generally have regard for others and try to care for one another.	Individuals will seek not only self-interest but also the best interests of society.
Liberty	One should be free to lead one's own life as one wants, free from interference.	Social compassion should outweigh individualistic competition. Individual liberty needs to be regulated and balanced by concern for collective interests.	Individuals should have wide entitlements to liberty, subject to reasonable state controls designed to protect and promote the public welfare.
Equality	Equality of opportunity is paramount.	Equality of condition is paramount.	Equality of opportunity and condition are both important in structuring a decent life in society.
Democracy	Individuals should be able to choose who governs them, but a government is best that has minimal impact on individual liberty.	The people should be able to choose who governs them, and society and its economy should be subject to the direction and control of democratically elected governments.	The people should be able to choose who governs them, and governments should promote both individual rights and interests and the social needs of the community.

	CONSERVATISM	SOCIAL DEMOCRACY	LIBERALISM
Materialism	Individuals naturally seek to acquire material possessions.	The wealth of society should be shared by the members of society.	Individuals will seek their own material self-interest, but so too must the state promote the material interests of the broader society.
Private vs. public property	One should be free to acquire and control one's own wealth. The private sector is and should be the driving force of the society and its economy.	The economy should be structured in the interests of the vast majority of people. Public ownership of strategic industries is often desired, although in recent decades state regulation rather than direct public ownership has become a more common policy option.	There should be a mixed economy based on a thriving private sector, along with a strong public sector to address matters of collective need. Some strategic industries should be under public ownership, but regulatory direction rather than direct ownership is now the more common policy option.
Free enterprise vs. state socio-economic control	Capitalism is the best form of organization for economic growth, wealth generation, and individual liberty.	The government should take the lead in setting and directing economic and social policies to promote the common welfare of society.	The state has a significant role to play in regulating the economy and in promoting social welfare policy.
Tradition	Traditions and social norms must be respected and upheld.	Social change should be evolutionary and democratic.	Social traditions should be respected, but society should always be seeking ways to progress.

Security Policy

- The public sector must support law and order and national security.
- Governments should be tough on crime, with an emphasis on punishment over rehabilitation for criminal convicts.
- Government should support a strong national defence. In a dangerous world, military power is the most important form of power in international relations.
- International security comes from the ability of the state to project its power onto the world stage in two forms: military capability and membership in international political and military alliances. A strong private sector able to compete globally through systems of free trade also projects power and therefore fosters security.

Social Policy

- Government should pass laws and design policies that promote the principles of individualism and individual liberty.
- Government should support family values and traditional social mores. This is emphasized in particular by **social conservatives.**
- Government should implement policies to advance individual responsibility.

THE SOCIAL DEMOCRATIC STATE

State Role

- The state should set and direct economic and social policies for the common welfare.
- The state should regulate the private sector to ensure that health and safety standards, labour rights, consumer protection, and environmental protection standards are met.

Economic Policy

- The state should encourage economic development and full employment.
- The public sector should regulate the private sector and should, if necessary, directly control economic activity through the use of Crown corporations.
- The state should advance economic nationalism and Canadian control of its own leading industries.
- The government should support a mixed economy.

Financial Policy

- The state should support fair and progressive taxation that places the tax burden more fully on those who can more easily bear the cost, including corporations.
- Taxation should be seen as a social obligation, the payment necessary to provide the goods and services needed by society.
- Government should be fiscally prudent but not shy away from public spending.

Security Policy

- Domestic security should come from strong social and economic policies. Crime is best dealt with through the preventative measures of a sound educational system, high employment, and an effective social welfare system.
- International security is best achieved through the promotion of social justice,

HARPER CONSERVATISM: RADICALLY RIGHT-WING OR MORE CENTRIST?

Was the Harper government fundamentally conservative or really more moderate and centrist? It's a tale of two perspectives.

The Fundamentalist Viewpoint

- Major reduction in taxation (cuts to GST, personal income tax, and corporate income tax) were effected
- Taxation became a "dirty word"
- Tough-on-crime policies became mainstream
- Long-gun registry was eliminated
- Restrictive approaches to the application of the Charter of Rights were supported
- Overall size and scope of the federal government was reduced
- Role of senior public servants in making public policy was diminished
- Long-form census was eliminated
- Gag orders on federal public servants became normal
- Partisan attacks against federal public servants and parliamentary watchdogs such as the Parliamentary Budget Officer, the federal Privacy Commissioner, the Chief Electoral Officer, and the Ethics Commissioner became usual

- Partisan attacks against the Chief Justice of the Canadian Supreme Court were seen
- Federal budget omnibus bills designed to limit parliamentary scrutiny of proposed federal legislation became usual
- Substantial deregulation of Canadian economy, especially in relation to natural resource extraction and pipeline industries, occurred
- Crown corporations (Canadian Wheat Board, Atlantic Canada Opportunities Agency, Canada Post, Canadian Broadcasting Corporation) were privatized/commercialized
- Strong climate change policy and any form of carbon tax/cap-and-trade policy were resisted
- Canadian foreign policy was realigned with greater emphasis on war/fighting over peacekeeping, promotion of foreign trade over promotion of human rights, resistance to effective international climate change policy, and fervent support for the state of Israel over a more balanced approach to the Israeli-Palestinian issue

The More Centrist Viewpoint

- Continued support for the Canada Health Act, though with capped federal funding
- Continued support for bilingualism and biculturalism policy
- Continued support for multiculturalism policy
- Continued support for federal equalization and regional development policy
- No federal initiatives to ban abortion

- No federal initiatives to reinstate capital punishment
- No federal initiatives to restrict immigration
- Continued restriction on the ownership of handguns
- No initiatives to privatize the Canadian Broadcasting Corporation
- Use of Keynesian economic policy (stimulus spending) during the recession of 2008–10

QUESTION PERIOD

If you are conservative-minded, how do you account for the Harper government's moderation on many matters? Was this just politics or a sign of something deeper? If so, what?

If you are centre-left in your thinking, did the Harper government fundamentally change Canada for the worse? Or have the core values of Canadian centrism survived? Can liberal/social democratic policy approaches be revived? If so, which ones would the Canadian public most readily support? How has the Trudeau government been dismantling the Harper legacy? And what will/should remain of this legacy?

Be prepared to support your positions with concrete arguments and examples.

democratic development, and economic improvement throughout the world.

Social Policy

- The state should guarantee that all citizens have equal access to core entitlements such as education, health care, social security (pensions, employment insurance, welfare benefits), and human rights.
- Government should respect the private sector but not be afraid to challenge it when necessary to advance the interests of society.
- Socio-economic change should be measured and gradual.
- The state should promote multiculturalism, social equality, and human rights.
- The Canadian government should promote social justice at home and abroad.

THE LIBERAL STATE

State Role

- The public sector should play a significant role in regulating the private sector.
- The state should regulate the private sector to ensure that health and safety standards, labour rights, consumer protection, and environmental protection standards are met.
- The public sector should promote the long-term best interests of the private sector while also advancing broader social and public interests.

Economic Policy

- The state should encourage economic development and full employment.
- The federal government should support national infrastructure development.

- The federal government should support the building of oil and gas pipelines as long as they meet all environmental and social safeguards.
- The state should advance Canadian economic nationalism.
- The government should support a mixed economy.

Financial Policy

- The state should support fair taxation under which the tax burden is placed more fully on those who can more easily bear the cost, including corporations, but taxes should never be allowed to become too high.
- The wealthy should be expected to pay higher taxes than middle and lower income Canadians because they have benefited most from life in this society.
- Governments should be fiscally prudent but not shy away from public spending.

Security Policy

- The state should be tough on crime but even tougher on the social causes of crime. It should promote sound education, a thriving economy with high employment rates, and strong social welfare protections in order to reduce criminality.
- International security requires a two-pronged approach: a strong national defence capacity coupled with international policies to promote economic development, social justice, and the expansion of liberal democracy throughout the world.

EVOLVING SOCIAL DEMOCRACY: POLICY OPTIONS

Shift Left

- Support new federal social programs such as national child care, First Nations development, abolition of university tuition, national pharmacare plan
- Challenge free trade agreements and promote regulated trade, with labour and environmental standards clauses
- Support a larger federal government with a greater presence in the lives of Canadians
- Support greater social justice policy to fight growing inequality
- Promote the public sector by defending the role and prestige of public servants
- Increase corporate taxes and individual taxes on the most wealthy
- Increase GST by 1 to 2 per cent
- Promote strong international environmental treaties
- Support strict CO_2 emission reduction standards
- Restrict further development of the Alberta oil sands
- Advance new, alternative green technologies and energy policies
- Restrict military spending
- Promote peacekeeping

Shift Right

- Accept Liberal socio-economic policies
- Accept existing free trade agreements
- Promote the role of the private sector by accepting that government is subordinate and designed to facilitate the economic goals of free enterprise
- Support corporate tax cuts
- Support cuts to GST
- Support a smaller federal government with a lessened impact on the lives of ordinary Canadians
- Support flexible, intensity-based emission standards
- Support the development of oil and natural gas pipelines to get these products to international markets
- Ensure environmental policies support existing economic opportunities
- Support tough-on-crime policy to promote justice in Canadian society
- Accept enhanced role for the military
- Promote peacemaking

QUESTION PERIOD

If the NDP moved to the left, would it ...

- Increase its base of support?
- Betray its core principles?
- Render itself unelectable?

If the NDP moved to the right, would it ...

- Increase its base of support?
- Make itself irrelevant?
- Become identical to the Liberals, leading to talk of a merger with that party?

Be prepared to support your position with concrete arguments.

Social Policy

- The state should guarantee that all citizens have equal rights to core entitlements such as education, health care, social security (pensions, employment insurance, welfare benefits), and human rights protection.

- Government should respect the private sector but not be afraid to challenge it when necessary to advance the interests of society.
- Socio-economic change should be measured and gradual.

EVOLVING LIBERALISM: POLICY OPTIONS

Maintain the Centre-Left

- Greater spending on social policy, health care, postsecondary education
- Renewed emphasis on Indigenous policy
- Promotion of environmental policy and greater stress on strict reductions to carbon emissions
- Focus on advancing social justice and human rights
- Greater concern about social inequality and public policies to combat this
- Greater willingness to increase federal revenues through taxation to generate income to devote to social needs
- Marrying humanitarian aid and social development initiatives to military action in such places as Iraq, Syria, and Libya
- Concern for international development
- Renewed commitment to peacekeeping

Shift Right

- Greater spending on tax cuts, business incentives, public debt reduction
- Greater concern for border security and illegal immigration
- Focus on industrial productivity, economic growth, job creation
- Interest in getting tough on crime and strengthening the Criminal Code
- Concern for national defence
- Support for US War on Terror

QUESTION PERIOD

If the Liberal Party maintained the centre-left, would it ...

- Increase its base of support?
- Ensure victory in the next election?
- Weaken its ability to win the next election?
- Marginalize the NDP?

If the Liberal Party moved to the right, would it ...

- Increase its base of support?
- Betray its core principles?
- Weaken its ability to win the next election?
- Threaten the Conservatives?
- Give new life to the NDP?

Be prepared to support your position with concrete arguments.

- The state should promote bilingualism and biculturalism, multiculturalism, social equality, and human rights.
- The Canadian government should promote social justice at home and abroad.

IDEAS, POLICY, AND THE ROLE OF THE STATE IN PRACTICE

Above, I've outlined various forms of political theory. But there is always a difference between theory and practice, so how do these ideas fare when they have to exist in the real world of politics and government? Conservative, social democratic, and liberal thought are all fundamental and legitimate elements of the political spectrum in this country. They are *fundamental* in that all three schools of thought have been instrumental, at various times and in different parts of the country, in shaping the way Canadians understand their society, economy, and politics. And they are *legitimate* in that all three exist within the realm of democratic thought; each approach is fully consistent with the principles and practices of parliamentary government, majority rule, respect for minority rights, free and fair elections, respect for human rights and freedoms, and obedience to the rule of law. Each can also claim a long and distinguished pedigree in our national history as having formed a part of our evolving understanding of what it means to be Canadian, of how and why Canadians should interact with one another, and of the role of the state in serving the social, economic, and governmental needs of this country (Horowitz 1996).

Although all three approaches are important elements of our political tradition, they have not been equally influential on how Canadians, and their governments, think and act.

THE TRIUMPH OF THE LIBERAL CENTRE

Throughout the twentieth century, modern liberalism was the most influential form of political thought and government practice in this country. The pre-eminence, even dominance, of liberal values can be attributed both to the breadth of the centrist liberal approach and to its flexibility—its willingness to borrow (some critics would say steal) ideas from across the political spectrum to produce a successful blend of political principle and practical results.

Liberalism is very much an **ideology of the centre**: it enlists the best and most reasonable ideas from conservatism on the right and Fabian socialism on the left in order to form an effective and coherent set of values and policy approaches. Its supporters see liberalism as an ideology of principled compromise and pragmatic wisdom—representative of, and appealing to, the moderate centre of political life. This political centre has become remarkable for its sound economic management—dedicated to regulated free enterprise, economic growth, and a mixed economy—and balanced support for a wide array of social, environmental, and cultural policies designed to serve the needs of all people.

The political attractiveness of such an approach is readily apparent in its ability to appeal across the ideological spectrum, and the Liberal Party of Canada turned that wide appeal to its electoral advantage over the past century. The party adopted modern liberalism (reform liberalism, as it was known at the time) at its 1919 convention and, under the leadership of William Lyon Mackenzie King, came to be the centrist party par excellence (Ball et al. 2010, 63–65; Whitaker 1977). It claimed the middle ground of Canadian politics and has rarely been pushed from that position since. The party has proven capable of borrowing from the left or right as circumstances require but always enveloping these accommodations in the mantle of liberal principle. And by dominating the centre, the Liberal Party likewise dominated federal electoral outcomes, demonstrating that most Canadians tend to share centrist political and ideological leanings. Liberal federal administrations prevailed for 72 years of the twentieth century, 43 of them between 1935 and 1984, the period during which modern society and the modern liberal state were born. The electorate thus saw fit to make the Liberal Party the most successful federal party over the past century (Ball et al. 2010; Dyck and Cochrane 2014), expressing generalized support for a mixed economy, Keynesian macro-economic management, progressive social welfare policy, and moderate taxation regimes that have come to characterize what it means to be Canadian. As Michael Harris (2014) and John Ibbitson (2015) have noted, however, a young Stephen Harper always bristled at this contention, believing that the liberal consensus in the country was really one promoted by metropolitan leftist elites who did not represent the real middle class of Canadians living in suburbia, small towns, and rural Canada. If he could ever get into power he was intent on reshaping Canada along more ideologically conservative lines.

The policies, programs, and structures of the federal government, particularly following World War II, reflected all the important elements of the modern liberal state. From the end of the war through to the mid-1980s, the country witnessed the vast growth of the state as the governments of Mackenzie King, Louis St. Laurent, Lester B. Pearson, and Pierre Elliott Trudeau created policies and programs designed to improve Canadian social and economic well-being. The full scope of these initiatives is quite astonishing. They ranged from a broad array of programs commonly referred to as the social safety net (family allowances, the Canada Pension Plan, the unemployment insurance system, disability insurance, and federal transfer funding to the provinces in support of provincially administered social welfare programs) to the establishment of a health care system in which all citizens have equal access to state-funded medical services regardless of province of residence or ability to pay. Such activist policies also included federal financial support for a comprehensive post-secondary system of colleges and universities, and for a variety of programs to promote development in disadvantaged regions of the country. These regional development initiatives came with a guarantee of federal support for financial equalization payments to the have-not provinces to enable them to provide essential public services equal to the national norm.

And the activist state created by these successive Liberal governments accomplished much more. Official bilingualism and biculturalism policy, dating from 1969, and multiculturalism policy, dating from 1972, promoted French- and English-language rights and the cultural interests of more recent immigrant groups. Human rights policies, including affirmative action and employment equity programs, were advanced by the Canadian

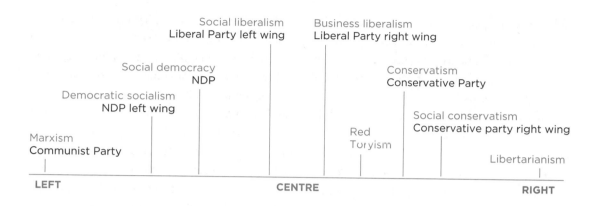

Figure 2.1 **The Canadian Political Spectrum**

Human Rights Commission, established in 1975. Cultural policy was promoted through such agencies as the CBC, the CRTC, the National Film Board, the Canada Council, and Sport Canada, benefiting interests as diverse as the music and film industries, amateur hockey, and the National Ballet of Canada.

Under Liberal leadership the federal government also became prominent in the economic life of the country after World War II. Successive Liberal governments practised a variation on Keynesian macro-economic management, pumping public monies into the economy via long-term policies of social spending, infrastructure development, and industrial subsidy, all with a dual purpose: they were intended not only to meet immediate social and industrial goals but also to prime the private sector and thus enhance economic activity, job creation, consumer confidence, production, and growth. Major economic infrastructure programs, for example, ranged from the Trans-Canada Highway system and the

TransCanada Pipeline of the 1950s to the steady development of a nationwide air transportation system in the 1960s and 70s. A variety of Crown corporations, regulatory agencies, economic development agencies, think tanks, and state programs were introduced with the purpose of enhancing economic performance, and by the 1980s federal Crown corporations and subsidiaries, regulatory agencies, and related economic development actors numbered well over 200.

All such government activity elevated the federal state (and eventually most provincial governments, too) in the ordinary life of the country. The public sector grew organizationally and financially, as the scope of its activity increased and its political and economic significance rose compared to the private sector. The cost of maintaining this level of government programming also grew, resulting in higher taxation rates or, as was more and more common from the mid-1970s to the mid-1990s, rising annual public sector deficit financing, contributing to the national debt. The impact of this trend is outlined and assessed in greater detail in later chapters. The important point here is that all such growth was justified by governments at the time as a desirably activist and progressive response to very real social and economic needs.

It is also worthy of note that state growth in the postwar decades was generally supported by all major political parties, as well as by the public. Indeed, it has long been argued that the electoral success of the Liberal Party throughout most of the second half of the twentieth century can be attributed to its correct understanding of mainstream Canadian public opinion. It reacted to the blend of progressive yet prudent, statist yet entrepreneurial, Keynesian, moderate-reform liberal thought adhered to by most citizens (Figure 2.1).

CONSERVATIVE VARIATIONS

The dominance of liberal ideology over these years had a significant impact on the fortunes and orientations of the Liberal Party's main challengers. The prevailing influence and electoral appeal of liberalism came to exert a profound moderating pull on the federal Progressive Conservative and New Democratic parties (Horowitz 1996, 156–60; Ball et al. 2010, 92–99, 152–60; Dyck and Cochrane 2014, 326–30). As it became abundantly clear that most Canadians had more or less progressively liberal and centrist political orientations, and that the Liberal Party was superbly positioned to reap parliamentary majorities from this wide bloc of public opinion, these other political parties became more centrist. From as early as the 1920s and through to the 1980s, this dynamic caused the parties of the left and right to take more moderate and liberal policy positions and—if and when they were able to win power—more moderate actions.

The Conservatives refashioned themselves numerous times over these years, even adding Progressive to their official title in the 1940s in an effort to signal to Canadians that the party was not reactionary in its economic thinking. In fact, the Conservative Party was never as conservative as its name implied; inspired by **Red Toryism**, it often endorsed direct state action in economic and social development. Examples include the National Policy and the construction of the Canadian Pacific Railway under the government of John A. Macdonald, the creation of the CBC under the government of R.B. Bennett, and the maintenance of Crown corporations inherited by Conservative governments such as that of John Diefenbaker.

It can be argued that from the 1950s to the 80s the Progressive Conservative Party was just as Keynesian as the Liberal Party. So pronounced was the policy convergence of the two mainstream federal parties following World War II that people often wondered whether they could be meaningfully distinguished on any substantive policy or program. The limited record of Conservative governments from the Great Depression to the Mulroney era (the Bennett government of 1930–35, the Diefenbaker government of 1957–63, the Clark government of 1979–80) suggests that there was little to differentiate the two parties other than the personalities of their leaders, internal party managerial competence, and the related ability to win majority governments: Liberals—generally very great; Progressive Conservatives—generally rather poor (Perlin 1980).

Conservative electoral success was much more prevalent at the provincial level, however, and various Progressive Conservative parties became well-established powers within particular provinces, while the Social Credit Party was a dominant force in Alberta from the 1930s through to the 1960s. In all cases, it is intriguing to note how relatively centrist and "liberal" such conservative governments became once they actually had to embrace the task of governing while also dealing with a Liberal federal government embarked upon progressive and activist state policies.

Progressive Conservative governments in the Maritimes, such as those of Robert Stanfield in Nova Scotia in the 1960s and Richard Hatfield in New Brunswick in the 1970s and 80s, were distinctly Red Tory in policy outlook, especially with regard to economic development initiatives, the creation of industrial and transportation infrastructure, and support for new health and social welfare programs subject to federal funding assistance. The Progressive Conservative government of Bill Davis in Ontario during the 1970s and early 80s was also noted for a variety of progressive social and economic policy initiatives: rent controls, the creation of GO Transit, environmental protection policies, and the steady elaboration of human rights protection and enforcement as the multicultural face of the province changed. The Progressive Conservative government of Peter Lougheed in Alberta in the 1970s and early 80s shared this moderate and even reformist mantle, with its support for the creation and elaboration of a national health care system based on substantial federal support of provincially administered hospitals, as well as its own foray into state intervention and direction through the Alberta Heritage Savings Trust Fund (based on oil and gas royalties), whose monies were used to invest in new and emerging primary, secondary, and tertiary industries within the province.

While all such moderate, centrist, and statist policies and programs can be attributed to the unique political conditions facing these governments, it should be borne in mind that all had to address public opinion that was essentially supportive of the activist federal state. No wonder even Progressive Conservative governments in the provinces came to replicate, albeit in more modest fashions, the interventionist federal state (Dyck 1996). All such moderate conservatism, however, would eventually come to be challenged by a new breed of much more ideologically motivated Conservative leaders starting with Preston Manning in Alberta, who established the Reform Party of Canada in 1987 to promote a more purist approach to conservative policy, followed by the Mike Harris Conservative government in Ontario from 1995 to 2002. And carefully watching and supporting these developments was Stephen Harper.

SOCIAL DEMOCRATIC VARIATIONS

A similar historical analysis applies to the New Democratic Party. While the NDP always espoused a social democratic policy orientation, its political rhetoric has moderated over the decades (Morton 1986; McLeod 1994; Whitehorn, 1996). Indeed, its forerunner, the Co-operative Commonwealth Federation (CCF), was founded in the depths of the Great Depression with an explicitly socialist mandate calling for massive state regulation of the economy, the nationalization of all major economic sectors (including the banks), and the eventual elimination of the capitalist system. Armed with such an idealistic vision of the left, the CCF was able to make itself a significant player in federal politics during the 1940s and 50s, becoming the dominant force in Saskatchewan provincial politics. The Saskatchewan CCF, under the leadership of Tommy Douglas, won the provincial election of 1944, inaugurating 20 years of uninterrupted CCF/NDP government in the Prairie province.

Such electoral and governmental success, however, was unmatched anywhere else in the country at either the federal or provincial level. By the mid-1950s the leadership of the CCF had recognized that mainstream Canadians, including the vast majority of working-class men and women, were moderate in their ideology and more liberal than socialist in outlook. If the party were to gain electoral success it would have to move closer to the centre of the political spectrum. This it did in the late 1950s and early 60s, amending its constitution to eliminate the controversial "eradication of capitalism" platform and stressing the need for all progressive and liberally minded Canadians to come together to help build a country founded on an active state but also comprising a vibrant private sector. As part of this political transformation the party name was changed to the New Democratic Party—emphasizing democracy over **socialism**.

This shift to the centre has been a significant development in Canadian political history. Once it won power in Saskatchewan in 1944 and was called upon to govern the province, the CCF under Premier Douglas proved to be more moderate and centrist than its own rhetoric had suggested. Capitalism was not abolished in Saskatchewan, nor was the continued viability of the private sector ever threatened. The CCF government in practice supported a balance of private and public sector leadership in running the economy, long before the official platform of the CCF/NDP came to endorse this political stance. The NDP has won power at various times in six provinces—British Columbia, Saskatchewan, Manitoba, Ontario, Nova Scotia, and Alberta—and in all instances their policy and program positions have been far from radical. Not one of these governments ever sought to "socialize" its province, and most came under attack from their own party loyalists and supporters for becoming too moderate, too willing to compromise on social democratic principles in an effort to retain public popularity and political support. The trials and tribulations of the Ontario NDP government of Bob Rae (1990–95) illustrate this point (Monahan 1995). The NDP government elected in Alberta in 2015, led by Premier Rachel Notley, also fits this pattern, with the newly elected premier taking pains during her first days in office to reassure Albertans and the national and international business community that her government, while being progressive, would support the core economic interests of the province and its focus on natural resource extraction, and recognizing the important place of the private sector in the economic life of the province.

This does not imply that the ability of these governments to provide effective social democratic governance was limited or compromised. Some of them, especially those in the West, were amongst the most progressive and influential provincial governments in Canadian history, and those in Saskatchewan were legendary for their pioneering role. They were

- first in establishing comprehensive, publicly funded medical care;
- first in establishing provincial human rights legislation;

- first in establishing postsecondary student loan programs; and
- a leader in promoting provincial Crown corporations and regulatory agencies to oversee the development and management of key economic sectors.

In all these matters, the CCF/NDP governments of Saskatchewan led the way, providing social and economic direction not only respected by most people in the province but also demonstrating to Canadians in general, and to other parties in particular, how governments could play a more active and beneficial role in the lives of citizens.

MAINTAINING THE LIBERAL CENTRE

These lessons were not lost on the federal Liberal Party. Its ability to borrow, adapt, refurbish, reform, reorder, and even steal popular ideas from other mainstream parties—whether right or, more often, left—and turn them into its own policies, platforms, and programs is another significant feature of Canadian political history. Adopting and adapting a popular political message while stripping the original messenger from the message itself is clearly an organizational skill of prime importance, and one finely honed by the federal Liberal Party over decades of practice (Wearing 1981; Clarkson 1996; Dyck and Cochrane 2014, 318–21).

Just as it was clear to the CCF/NDP leadership that the party had to move toward the centre if it ever wished to get elected, so the federal Liberal leadership gradually realized that some of the policy positions advocated by the CCF/NDP—unemployment insurance, old age pensions, family allowances, welfare entitlements, labour

law reform, and national health insurance—had wide and growing popular appeal. If the Liberals could champion these causes as their own while reassuring Canadians that such reforms would be introduced only in measured, pragmatic, and economically viable ways, reasoned Liberal strategists, then the party itself could gain the support of voters seeking progressive policies while keeping the support of those who wanted social and economic prudence. Thus, the Liberals adopted a classic centrist party stance: they presented themselves as the party of sound practical and managerial judgement, capable of running a moderate mixed economy effectively while also being receptive to the new ideas, concerns, principles, and policies ascendant in political discourse and gaining widespread favour.

And so they were trusted by the vast majority of citizens to offer sound, stable, and prudent social and economic management, in no way dangerous to economic health or the existing social system. Furthermore, implicit in this was a promise for the future, that when social consensus for new ways of addressing social and economic problems arose, the state would be prepared to address those concerns and deliver popular and progressive policy with effective management.

THE SHIFTING CENTRE

To understand the political undercurrents of public policy development and public sector management, we must realize not only that parties can and do shift their positions along the axis of the political spectrum but also that the centre of the axis can itself move left or right as prevailing social

TABLE 2.2

Federal Governments and Prime Ministers since 1900

YEARS IN POWER	PARTY	PRIME MINISTER
1900–11	Liberal	Wilfrid Laurier
1911–17	Conservative	Robert Borden
1917–20	Unionist*	Robert Borden
1920–21	Conservative	Arthur Meighen
1921–26	Liberal	William Lyon Mackenzie King
1926	Conservative	Arthur Meighen
1926–30	Liberal	William Lyon Mackenzie King
1930–35	Conservative	R.B. Bennett
1935–48	Liberal	William Lyon Mackenzie King
1948–57	Liberal	Louis St. Laurent
1957–63	Progressive Conservative	John Diefenbaker
1963–68	Liberal	Lester B. Pearson
1968–79	Liberal	Pierre Elliott Trudeau
1979–80	Progressive Conservative	Joe Clark
1980–84	Liberal	Pierre Elliott Trudeau
1984	Liberal	John Turner
1984–93	Progressive Conservative	Brian Mulroney
1993	Progressive Conservative	Kim Campbell
1993–2003	Liberal	Jean Chrétien
2003–06	Liberal	Paul Martin
2006–15	Conservative	Stephen Harper
2015–	Liberal	Justin Trudeau

* Conservative–Liberal wartime coalition

attitudes change. The point is simple, yet it has profound implications for parties, governments, and the public they serve.

History has demonstrated that the liberal centre of the Canadian political spectrum has been the predominant ground for building public support. As we have just seen, the success with which the Liberal Party held the centre led the other leading parties to moderate—to "liberalize"—their platforms to appeal to the majority of voters.

But the centre is not anchored in an unchanging moderate liberal environment. It moves in response to changing social and economic ideas and so must be defined relative to the times. In other words, the centre is defined in terms of the political values of the majority, and its nature depends on the desired nature of society, the economy, and the role of the state. Since most major parties want to dominate the central political ground because it is where, by definition, most of the population and thus most of the votes are to be found, we can see a gradual transformation of political platforms and party policy over the past century (Dyck and Cochrane 2014, 328–30). And the centre has been shifting to the right over the last 40 years. The **social liberalism** of the Pierre Trudeau days was slowly eclipsed by the revived conservatism of the Mulroney government and the **business liberalism** of the Chrétien and Martin governments. With the election of the Harper Conservative government in 2006, Canadians witnessed the rise of a prime minister with a distinctly ideological approach to governing: Prime Minister Harper very much wanted to roll back the liberal features of the state in Canada while seeking to make Canada ever more conservative in its laws, policies, approaches to politics and government,

and in the way Canadians think about themselves and their relationship to one another and the state. An intriguing debate soon developed as to whether Canada still had a predominantly liberal political culture or whether we became a country better described as conservative (Ibbitson 2015; Boessenkool 2015).

We will delve into these issues shortly, but to comprehend where we are now and the degree to which Canadian political culture may have changed in the past decades we have to know from where we have come. Full coverage on the historical evolution of Canadian political culture in the twentieth century and the shifting centre in Canadian political life is to be found on the Thinking Government website. You are encouraged to read it. The highlights of this history are presented below.

THE LAISSEZ-FAIRE DECADES: 1900–1930s

- Political culture predominantly conservative
- Strong belief in free enterprise, capitalism, market economics
- Economy largely unregulated
- Era of small governments with limited impact on the economy
- Era of minimal taxation; income tax introduced in 1918 as a "temporary" wartime measure
- Apart from Workman's Compensation, few public social security systems
- Federal Liberals in 1919, led by Mackenzie King, endorse social liberalism but, through 1920s and 1930s, more rhetoric than reality

THE EFFECTS OF DEPRESSION AND WAR: THE 1930s AND 1940s

- Economic collapse, widespread poverty, social malaise
- The system wasn't working
- The CCF becomes the voice of democratic socialism
- World War II brings sense of social purpose
- World War II introduces the command economy
- The federal government takes the lead in directing the economy to work for the war effort; Keynesian economics in full swing
- Mackenzie King government promises there will be no return to the Depression after the war; the era of social liberalism will begin
- Government policies could advance social welfare
- National unemployment insurance system introduced in 1940
- National labour relations system recognizing collective bargaining between labour unions and management introduced in 1944
- National family allowance system introduced in 1945

SOCIAL LIBERALISM: THE 1950s TO THE 1980s

- Public health care first introduced in Saskatchewan in 1946
- Federal old age security plan introduced in 1952
- Federal-provincial system of equalization introduced in 1957
- Canada Pension Plan introduced in 1965
- National federal-provincial health insurance system introduced in 1968

- Official bilingualism introduced in 1969
- Official multiculturalism introduced in 1971
- Canadian Human Rights Act introduced in 1977
- Canadian Charter of Rights and Freedoms becomes law in 1982
- Federal employment equity policy established in 1986
- Through these years government was seen, by many, as an agent of social progress
- By the 1980s the Canadian social security system had been built

THE CENTRE SHIFTS RIGHT: THE 1980s TO 2006

THE MULRONEY GOVERNMENT: 1984–93

- Growing concern about deficits and debt
- Growing belief that government was too big, too bloated, too expensive
- Growing belief that government wasn't the solution to problems, it was the problem
- Growing belief that the private sector needed to be promoted, that free enterprise needed to be unshackled
- Federal government promoted privatization of federal Crown corporations, most notably Air Canada, Canadian National Railways, Petro-Canada
- Federal government promoted deregulation of the economy, lesser regulation on Canadian businesses
- Federal government promoted Canada–United States Free Trade Agreement, 1989

- Federal government established the goods and services tax (GST) in 1990 as a means of eliminating the federal deficit

THE CHRÉTIEN GOVERNMENT: 1993–2003

- Although campaigning on the left in the 1993 election, Chrétien quickly moved to the right once in office
- Federal government endorsed North American Free Trade Agreement, 1994
- Federal government maintained the GST (although Chrétien had promised to "axe the tax" in the 1993 election)
- Federal government promised in 1995 to eliminate the federal deficit of $43 billion
- Between 1995 and 1997 the federal government balanced the budget through a combination of tax revenues gained from a growing national economy, devoting surplus billions of dollars from the employment insurance system to deficit reduction, and mandating major cutbacks to the federal public service through the system of Program Review
- Between 1995 and 1999, Program Review led to the elimination of 39,444 full-time federal public service jobs (18.1 per cent of the total federal public service)
- The Chrétien government continued the processes of privatization of federal Crown corporations and the deregulation of the Canadian economy
- With the advent of healthy government surpluses beginning in 1997, the bulk of surplus revenues went to tax cuts for individuals and corporations, as well as paying down the national debt

- The Chrétien government signed the Kyoto Accord in 1997 but failed to live up to its commitments respecting greenhouse gas emission reductions
- Between 2000 and 2005 $100 billion was spent on individual and corporate tax cuts
- Although the Chrétien government three times promised a national public day care system (during the elections of 1993, 1997, and 2000), it never delivered on this promise

THE MARTIN GOVERNMENT: 2004–06

- Maintained the focus on tax cuts and paying down the national debt
- Maintained the focus on deregulation of the national economy
- Maintained the support for "business-friendly" economic and regulatory policies
- Supported major spending initiatives for health care ($75 billion over 10 years) and Aboriginal policy (the $5 billion Kelowna Accord), and began to make good on the long-promised national public child care system, devoting $5 billion to this initiative

THE HARPER GOVERNMENT

In the federal election of 2006, the Conservative Party led by Stephen Harper won a minority government, marking the advent of one of the most controversial periods in Canadian politics and government. The Conservatives ran on a very disciplined policy platform, promising

- to cut the GST by two percentage points
- to cut individual and corporate tax rates
- to bring in a Federal Accountability Act

- to provide tax credits to families needing day care
- to get tough on crime
- to increase funding to the Canadian military

This conservative agenda resonated with a plurality of Canadians, and once in power Harper quickly moved to make good on all his campaign promises. By the fall of 2008 his government could claim success on all these matters as well as a series of other conservative initiatives:

- strong support for the United States in the War on Terror
- continued commitment to the NATO mission in Afghanistan
- fervent defence of Israel and its security needs
- promotion of free trade with the United States and other countries
- promotion of increased trade relations with China and India
- support for the Canadian oil and gas industry
- climate change policy that supported the use of carbon emission intensity targets and harmonization of Canadian and American environmental policies
- a diminished role for the federal government through downsizing, privatization, and deregulation
- the downplaying of federal social welfare policy and concomitant support for traditional family values, such as individual responsibility, self-help, private charity, religious marriage, and disciplined child rearing
- recognition that the provinces should take the lead in health, education, and social welfare policies (Flanagan 2009; Plamondon 2009)

The Harper government emphasized its commitment to a smaller government that taxes less, is less of a burden on the private sector, and favours free enterprise and individual liberty. Through such policies, it sought to reorient Canadian politics and public policy to the right on the ideological spectrum. The Conservative Party won re-election to another minority government in 2008, although with an increased seat count, and then, in 2011, Stephen Harper won his long-coveted prize: a strong, stable national majority government. Freed from the limitations of a minority government, Prime Minister Harper had the power to put his own distinctive stamp on Canadian politics and government.

And this he did. According to analysts such as Bricker and Ibbitson (2013), Ibbitson (2015), and Boessenkool (2015), the Harper government continued its deliberate and well-planned shift of the centre rightward, leading to a fundamental reorientation of Canadian political culture. As Ibbitson (2015) stressed, we are now a much more conservative country than at any point in Canadian history, and it will be hard for any future government of whatever political stripe to undo much of what Stephen Harper has wrought. The conservative accomplishments of the Harper government are many:

- An emphasis on individual and corporate tax cuts, and the vilification of any idea that taxes should ever be increased. To Stephen Harper, there is no such thing as a good tax.

- An emphasis on tough-on-crime policies, stressing the importance of heightened punishment over convict rehabilitation, the necessity of mandatory minimum sentences, the need to fetter judicial discretion in criminal sentencing, and the promotion of the idea that, despite a steady decrease in crime rates since the 1960s, Canadians need to fear criminality; that crime is caused by evil-doers; that crime has no sociological antecedents such as poverty, weak child rearing, poor schooling, or early childhood education and socialization; and any attempt to challenge any of these ideas is to be labelled "soft on crime."
- A downsizing of the federal government and privatization of Crown corporations such as the Canadian Wheat Board, Atomic Energy of Canada Limited, and Enterprise Cape Breton Corporation, with the related initiative of downplaying the role of the federal public service as a leader in policy making in favour of policy making coming from the political realm of the Prime Minister's Office. Coupled to these realities were the government's aims to limit the ability of public servants to speak publicly about their research; to impose strict, centrally directed message control over all communications coming from the federal public service; and to engage in direct partisan attacks against any public servant, especially Officers of Parliament such as the Parliamentary Budget Officer or the Chief Electoral Officer, who would challenge government policy initiatives.
- An emphasis on oil and gas development and the building of pipelines.
- Criticism of national and international climate change initiatives that would have the effect of reducing reliance on carbon fuels, of imposing strict limits on greenhouse gas emissions, and of imposing economic penalties on air pollution via some form of carbon taxation or a system of cap-and-trade regulation of carbon emissions.
- The use of omnibus budget bills to pack dozens upon dozens of legislative changes into scores of usually unrelated federal laws and policies. Such bills often ran to hundreds of pages of technical detail and resulted in a single Yes or No vote, with MPs having limited opportunity to scrutinize and assess these many legislative changes or offer constructive criticism of government planning.
- The focus of Canadian foreign policy being rooted both to the promotion of Canadian trade and commerce over the promotion of international human rights, and the need to assert Canadian interests on the world stage with military force and the support of key allies. This more belligerent approach to foreign policy downplayed the once-traditional approach of Canadian peacekeeping while favouring combat missions in Iraq and Syria in the never-ending fight against global jihadi terrorism, fervent and one-dimensional support for the official Israeli government position in the Israeli-Palestinian conflict, and unquestioning support for Ukraine in the Ukraine/Russia conflict.

IDEOLOGY AND THE HARPER GOVERNMENT

Many critics of Stephen Harper viewed his government as unrelentingly right wing, fundamentally changing the nature of Canadian politics and society and laying the groundwork for a much more conservative, and meaner, country. To many strict conservatives, however, the Harper government has a history of disappointment: a conservative in name but often betraying true conservative values and policies in practice. Here's a snapshot of the debate.

	TOO CONSERVATIVE	TOO LIBERAL
Style of governance	• Dismissive of opposition, parliamentary traditions • Used prorogation to avoid non-confidence votes • Excessive use of omnibus bills to obstruct parliamentary oversight of legislation • Authoritarian style of governing • Disrespectful of federal public service • Promoting American-style negative politics	• Size of government too big • Little decentralization of power • No limitation on equalization policy
Security	• Excessive military spending	• Limited action on pro-gun laws
Foreign policy	• Too militaristic an approach to international terrorism • No longer an "honest broker" in the Middle East • Too close to Israel	• Not tough enough on jihadi terrorism • Not tough enough on Putin and Russia • More military spending required for national defence
Economic policy	• Excessive tax cuts • Poor management of economy • Excessive reliance on/promotion of oil and gas industry • Weak promotion/support of manufacturing sector	• Inadequate tax cuts • Promoted Keynesian economics • Return to deficit financing • National debt increasing • No privatization of CBC • No privatization of health care
Social policy	• Killed national day care policy • Obstructive environmental policies • Reduced funding to social advocacy groups • Killed Kelowna Accord on Aboriginal policy	• No restrictions on abortion • No ban on gay marriage • No action on capital punishment

QUESTION PERIOD

- Was the Harper government committed to conservatism? Or to pragmatism? Support your argument.
- Which do you see as more at play in the Harper government: liberal or conservative ideology? Or was there a blend of both?
- What does this say about the art of governing in this country?

- A focus on the War on Terror that also resulted in unprecedented initiatives by the Harper Government found in 2015's Bill C-51 (supported by the Liberal Party) to dramatically enhance Canadian police and security agency powers to engage in surveillance, disruption, and detention of suspected terrorists or terrorist sympathizers within Canada. Terrorism was defined broadly to include threats to harm Canadians and Canadian economic interests, and these additional security powers were subjected to minimal judicial and parliamentary oversight.

While commentators such as Flanagan (2009), Plamondon (2009), Harris (2014), and Ibbitson (2015) have found Harper to be quite effective in these tasks, it is important to note the staying power of certain key liberal dynamics in his government's public policy:

- Abortion remained legal.
- The Canada Health Act remained in place, although subject to federal funding increases limited to the percentage growth of national GDP.
- Official bilingualism policy remained in place.
- Federal multiculturalism policy remained in place.
- Federal human rights legislation remained in place.
- CBC funding was reduced, but the institution remained in place as a federal Crown corporation.
- Canada Post remained a Crown corporation, although with a more commercialized focus of service delivery.

- Federal environmental protection legislation was amended and made more limited, but not eliminated.
- Capital punishment remains a prohibited form of tough-on-crime policy.
- Although the long-gun registry has been eliminated, the federal government still continues to impose very restrictive and prohibitive laws concerning handgun ownership in comparison to American gun laws.

IDEAS, POLICY, AND THE FUTURE ROLE OF THE STATE

Future chapters address contemporary federal financial and human resources management issues in more detail; here we simply recognize the staying power of core features of Canadian public policy and public administration, dating back decades. Even with a Conservative government dedicated to shifting public policy to the right, we still see the limits to such trends. In other words, the core features of the liberal centre of public policy remain highly prized by most Canadians, such that a Conservative government had to tread carefully for fear of alienating the very people it needed to attract to its cause.

It is noteworthy that from the very outset of Stephen Harper's quest for the prime ministership he let it be known that a government led by him would not legislate on abortion, would not diminish bilingualism or multiculturalism policy, would support the Canada Health Act, would promote Canadian human rights policy, and would safeguard the basics of health, safety, and environmental protection legislation. Critics can and will challenge how successfully he adhered to these policy ambitions, especially in light of the disaster that occurred with the train derailment and explosion at Lac Mégantic in Quebec in 2013, ongoing concerns about the regulatory effectiveness of the Canada Food Inspection Agency, and the cutbacks to the federal system of environmental assessment of new industrial initiatives, especially in relation to the oil and gas industry and the construction of related pipelines. We see here, however, a Conservative leader and government still recognizing the significance of the liberal centre even as it endeavoured to shift the country rightward.

A telling indication of the continuing importance of the liberal centre in Canadian politics and government during the Harper years was the federal budget of 2009. As Canada was slipping into the recession of 2009–10, the government brought forth a stimulus budget, very much demanded by the opposition parties, launching an action plan to pump $55 billion into the Canadian economy between 2009 and 2011. Much of this federal spending was designated to federal, provincial, and municipal infrastructure, along with support for the automobile industry and for Canadians needing employment insurance assistance. And all this spending was to be funded through deficit financing.

After years of denouncing deficit spending, the Harper government initiated a plan that envisioned federal deficits until 2014–15. It defended these initiatives as smart and necessary policies to ameliorate the worst effects of the recession and to help Canadian industries get back to growth. The opposition parties and many in the national media, however, were quick to note that the stimulus package was a classic example of Keynesian planning: the state was to play the lead in pumping money into an ailing economy to ease the pain of unemployment and spur growth when the private sector could not. As such, a progressive role for the state was vindicated, and even the Conservative government was compelled to realize that there were times when the federal government had to take the lead in serving national economic and social interests.

As the Harper government settled into power it was constantly assailed by the opposition parties. The federal Liberal and New Democratic parties denounced it for bringing forth policies such as the two percentage point cut to the GST, cuts to the CBC, and moves to privatize the Canadian Wheat Board and Atomic Energy of Canada Limited—seeing them as evidence of a desire to reduce the presence of the state. And while the Conservatives refrained from legislating on abortion, all the opposition parties stressed that such restraint in this and other policy fields was probably only due to fear of the consequences rather than any belief in the right of women to control their own bodies. All of them attacked the government for reneging on the terms of the Kyoto Accord, for taking no serious initiatives to actually reduce Canada's carbon footprint, and for working to obstruct and weaken international agreements on climate change policy.

In many instances, however, opposition criticism was simply directed at the style of Stephen Harper's leadership. He was often censured for an autocratic and authoritarian style of leadership, and for being dismissive of criticism, closed to alternative ideas, and excessively partisan. The issues of leadership

WILL STEPHEN HARPER LEAVE A LEGACY?

Between 2006 and 2015 the Conservative government of Stephen Harper promoted many policy initiatives. How many of these will survive the reign of Justin Trudeau?

- The two percentage point cut to the GST
- Cuts to individual and corporate tax rates
- Tax credits for family day care
- Tough-on-crime policies/mandatory minimum sentences
- Elimination of the long-gun registry
- Elimination of the long-form census
- Elimination of the per-vote subsidy for political parties
- Strong support for the US-led War on Terror
- Funding increases for the Canadian military
- Fervent defence of Israel
- Promotion of free trade agreements
- Great support for the Canadian oil and gas industry

- Resistance to climate change policy that would harm the Canadian oil and gas industry
- Privatization/commercialization of federal Crown corporations
- Reduced funding for the CBC
- Downplaying the policy role of the federal public service
- Centralized decision making in the Prime Minister's Office

As 2015 recedes into history, reflect on this list and note the degree to which the Trudeau government is downplaying, altering, and eliminating these legacy items. But note what remains.

and accountability are the focus of later chapters, but it bears mention that the very tightly disciplined, highly centralized command-and-control approach to leadership exhibited by Harper—in which all key decisions in his government emanated from his office—did not begin with him. We will study the origins of this approach to leadership in the next two chapters.

TRUDEAU REDUX

If one needs further evidence of the continuing influence of liberal-centrist ideas and policies in Canadian politics, look no further than the results of the 2015 federal election. While the Trudeau Liberals won with only 39.5 per cent of the vote, this victory was a resounding defeat for the Conservatives. Stephen Harper, the sitting prime minister, was only able to garner 31.2 per cent of the popular vote, compared to 39.6 per cent in 2011, meaning that he had lost moderate swing voters and could only claim the support of dyed-in-the-wool Conservatives. This percentage is certainly considerable in Canadian politics but it is, on its own, incapable of winning the Conservative Party a majority government. And the Canadians voting against the Conservative government, and very much voting against Stephen Harper himself, accounted for the vast majority of Canadian voters. To the Liberal popular vote numbers were added the 19.7 per cent of Canadians who were New

Democratic supporters, 6.0 per cent who were Bloc Québécois voters, and 3.4 per cent who were Green supporters. Fully 68 per cent of Canadians who cast ballots voted in opposition to the Harper government.

With the rise to power of the Liberals under the leadership of Justin Trudeau, Canadians witnessed the return of a traditional Liberal government with traditional liberal values and instincts. The Trudeau Liberals came to Ottawa promising

- a middle class tax cut
- tax increases on the wealthiest Canadians (those earning over $200,000 per year)
- $60 billion in infrastructure spending over three years
- modest federal deficits in the $10 billion per year range
- balanced federal budget by 2019
- stronger environmental regulations
- serious action on climate change and major greenhouse gas emission reduction targets
- to get Canadian oil and natural gas to international markets through the construction of pipelines to tidewater, with these pipelines meeting all environmental and social concerns
- to launch a national inquiry into missing and murdered Indigenous women
- to engage with Indigenous leaders, provincial premiers, and municipal leaders
- to reinstate the long-form census
- to re-establish a respectful working rapport with the federal public service
- to reform federal anti-terror legislation (Bill C-51) to enhance Charter protections and parliamentary oversight

- to legalize and tax marijuana sales and possession
- to increase funding for the CBC and arts organizations
- to reform Canadian election laws so that the 2015 election would be the last one run under the single-member plurality (first-past-the-post) system
- to promote greater openness, transparency, and accountability in government, inclusive of greater accessibility by and to the media
- to limit the use of omnibus budget bills
- to make the Canadian government and cabinet more reflective of the diversity of Canadian society
- to withdraw Canadian CF-18s from the air war against ISIS in Iraq and Syria while enhancing Canada's military training mission for Iraqi Kurdish forces and promoting greater humanitarian relief
- to settle 50,000 Syrian refugees in Canada by the end of 2016
- to reassess the need for F-35 fighter jets for the RCAF
- to promote Canadian involvement in UN peacekeeping missions while re-engaging in diplomatic relations with such countries as Iran and Russia

This list, exhaustive and detailed, was a reflection of the pent-up liberal desire for change that was alive in the country by 2015, and it represented a wave of reformist ideals that the Harper Conservatives could not denounce into oblivion. Rather, it was these ideals, and the vast numbers of Canadians who were moved by them, that washed away the Conservative government. Justin Trudeau rode this wave of reform into power, meaning that he began his mandate with great expectations upon his shoulders. Such expectations, however, can soon lead to bitter disappointment if people do not see those expectations being fulfilled by new government policies, programs, and spending commitments. Justin Trudeau set the bar high for himself and his government in the fall of 2015. If he is to deserve re-election in 2019, he will need to fulfill most of these commitments he made to Canadians. Look at the above list of commitments and think about whether they have been achieved or not.

THE RECORD

Regardless of the rise and fall of parties and governments, two points remain fundamental. The first is that ideological beliefs continue to be important to our political evolution and the work we expect our governments to do. While the centre of Canadian political thought remains dominated by liberal values, it is far from static, being susceptible to influence from both the right and the left. Past Canadian governments have generally taken a moderate liberal centrist policy and program approach, but the centre of the political spectrum has shifted as social and political beliefs about the role of the state have changed. Over the three decades leading up to 2015 the centre moved right. As of 2015, however, we witnessed a dramatic shift to the centre-left. Canadians of a liberal-left orientation applauded this move; more conservative-minded persons expressed concern if not dismay at what they were seeing. Such is politics.

The second point follows from the first. The role of the state is central to all political and ideological discourse in this country, and whichever the party is that forms the government, certain issues always dominate the national debate:

- the nature of the ideal state and the degree to which the current state meets this ideal in practice;
- the public responsiveness of government and the degree to which bureaucratic authority is subject to democratic control;
- the ability of government departments, agencies, and Crown corporations to deliver mandated policies economically, efficiently, effectively, ethically, and accountably; and
- the quality of leadership exhibited by politicians and senior public servants.

These points attest to the importance of public sector management. Regardless of what a government tries to accomplish in terms of policy and programs, effective management of the state is crucial. A close study of the evolution, nature, and current dynamics of public sector management is therefore at the forefront as we review and assess the inner workings of Canadian government in the following chapters.

REFERENCES AND SUGGESTED READING

Adams, Michael. 2003. *Fire and Ice: The United States, Canada, and the Myth of Converging Values.* Toronto: Penguin.

Bell, David. 2008. "Political Culture in Canada." In *Canadian Politics in the 21st Century*, 7th ed., edited by Michael Whittington and Glen Williams, 228–59. Toronto: Thomson Nelson.

Ball, Terence, Richard Dagger, William Christian, and Colin Campbell. 2010. *Political Ideologies and the Democratic Ideal.* 2nd Canadian ed. Toronto: Pearson Canada.

Barlow, Maude, and Bruce Campbell. 1991. *Take Back the Nation.* Toronto: Key Porter Books.

Bazowski, Raymond. 1999. "Contrasting Ideologies in Canada: What's Left? What's Right?" In *Canadian Politics*, 3rd ed., edited by James Bickerton and Alain-G. Gagnon, 79–108. Toronto: University of Toronto Press.

Belous, Richard S., and Jonathan Lemco. 1995. "The NAFTA Development Model of Combining High- and Low-Wage Areas: An Introduction." In *NAFTA as Model of Development: The Benefits and Costs of Merging High- and Low-Wage Areas*, edited by Richard S. Belous and Jonathan Lemco, 1–20. Albany: SUNY Press.

Boessenkool, Ken. 2015. "Ordered Liberty: How Harper's Philosophy Transformed Canada for the Better." In *Policy Options*. Montreal: IRPP. http://policyoptions.irpp.org/2015/12/01/harper.

Bricker, Darrell, and John Ibbitson. 2013. *The Big Shift: The Seismic Change in Canadian Politics, Business, and Culture and What It Means for Our Future.* Toronto: Harper Collins.

Clarkson, Stephen. 1996. "The Liberal Party of Canada: Pragmatism versus Principle." In *Party Politics in Canada*, 7th ed., edited by Hugh G. Thorburn, 262–79. Scarborough, ON: Prentice Hall Canada.

Delacourt, Susan. 2003. *Juggernaut: Paul Martin's Campaign for Chrétien's Crown.* Toronto: McClelland and Stewart.

Dobrowolsky, Alexandra. 2000. "Political Parties: Teletubby Politics, the Third Way, and Democratic Challenge(r)s." In *Canadian Politics in the 21st Century*, edited by Michael Whittington and Glen Williams, 131–58. Toronto: Nelson.

Doern, G. Bruce. 1978. "Introduction: The Regulatory Process in Canada." In *The Regulatory Process in Canada*, edited by G. Bruce Doern, 1–33. Toronto: Macmillan Canada.

Dyck, Rand. 1996. *Provincial Politics in Canada: Towards the Turn of the Century.* 3rd ed. Scarborough, ON: Prentice Hall Canada.

———, Rand, and Christopher Cochrane. 2014. *Canadian Politics: Critical Approaches.* 7th ed. Toronto: Nelson.

Flanagan, Tom. 2009. *Harper's Team: Behind the Scenes in the Conservative Rise to Power.* 2nd ed. Montreal: McGill-Queen's University Press.

Gagnon, Alain-G., and A. Brian Tanguay, eds. 2006. *Canadian Parties in Transition.* 3rd ed. Toronto: University of Toronto Press.

Gibbins, Roger, and Loleen Youngman. 1996. *Mindscapes: Political Ideologies towards the 21st Century*. Toronto: McGraw-Hill Ryerson.

Gollner, Andrew B., and Daniel Salée, eds. 1988. *Canada under Mulroney: An End of Term Report*. Montreal: Véhicule Press.

Gray, John. 2003. *Paul Martin: The Power of Ambition*. Toronto: Key Porter Books.

Greenspon, Edward, and Anthony Wilson-Smith. 1997. *Double Vision: The Inside Story of the Liberals in Power*. Toronto: Seal Books.

Harris, Michael. 2014. *Party of One: Stephen Harper and Canada's Radical Makeover*. Toronto: Viking.

Horowitz, Gad. 1996. "Conservatism, Liberalism and Socialism in Canada: An Interpretation." In *Party Politics in Canada*, 7th ed., edited by Hugh G. Thorburn, 146–62. Scarborough, ON: Prentice Hall Canada.

Ibbitson, John. 2015. *Stephen Harper*. Toronto: Signal/McClelland and Stewart.

Johnson, William. 2005. *Stephen Harper and the Future of Canada*. Toronto: McClelland and Stewart.

Johnston, Larry. 1996. *Ideologies: An Analytic and Contextual Approach*. Toronto: University of Toronto Press.

Martin, Lawrence. 2010. *Harperland: The Politics of Control*. Toronto: Viking Canada.

McLeod, Ian. 1994. *Under Siege: The Federal NDP in the Nineties*. Toronto: James Lorimer.

McQuaig, Linda. 1995. *Shooting the Hippo: Death by Deficit and Other Canadian Myths*. Toronto: Penguin Books.

———. 1999. *The Cult of Impotence: Selling the Myth of Powerlessness in the Global Economy*. Toronto: Penguin Books.

Monahan, Patrick. 1995. *Storming the Pink Palace: The NDP in Power: A Cautionary Tale*. Toronto: Lester Publishing.

Morton, Desmond. 1986. *The New Democrats 1961–1986: The Politics of Change*. Toronto: Copp Clark Pitman.

Nelson, Ralph. 1995. "Ideologies." In *Introductory Readings in Canadian Government and Politics*, 2nd ed., edited by Robert M. Krause and R.H. Wagenberg, 25–40. Toronto: Copp Clark.

Perlin, George. 1980. *The Tory Syndrome: Leadership Politics in the Progressive Conservative Party*. Montreal: McGill-Queen's University Press.

Plamondon, Bob. 2009. *Blue Thunder: The Truth about Conservatives from Macdonald to Harper*. Toronto: Key Porter Books.

Rae, Bob. 2015. *What's Happened to Politics?* Toronto: Simon and Schuster.

Thorburn, H.G., and Alan Whitehorn, eds. 2001. *Party Politics in Canada*. 8th ed. Scarborough, ON: Prentice Hall Canada.

Walker, Michael A. 1993. "Free Trade and the Future of North America." In *Beyond NAFTA: An Economic, Political and Sociological Perspective*, edited by A.R. Riggs and Tom Velk, 13–21. Vancouver: Fraser Institute.

Wearing, Joseph. 1981. *The L-Shaped Party: The Liberal Party of Canada 1958–1980*. Toronto: McGraw-Hill Ryerson.

Whitaker, Reginald. 1977. *The Government Party: Organizing and Financing the Liberal Party of Canada 1930–1958*. Toronto: University of Toronto Press.

———. 1996. "Party and State in the Liberal Era." In *Party Politics in Canada*, 7th ed., edited by Hugh G. Thorburn, 249–61. Scarborough, ON: Prentice Hall Canada.

Whitehorn, Alan. 1996. "Audrey McLaughlin and the Decline of the Federal NDP." In *Party Politics in Canada*, 7th ed., edited by Hugh G. Thorburn, 315–35. Scarborough, ON: Prentice Hall Canada.

Wiseman, Nelson. 2007. *In Search of Canadian Political Culture*. Vancouver: UBC Press.

Woolstencroft, Peter. 1996. "The Progressive Conservative Party." In *Party Politics in Canada*, 7th ed., edited by Hugh G. Thorburn, 280–305. Scarborough, ON: Prentice Hall Canada.

RELATED WEBSITES

POLITICAL PARTIES

Bloc Québécois. www.blocquebecois.org

Conservative Party of Canada. www.conservative.ca

Green Party of Canada. www.greenparty.ca

Liberal Party of Canada. www.liberal.ca

New Democratic Party. www.ndp.ca

POLITICAL INFORMATION

Canoe. www.canoe.ca

The Hill Times. www.hilltimes.com

Canadian Broadcasting Corporation. www.cbc.ca

University of British Columbia Library, Political Science. http://guides.library.ubc.ca/politicalscience

CHAPTER 3

Institutions of Governance

A form of government that is not the result of a long sequence of shared experiences, efforts, and endeavours can never take root.

–Napoleon, 1803

After reading this chapter and its related web pages you will be able to

- identify the key powers and roles of the prime minister;
- understand how prime ministers build cabinets;
- appreciate the scope of ministerial duty and responsibility;
- describe the structure and functions of departments; and
- identify the roles and purposes of Crown corporations and regulatory agencies.

3   Institutions of Governance

The executive institutions of the federal government are intricate. Pioneering scholar of leadership Warren Bennis once remarked, "Government is like an onion. To understand it, you have to peel through many different layers. Most outsiders never get beyond the first or second layer." At the apex of power stand the pre-eminent decision-making authorities: the **prime minister**, **cabinet**, government departments, the senior management of the public service, and—to the uninitiated—an often bewildering variety of **cabinet committees** and **central agencies**, all mandated with providing leadership to the federal government and, thereby, to the Canadian people. These authorities perform the executive tasks demanded of any managerial body: strategic priority setting; policy and program direction, making, and implementation; sound management; and the creation of accountability structures to hold those who exercise power responsible for their actions. But this is a public management system at the head of a democratic government and therefore it must also ensure that ultimate responsibility is borne by democratically elected representatives of the people.

These obligations impose important challenges not only for those working in government but also for those seeking to understand it. How is the executive command system of the federal government organized? Who are the pivotal actors? What mechanisms does the system employ? Does it indeed have sound managerial capacity, especially in relation to priority setting, program implementation, and policy and program review and analysis?

And what about power relations within the executive? How do the roles and responsibilities of elected cabinet ministers relate to those of unelected senior public sector managers? Do such officials exercise too much power, and can a more effective balance be found between politicians and bureaucrats? Finally, what is the nature of prime ministerial authority, how has it evolved in recent decades, and what are we to make of the increasing centralization of executive power?

The dynamic centre of government resides in power relations within the federal executive. To understand that truism, we will explore the evolution of the executive structure over the past six decades—especially in the Pierre Trudeau, Brian Mulroney, Jean Chrétien, and Stephen Harper governments—and the command system of decision making found in the Justin Trudeau **ministry**.

THE POLITICAL EXECUTIVE

The cabinet is the central executive decision-making body of the federal state, and directing it is a minister above all others—the prime minister. Together they form the political executive. The prime minister, the head of government, is the most influential person in the federal state. All analyses of Canadian government thus come to revolve around the composition and exercise of prime ministerial authority.

It is therefore perhaps surprising that the responsibilities of the executive institutions are nowhere codified within the constitution (Monahan 2006, chap. 3). Rather, the office of prime minister and the organization of cabinet exist within the realm of constitutional conventions, uncodified yet immensely strong traditions that flesh out the skeletal constitutional text. In the Constitution Act, 1867, formal executive power in and over Canada is vested in Her Majesty the Queen and is officially exercised by the governor general. Section 13 of the Constitution Act, 1867 also provides for the establishment of the **Privy Council**, to be appointed by the governor general to "aid and advise" that official in the exercise of executive duties, while also stipulating that the exercise of all general powers by the governor general "shall be construed as the Governor General acting by and with the Advice of the Queen's Privy Council for Canada."

In the formal language of the Constitution Act, 1867, the Privy Council is thus designated as the body that will exercise the *de facto* ("in fact," whether or not recognized legally) executive authority in the country as opposed to the *de jure* ("by right," fully legal) executive power of the Crown. This is in keeping with the traditions and practices of British parliamentary democracy. In formal constitutional law, the Privy Council is the advisory body to the governor general, but important constitutional conventions have grown up around the exercise of Crown powers and those of the Council, and it is here we must look to understand the emergence of real political power in this country.

When making appointments to the Privy Council, the governor general draws from the ranks of the party commanding the confidence of the House of Commons. This is not a matter of law but of convention and takes place with almost the

same force of expectation as if it were law. It is also the only practicable course of action. The leader of the governing party becomes the prime minister, *primus inter pares*—the first among equals—within the Privy Council. Appointment to the Privy Council is thus contingent on one's party winning an election, gaining either a majority or at least a plurality of the seats in the House of Commons. Democratic victory entitles the winning party to form a government by assuming command of the Privy Council, which will aid and advise the governor general in the exercise of all executive authority within the ambit of the federal state. A further constitutional convention stipulates that, in the exercise of such executive power, the governor general shall generally follow such advice as orders, thus making the Privy Council itself, and not the governor general, the effective executive authority in the state.

Appointments to the Privy Council are lifelong, an honorary testament to the importance of the appointee in the public life of the country. With lifelong appointments, however, the full membership of the Council naturally becomes quite large. As of 2016 the full Privy Council had 390 members. This, of course, is a wholly unworkable size for an executive advisory body, especially when its composition makes it susceptible to political dissension. Eight of the last nine prime ministers are still living, representing governments of various political stripes dating back to the late 1970s, and all of them have a spot on the Council. Thus, the convention has become that only privy councillors selected from the current parliament act as the *de facto* advisers of the governor general, forming the real executive within the country. This stipulation effectively turns current members into an

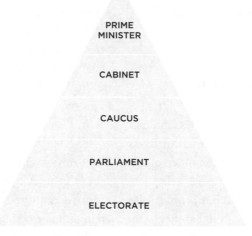

Figure 3.1 **The Political Hierarchy**

executive committee—a cabinet—of the full Privy Council. Chaired by the prime minister, the cabinet exercises full executive authority in and over the federal state.

The formal appointment process of the cabinet bears scrutiny for what it tells us both about the powers of the prime minister and about the political demands placed on him or her in establishing a broadly representative executive governing authority (Jackson and Jackson 2009, 274–75; Webber 2015, 92–97). Following an election, the governor general calls on the leader of the winning party to form a government. The governor general appoints this person to the Privy Council and bestows on him or her the title "the Right Honourable," at which point he or she becomes prime minister. The prime minister then "advises" (that is, orders) the governor general to make other appointments to the Privy Council as a cabinet to assist in the

exercise of government power. Those selected are usually appointed as ministers of the Crown, each responsible for the leadership and oversight of a department (referred to as a **portfolio**), and given the title "the Honourable." The prime minister can also "recommend" the appointment of ministers of state to the Privy Council. These appointees act as junior ministers, not administering portfolios of their own but serving as assistants to other, more senior ministers.

The senior ministers, along with the prime minister, compose the cabinet proper. If ministers of state are appointed to the Privy Council, they are not full members of cabinet or full participants in its meetings. Rather, they constitute part of what is known as the governing ministry, within which the cabinet remains the executive authority (Aucoin 1999, 113). Once sworn into office, the cabinet becomes the power centre of the federal government, exercising full executive authority throughout the federal state and the country overall. At the apex of this power system stands the prime minister (Figure 3.1).

THE PRIME MINISTER

While the cabinet is the heart of the Canadian government, dominant executive authority is found not so much there as in the office of the prime minister. Contrary to the traditional aphorism that the prime minister is but *primus inter pares*, in truth the PM rules the cabinet. Any claim to equality with other cabinet colleagues is a polite but hollow pretence. As Rand Dyck and Christopher Cochrane (2014, 525–30) have argued, the enormous authority of the prime minister within cabinet can be observed through a variety of powers, privileges, and responsibilities that can be reduced to six points.

LEADING THE GOVERNING PARTY

The prime minister is the leader of the governing party. The political significance of this cannot be underestimated. To win first a party leadership and then an election is no small feat, as any opposition leader would attest. The prime minister has built the party membership, influenced its candidates, imbued it with a political and ideological message, and inspired both its members and at least a plurality of Canadian voters. In the acid test of party politics, that takes those most cherished attributes—political leadership and electoral success.

Thus, the PM will have set a personal stamp on the party, establishing bonds of loyalty with party members in general and the government **caucus**

in particular. An inspirational and successful "commander-in-chief" makes followers want to be a part of his or her vision for the country, to serve as loyal "lieutenants." The most fundamental characteristic of successful leadership—a committed and enthusiastic following—inheres in any prime minister by simple virtue of having gained access to the office.

SELECTING A CABINET

The prime minister has the exclusive power to select a cabinet and alone possesses the privilege of instructing the governor general on whom to appoint. In selecting a cabinet, a prime minister will be influenced by constitutional conventions and political assumptions, but the power of choice nonetheless gives a prime minister extraordinary influence over the elected party members—the caucus—and cabinet. The prime minister alone decides who from within the parliamentary caucus will gain a seat at the cabinet table, and the cabinet so chosen will in turn reflect the PM's goals, ambitions, and desires for the party and government.

Cabinet membership also reflects a leader's sense of who is most capable of the job, most experienced in political leadership, most loyal and deserving of promotion, and who is a rising star and future inheritor of the current prime minister's legacy. And, finally, the PM's cabinet appointments must also be understood in a negative sense, as a power of dismissal. The prime minister alone has the full and final power to ask for the resignation of a minister or to dismiss the minister. All ministers serve "at the pleasure" of the PM, and all know that their continuation in office depends on maintaining his or her trust and support.

THE PRIME MINISTER'S KEY POWERS AND RESPONSIBILITIES

- Head of government
- Governing party leader
- Cabinet leader, responsible for its selection
- Chief government policy maker
- Chief architect of government structure
- Responsible for appointment of senior executive and judicial officials
- Special direction and oversight relationship to the clerk of the Privy Council with regard to managing the public service and administering policy agenda

- Special relationship to the governor general, issuing direction with respect to calling elections and proroguing parliament
- Government leader in parliament
- Chief communicator of the government
- Chief international representative of the country

SHAPING THE DECISION-MAKING STRUCTURE

The prime minister is also the chief architect of the structure of the government and the cabinet decision-making system. It is the prime minister who determines the number of departments and the scope and nature of these portfolios, sometimes creating new ones and sometimes disbanding others or amalgamating them into other departments. The prime minister is instrumental in deciding the future of regulatory agencies and Crown corporations: should one be created, modified, privatized, or abolished?

Beyond such general matters of government structure, the PM is responsible for the organization of cabinet and the systems of determining policy and making decisions. Each prime minister brings a personal style to cabinet administration, but in the past 50 years efforts to improve the quality and accountability of cabinet decision making have fundamentally transformed its nature and operation. A study of cabinets past and present reveals a seemingly Byzantine system of committees and central agencies designed to coordinate and assist in the process of determining policy priorities, and of complex power relations between senior public servants, senior political advisors, ministers, and the prime minister. Any period of Canadian political history reveals a fundamental political truth: the PM is the predominant figure in every government—always the cabinet maker, always the head of the cabinet, always the chair of the most important cabinet committees, and always the chief policy maker. Because his or her influence is so pronounced, we come quite reasonably to speak of "Trudeau's government," "Mulroney's administration," or "Harper's ministry."

MAKING APPOINTMENTS

The prime minister is vested with wide authority to make appointments within the government and to other state institutions. While the power to appoint cabinet ministers is the most readily apparent, the prime minister also appoints the governor general and the provincial lieutenant-governors; the members of the Senate; the judges of the Supreme Court of Canada, the Federal Court of Canada, and the provincial superior courts; and all Canadian ambassadors abroad.

But possibly even more important than such high-profile appointments as these, the PM also has full discretionary power to appoint the most senior ranks of the federal public service: the heads of federal regulatory agencies and Crown corporations and those who will serve as deputy ministers—the senior public service heads—within each government department. Finally, the prime minister alone has the power to appoint the most senior public servant in the country—the **clerk of the Privy Council** and the secretary to cabinet, who is the official head of the public service of Canada. Here, the PM has the greatest capacity to directly shape and control the government's policy, to set its ideological and managerial tenor, and to order its administrative working.

LEADING PARLIAMENT AND DIRECTING THE GOVERNOR GENERAL

A prime minister's power is related to his or her special role in parliament and link with the governor general. As head of government and of the governing party, the prime minister is the central figure in the House of Commons. The PM sets the tone of parliament and in the daily Question Period is ordinarily the target of opposition attacks and the chief advocate and defender of government policy. Although the prime minister does not attend most of the routine debates in the House of Commons due to time constraints, the proposed legislation emanating from the cabinet sets the Commons agenda, and the convention of party loyalty and discipline influences all government **backbenchers**, who routinely support government policy and vote according to the wishes of the PM and cabinet.

Should any backbencher break ranks with party discipline, the prime minister has an ample array of political weapons with which to punish such an act of disloyalty: private or public reprimand and rebuke, loss of party privileges, expulsion from caucus, or even expulsion from the party altogether. Such actions are of course rare, since most backbenchers are eager to demonstrate their loyalty not only ideologically but also as a way to illustrate their ability to serve the party, thereby attracting the attention of the PM and senior advisors when it comes to future cabinet appointments.

The parliamentary influence of the prime minister is also observed in his or her relationship to the governor general. The power of "advising" in the exercise of executive powers is felt most deeply in reference to the dissolution of parliament and calling of a general election. It is the PM who, as a constitutional rule, possesses the real power to order the termination of a parliamentary sitting and the issuance of writs for new elections. As is often said of politics, timing is everything, and here we observe the PM in sole control of one of the most important political and governmental tools— the timing of the next election.

COMMUNICATING THE GOVERNMENT MESSAGE

The prime minister is the chief communicator for the government abroad and at home. Within the world of international relations the PM is the primary Canadian diplomat, making decisions about our foreign policy and representing Canada at major bilateral meetings with the American president, annual G8 and G20 summits, Commonwealth and Francophonie meetings, and at some United Nations events. On the national stage, the PM acts as the chief public relations officer of the government, carrying the message of the government throughout the country. The prime minister is the ultimate link between the government and the national media as it covers the news and provides journalistic analysis. He or she is expected to engage in press conferences, parliamentary "scrums," and routine interviews with the media, all as a means of advancing and defending the message of the government to the public.

In an era marked by the decline of political party organizations, the growing concentration of power in the hands of party leaders, and the overwhelming influence of television on political life, the leadership role of the PM cannot be underestimated. He or she becomes the living embodiment of government, and this is very much how modern prime ministers wish to be perceived. They are the driving force, the central actor on the political stage, giving direction and meaning to the work of government. They see themselves as the "great communicators" for their governments and try to establish a special rapport with the people of Canada through successful use of the media.

Since the Pierre Trudeau years, this relationship with the Canadian public has become very personal—a bond of trust between the PM as an individual and the general public. Prime ministers must maintain the trust of their parties and followers, but even more so of the country as a whole.

When prime ministers begin to lose such public trust and loyalty, the end of their political careers is at hand.

FORMING A CABINET

SELECTION

The prime minister is the heart and soul, intellect and muscle, of any government. But the PM needs the assistance of ministers, so **cabinet selection** is the first exercise of power. Although the PM is solely responsible for the selection of **cabinet ministers**, several constitutional and political conventions have developed to govern this exercise of prime ministerial authority. In appointing a cabinet every prime minister must address certain realities (Aucoin 1995, 175–78; Dyck and Cochrane 2014, 531–35; Mintz, Tossutti, and Dunn 2014, 428–31).

Choosing from the Elected

The first constraint on the PM's power is that, as a general rule, cabinet ministers must be selected from governing party members holding seats within parliament. This derives from the principle of responsible government: the exercise of government power should ultimately be the preserve of democratically elected politicians answerable and accountable for their actions before parliament. In this sense, the prime minister and cabinet are first and foremost members of parliament (MPs), elected representatives of the people, leading the party that commands the confidence of the House of Commons. They have a right to power only for as long as their government can maintain majority support on the floor of the Commons. An

HOW DO YOU BUILD A CABINET?

A cabinet minister should
- hold a seat in the House of Commons
- be appointed on merit

The cabinet as a whole should reflect
- the ideological diversity of the governing party
- provincial and regional diversity
- provincial representation proportionate to population
- French and English representation
- equitable representation of women
- equitable representation of ethnic, visible, and other minorities
- equitable representation of religious groups

Choosing from the Unelected

But there can be exceptions. A cabinet minister does not *necessarily* have to come from the House of Commons. A prime minister may appoint a member of the Senate to cabinet and may even, on rare occasions, appoint an "ordinary" citizen as a minister. These are exceptions to the "Commons' rule." In the first case, prime ministers in the past have usually appointed one senator from the governing party as the government's Senate representative in the cabinet. While this position is usually considered honorary, such a senator does sometimes rise to regional prominence. In the aftermath of the federal election of 1997, for example, the Liberal Party was left without a single seat in Nova Scotia. In such circumstances the prime minister is expected to "reach into the Senate" for a party loyalist coming from the part of the country in question. In this case, Prime Minister Chrétien appointed Liberal Senator Al Graham to the cabinet as both the government representative in the Senate and as the cabinet representative for Nova Scotia. It's noteworthy, however, that in 2015 Justin Trudeau refrained from having a Senate representative in cabinet as a means of distancing his government from that body, now largely discredited due to its lack of democratic legitimacy.

In the second, even rarer case, a prime minister may appoint an unelected citizen. This person is invariably someone with strong party and policy credentials whom the prime minister wishes to see in cabinet for immediate political reasons. It is understood that the person so appointed must undertake to win a seat in the House of Commons as quickly as possible, and that the appointee who fails to do so must promptly resign from cabinet. In

understanding of the constitutional basis for the cabinet explains the democratic foundations of cabinet government as well as the significance of party discipline. It is all important to the continued life of any government.

Because the PM must choose cabinet members from among MPs, a common sense rule follows: he or she will look to the party caucus as the main source of cabinet material. From 1867 on, this has been the general practice for obvious constitutional and political reasons. Cabinet ministers selected from the ranks of the governing party in the Commons have won democratic election and are directly answerable to the opposition parties for their exercise of power. Their selection satisfies the requirements of responsible government.

1996, Stéphane Dion entered cabinet in this fashion as a new representative from Quebec, later winning his Montreal seat in a by-election.

Choosing from Experience and among Rivals

In selecting cabinet ministers, all prime ministers have been motivated by party and cabinet politics, provincial representation, socio-demographic representativeness, and individual talent. They usually see the wisdom in appointing veteran MPs to cabinet, especially those with previous cabinet experience. Knowledge is a form of power, and all prime ministers want to benefit from the collective experience of their ministers. Prime ministers will also tend to appoint the senior leaders of caucus, including MPs who ran for the party leadership but lost.

As Dyck and Cochrane (2014, 532) assert, prime ministers often find it better to have past and present leadership rivals inside cabinet, and thus subject to the constraints of cabinet loyalty and confidentiality, than outside, where they are freer to criticize. It is no surprise that Jean Chrétien named former party leader hopeful Paul Martin minister of finance in 1993 and kept him there throughout his first two terms in office. Likewise, when Stephen Harper became prime minister in 2006 he appointed one-time leadership rival Peter MacKay to his cabinet, where he served in a variety of senior roles, including minister of defence. Stockwell Day, a former leader of the Reform Party, was also appointed to the Harper cabinet, serving in numerous roles, such as president of the Treasury Board of Canada. In 2015 Justin Trudeau had no real rivals to his leadership, so he did not have to worry about this issue.

Choosing Ideologically

All prime ministers are also concerned with the ideological composition of their cabinet in relation to the relative diversity of political opinion within the party. Just as all federal political parties have left, centre, and right wings, relatively speaking, so too will prime ministers tend to want such ideological diversity reflected in the cabinet to make it broadly representative of the sweep of opinion found within the party. Each prime minister, however, will fashion such representativeness to achieve the balance of opinion most desirable and effective in developing and implementing his or her public policy.

Choosing Regionally

Beyond internal party ideological representation is the ideal that every province and each major region of the country should be recognized within a "balanced" cabinet. This principle—recognizing the fact of federalism and the importance of provinces and regionalism in the governance of the Canadian state—has come to be a defining feature of federal cabinet composition. All prime ministers in Canadian history have sought equitable and balanced regional representation in cabinet, constrained only by the availability of caucus members from each province.

In an ideal world, the prime minister wants a strong caucus deriving from all 10 provinces, each being home to a good number of government MPs. The PM can then appoint a provincially representative cabinet, with the more populous provinces having proportionately greater representation. Ontario tends to have the most, followed closely by Quebec. British Columbia and Alberta follow, if numbers permit, with mid-range numbers of cabinet ministers, while the less populous provinces usually find themselves with one or two ministers each (Table 3.1).

A prime minister's task, of course, is made much more difficult when the caucus is not representative of all provinces. A governing party may have few or no elected members from some provinces and scant caucus representation across whole regions. Since the Pierre Trudeau years, the federal Liberals were weak in the West, while following the collapse of the Mulroney government in 1993 the Conservatives have had limited representation in

Quebec. This meant that neither the 1993 Chrétien Liberal government nor the Harper Conservative government of 2006 were fully regionally representative. In 2015 the Liberals made inroads into the West, meaning that Prime Minister Justin Trudeau was able to name cabinet ministers from every province.

Another important political dynamic is that concern for provincial or regional representation can, at times, outweigh or even overwhelm concern for political knowledge and experience in cabinet selection. Simply put, if a province returns only one government MP, that person, regardless of education, background, and experience, is almost guaranteed a seat in cabinet thanks to the representational principle. At the same time, if another province has returned a large contingent of government MPs, such as Ontario's 100 Liberals from 103 ridings in 2000, the vast majority have no realistic hope of ever getting into cabinet. Caucus members from the larger province, disadvantaged by the working of this representational logic, may begin to look to the single caucus member from the other province, now holding a cabinet position, with quiet resentment. The left-out members may feel, with some justification, that they are each individually better suited for the job than the cabinet member who holds the position only by virtue of province of origin.

There are two basic lessons to be derived from this. One is the importance of regional representation in cabinet composition. The other is that cabinet selection often breeds resentment and rivalry between the "ins" and the "outs." It is a fallacy that government parties always unite loyally behind their cabinet. While the government demands that unity and loyalty be the public face

TABLE 3.1

Cabinet Membership by Province/ Territory, 2016

PROVINCE/TERRITORY	MINISTERS
Ontario	11
Quebec	7
British Columbia	3
Alberta	2
Manitoba	2
New Brunswick	1
Saskatchewan	1
Nova Scotia	1
Nunavut	1
Prince Edward Island	1
Newfoundland and Labrador	1
Northwest Territories	0
Yukon	0
Total	31

Note: Data as of February 15, 2016.

of the party, more often than not, behind closed doors, the governing party is marked by divisions and rivalries between caucus members and certain ministers. And while most caucus members usually can be counted on to demonstrate loyalty to the PM, such a display of loyalty and support will not be extended equally to all other members of cabinet.

Choosing Demographically

Although provincial and regional representation is the major consideration in cabinet composition, other socio-demographic concerns have also become significant. All prime ministers have traditionally sought a balance in cabinet between francophones and anglophones, with the former receiving around one-third of cabinet seats to the latter's two-thirds. Prime ministers will also strive for regional balance within these groups, seeking to appoint a certain number of French Canadians from outside Quebec (Acadians or Franco-Ontarians, for example, such as Dominic LeBlanc from New Brunswick in 2015), as well as at least one English Canadian from Quebec (Lawrence Cannon in 2006 and 2008, for example).

The other traditional demographic consideration dating from the time of Confederation is religious balance. Prime ministers establish a rough balance between Roman Catholics and Protestants and a similar sub-balance among the various major Protestant denominations. Over the past century, as religious tolerance has grown within the country, the Jewish community has been represented in cabinet whenever possible. Since the appointment of Herb Gray to the Trudeau cabinet in 1969, Jews have traditionally held one to two cabinet seats (Dyck and Cochrane 2014, 534).

In more recent decades, prime ministers have accommodated concern for gender equality and multiculturalism in their cabinets to a certain extent. A woman first entered the federal cabinet in 1957, when Ellen Fairclough was appointed to the Diefenbaker government, and since then the representation of women in cabinet has slowly grown to the point that in the past two decades they have accounted for roughly 15 to 25 per cent of the total. In 2015, Justin Trudeau made history, finally, in appointing a gender-equal cabinet with 15 of its 30 ministers being female. The prime minister himself counts as the 31st member of cabinet.

Similar evolutionary changes are also to be observed with respect to the representation of ethnic and visible minorities. Whereas the cabinets of Macdonald, Laurier, or Mackenzie King held no such minorities because they simply were not represented in most political parties or government caucuses, this slowly began to change after World War II. Members of European ethnic groups other than French or English began to enter cabinets in the 1950s and 60s, and since then such non-visible minority representation has been taken for granted in federal cabinets. In 2015 Justin Trudeau again made history appointing a record number of four Sikhs to cabinet, including Harjit Singh Sajjan as minister of national defence. Jody Wilson-Raybould also became the country's first Indigenous minister of justice and attorney general, while Maryam Monsef became the first ever Afghan-born cabinet member (minister of democratic institutions). But further progress is still called for. Despite its historic firsts, this cabinet has no members from the East Asian, African Canadian, Southeast Asian, or Latin American communities.

Choosing on Merit

While prime ministers are constrained by both long-established and newly developing expectations of representation, they must balance such demands with individual capabilities, demonstrated merit, and fitness for responsibilities to come. All prime ministers want strong cabinets staffed by ministers with a combination of intelligence, training, experience, determination, social vision, and political acumen. A cabinet appointment is an entrée into the elite ranks of government, a call to the executive leadership of the country. For most politicians, it is what they have dreamed about, and for the vast majority of those privileged to "get the call," the cabinet appointment will be the pinnacle of their political careers.

Given the magnitude of the decision, all prime ministers treat the appointment process with great care, and though the exigencies of provincial/ regional or socio-demographic representation may mean that some cabinet ministers lack ideal qualifications, such appointments tend to be the exceptions to the rule. Prime ministers need and want exceptionally talented cabinet ministers and will work hard to fashion and maintain such a team.

Choosing by Performance

Finally, if it is difficult for an MP to get into cabinet, it is even more difficult to stay there. Cabinet ministers must perform well, and regardless of how they got in, if ministers prove incapable or come to be viewed by the PM as more of a detriment than an asset to the government, they won't last long. With the prime minister's sole power to appoint comes the sole power to remove a "failing" minister and to replace that person with another aspiring caucus member eager to enter the limelight.

And all ministers know this. So long as they can demonstrate sound ministerial leadership, their position is assured, and they can even rise within the senior ranks of the party and government. But should they seriously falter, weakening the political capital of both the government and the party, they will find themselves subject to deep criticism within their own caucus and will lose in the scramble of others claiming to be better able to serve the government and the prime minister.

SIZE

The prime minister also has the authority to dictate the size of the cabinet and its organizational structure (Aucoin 1999, 117–19; Dyck and Cochrane 2014, 535–40; Mintz, Tossutti, and Dunn 2014, 431–33). Cabinet size has varied greatly since Confederation, steadily increasing over the twentieth century until the 1990s. In 1867 the first cabinet of John A. Macdonald had 13 departments and ministers, and subsequent cabinets stood around this number until the 1920s. From 1920 to 1960 the progressive liberal state slowly emerged, and as the role of the state evolved and expanded, so did the size of the federal government. By 1960 the number of departments and ministers stood at around 20, which increased to about 30 under Pierre Trudeau. Mulroney's cabinet in the mid-1980s reached an all-time high of 40 ministers (Table 3.2).

The trend began to reverse in the 1990s with the short-lived government of Kim Campbell, who reduced her cabinet to 24 ministers as a demonstration of her government's commitment to financial restraint and downsizing the public sector. With his advent to power in 1993, Jean

TABLE 3.2

Federal Government Departments, 1867, 1984, 2015

FIRST MACDONALD MINISTRY, 1867	FIRST MULRONEY MINISTRY, 1984	JUSTIN TRUDEAU MINISTRY, 2015
Agriculture	Agriculture	Agriculture and Agri-food
Customs	Communications	Canadian Heritage
Finance	Consumer and Corporate Affairs	Employment, Workforce Development and Labour
Inland Revenue	Defence	Environment and Climate Change
Justice	Employment and Immigration	Families, Children and Social Development
Marine and Fisheries	Energy, Mines and Resources	Finance
Militia and Defence	Environment	Fisheries, Oceans and Canadian Coast Guard
Post Office	External Affairs	Foreign Affairs
Privy Council	External Relations	Health
Public Works	Finance	Immigration, Refugees and Citizenship
Secretary of State	Fisheries and Oceans	Indigenous and Northern Affairs
Secretary of State for Provinces	Fitness and Amateur Sport	Innovation, Science and Economic Development
	Forestry	Justice and Attorney General
	Health and Welfare	National Defence
	Indian Affairs and Northern Development	Public Safety and Emergency Preparedness
	International Trade	Public Services and Procurement
	Justice and Attorney General	Transport
	Labour	Treasury Board
	Multiculturalism	Veterans Affairs
	National Revenue	
	Public Works	
	Regional Industrial Expansion	
	Secretary of State	
	Science and Technology	
	Small Business	
	Solicitor General	
	Supply and Services	
	Tourism	
	Transport	
	Treasury Board	
	Veterans Affairs	
	Youth	

Sources: Canada, Privy Council Office 2015; Hodgetts 1973, 89; Landes 1987, 104.

Chrétien maintained this smaller and supposedly more efficient cabinet while launching a significant alteration of central government administration.

Whereas in the past all ministers had been full members of cabinet, after 1993 Chrétien followed the British model of ministry organization, with two types of ministers: department ministers and secretaries of state. In 1993 Chrétien appointed 22 ministers to head government departments, and these ministers constituted the full cabinet; he also appointed eight secretaries of state to assist department ministers. They were ministers of the Crown sworn into the Privy Council and bound by all the rules of cabinet collective responsibility, but they were not full ministers as they did not possess department portfolios, were not entitled to attend all cabinet meetings, and received neither the salary nor the staff support of full ministers. The Chrétien ministry numbered 30, with 22 in cabinet proper. In 1997 it grew to 37, with 29 full ministers and 8 secretaries of state.

When Stephen Harper became prime minister in February 2006 he maintained the ministry form of cabinet organization while doing away with secretaries of state. All members of Stephen Harper's cabinet were to be full ministers of the Crown. In 2006, in an effort to demonstrate leadership difference from the previous Liberal governments, Harper reduced the size of cabinet to 27. In 2007, however, facing the pressure of governmental work, he added five junior ministers, initially termed secretaries of state and eventually renamed ministers of state. These officials are members of the ministry but not full members of cabinet. Following the election of 2008 the cabinet grew to 38 members, and, after the May 2011 election, the cabinet consisted of 39 members: 25 ministers, the leader of the government in the Senate, the leader of the government in the House of Commons, 11 ministers of state, and, of course, the prime minister (Figure 3.2).

Following his electoral victory in October 2015, Justin Trudeau established a smaller cabinet than that of Stephen Harper. With 31 members including himself, this cabinet was more akin to the first cabinets of both Chrétien and Harper. New prime ministers always like to say that their administrations will be leaner than their immediate predecessor. But history also shows that cabinet membership tends to grow over time as the workload on ministers becomes crushing and the prime minister wishes to reward more valued members of his or her caucus. Also noteworthy of the Trudeau cabinet of 2015 was its historic claim to gender equity.

MINISTERIAL ROLES AND RESPONSIBILITIES

When appointed to cabinet, full ministers are given one or more departments to manage. As the political heads of these portfolios, they are officially accountable to the government, to parliament, and to the Canadian people for all the decisions and actions of their departments and of all the regulatory agencies and Crown corporations reporting to those departments (Archer et al. 1999, 241–43; Jackson and Jackson 2009, 287–88).

Within the British parliamentary tradition, **ministerial responsibility** involves two distinct yet related concepts. First, individual ministerial responsibility, as noted above, means that the minister

Note: Data as of 19 May 2011.

Figure 3.2a **The Harper Cabinet, 2011**

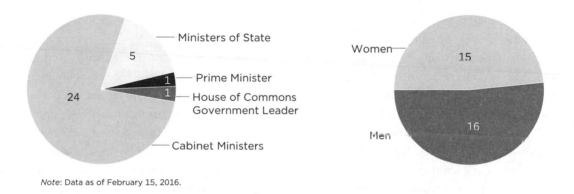

Note: Data as of February 15, 2016.

Figure 3.2b **The Trudeau Cabinet, 2015**

- is individually responsible for the running of his or her department(s);
- is ultimately responsible, before parliament, for the policy and program development of the department(s);
- is accountable for all decisions made by the department(s) while he or she is in charge.

Thus, if need be, the minister is expected to stand in the House of Commons and answer questions from the opposition parties about departmental operations and to explain departmental actions before the media. And if allegations of gross ministerial or departmental incompetence or corruption cannot be defended satisfactorily, the minister is

MINISTERIAL RESPONSIBILITIES

Individual

- Ministers are individually responsible to parliament for the operation of their departments.
- Ministers must answer to parliament for the policy and program developments in their departments.
- Ministers must explain and defend the actions of their departments to parliament.
- Ministers must be prepared to resign if gross ministerial or departmental incompetence is found on their watch.

Collective

- Ministers bear collective responsibility for the final approval of government policy.
- Ministers are expected to support government legislation in parliament.
- Ministers are expected to promote and defend all government policies and programs in public and to resign if they cannot do so in good faith.

expected to resign so that parliamentary and public trust in the government can be rebuilt.

The second concept, much less understood by the public, is collective ministerial responsibility. This necessitates that all ministers, together, support all cabinet decisions and actions. Ministers not only bring discrete departmental concerns, policy issues, and proposed legislation to cabinet for discussion and approval; they are collectively responsible for the executive governance of the country as a whole. All ministers thus bear formal common responsibility for the development of government policy, the approval of draft legislation, the adoption of orders-in-council, and the management of the nation's finances and public personnel systems. In a spirit of "all for one and one for all," each cabinet minister is expected to share an interest in policy and program developments beyond those in his or her own portfolio, to engage in all full cabinet discussions on a host of issues, and to bring considered judgement to

general cabinet business (Mintz, Tossutti, and Dunn 2014, 420–23).

Cabinet, then, must be understood in collective terms. Individual ministers may propose department policy and program initiatives, but cabinet, either as a whole or through its subcommittees, has the right and duty to dispose of these matters as it deems fit. Cabinet discussions can take many forms, but they are meant to be an exercise in collective decision making under the leadership of the prime minister. The prime minister controls the agendas of full cabinet and key cabinet committee meetings and usually seeks the input of all members with respect to agenda items. Cabinet discussions are meant to be frank analyses of

- policy and program options;
- the desired course of government action;
- weaknesses, problems, and dangers confronting government; and
- the best means of overcoming these difficulties.

All cabinet deliberations are strictly confidential. Such secrecy is meant to ensure not only that individual ministers and senior officials can speak their minds freely but that the cabinet as a whole can debate the pros and cons of proposed courses of action, openly assessing their policy and political strengths and weaknesses without fear of publicity prior to making formal decisions.

DECISION MAKING IN CABINET

While the substance of cabinet discussions is secret, we can glean something of their style from the memoirs of former ministers and prime ministers. Cabinet documents themselves are kept confidential for 30 years. Chapter 4 offers a detailed review of the development of modern cabinet decision-making systems, but before we undertake a close assessment, it is helpful to understand the workings of cabinet more generally (Bakvis and MacDonald 1993, 53–57; Jackson and Jackson 2009, 287–91; Dyck and Cochrane 2014, 531–40).

Most prime ministers have preferred to let cabinet engage in wide-open discussion on policy and program proposals, canvassing all possible governmental, political, and socio-economic considerations. It has also been quite common for prime ministers to play a passive role in such free-flowing discussions, often sitting back as ministers hash over the political and administrative pros and cons of a policy matter. In such scenarios, prime ministerial intervention comes in two versions: either toward the end of a discussion, when the PM will summarize the salient points of consideration and his or her sense of the emerging consensus; or in the midst of the debate, when the PM will stress his or her interest in a desired outcome. As Donald Savoie (1999, 84–86) has written of the cabinet meetings of the Pierre Trudeau government, the discussion often resembled a university seminar.

What we know about Stephen Harper's style of governing is that his cabinet meetings would never be described as "university seminars." As both Michael Harris (2014) and John Ibbitson (2015) have noted, Prime Minister Harper's approach to decision making was always highly controlled, authoritarian, and very much top-down. From the inauguration of his first cabinet in 2006 he let it be known to all his ministers that he was the key decision maker in his government, with ministers playing distinct subordinate roles mainly focusing on delivering messages to the public that had already been predetermined by the prime minister and his close advisors in the Prime Minister's Office. Ibbitson, a more favourable commentator on the Harper years than Harris, admits that the Harper cabinet "functioned largely as a talking shop and a rubber stamp." This prime minister showed little patience with meetings of full cabinet because almost all important government decisions had already been made prior to these meetings. All major decisions would be made by select cabinet committees (to be looked at in the next chapter), with the members of these committees handpicked by the prime minister. "When it came to priorities and planning," writes Ibbitson, "the prime minister handles those files himself" (2015, 234).

Justin Trudeau came to power in the fall of 2015 promising to do things very differently from Stephen Harper, with a cabinet and government that would be far more open, transparent, responsive, and accountable to the Canadian people. At the time of writing the "new" Trudeau government is only settling down to the process of governing, so it is too early to assess its art of governing.

Check the Thinking Government website for more recent commentary. One thing history has shown us, however, is that for all the rhetoric of new prime ministers in offering better government, the prime minister remains the number one decision maker in government. All leading approaches and vital decisions emanate from the prime minister, the strategic centre of the government and the key driving force in the cabinet. It is highly unlikely that Justin Trudeau's style of leadership will diverge from this reality for he, and he alone, is the prime minister, the prime mover, the first amongst equals.

Of course, not all ministers are equal in the eyes of the PM or other ministers in terms of experience, length of cabinet service, knowledge of the given policy field, or intellectual sophistication, so their opinions carry different weight. But it has been extremely rare for deliberations to result in a formal vote. Prime ministers have routinely sought consensus—and that emerges sometimes quickly, sometimes more slowly. The reticence to hold votes is easily understood: no prime minister wants to see a minority bloc challenged and defeated by a majority, as it would run counter to the ideal of cabinet as a unified executive force. The concept of collective ministerial responsibility, according to which all ministers must support all cabinet decisions and actions, means that prime ministers want their cabinets to achieve consensus on most policy matters.

Consensus leads ministers to feel themselves a positive part of all decisions taken by cabinet. Furthermore, a system of voting would run the risk of establishing a false equality among ministers, even the prime minister. No prime minister has or ever would accept such a procedure, hence the quest for cabinet consensus under firm prime ministerial leadership.

Once a cabinet decision has been made—a consensus with which the PM is comfortable—the principle of collective responsibility necessitates that ministers close ranks and endorse it as their own. The opposition and media would pounce on any hint of division as a sign of government weakness, and a unified front signals to the entire public service that the executive is strong, that it is committed to the ends it is advancing. An individual minister who cannot support a decision so reached must resign, and although such resignations are rare, the fact that they do occasionally happen shows all the more clearly the collective nature of cabinet decision making.

MINISTERS AS MEMBERS OF PARLIAMENT

Ministerial roles and responsibilities extend beyond department and cabinet responsibilities (Savoie 1999, 240–48; Tardi 2010, 31–32). A minister remains an MP and a caucus member and becomes a much more significant actor within the governing party (Figure 3.4). Ministers must continue to bear all the duties expected of MPs: they take part in Question Period, parliamentary debates, and parliamentary committee meetings, especially in relation to their departmental responsibilities; they continue with routine constituency work, fulfilling the role of local representative for the home riding and ombudsperson for constituents seeking assistance with the federal bureaucracy. All ministers know, or should know, they must assure local electors that, notwithstanding their larger national responsibilities, they remember where they came

Individual ministerial duties

Collective ministerial duties

Member of the governing caucus

Member of the party

Member of parliament

Figure 3.3 **The Responsibilities of a Cabinet Minister**

from, whom they directly represent in parliament, and whose support they need in the next election.

Ministers also remain members of the government caucus and are expected to maintain a close and open relationship with it, being available to discuss government policy and administrative matters, maintaining and building backbench awareness of and support for the activities of government. This liaison is significant to the long-term success of any minister, especially if he or she hopes to be promoted to more important cabinet positions, with even more advanced and demanding leadership requirements. Ministers who ignore the caucus do so at their political peril.

Ministers are seen as primary or secondary party leaders, depending on their portfolios and experience, as loyal lieutenants to the prime minister, and some as future party leaders. Ministers are definitely perceived as spokespeople within cabinet for their home province and region, some indeed owing their presence in cabinet to that role. Other ministers also represent the concerns of women, visible and ethnic minorities, religious minorities, people with disabilities, or Indigenous Canadians.

Whatever role a minister has must be effectively performed not only within the government but also within the party. In practice this means the minister must attend innumerable caucus and party events to promote everything from regional concerns and policy interests to the program ambitions of the social groups the minister is deemed to represent.

It seems a crushing workload. As ministers have long recognized, they could devote 24 hours a day, seven days a week to their portfolios and still not accomplish everything they want to. And what about the pressing demands of constituents, parliament, caucus, and the party? In this environment of competing obligations, time is often a minister's most precious commodity. And of course, ministers also have personal lives. Most yearn for more time with family and friends, cherishing time away from the glare and heat of public responsibilities. And at worst, as Steve Paikin (2003) has documented, the demands of public life can lead to such stress-related problems as the alienation of friends and family members, marriage breakdown, and self-destructive behaviour such as alcohol and drug abuse.

When you think of ministers, reflect for a moment on the stresses and time demands they face, and the sacrifices they must make as their private lives are reconfigured by public duties.

THE BUREAUCRATIC EXECUTIVE

Central to government organization in this country are two types of institution: **departments** and **Crown agencies**. The former are better known, but the latter are also very significant (Tardi 2010, 29–31; Dyck and Cochrane 2014, 555–58; Mintz, Tossutti, and Dunn 2014, 485–90).

Government departments, each headed by a minister, fulfill the chief roles of public sector management. As a prime minister and cabinet make decisions—the what, how, where, and when of modifying programs and initiating policies—they look primarily to departments for the means to these ends. Crown agencies, by contrast, are organizations such as Crown corporations, regulatory bodies, and other service institutions specifically designed to be substantially independent from the government of the day in their routine operations. They develop and implement special policies and programs that require such independence. These two forms of bureaucratic executive institution are examined in turn.

GOVERNMENT DEPARTMENTS

Departments are the workhorses of government, and each has four generic functions:

- policy administration
- policy development
- research, analysis, and record keeping
- communication and liaison

POLICY ADMINISTRATION

First, a department delivers programs within its field of jurisdiction. When a new policy is developed, usually the pertinent department is given responsibility for transforming it into a program: the series of discrete operational tasks and goals that link the department (i.e., the government) to those whom the policy is designed to serve. Thus, departments act as the operational "conveyor belts" of government activity, taking policies and seeing that they are applied within society. But while departments put the work of the current government into practice, most of the programs they implement in fact derive from the policy initiatives of previous governments.

When any government comes into power, it inherits not a bureaucratic vacuum but a full-fledged system of policies and programs across the whole breadth of government activity in any given field, along with administrative divisions fully engaged in maintaining them. The new government can of course alter these functioning policies and programs, but it is rare for one to fundamentally transform *all* such activities. On the one hand, such a task would be absolutely enormous, entailing disruption of monumental proportions to the routine workings of government. On the other, it would be administratively and politically undesirable, indeed foolish. Programs all have established beneficiaries, accustomed to these particular state services, and most are valuable in that they serve long-recognized public needs.

Within any government, then, the influence of earlier decisions is present from the outset. In fact, the vast majority of any government's work involves the implementation of programs promulgated by its predecessors. In this sense all governments are incrementalist, rooting their administration in the policy decisions of the past.

This means that the current government can continue policies without any substantial analysis or administrative review. The Mulroney government inherited the Pierre Trudeau government's policies and programs respecting bilingualism and biculturalism, program funding and equalization payments to the provinces, health care, regional development, immigration and citizenship, human rights, and agricultural subsidy, just as the Chrétien government inherited the Mulroney government's policies and programs in foreign affairs and defence, environmental issues, income security, health care, the GST, and free trade. And despite Stephen Harper's desire to be different from the Chrétien and Martin governments, his government inherited a fully functioning set of Liberal policies and programs for public health care, federal equalization and regional development, public funding for the CBC, gun control, same-sex marriage, and access to abortion.

Although the Harper government inherited a whole set of Liberal policies and programs in 2006, it quickly moved to implement sweeping changes, as outlined in the previous chapters, to make Canada generally more conservative. The government of Justin Trudeau, in turn, inherited Harper's policies, from tax cuts and a belief in a smaller federal government, to a limited climate change policy, ongoing support for the oil and gas sector, and a more belligerent foreign policy. The Trudeau government quickly began distancing

DISPATCH BOX

KEY DEPARTMENT FUNCTIONS

- Delivering programs and services
- Conducting research and policy analysis
- Maintaining records
- Communicating internally and engaging in liaison with other, related interests
- Adhering to all financial management rules and regulations
- Adhering to human resources rules and regulations
- Training departmental staff

itself from many of these policies, stressing the need to re-engage with the world community on climate change policy, the promotion of a foreign policy more geared to international collaboration over conflict, and more moderate and centrist social and economic policies at home. But Harper-era free trade agreements remained a priority of the new government, as did the desire to promote the oil and gas industry through pipeline development, all the while stressing the need to do this in an environmentally sustainable manner.

POLICY DEVELOPMENT

Another vital function of departments is policy development. Each department becomes expert within its field in dealing with

- the operational strengths and weaknesses of existing policies and programs;
- the continuing needs of individual citizens, interest groups, or business corporations as clients of the department; and

- the potential for new state action to enhance government effectiveness in that field.

Information is communicated up the chain of departmental command from front-line field office workers and middle-level managers to senior management and policy advisors. These officials assess the accumulated departmental knowledge and develop either reforms of existing policies and programs—the fine-tuning of current practices—or wholly new ones to address concerns they deem important. It is not unusual for significant modifications to be made to most policies and programs as departments refine their work, discerning better ways to deliver regional development policy, for example, or to maintain an effective military, or to promote social welfare policy or a fairer system of taxation.

This process of reform, adjustment, renewal, and creation is of course closely tied to the leadership interests of the department's minister. Each minister arrives with ideas about how a department can perform its role and strengthen its policy more effectively. Every minister wants to work closely with senior management to assess policy strengths and weaknesses and determine improvements. Of course, there is no guarantee that a minister and senior staff will see eye to eye in the process. At times ministers see departmental interests in certain reforms as essentially administrative and technical and thus of insufficient political interest to merit their deep attention. At other times senior staff and a minister disagree over the substance of reform proposals. Although each minister is the formal head of his or her department, the power and influence flowing between ministers and their senior department managers

involve sophisticated interaction. And ministers do not always get their way.

RESEARCH, ANALYSIS, AND RECORD KEEPING

Departments must perform ongoing research, analysis, and record keeping to maintain their institutional memory. Departments are intricate bureaucratic entities active within a political world where, to quote Max Weber, "knowledge is power." Departments keep records of all their policy and program initiatives and of previous and continuing studies. They also routinely analyze the activities of other departments with similar portfolios in other governments, both in this country and abroad. Thus, the federal Department of Environment maintains close contact with provincial environmental departments, sharing information and assessing best practices. Likewise, the Department of National Defence maintains close contact with its counterparts in other countries, especially those of our NATO allies, analyzing their defence strategies and developing Canadian military training, organization, and equipment to dovetail with their needs. One can appreciate how these bureaucracies come to be associated with flurries of documents and papers flowing back and forth and accumulating in department files.

No department can function effectively without detailed knowledge of its field of operation—whether of current administrative practices, technical improvements, or strategic policy options—or records of its own actions undertaken or decided against. The department must know itself: why its field has evolved as it has, why certain policies and programs were advanced and implemented and to what effect, and why others were rejected.

Understanding lack of action is often as instructive as comprehending the logic of initiatives put into practice, because those that were contemplated but eventually rejected illustrate assessments of costs and benefits and strengths and weaknesses, all crucial to understanding how, administratively, and why, politically, a department operates as it does. When a minister seeks to do something new, it is unlikely that the department has not already considered the proposal at some point in the near or distant past, providing a body of knowledge from which to build.

COMMUNICATION AND LIAISON

Closely tied to research, analysis, and record keeping is the fourth function of departments: communication and liaison with others interested in their work. These others encompass a host of government and non-government organizations, policy and program stakeholders, parliamentary actors, the media, and citizens. Departments must communicate about almost everything they do. They provide information and services to citizens (clients) entitled to a service; they conduct liaison with business and other public interest groups; and they keep MPs and the media up to date about the activities of the department. They interact closely with parliamentary officials at the Office of the Auditor General, the Office of the Commissioner of Official Languages, and the Office of the Privacy Commissioner, to name a few. And of course they maintain very close lines of communication with other federal and provincial departments whose work touches on theirs, with related departments of foreign governments, and with all the cabinet committees and central agencies to be introduced in the next chapter.

The primary communicative goals of any department are

- to gain information relevant to its duties;
- to maintain close communication with clients and those concerned with departmental policy development and program delivery;
- to facilitate feedback channels that enable department officials to become aware of emerging policy and program problems, and to respond quickly;
- to establish effective liaison with all important government and parliamentary actors; and
- to maintain such links with other relevant actors within domestic and foreign governments.

To accomplish all this, department members are expected to possess excellent communication skills, enabling them to accumulate and synthesize information and to channel this intelligence to those who need it.

DEPARTMENTAL STRUCTURE

Numerous authors have developed more or less intricate typologies of departmental organization; one can choose from the works of Kernaghan and Siegel (1999, 203–7), Jackson and Jackson (2009, 359), and Inwood (2011, 130–35), for example. However, a simpler outline of departmental form and function assigns two broad categories—service departments or support departments—according to their relationship with either the government or the public (Figure 3.5).

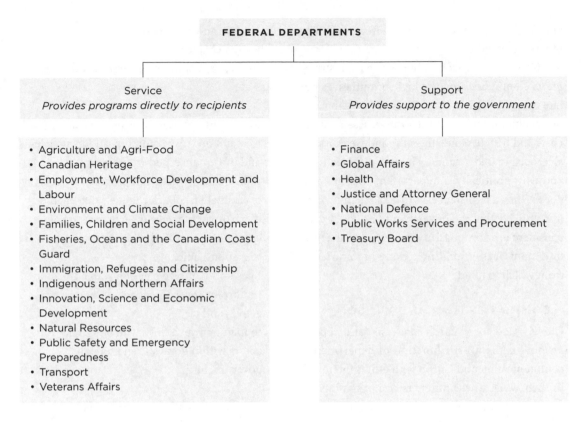

FEDERAL DEPARTMENTS

Service
Provides programs directly to recipients

- Agriculture and Agri-Food
- Canadian Heritage
- Employment, Workforce Development and Labour
- Environment and Climate Change
- Families, Children and Social Development
- Fisheries, Oceans and the Canadian Coast Guard
- Immigration, Refugees and Citizenship
- Indigenous and Northern Affairs
- Innovation, Science and Economic Development
- Natural Resources
- Public Safety and Emergency Preparedness
- Transport
- Veterans Affairs

Support
Provides support to the government

- Finance
- Global Affairs
- Health
- Justice and Attorney General
- National Defence
- Public Works Services and Procurement
- Treasury Board

Figure 3.4 **Departmental Structure**

Service Departments

The majority are best understood as "line" or "operational" **service departments**, because their primary responsibility is to provide services directly to the public or to specific client groups within the public. The Department of Agriculture and Agri-Food, for example, provides programs and funding in aid of Canadian farmers and the food production industry, just as the Department of Fisheries, Oceans and the Canadian Coast Guard has a mandate to support the Canadian fishing industry with financial measures that assist fishers, by regulating fish stocks and fishing practices, and by licensing and overseeing those involved in the fishery. The Departments of Immigration, Refugees and Citizenship; Indigenous and Northern Affairs; Industry; and Innovation, Science and Economic Development provide a wide variety of services to many constituencies of Canadians: the reception and integration of new Canadians; cooperation with First Nations governments for the provision of social and economic services guaranteed by treaties; financial support, training, and business advice for entrepreneurs; and the provision of training for jobs and skills development for all citizens.

In 1999 the ranking of service departments was significantly altered when the federal government transformed Revenue Canada, traditionally responsible for taxation, customs and tariff policy, and tax collection, into a special operating agency of the federal government now known as the Canada Revenue Agency. This agency is no longer a government department, and the more than 40,000 employees who work there are officially no longer employed by the Treasury Board, meaning that they are no longer classed as members of the public service. The federal government asserts that it has reduced the size of the public service by that number of employees, when in fact they still have government jobs, but within an agency that acts as its own employer. This innovation is evidence both of the degree to which departmental forms are subject to change and also of the political considerations inherent in reforming the structure of the federal government.

Program implementation and delivery frequently require a department to have offices dispersed across the country's vast geography. If you have bought postage stamps, received employment insurance benefits, taken a job training program, or got a small business development loan, you've encountered a government department. But service departments, though the largest and most popularly known, are not necessarily the most influential within government.

Support Departments

A smaller number of departments have primary responsibility for providing policy and program assistance more to the government itself than to the general public. These **support departments** include such diverse bodies as Finance, Global Affairs, Health, Justice and Attorney General, National Defence, Treasury Board, and Public Services and Procurement. They provide either administrative or policy services, or some combination of the two, to the government itself.

Global Affairs, for example, has the gargantuan task of providing the government with all services dealing with Canada's relations with the broader world, extending from diplomatic and consular work to intelligence gathering, and from representing and supporting state interests abroad to promoting Canadian trade, commerce, and investment globally. Public Services and Procurement provides, maintains, and disposes of all government properties and goods and services—from pens, paper, and office equipment to automobiles, trucks, and civilian aircraft needed by other government departments and their officials.

Other support departments, such as Finance, Health, and Justice and Attorney General, supply the government with intelligence and policy options within their specific fields. When the government, and specifically the cabinet, needs detailed information about the state of the economy and the track record of budgetary matters and economic policies, it turns to the Department of Finance. Likewise, when it needs advice and information about the health care system, health care programming in the provinces, and the degree of provincial compliance with the standards of the Canada Health Act, it turns to the Department of Health.

It is these departments, not their service counterparts, that play a most powerful role as the information and intelligence links between the social, economic, and political life of Canada and the policy makers in the federal government (Tardi 2010, 34–40).

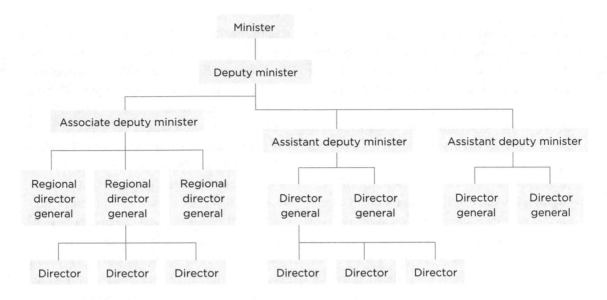

Figure 3.5 **Departmental Hierarchy**

Most support departments are smaller than their service counterparts, with fewer staff and smaller operating budgets, and each is geographically tied to the nation's capital. This is especially true of Finance, Global Affairs, Health, and Justice and Attorney General, but less so of Public Services and Procurement. Although headquartered in the capital region, this last one has a larger staff than the other support departments, forcing it to spread out somewhat.

The exception, of course, is National Defence. While it is clearly a support department in that it is mandated to provide the government with military support when requested and its personnel generally do not provide services directly to the public, it is neither small, nor inexpensive, nor geographically concentrated. With a personnel complement of 68,000, it has the largest departmental staff in the federal government, and it is dispersed across

military bases throughout the country as well as on active service overseas. And, with its unique equipment and facilities requirements, it possesses one of the largest budgets of any federal department.

DEPARTMENTAL HIERARCHY, SIZE, AND MAGNITUDE

All departments are hierarchical and pyramidal (Figure 3.6). They are multilayered bureaucracies with an operational base much larger than their middle-management layer of directors and directors general and an even smaller number of senior managers—associate deputy ministers and assistant deputy ministers—who constitute the leading administrative and policy actors within the department headquarters in Ottawa. At the apex of department power and authority stands the minister and, just below him or her, the deputy minister: the most senior public servant within the department. This hierarchical structure is common throughout all governments both in this country and abroad.

The institutional form is valuable for its ability to provide both a clear line of managerial command and control from the top down and, in theory, a clear line of information from field-level operations and regional offices up to senior management in the headquarters. Of course, Canadian government history is replete with examples of communication breaking down for various reasons, leading to all sorts of government and political problems. In 2010–11, for example, a senior aide in Prime Minister Harper's own office, Bruce Carson, was allegedly involved in influence peddling and conflicts of interest. More troubling was that Carson was a disbarred lawyer who had been convicted of fraud. The prime minister had to admit that he did not know how Carson passed his security clearance and that he would not have approved his hiring had he known about the aide's past. The prime minister also claimed that officials in the PMO had failed to communicate effectively among themselves and to the prime minister (CBC 2011). In a similar fashion, in 2013, Prime Minister Harper's office corroborated media reports that the PM's chief of staff, Nigel Wright, had personally given Conservative Senator Mike Duffy (who was facing allegations of unethical conduct), $90,000 to pay back questionable expenses. This revelation set off a media storm that went on for more than three years, witnessing a police investigation into Wright's actions, corruption charges being brought against Senator Duffy, and a cloud of suspicion hanging over the behaviour of the prime minister (CBC 2015). Yet no government has tried to fundamentally transform this system of organizing government work. As is often said within government, the system is fine—the problems are with the people who run it.

In understanding departments, it is useful to consider size and operational magnitude. Most service departments of necessity possess a massive staff of junior and middle managers spread across regional and local offices. Departments such as Agriculture and Agri-Food and Employment, Workforce Development and Labour employ thousands of public servants, most of whom work in offices found in all the major and in many minor urban locations across the country. Other departments, such as Fisheries, Oceans and the Canadian Coast Guard, and Immigration, Refugees and Citizenship, also employ thousands, with field-level employees assigned to more territorially specific parts of the country—the east and west coasts for Fisheries, Oceans and the Canadian Coast Guard and the major urban centres and international entry points for Immigration, Refugees and Citizenship. Likewise, officials in the Departments of Environment and Climate Change; Innovation, Science and Economic Development; and Transport are dispersed across the country, as are most of the service personnel in National Defence.

Senior management faces a real challenge in showing leadership, maintaining effective communications, and generally exerting command and control of large numbers of staff over a country this size. Though the advent of modern telecommunications has clearly helped, the issue is always of concern to those at office headquarters in Ottawa–Gatineau. Often those at both ends of the chain lament the inability of the "other side" to fully comprehend and appreciate the organizational and administrative difficulties they face.

The sheer magnitude of ordinary departmental decision making also poses an enormous challenge. Any service department operates dozens of separate programs, providing services to the many individuals, interest groups, and/or businesses within its purview. On any given day, a department interacts with thousands of citizens/clients and its officials make thousands of decisions about

- entitlement to services;
- the nature of services owed to any given citizen, group, or corporation;
- the delivery or non-delivery of services;
- the obligations of citizens, groups, or corporations to the department; and
- the future needs of citizens.

Service departments thus interact with clients routinely, and their staff and junior management make most of the decisions about how to apply the programs that flow from policy directions received from supervisors and more senior management. Senior management, for its part, routinely fine-tunes the programming and assesses program and policy strengths and weaknesses, administrative and managerial capabilities, new initiatives, and ongoing financial and personnel management issues. In short, senior management is occupied with scores of pressing matters requiring countless decisions on a daily basis. And this is also the case with the support departments, although on a smaller scale.

Any department is thereby awash in decision making, from the most bureaucratically routine to the most politically significant. The departments are, in both theory and practice, the key actors for linking a government to the country it serves, and departmental decision making constitutes a significant proportion of the substance of public sector management.

CROWN AGENCIES

Distinct from government departments are Crown agencies (Barker 2008, chaps. 6, 7; Inwood 2011, chap. 5; Dyck and Cochrane 2014, 565–70). There are some 400 federal Crown agencies in this country and an even larger number of provincial ones, active in a wide variety of policy fields. Federal Crown corporations such as Canada Post, the CBC, VIA Rail, and the National Film Board (NFB) are more widely known, but regulatory agencies such as the CRTC, the Canadian Industrial Relations Board, the National Transportation Safety Board, and the Immigration and Refugee Board are also major agencies. Special agencies such as Elections Canada, the Public Service Commission, and the RCMP also deserve mention.

Crown corporations, regulatory agencies, and special agencies share common organizational characteristics:

- They are designed to be relatively independent of government.
- They are organized differently from government departments.
- They are not subject to departmental systems of accountability, financial management, or personnel administration.

MAJOR FEDERAL CROWN CORPORATIONS, 2016

Atlantic Canada Opportunities Agency

Bank of Canada

Canada Mortgage and Housing Corporation

Canada Post Corporation

Canadian Broadcasting Corporation

Canadian Commercial Corporation

Export Development Canada

Farm Credit Corporation

Federal Business Development Bank of Canada

Marine Atlantic

National Arts Centre Corporation

National Film Board

National Gallery of Canada

Royal Canadian Mint

St. Lawrence Seaway Management Corporation

Telefilm Canada

VIA Rail

Western Economic Diversification Canada

All agencies exist as unique institutions possessing special commercial, legal, or administrative relationships to the government and the public.

CROWN CORPORATIONS

Crown corporations either provide commercial services to Canadians or interact with citizens and businesses in a corporate-like fashion. Crown corporations such as Air Canada, Canadian National Railway (CN), and Petro-Canada were designed to enter a field of commercial activity—air and rail transportation, oil and gas exploration, refining, and marketing—and to promote the public interest by providing services to the public. Such service delivery often comes into direct competition with existing private sector service providers, as can be observed in CBC-TV's relationship to CTV and Shaw Media (formerly CanWest Global).

Other Crown corporations do not have a direct commercial and competitive mandate but are expected to act in a cost-effective and "business-like" manner, either in managing a state monopoly or in delivering special services to individual citizens or business ventures. Examples of the former are Atomic Energy of Canada Limited, Canada Post, and the Royal Canadian Mint. Examples of the latter are the NFB, Export Development Canada, Farm Credit Canada, the Business Development Bank of Canada (BDBC), and the St. Lawrence Seaway Management Corporation, as well as such regional development corporations as the Atlantic Canada Opportunities Agency (ACOA) and Western Economic Diversification Canada.

Governments usually have several motives for establishing Crown corporations. One, obviously, is for the state to play an important role in the management of a particular field of commercial activity deemed to be of national significance, while more specific motives include

- defending traditional forms of economic activity and service delivery (Canada Post, Canada Mortgage and Housing Corporation, the Canadian Wheat Board);

- promoting new industrial and commercial activity (Petro-Canada, ACOA, Western Economic Diversification Canada, BDBC, CBC); and
- ensuring the delivery of important services nationwide (Air Canada, CN, VIA Rail).

Stemming from Canadian economic nationalism, we had CN, Air Canada, Petro-Canada, and de Havilland. From the promotion and defence of Canadian culture we have the CBC, NFB, and the National Gallery of Canada.

The Benefits of Independence

Once a government decides to enter a field of commercial or entrepreneurial activity, what advantages distinguish the Crown corporation? It is operationally independent from the routine financial and personnel management rules and regulations associated with government departments. The corporation can undertake its own hiring and personnel management practices, free from the restrictions and controls of regular departments. It can engage in business undertakings, commercial transactions, and financial management free from the multifarious systems of departmental budgeting. Its board of directors can be chosen from the private sector or the general community, among those who have an interest in the mission of the corporation, rather than from the public service. The operational heads of Crown corporations are generally drawn from outside the ranks of government and appointed by the PM and cabinet to serve for three, five, or seven years. Once appointed, a board is free to hire senior management, again from outside the permanent public service, bringing in people with expertise in the relevant field of activity. Thus, the CBC is staffed by people knowledgeable in radio and television broadcasting, for example, and the Canadian Wheat Board management was skilled in agricultural

DISPATCH BOX

MAJOR FEDERAL CROWN CORPORATION PRIVATIZATIONS, 1980S TO 2015

Air Canada	Terra Nova Telecommunication
Atomic Energy of Canada Limited	Canadian Wheat Board
Canada Communications Group	de Havilland Aircraft
Canada Development Corporation	Eldorado Nuclear
Canadair	Fishery Products International
Canadian Arsenals	Northern Canada Power Commission
Canadian National Railway (CN)	Northern Transportation Company
CN subsidiaries	Petro-Canada
CN Hotels	Teleglobe Canada
CPCN Telecommunications (part owned by CN)	Telesat
Northwestel	

economics, supply management, and international grain marketing.

Operational independence is also vitally important to the policy and program development function of Crown corporations, which exist at arm's length from the government of the day so that partisan political interests do not interfere with professional managerial judgement. For example, it has long been recognized that the decision making of the CBC, especially in relation to news and public affairs broadcasting, should not be subject to direct or even indirect government influence. The credibility of the CBC as a public broadcaster hinges on its ability to be, and to be seen to be, an independent actor insofar as its broadcasting initiatives are concerned. Similar interests respecting operational autonomy are inherent in Crown corporations as diverse as the Federal Business Development Bank, VIA Rail, and Canada Post.

An arm's-length relationship can also insulate the government from political controversies. When a Crown corporation makes decisions that invite divisive commentary and public criticism, such as when Canada Post raises postal rates or VIA Rail reduces levels of passenger rail service, the government will be quite content to state that the matter is an operational decision fully within the jurisdiction of the corporation and that it is inappropriate for the government to intervene.

That being said, cabinet ministers sometimes sense a political advantage in trying to influence a Crown corporation, often to the consternation of corporation senior management. In the fall of 2007, for example, Atomic Energy of Canada Limited (AECL) shut down its Chalk River nuclear reactor in compliance with regulatory orders issued by the Canadian Nuclear Safety Commission.

The shutdown effectively halted production of 60 per cent of the world's medical isotopes. Even though AECL and the leadership of the Canadian Nuclear Safety Commission asserted that the facility required upgrading, the Harper government ordered AECL to restart the Chalk River reactor. When the Canadian Nuclear Safety Commission refused to authorize the move, the government brought forward emergency legislation with all-party support mandating the reopening of the facility. In January 2008 the Harper government terminated the employment of the head of the Canadian Nuclear Safety Commission (CBC 2008). As this narrative suggests, the operational independence of these institutions is, in certain respects, contingent on ministerial self-restraint: their willingness to leave administrative and technocratic decision making up to the executives who manage these agencies.

The formal and informal relationships between Crown corporations and the government are quite special. Crown corporations are established by legislation that provides the broad policy mandate of each corporation, which is approved by parliament, but the exercise of this mandate is left to its management and staff. Furthermore, no corporation is directly responsible to a single minister; each reports annually to parliament on its work. Some corporations receive annual contributions from the government to fund their programs in whole or in part. Such is the case with the CBC, ACOA, and Western Economic Diversification Canada. Other corporations, such as Canada Post, VIA Rail, and, before their privatization, Petro-Canada, Air Canada, and CN, are financially self-sufficient, deriving their operational revenue from the sale of services.

The Drive to Privatize

Over the past three decades most Crown corporations have confronted the issue of **privatization** (Barker 2008, chap. 6; Inwood 2011, chap. 5) as governments divest themselves of corporations and sell them to private investors. Privatization can take more than one form. A single private business venture can purchase a Crown corporation outright (e.g., de Havilland was purchased by Boeing and later resold to Bombardier, and Teleglobe Canada was sold to Memotec Data). Or the government can decide to offer publicly traded shares of a Crown corporation (e.g. Air Canada, Petro-Canada, and CN). In the latter, more common case, the government can impose restrictions on the proportion of the corporation that any one purchaser can control and on the number of shares that can be held by non-Canadian interests. It can also retain a minority stock interest in the privatized corporation, as has been the case with Air Canada and Petro-Canada, though most governments following this option tend to stress that their minority interests are "non-voting" in terms of shareholder decision making.

Privatization is controversial. Advocates, usually representing a right-of-centre ideological perspective, make both practical and philosophical arguments in favour of it. They emphasize that many Crown corporations are uneconomical and inefficient, tending to waste public monies. Supporters also assert the importance of raising public revenues through the sale process, often billions of dollars. These monies can then be earmarked for national deficit or debt reduction. Finally, and perhaps most important, they argue that governments simply should not be in the business of owning and operating commercial enterprises. They assert that such activity is best undertaken by the private sector operating under the discipline of the profit motive, and that government can best promote a climate of free enterprise and market economics by dismantling Crown corporations.

Critics of privatization challenge all these points, also with a variety of practical and philosophical arguments. They stress, usually from a left-of-centre ideological perspective, that many Crown corporations are cost effective and efficient, often generating substantial profits for the state (as was the case with Petro-Canada and still is with Canada Post and provincial power utilities and liquor distribution corporations). Defenders point to political interference and weak management systems to explain the poor performance of Crown corporations that have failed to achieve profitability, such as de Havilland, Canadair, and the Cape Breton Development Corporation. They highlight several key ideas:

- Crown corporations were established for valid public policy reasons.
- They provide important services that the private sector either can't or won't offer either to the country overall or to particular regions.
- The CBC, the NFB, CN, Air Canada, VIA Rail, and Petro-Canada did or do or should strengthen Canadian culture, advance Canadian nationalism, and defend Canadian economic sovereignty.

Defenders of Crown corporations argue that privatization is, at best, a simplistic way of raising public revenues to deal with deficit and debt

SHOULD MORE CROWN CORPORATIONS BE PRIVATIZED?

After a substantial number of privatizations of federal Crown corporations in the 1990s, the pace slowed by 2000 but picked up again with the advent of the Conservative government led by Stephen Harper. His government privatized the Canadian Wheat Board in 2015, and folded Enterprise Cape Breton Corporation into ACOA in 2014, while largely turning over Atomic Energy of Canada Limited to private ownership by 2014. And there is interest in conservative circles for further privatizations.

THE CANDIDATES

Canadian Broadcasting Corporation

The CBC is a national television, radio, and web broadcaster funded by the federal government and in direct competition with private broadcasters. The CBC needs greater investment to enhance its programming. Privatization could bring it additional revenues to promote program development while eliminating public competition with private industries. Remaining public would allow it to continue its mandate to promote Canadian arts and entertainment, and deliver impartial news and public affairs broadcasting. Conservative critics have long argued that the CBC is an elitist institution with a liberal bias.

Canada Post

This is the national mail carrier, providing mail and parcel post delivery services across the country, but new technologies and alternative service providers have weakened this Crown corporation's economic viability. Fewer Canadians send "snail-mail" letters to one another, preferring the convenience and speed of email, while private courier services have eaten into Canada Post's parcel service. In seeking to curtail costs, Canada Post has moved to eliminate door-to-door service, but critics say this just further weakens the ability of the corporation to provide a needed public service to Canadians. Is this service still needed?

VIA Rail

VIA Rail is the national passenger railway service in Canada and the last vestige of the once-mighty Canadian National Railways. CN was privatized in 1995, while its passenger service was retained as a separate Crown corporation on the basis that such service fulfilled an important public need. But VIA Rail has struggled with issues of declining ridership and rising costs. Most VIA Rail services are now found in the Windsor–Quebec City corridor, the most populous area of Canada, leaving the rest of the country with limited to no passenger rail service. Is this fair? Does Canada need such a limited rail service, or would we be better to invest scarce transportation dollars in improved highways? Or should we expand the passenger rail service with high-speed trains as a way of moving people around quickly and in a more environmentally friendly way?

THE OPTIONS

[ ] **More privatization.** For which corporations? Why? Are there any that should *not* be privatized? Why not?

[ ] **Less privatization.** Why? Should some former Crown corporations be renationalized? Which ones and why? Should any remain privatized? Why?

problems, akin to selling off family heirlooms to pay the mortgage. They note that potential private sector investors want to buy only profitable or potentially profitable Crown corporations—raising the question why a government should divest itself of such attractive assets. Of course, privatization is motivated by conservative thought, just as support for a continued state presence in the economy via Crown corporations is motivated by reform liberal or Fabian socialist views.

As mentioned in the previous chapter, the 1980s and 90s were marked by a general rightward shift in the centre ground of Canadian politics: the election of the Progressive Conservatives under Brian Mulroney in 1984 and of a rather conservative Liberal government under Jean Chrétien in 1993. During these years many federal Crown corporations were privatized, including such major ones as Air Canada, Canadair, de Havilland, Eldorado Nuclear, Teleglobe Canada, Petro-Canada, and CN. Although the CBC was not part of this privatization wave, it remains a speculative target; the Canadian Alliance party suggested, during the federal election of 2000, that CBC-TV be considered for divestiture.

Since 2006 the Harper government promoted the privatization of AECL, the Canadian Wheat Board, and Enterprise Cape Breton Corporation. All Crown corporations were expected to be more commercialized and more subject to market economics, with Canada Post especially facing pressure to show profits. As well, many conservative ideologues continued to support the privatization of the CBC. With the election of the Trudeau Liberal government in 2015 the push for privatizations within the federal government have likely subsided for some time. But the commercialization of Crown corporations like Canada Post, the CBC, and VIA Rail will probably continue. And it is highly unlikely that the Trudeau government will undo the Harper government's privatizations of the Canadian Wheat Board and Atomic Energy of Canada Limited, or the elimination of Enterprise Cape Breton Corporation.

REGULATORY AGENCIES

Regulatory agencies are the second type of Crown agency in this country (Barker 2008, chap. 7; Dyck and Cochrane 2014, 567–70). Although regulatory agencies share certain organizational features with Crown corporations—namely, quasi-independence from government and separate systems for appointments and financial and personnel management—they are significantly different.

Whereas Crown corporations engage in specific commercial or economic transactions with individuals or other businesses, regulatory agencies develop and implement general forms of economic and social regulation across wide fields of activity, as prescribed by law. Regulation itself refers to rules and standards developed by either government agencies or departments and generally approved by parliament. It is designed to govern the actions of all individuals, groups, businesses, or even federal government bodies within a given socio-economic field. As highlighted in Chapter 1, state regulation can encompass everything from occupational health and safety standards, product quality and safety standards, occupational and professional licensing requirements, and environmental protection standards to labour relations and the protection of human rights. Government regulation falls into three broad types: economic, social, and environmental.

MAJOR FEDERAL REGULATORY AGENCIES, 2016

Canadian Agricultural Review Tribunal
Canadian Dairy Commission
Canadian Environmental Assessment Agency
Canadian Food Inspection Agency
Canadian Human Rights Commission
Canadian International Trade Tribunal
Canadian Nuclear Safety Commission
Canadian Pension Plan Investment Board
Canadian Radio-television and Telecommunications
   Commission
Canadian Transportation Agency
Competition Tribunal

Immigration and Refugee Board of Canada
Indian Claims Commission
International Joint Commission
National Capital Commission
National Energy Board
National Parole Board
Pension Appeals Board
Privacy Commission of Canada
Public Service Staff Relations Board
Security Intelligence Review Committee
Standards Council of Canada
Transportation Safety Board of Canada

Economic Regulation

Economic regulation deals with such matters as price and tariff setting and oversight, product supply management, market entry and conditions of service, product content, and methods of production. Federal regulatory agencies such as Investment Canada, the National Energy Board (NEB), the Canadian Transportation Agency, and the Canadian International Trade Tribunal address the desirability of mega-corporate mergers involving foreign companies, the construction of oil and gas pipelines and the nature of their distribution networks, the restriction and punishment of "economic dumping" by foreign firms into the Canadian marketplace, and service standards and price competition in the transportation industry.

Social Regulation

Social regulation deals with matters such as labour standards, health and safety provisions, protection of human rights entitlements, and support of Canadian culture. For example, the Canadian Industrial Relations Board, the Canadian Food Inspection Agency, the Canadian Human Rights Commission, and the CRTC regulate the collective bargaining and industrial dispute resolution system for firms subject to federal labour law, food production quality control, adherence to and respect for federal human rights law, and the advancement of Canadian content in television and radio broadcasting.

The activities of all these agencies have distinct economic overtones for affected businesses, illustrating that in practice there is no simple demarcation between economic and social regulation. The CRTC terms and conditions of television and radio broadcast licence renewals, for example, have a social impact on the amount of Canadian broadcast content, but this carries a financial obligation for the licence holders to utilize and create Canadian programming while limiting, in a relative sense, the use of already existing and less expensive foreign (usually American) content.

To defenders of regulatory initiatives, however, these are the costs of doing business in this country, an activity that carries important social obligations. They also point out that Canadian content regulation has the intended desirable effect of encouraging the economic activity of those who produce Canadian radio and television content, namely, artists, actors, performers, writers, and the whole gamut of people involved in broadcast production.

Environmental Regulation

A similar logic applies in environmental regulation. The Canadian Environmental Assessment Agency is required to conduct comprehensive reviews of all major economic development projects within the federal sphere of jurisdiction that might have environmental consequences. The agency is called upon to study the environmental impact of initiatives such as natural gas pipeline construction in Nova Scotia and New Brunswick (in conjunction with hearings of the NEB), fish habitat restoration projects in coastal British Columbia and Yukon, ski development projects in national parks across the country, and low-level military jet flight training in Labrador.

Although the appraisal, modification, and ultimate approval or disapproval of planned developments have a direct impact on the quality of the environment, such decisions also have immediate and long-term economic consequences for those interested in the business side of these ventures. Again, this illustrates the interconnectedness of the environmental, economic, and social spheres. These activities are important to

Canadians, and regulatory bodies must advance the public interest through their work.

The Benefits of Independence

As with Crown corporations, regulatory agencies possess an arm's-length relationship with government, but their relative autonomy is demanded by the special legal role they fulfill rather than by corporate interest. Regulatory agencies are mandated to develop and implement standards in their field of jurisdiction, regardless of the source of activity. Thus, the CRTC regulates the public CBC equally with the private CTV and Shaw Media; the Canadian Human Rights Commission has jurisdiction over all employers and employees subject to federal regulation in Canada, including everyone in the federal public service.

Regulatory agencies are quasi-judicial entities in that their decision making has legal authority. They must apply the legal provisions in their enabling statutes case by case to decide whether individuals, groups, corporations, or government bodies conform with established regulatory rules and practices as understood and applied by the agencies. Their final decisions carry the force of law, enabling some actors to continue legally with a desired course of action while requiring others to desist or to change their practices.

Because of the legal nature of their work, regulatory agencies require a quasi-independent status, free from any political intervention. They must be free from any real or perceived bias emanating from their organizational link to government. Although governments can establish agencies and their mandates, amend them through legislation, appoint their boards of directors or commissions, and on special occasions issue them with policy directives, they are nonetheless forbidden from intervening in any particular case before an agency outside of normal hearing procedures. In fact, any such intervention is illegal and subject to punishment.

As is true with respect to Crown corporations, however, the buffer between agency and government benefits both sides. It permits ministers to claim that certain "hot" political issues—such as **pay equity**, environmental disputes, or broadcast licensing—are legal issues to be put before regulatory agencies and are thus beyond the realm of ministerial action. Governments can be quite happy to transfer responsibility for decision making in these spheres to other duly constituted authorities.

The Drive to Deregulate

Just as Crown corporations have been at the centre of much political debate over the past three decades with respect to privatization, certain regulatory agencies have been subject to controversy over **deregulation**. Both these policy dynamics evolve from the rightward shift in political discourse. Deregulation refers to a government's move to diminish or eliminate regulatory provisions governing a certain field of activity that was hitherto subject to them. It is perceived by its generally right-of-centre advocates as a means, once again, of promoting free enterprise, enhancing the private sector, and lessening the administrative and economic burden borne by private firms.

In contrast, deregulation is seen by its generally left-of-centre critics as an ideologically motivated attack on the role of the state, leading to a weakening of the public interest with respect to economic, social, and environmental policy.

However, while the Mulroney and Chrétien governments both substantially deregulated federal economic activities, the overall impact has been much less than the impact of privatization over the same period. In the 1980s and 90s, most large federal Crown corporations in this country were privatized, but major federal regulatory agencies were not. Deregulation as a major concern of public policy was accentuated under the Harper Conservative government from 2006 to 2015 and was most felt in

- oil and gas production, pricing, and export;
- the loosening of environmental regulations respecting oil and gas pipeline construction;
- foreign investment screening;
- financial services administration;
- the elimination of restrictions on competition in the transportation industry, in particular air, rail, and trucking; and
- the promotion of industrial self-regulation in such matters as food safety, transportation safety, and natural resource extraction.

Despite these significant examples of deregulation, however, the regulatory scope of the federal state remains substantial. In terms of economic policy, bodies such as the Atomic Energy Control Board, the Canadian Labour Relations Board, the NEB, Investment Canada, the National Transportation Safety Board, and the Canadian Tariff Board remain intact, and the major social and environmental policy agencies already mentioned are also still in place, if with reduced regulatory scope and capacity.

Regulatory policy remains a significant aspect of the Canadian state presence, and the work of these agencies is a major component of the federal public sector management system. Rather than viewing deregulation itself as a threat to the role of the state, it can be argued that systematic budget cutting and the downloading of regulatory responsibilities to other levels of government and to the private sector has posed a greater threat to the federal regulatory system than has any direct deregulatory initiative. It's noteworthy that the Justin Trudeau government came to power promising to strengthen environmental regulations, especially in relation to the building of new oil and natural gas pipelines, as a means of not only protecting the environment but also establishing the "social licence" necessary for gaining the public trust and support needed for these major national infrastructure projects to be built. In this sense, corporate Canada needs strong regulatory frameworks for its own long-term economic viability.

SPECIAL AGENCIES

Special agencies also fall under the general rubric of Crown agencies (Jackson and Jackson 2009, 361), and quite a few unique public bodies provide special services either to the government or to the public, or to both. These bodies are neither departments nor Crown corporations, nor even regulatory agencies. They fall into two categories: permanent and temporary. In the first are entities such as Elections Canada, the Public Service Commission of Canada, the Office of the Commissioner of Official Languages, Statistics Canada, Library and Archives Canada, the RCMP, and the Canadian Security Intelligence Service. All these agencies provide services that are either unique or politically or legally sensitive enough to require quasi-independence from the government. In the temporary category are organizations such as royal commissions and special policy task forces.

All such agencies play an important role in the broad process of government. Permanent special agencies are vital elements in the delivery of public services within their fields of jurisdiction.

Departments, Crown corporations, regulatory agencies, and special agencies constitute the principal institutions of the federal public service. Governments rely on them to deliver most policies and programs, and thus they form the primary link between government and the public, and between the elected executive and the professional bureaucracy. To what degree, then, are they held accountable for their work?

Crown agencies are quasi-independent administrative actors, specifically designed to be substantially autonomous from government in their routine operations. Yet they are state institutions, mandated by government to develop and implement public policies. And departments are the workhorses of government, vested under the authority of ministers of the Crown and falling under the collective political control of the prime minister and cabinet. Yet they are massive bureaucracies that administer detailed policies and programs. How and to what degree are they subject to effective political and managerial control to ensure that ultimate authority rests in the hands of elected, and thus democratically responsible, officials? These questions go to the heart of power relations in government and the relationship of democracy and bureaucracy.

REFERENCES AND SUGGESTED READING

Adie, Robert F., and Paul G. Thomas. 1987. *Canadian Public Administration: Problematical Perspectives.* 2nd ed. Scarborough, ON: Prentice Hall Canada.

Archer, Keith, Roger Gibbins, Rainer Knopff, and Leslie A. Pal. 1999. *Parameters of Power: Canada's Political Institutions.* 2nd ed. Toronto: Nelson.

Aucoin, Peter. 1995. "The Prime Minister and Cabinet." In *Introductory Readings in Canadian Government and Politics*, 2nd ed., edited by Robert M. Krause and R.H. Wagenberg, 169–92. Toronto: Copp Clark.

———. 1999. "Prime Minister and Cabinet: Power at the Apex." In *Canadian Politics*, 3rd ed., edited by James Bickerton and Alain-G. Gagnon, 109–28. Toronto: University of Toronto Press.

Bakvis, Herman, and David MacDonald. 1993. "The Canadian Cabinet: Organization, Decision-Rules, and Policy Impact." In *Governing Canada: Institutions and Public Policy*, edited by Michael M. Atkinson, 47–80. Toronto: Harcourt Brace.

Barker, Paul. 2008. *Public Administration in Canada: Brief Edition.* Toronto: Nelson.

Canada, Privy Council Office. 2015. The Canadian Ministry (Current). pm.gc/sites/pm/files/docs/cabinet.pdf .

CBC. 2008. "Nuclear Safety Watchdog Head Fired for 'Lack of Leadership': Minister." January 16. www.cbc.ca/news/canada/story/2008/01/16/keen-firing.html.

———. 2011. "Carson's Recruiters Knew of PMO Aide's Criminal Past." March 18. www.cbc.ca/news/canada/calgary/carson-s-recruiters-knew-of-pmo-aide-s-criminal-past-1.977463

———. 2015. "Mike Duffy Trial: Chronology of the Senate Expense Scandal Saga." August 12. www.cbc.ca/beta/news/politics/mike-duffy-trial-chronology-of-the-senate-expense-scandal-saga.html.

Delacourt, Susan. 2003. *Juggernaut: Paul Martin's Campaign for Chrétien's Crown*. Toronto: McClelland and Stewart.

Dyck, Rand, and Christopher Cochrane. 2014. *Canadian Politics: Critical Approaches*. 7th ed. Toronto: Nelson.

Gray, John. 2003. *Paul Martin: The Power of Ambition*. Toronto: Key Porter Books.

Harris, Michael. 2014. *Party of One: Stephen Harper and Canada's Radical Makeover*. Toronto: Viking.

Hodgetts, J.E. 1973. *The Canadian Public Service: A Physiology of Government 1867–1970*. Toronto: University of Toronto Press.

Ibbitson, John. 2015. *Stephen Harper*. Toronto: Signal/McClelland and Stewart.

Inwood, Gregory J. 2011. *Understanding Canadian Public Administration: An Introduction to Theory and Practice*. 4th ed. Toronto: Pearson Education.

Jackson, Robert J., and Doreen Jackson. 2009. *Politics in Canada: Culture, Institutions, Behaviour and Public Policy*. 7th ed. Toronto: Pearson Prentice Hall Canada.

Kernaghan, Kenneth. 2010. "East Block and Westminster: Conventions, Values and Public Service." In *The Handbook of Canadian Public Administration*, edited by Christopher Dunn, 289–304. Toronto: Oxford University Press.

———, and David Siegel. 1999. *Public Administration in Canada: A Text*. 4th ed. Toronto: Nelson.

Landes, Ronald G. 1987. *The Canadian Polity: A Comparative Introduction*. 2nd ed. Scarborough, ON: Prentice Hall Canada.

Mintz, Eric, Livianna Tossutti, and Christopher Dunn. 2014. *Canada's Politics: Democracy, Diversity and Good Governance*. 2nd ed. Toronto: Pearson.

Monahan, Patrick. 2006. *Constitutional Law*. 3rd ed. Toronto: Irwin Law.

Paikin, Steve. 2003. *The Dark Side: The Personal Price of Political Life*. Toronto: Viking Canada.

Savoie, Donald J. 1999. *Governing from the Centre: The Concentration of Power in Canadian Politics*. Toronto: University of Toronto Press.

Tardi, Gregory. 2010. "Departments and Other Institutions of Government." In *The Handbook of Canadian Public Administration*, 2nd ed., edited by Christopher Dunn, 25–52. Toronto: Oxford University Press.

Webber, Jeremy. 2015. *The Constitution of Canada: A Contextual Analysis*. Oxford: Hart Publishing.

Whittington, Michael S. 2000. "The Prime Minister, Cabinet, and the Executive Power in Canada." In *Canadian Politics in the 21st Century*, edited by Michael Whittington and Glen Williams, 31–54. Toronto: Nelson.

Wiseman, Nelson, and David Whorley. 2002. "Lessons on the Centrality of Politics from Canadian Crown Enterprises." In *The Handbook of Canadian Public Administration*, edited by Christopher Dunn, 382–96. Toronto: Oxford University Press.

RELATED WEBSITES

Government of Canada. www.canada.ca
Prime Minister of Canada. www.pm.gc.ca
Privy Council Office. www.pco-bcp.gc.ca/premier.asp

CROWN CORPORATIONS

Canada Post. www.canadapost.ca/web/en/home.page.
Canada Mortgage and Housing Corporation. www.cmhc-schl.gc.ca
Canadian Broadcasting Corporation. www.cbc.ca
Export Development Canada. www.edc.ca/pages/default.aspx.
Royal Canadian Mint. www.mint.ca/store/template/home.jsp.

REGULATORY AGENCIES

Canada Industrial Relations Board. www.cirb-ccri.gc.ca/eic/site/047.nsf/Intro.
Canadian Radio-television and Telecommunications Commission. www.crtc.gc.ca
Immigration and Refugee Board. www.lrb-cisr.gc.ca/pages/default.aspx.
Transportation Safety Board of Canada. www.tsb.gc.ca

SPECIAL AGENCIES

Elections Canada. www.elections.ca
Public Service Commission of Canada. www.psc-cfp.gc.ca
Royal Canadian Mounted Police. www.rcmp-grc.gc.ca

CHAPTER 4

Ministers and Cabinet Decision-Making Systems

Man is by nature a political animal.

–Aristotle, c. 350 BCE

After reading this chapter and its related web pages you will be able to

- describe how deputy ministers are appointed and what their duties are;
- analyze the minister–deputy minister relationship;
- describe departmentalized and institutionalized cabinet systems;
- explain the purpose of cabinet committees and central agencies and how they work;
- debate the strengths and weaknesses of the current cabinet decision-making process;
- identify the prime ministerial prerogative in decision making; and
- analyze the command mode of cabinet decision making.

4   Ministers and Cabinet Decision-Making Systems

The last chapter defined the main actors and institutions constituting the heart of the executive system in Ottawa. We turn now to the power relations between them and to questions of political authority, ministerial responsibility, government accountability, and central executive control. In other words, we explore the tension between democracy and bureaucracy and between the desire for open and responsible government and the growing command and control mode of government. We have seen that departments are staffed by many hundreds of employees, who administer dozens upon dozens of programs and make thousands upon thousands of decisions, large and small. Departments are the central administrative entities of any government, and at the head of each stands a minister. The minister is the formal leader of the department, bearing individual responsibility for all its actions. As a democratically elected member of parliament (MP) and a member of cabinet, the minister also serves a leading role in the democratic system. The principles of responsible government dictate that executive power is vested in the party that has a commanding number of seats in parliament. Executive power within each department is constitutionally placed within the hands of an MP who is individually responsible to parliament, and thus to the Canadian people he or she represents in parliament. The vast power and authority of the federal bureaucracy are therefore subject to the democratic control of elected members of cabinet, and these officials are themselves subject to the oversight of parliament.

Despite the formal logic of these constitutional relationships, a practical problem lurks within this system of duties and responsibilities, and it has been at the centre of organizational reform initiatives for the better part of six decades. Simply put, can ministers really be expected to bear full responsibility for everything their departments do? What about the many routine operations of which the minister may be wholly unaware? Is this level of responsibility an unrealistic burden? If so, who else should assume it? And if it is more appropriate to place the expectation on senior management, how would the new power relationship between ministers and managers reflect the democratic principles of responsible government and accountability?

Those in the senior ranks of government understand that no minister can hope to oversee a department single-handedly. For one thing, it would call for Herculean effort and time to master the operational decision making and programs of any department and to take responsibility for them all. (And the task would of course be in addition to all the other responsibilities borne by cabinet ministers, as outlined in Chapter 3.) For another, such an undertaking assumes that the minister is actually expert in public administration and management and in the intricate details of the departmental policy field. To assume that either condition is viable, or even desirable, is idealistic at best.

Rather than viewing a minister as the hands-on supervisor of a department, then, it is more accurate to see the role as that of political head: the most senior departmental official, officially responsible

PRIME
MINISTER

CLERK OF THE
PRIVY COUNCIL

MINISTERS

DEPUTY MINISTERS

DEPARTMENTS

PUBLIC

Figure 4.1 **The Prime Minister and the Bureaucratic Hierarchy**

to cabinet and parliament for policy development and evolution and program implementation (Dyck and Cochrane 2014, 557; Savoie 2015, 44–49). In this sense—clearly the one prime ministers have long understood as the proper role for their ministers— the person appointed is neither an operational manager nor the main expert in department policy.

The minister instead functions as a "gifted generalist." He or she is the political leader who charts departmental direction in keeping with the strategic direction of the government overall and acts as a liaison between the bureaucracy and the political centre, but doesn't perform the hands-on tasks that move the department in that direction (see Figure 4.1). As professor of public affairs E.S. Savas once remarked, the word *government* "is from the Greek word, which means 'to steer.' The job of government is to steer, not to row the boat. Delivering services is rowing and government is not very good at rowing."

WHAT DOES A DEPUTY MINISTER DO?

As is true of any complex organization, every department needs senior officials to conduct its operational, managerial, and policy analysis tasks. Senior management meets these needs, and the most important senior manager is the department **deputy minister** (DM). Whereas the minister is the political head of the department, the deputy minister is its administrative head and chief manager, responsible to the minister and prime minister for

• administration of policies and programs;

DEPUTY MINISTERIAL RESPONSIBILITIES

Administration

- Responsible to the prime minister for the operation of a department
- Administrative head and chief manager of the department
- Financial management
- Oversight of departmental legal obligations

Policy

- Chief policy adviser to the minister
- New policy and program development and implementation
- Implementation of existing policies and programs

Communication

- Chief communicator for the department
- Liaison with other departments, agencies, institutions, and interest groups
- Rapport with clerk of the Privy Council regarding department operations

Personnel

- Leadership, motivation, and strategic direction
- Personnel management, training, and development

- development and assessment of policy initiatives;
- liaison and communication; and
- attention to routine departmental needs for financial, personnel, and legal administration.

The deputy minister, not the minister, is responsible for ensuring that the department is able to fulfill its many duties. He or she is the official expert in public sector management and all aspects of policy making with respect to the department portfolio (Bourgault 2002, 431–34; Barker 2008, 178–80; Dyck and Cochrane 2014, 557–58).

Deputy ministers are assisted by other senior managers just one or two steps beneath them in the hierarchy. Associate and assistant deputy ministers (both sometimes referred to as ADMs) are in charge of one of the main functional divisions within a department—operations, finance, personnel, or policy—and typically are expert in their fields of jurisdiction. **Associate deputy ministers** are the more senior; departments usually have one or two, who work closely with the deputy minister on policy and operational matters affecting the entire department. In large departments, from seven to ten **assistant deputy ministers** support the work of the deputy minister and associate deputy ministers. Assistant deputy ministers have specialized policy, operational, or administrative portfolios and are thus the chief specialists for each of the functional subgroups. They are assisted by a variety of other senior managers whose duties are to manage the work of their given branches and to supervise program directors, staff, and regional offices across the country.

Within this hierarchy, the deputy minister thus stands in direct command and control of a set of officials who form the executive heart of the department. This group oversees policy and program implementation and addresses matters that form the daily, weekly, and monthly routine. They also manage issues that arise as general directives are applied to specific cases and as particular program entitlements or duties have to be interpreted and delivered to clients, corporations, or citizens. The deputy minister

- leads managers and their staffs by assigning their tasks and setting broad strategic goals.
- provides direction, support, and inspiration.
- ensures that senior managers have the financial, personnel, and legal resources necessary to do their jobs effectively.

The deputy minister stands at the apex not only of a large operational bureaucracy but also of a powerful information-gathering and intelligence-formulating apparatus. Within a bureaucratic system in which knowledge is very often power, he or she is in a position both to receive intelligence and advice from senior staff and to transmit directives and suggestions back to these officials and their staff. Because they are responsible for the actual running of the organization, all deputies possess a close and important relationship to their ministers.

APPOINTING A DEPUTY MINISTER

Although each deputy minister is operationally responsible to the minister, it is important to remember that he or she is appointed not by the minister but "at the pleasure of the prime minister." Acting with the advice of the **clerk of the Privy Council**, it is the prime minister who appoints deputies, usually from the ranks of associate or assistant deputy ministers; who shifts them from portfolio to portfolio; and who, if necessary, removes them from office.

As the head of the public service, the clerk of the Privy Council acts as the linchpin between the political world of the cabinet and the administrative sphere of departments. A deputy is removed from office when a prime minister, usually newly elected, deems such a move necessary to ensure smooth implementation of the policy agenda and to assure the minister in question that the most senior administrative ranks of the department are committed to working with him or her.

This appointment of deputy ministers has four practical characteristics: deputy ministers come from the professional public service; they function as the non-partisan head of the department; they are responsible to the prime minister; and they are insulated from the power of the minister they serve (Bourgault 2002, 435–37; Inwood 2011, 142–44).

THE CANDIDATE POOL

Deputy ministers are senior public servants with decades of experience within various branches of the government, gaining promotion through the ranks of management, and exercising ever greater responsibilities. To be appointed deputy minister is, to almost every public sector manager, the pinnacle of one's career, the crowning professional reward following years of hard work and faithful government service.

The career path means that most people are in their fifties when they receive their first appointment to the deputy ranks. Once appointed, deputies are eligible for lateral transfers from one department to another, meaning that some gain extensive experience in a number of departments during their years of deputy service. Most, however, remain in one department for five to six years, a much longer continuity of service than the minister, who serves for an average of three to four years. This difference becomes quite important in assessing the power relations between ministers and their deputies.

LACK OF PARTISANSHIP

The deputy minister will be the non-partisan head of the department, bringing to it professional managerial judgement gained from years of practical experience in how the department can be best managed, its programs best implemented and administered, and its policies best developed. As deputy ministers are the senior administrative heads of departments, they bring to their work the virtues of neutral bureaucratic expertise and the independent wisdom of the professional public service.

RESPONSIBILITY TO THE PRIME MINISTER

Although deputies directly serve a minister, they nevertheless owe primary responsibility to the prime minister, who wants to know that a department is administered economically, efficiently, and effectively. The deputy is the person both to assure the prime minister that the department is capable of advancing the policy and program agenda and to guarantee that its senior management faithfully serves and protects the interests of the minister.

INSULARITY FROM THE MINISTER

The deputy serves the minister, is responsible to the minister, and is formally subordinate to the minister yet is not subject to the minister's power and authority. The point here is nuanced, but significant. The deputy minister is a professional colleague to the minister—an administrator and adviser to the minister, who enables and assists the minister in "steering" the administrative apparatus of the department.

MINISTERS AND THEIR DEPUTIES

The relationship between ministers and their deputies is crucial in the power relations in any government, and these relationships are complex. The deputy minister's general duty is to serve the minister not only by attending to routine management but also by providing non-partisan professional advice. The deputy is well versed in the policy environment confronting the department and is called upon by the minister to provide expert opinion on the strengths and weaknesses of current policies, to assess policy reform proposals from all interested parties and groups (including those of the minister and the governing party), and to propose and assess new policy initiatives emanating from senior department managers.

The deputy minister walks a fine line, with a close eye on both the administrative interests of the department and the political interests of the governing party. Deputies tend to stress the former while being fully cognizant of the need to embrace the latter once a departmental and ministerial consensus has emerged over a given policy approach. Their opinions are based on

- the professional experience of the department's portfolio;
- the likelihood that particular policies and programs will meet their goals given the specified means; and
- the capacity of the department to implement new proposals with existing or newly established means.

The deputy must be free to offer frank commentary on the administrative, legal, and even broad political (as distinct from partisan) merits and demerits of policy proposals, as well as on the organizational means of achieving them. Deputies need to be critical analysts of all new policy ideas, whatever source they come from, including the minister. And yet they are also expected to

- serve the minister;
- assist in the development of policies and programs desired by the minister, the cabinet, and the prime minister; and
- ensure that new initiatives are consistent with the professional norms and administrative capabilities of the department.

The balance between the administrative and political sides of policy development is never easy, calling for great sensitivity on both sides. Ministers and deputy ministers need each other, and each brings special skills and capabilities, but also limitations, to the decision-making process. The minister is always key, the political head of the department, with a vital interest in the development of initiatives that support both overall government priorities and an individual policy agenda. This point bears close attention; a minister brings to the portfolio a clear but limited set of objectives. Most realize that they will be in their portfolios for three to four years and will be fortunate to secure one or two significant new initiatives during this time. They are therefore very careful when selecting the issues they will pursue, and they take a highly strategic approach to their role within their departments (Savoie 1999, 240–48). It follows that ministers tend to refrain from day-to-day administration, correctly sensing that they have neither the time, the expertise, nor the interest to address the plethora of routine matters. Leaving these to senior department officials liberates the minister to concentrate on strategic initiatives.

Nevertheless, the minister must turn to the deputy for assistance with such initiatives too. The deputy minister can bring expertise and wisdom to bear and is expected, even required, to advise the minister, however unwelcome some of the advice may be. The deputy is likewise expected to be dispassionate with respect to policy initiatives emerging from other sources, including the department itself. A deputy never properly serves the minister by being a "yes" person. Deputies must give detailed and critical advice and be able to ask that an issue be reconsidered on theoretical, operational, legal, or managerial grounds. Here is where the deputy's personal and professional insulation from the minister comes into play.

All deputies know that their duty is to turn the minister's ideas into policy statements and viable programs. While this requires professional expertise, it also calls for flexibility in serving a variety of political masters over time. As they come to power, new parties bring their own political and ideological perspectives, and their ministers take these "new" ideas and turn them into policy and program reality. Deputies play a very significant non-partisan advisory role in this process, regardless of the party in power or the policy approach of the new government. The deputy must always advance sound advice toward fulfilling the aims of the minister while also identifying any administrative, operational, or legal constraints.

A DUTY TO ONE'S MINISTER

In this sense, as Robert Adie and Paul Thomas (1987, 166–67) have written, deputies understand that their first duty to their minister is to keep him or her "out of trouble" by managing the department well: maintaining effective and positive communications and quickly, smoothly, and (one hopes) quietly solving problems as they arise. No minister wants to deal with major administrative problems, and no deputy wants to admit that the departmental administration is malfunctioning badly enough to require ministerial attention—inevitably at the expense of the minister's own strategic policy agenda. Donald Savoie's (2015, 102–5) assessment of contemporary power relations in Ottawa between ministers and their deputies, while noting certain significant changes in the power relations between these actors that we will address toward the end of this chapter, confirms the lasting truth of Adie and Thomas's point.

The second duty is to assist the minister in the development, cabinet approval, and departmental implementation of the policy agenda. A minister's political leadership will be judged on results, and the success or failure of a minister also reflects on the professional success or failure of senior officials themselves. As chief policy advisers to their ministers, deputies must provide professional and non-partisan policy advice while assisting their ministers in fulfilling their policy and program objectives. The task requires the skills of a capable administrator, negotiator, listener, policy analyst, politician, communications expert, and diplomat. It is far from easy, but it can bring great professional satisfaction.

THE AUTHORITY DILEMMA

Deputy ministers are assisted by a variety of associate and assistant deputy ministers and other senior management officials. These are the public servants who manage the routine departmental administration and program implementation as well as all the standard research, policy and program analysis, and departmental communication and liaison functions. And, as outlined above, this core group of deputies and assistant and associate deputies has a major role to play in the policy-advisory and policy-making function of the department.

This raises some troubling questions: Does the predominance of senior officials—all of whom are permanent public servants—within the operational life of departments mean that these essential institutions are more subject to the influence and control of unelected bureaucrats than of elected politicians? Does their combination of departmental longevity, administrative knowledge, and policy and program expertise overshadow the roles of elected ministers? Can the interests of bureaucracy and democracy be balanced to ensure that those involved know their legitimate roles and their limitations?

THE DEPARTMENTALIZED CABINET

This tension between bureaucracy and democracy has long been a feature of Canadian government life, influencing the structure of cabinet decision making for the better part of the last half-century. The current decision-making system, with its unique institutions and processes, has evolved over this period, so it is helpful to review how the modern cabinet has come to be.

For most of the twentieth century, Canadian prime ministers (and premiers) ran their governments through what J. Stefan Dupré (1987) has termed a **departmentalized cabinet system**. A full analytical description of the working of this system is to be found on the Thinking Government website. The key traits of the system were as follows:

- Each minister was responsible for his or her own department.
- Each department functioned on its own, with few formal links to any other.
- Policy making was largely incremental with little long-range planning.
- Cabinet possessed few coordinating mechanisms.
- The PM alone was responsible for coordination and systemic planning.
- Ministers and their departments were fairly autonomous.
- Policy making operated in departmental silos
- Strong cabinet ministers could wield great authority over their department and its policy field.
- Weaker cabinet ministers would come to be reliant/dependent upon strong DMs.
- Strong DMs could wield enormous power and influence in this system.
- By the end of World War II, DMs were being referred to as **mandarins**.
- By the 1960s the democratic legitimacy of the departmentalized cabinet system was being called into question.

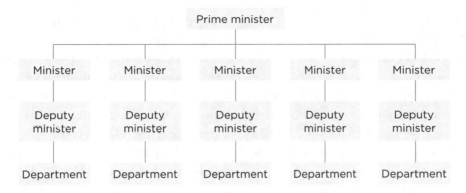

Figure 4.2 **Departmental Hierarchy**

THE INSTITUTIONALIZED CABINET

The origins of the modern **institutionalized cabinet** can be traced to the 1960s and the government of Lester Pearson (Dupré 1987, 236–58; Dunn 2002, 318–21). On coming to power in 1963, Pearson sought to reform the unstructured and chaotic cabinet procedures of the Diefenbaker era (Van Loon and Whittington 1987, 473) with a new approach to executive action that offered greater systematization to decision making while enhancing the power of elected ministers vis-à-vis unelected senior officials, including deputies (Bakvis and MacDonald 1993, 54–57; Thomas 1999, 132–38). Pearson inaugurated a permanent system of standing cabinet committees staffed by ministers themselves. Each committee was given responsibility for developing recommendations with respect to a broad jurisdictional field spanning the portfolios of several related departments. Full cabinet, in turn, met to discuss these policy and program recommendations and to endorse those the ministers collectively desired as government initiatives. A full analytical assessment of the institutionalized cabinet system can be found on the Thinking

Government website. Certain core dynamics of this system are noteworthy:

- The **Priorities and Planning Committee** (P&P) was the key coordinating committee of cabinet, overseeing and directing the work of all other committees.
- P&P was the only committee chaired by the PM, with all other members being the chairs of the other cabinet committees.
- The institutionalized cabinet system was designed to ensure that elected ministers and not unelected DMs were the makers of policy.
- This system was also designed to promote top-down, centralized, systematic, and rational decision making.
- The institutionalized cabinet was also provided with alternative sources of advice respecting policy making and assessing program administration different from government departments.
- These other institutions came to be known as **central agencies**.

HOW AN INSTITUTIONALIZED CABINET WORKS

While the cabinet structures of the Pierre Trudeau, Clark, Turner, Mulroney, Campbell, Chrétien, Martin, and Harper governments differ, they are all characterized as institutionalized cabinets. The following is an overview of the nature and working of such a cabinet system.

CABINET COMMITTEES

The institutionalized cabinet system groups departments into spheres of policy and program interests, and the ministers of these "sister" departments sit on a given **cabinet committee**. Departments of health, labour, human resources, and environment, for example, which share broad social policy interests, can be grouped under a cabinet committee on social development. Finance, industry, trade and commerce, transportation, and regional development, on the other hand, can be united under a cabinet committee on economic development. Similar subdivisions have been formed with respect to foreign and defence policy; security and intelligence; government operations and public works; communications; and treasury policy. In this system, most portfolios require the minister to sit on more than one cabinet committee. For example, the minister of global affairs sits on the committee for both foreign and defence policy and for security and intelligence; the minister of citizenship and immigration sits on the committees for social development, communications, and government operations. Several other cabinet committees have been common as well, such as legislation and house planning, public service, and

a special committee of council (to deal with order-in-council appointments).

Each prime minister has full discretion to establish, disband, or reconfigure cabinet committees—hence, a committee on national unity and constitutional reform during the later Trudeau and the Mulroney years, and committees on operations and expenditure review during Mulroney's second term. In that term, Mulroney presided over a cabinet of 40 ministers allocated into some 11 separate committees (see Figure 4.3).

Regardless of their focus, cabinet committees share certain basic functions. First and foremost they provide a forum for ministers with complementary portfolios to discuss policy and program concerns and developments of mutual interest. Over time, the committees also became a locus of discussions about departmental budget allocations under the **policy and expenditure management system** (PEMS), outlined in Chapter 6. A committee enabled its members to address not only new initiatives but also all government actions within its jurisdiction. In this way, policy and program administration and development became more collectivist. Gone were the days when a policy initiative emanating from a single department could become law with only the most cursory attention from other ministers. Now, all ministers were expected to debate the initiatives of sister departments and come to a consensus about which should go to full cabinet for ratification.

And gone were the days when a strong deputy could exert inordinate influence over a single cabinet minister, and thus over the department and its policy agenda. Now, each minister acted as a check and balance on the actions of another and, hence, on his or her deputy. The committee also

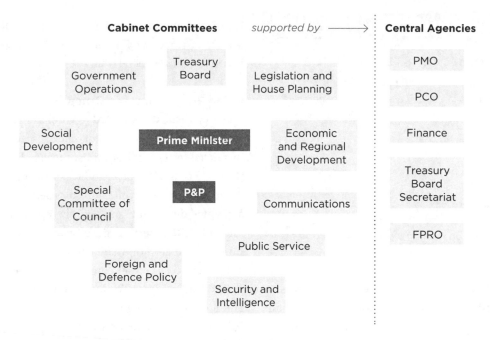

Cabinet Committees   *supported by* ⟶   **Central Agencies**

Government Operations

Treasury Board

Legislation and House Planning

PMO

PCO

Social Development

Prime Minister

Economic and Regional Development

Finance

Special Committee of Council

P&P

Communications

Treasury Board Secretariat

Public Service

FPRO

Foreign and Defence Policy

Security and Intelligence

Figure 4.3 **Institutionalized Cabinet System, 1986**
Source: Clark, 1985, 474.

gave any minister who was having problems with a deputy a way to discuss the difficulty and gain the confidential advice of colleagues.

In simple terms, committees operated on the principle that more heads are better than one in discussing policy. The process meant that policy proposals stood or fell on the judgement of democratically elected officials, theoretically enhancing the role of ministers and diminishing the influence and power of senior department management.

PRIORITIES AND PLANNING

The P&P became the leading committee within cabinet from the mid-1960s to the early 1990s (Van Loon and Whittington 1987, 472–81). It was the one committee chaired by the prime minister as a matter of course, and its members consisted

of the chairs of all the other cabinet committees, the minister of finance, and other senior ministers selected by the prime minister. During the Pierre Trudeau and Mulroney years, the P&P became the central decision-making body of cabinet, with six main functions:

- setting long-range priorities
- tackling short-term political crises
- establishing broad goals and objectives for the other standing cabinet committees
- reviewing all standing committee decisions and resolving disputes
- setting budgetary parameters under the PEMS for committees and departments
- establishing policy and program initiatives in the name of the full cabinet

THE PRIME MINISTER'S OFFICE

The Prime Minister's Office provides the following types of advice to the prime minister:

- Policy advice
- Research advice
- Communications advice
- Operational advice
- Scheduling advice
- Media advice
- Partisan advice
- Advice on dealing with political problems

With the heightened executive leadership afforded by P&P and the more specialized and targeted executive decision making provided by the standing committees, the full cabinet lost its pre-eminence as the central decision-making body. Rather than meeting regularly to review matters and make final decisions, the full cabinet met only to ratify decisions already established by standing committees and approved by P&P.

CENTRAL AGENCIES

Alongside the cabinet committees is the other half of the institutionalized system: a set of advisory bodies that provide the cabinet or the prime minister with detailed information and intelligence (Whitaker 1995; Thomas 1999). Although some central agencies, such as the Privy Council Office, long predated the Pierre Trudeau cabinet, the central agency system as we now know it came into existence under his government and remains largely intact to this day.

Four central agencies rose to prominence, each with its own composition and unique role: the Prime Minister's Office, the Privy Council Office, the Department of Finance, and the Treasury Board of Canada Secretariat.

The Prime Minister's Office

The **Prime Minister's Office** (PMO), as the name suggests, is an organization of officials specifically mandated to serve the administrative, policy, and political needs of the prime minister. The members of the PMO are the prime minister's personal staff, appointed directly by, and entirely responsible to, him or her. They serve at the pleasure of the prime minister and are not members of the permanent public service. The staff complement of the PMO varies. Under Pierre Trudeau it was around 100, and it peaked at roughly 120 under Mulroney in 1985–86. Chrétien held his PMO to 63 during his first term, raising it to 83 by the end of his second (Thomas 1999, 133, 140). Paul Martin aimed for an even leaner staff complement, with just 73 in the PMO in 2006. Stephen Harper increased the size of his PMO to 94 persons as of 2015, 38 per cent more than Martin's figure (McGregor 2014).

The senior ranks of the PMO usually consist of a chief of staff, a senior policy adviser, a research director, a director of communications, and a director of operations (Figure 4.4). They are hand-picked by the prime minister and usually are long-time friends and colleagues whose political opinions and instincts are dependable and who are committed to furthering the vision of the prime minister. Not surprisingly, many have served as chief strategists in the most recent election.

The PMO offers administrative assistance as well as advice. It deals with correspondence, media communications and relations, advice on partisan appointments, organization of public

Source: Data from Government Electronic Directory Services.

Figure 4.4 **Senior Officials in the PMO**

appearances, and drafting of speeches. Above and beyond immediate business, however, senior PMO staff are focused on keeping the prime minister in office and therefore providing directly political and partisan advice about

- how the PM should address leading issues;
- how the PM should be developing policy;
- how the PM should be directing ministers and other senior officials in the development of the government's policy and program agenda;

- what decisions the PM should make or refrain from making;
- how the PM should relate to other ministers, caucus members, opposition leaders, and opposition parties;
- how the PM should deal with the media and what sort of public image he or she should foster;
- what type of message the PM should send to the Canadian public and to major interest groups; and
- who the PM should meet with, talk to, and deal with in the pursuit of the policy agenda.

In this sense, as Paul Thomas has written, the PMO plays the role of a "political switchboard," plugging the prime minister into a host of communication links with the caucus and party, other government officials, the media, and the vast array of interest groups concerned with government policy (1999, 141).

The Privy Council Office

In contrast to the PMO's explicitly political and partisan role, the **Privy Council Office** (PCO) gives administrative support and policy advice to the entire cabinet (Dyck and Cochrane 2014, 541–43). It is staffed by career public servants, and its head, the clerk of the Privy Council and secretary to cabinet, is the most senior public servant in the country and official head of the public service of Canada. The clerk is appointed by the prime minister and, as a rule, drawn from the ranks of senior department deputies. For a deputy minister to be appointed clerk is to reach the pinnacle of a public service career.

First and above all, the PCO provides logistical support to cabinet and its committees—developing agendas, organizing meetings, preparing informational material and analytical briefing notes for ministers, taking and circulating minutes, and disseminating cabinet and committee decisions. The PCO also performs a review and analysis function, providing ministers and the prime minister with assessments of current policies and programs and analyses of new options. Beyond these matters, the PCO has a general responsibility for overseeing the "machinery of government and the appointment of senior public service personnel" (Dyck and Cochrane 2014, 542). In 1993 the PCO was given jurisdiction over federal–provincial relations,

providing advice to the cabinet in this area when the Federal–Provincial Relations Office (FPRO) was reincorporated into the PCO. Prior to this the FPRO had been a separate central agency, providing the Trudeau and Mulroney governments with expert advice on federal–provincial constitutional negotiations.

As of 2015 the Privy Council Office usually employed 727 public servants, assigned to offices such as operations, plans and consultations, management priorities, and senior personnel secretariat. It is also divided into policy branches: foreign and defence policy, security and intelligence, Indigenous affairs, economic and regional development policy, social development policy, regulatory affairs and orders-in-council, legislation and house planning and counsel, machinery of government, and financial planning and analysis. It is evident from this brief list that the PCO is designed to address policy and program matters spanning the full range of government responsibilities. The officials in these offices and branches are some of the most influential public servants in the country, operating at one of the nerve centres of federal government decision making (Treasury Board Secretariat 2015).

The Clerk of the Privy Council

The clerk of the Privy Council and secretary to cabinet oversees one of the most important organizations in the federal government and bears three major and related responsibilities:

- deputy minister to the prime minister
- secretary to the cabinet
- head of the federal public service

In the first role, the clerk meets daily with the prime minister to review ongoing issues and offer non-partisan advice on policy development and related administrative requirements, and on the organization and operation of government decision-making systems themselves. The clerk helps the prime minister in

- structuring cabinet committees;
- structuring and restructuring department portfolios and functions;
- appointing senior public servants; and
- appointing, promoting, demoting, or even removing deputy ministers.

As secretary to the cabinet, the clerk assists its ministers in cabinet and committee organization and operations, ensuring that

- the cabinet and committees receive briefing materials, policy and program analyses, and administrative-operational reviews.
- ministers are privy to relevant information.
- the paper flow into and out of cabinet and committees is detailed, accurate, efficient, and strictly confidential.

Finally, as head of the public service, the clerk is responsible to the prime minister for the overall administrative operations of the federal government, ensuring that

- departments are well organized and staffed;
- senior officials are competent; and
- department employees are trained and motivated.

The clerk is intimately involved in all major reforms to improve the operational efficiency of the public service. The clerk also assists the prime minister in making senior executive appointments to federal Crown corporations and regulatory agencies, and maintains a "watching brief" over all such agencies, reporting to the prime minister on their strengths and weaknesses while respecting their operational autonomy. The clerk assesses the managerial and political environments Crown corporations face and the need for senior appointments, legislative review, and, in rare instances, policy directives to agency boards of directors.

The Department of Finance

The **Department of Finance** is a regular government department under the category of central support departments, but it also acts as a central agency in its role as macro-economic policy adviser to the prime minister and cabinet on all matters touching upon government revenues and expenses—meaning almost everything the government does (Dyck and Cochrane 2014, 543). As Greg Inwood (2011, 136–37) asserts, this department's jurisdictional role over the economy and its financial management of the government make it in many respects "the most powerful actor in the federal government," elevating its minister to become second only to the prime minister in political significance and government power.

Finance has a number of major responsibilities, any one of which would make it significant. When combined, they make it a heavyweight in the world of power politics. First, the department provides the prime minister and cabinet with most of its macro-economic information about the health of the national economy and the effects of government activity in general, and taxation policies in particular, on the viability of the economy and the private sector.

Second, in very close consultation with the prime minister, the department and its minister develop the government's annual budget. Officials from Finance advise the prime minister and relevant cabinet ministers on taxation policy, predicted multiyear revenue streams, and desirable government expenditure parameters. In consultation with the top political leadership and senior officials in the other departments, Finance crafts a budget that

- establishes federal corporate and personal tax policy (increases, decreases, or marginal modifications).
- addresses deficit and debt management.
- provides a multiyear government revenue stream and broad fiscal framework for revenue management in terms of deficit and/or debt reduction, taxation reductions, program funding, and new program development.

Finance is a coordinating hub in the government; as part of its budgetary responsibility, its officials must communicate with senior officials from every other department to find out about their expenditure requirements and spending goals and to convey the government's view of the fiscal climate and the parameters for program expenditure. Finance thus brings significant influence to bear on the development of social, cultural, and environmental policies and their economic consequences.

Third, beyond its macro-economic and financial management duties, Finance provides advice to the cabinet about

DISPATCH BOX

DEPARTMENT OF FINANCE RESPONSIBILITIES

Government financial management
Development of annual budget
Budget coordination with departments
Advice to the prime minister and cabinet on

- economic policy
- tax policy
- international trade
- NAFTA
- deficit management
- debt repayment

- international trade and tariff policy, including management of foreign trade treaties such as NAFTA;
- foreign borrowing and debt repayment;
- overseeing the national debt; and
- balance of payments and foreign exchange.

Finance fulfills all these roles and wields enormous power and influence through the work of 743 public servants as of 2015. These officials, the self-perceived guardians of sound financial management, form an elite within the federal bureaucracy, as much feared as respected by the public servants and ministers who must interact with them. As Inwood (2011, 136) suggests, such is the authority of those who control the purse strings.

The Treasury Board of Canada

The **Treasury Board of Canada** (TB) and its administrative arm, the **Treasury Board of Canada Secretariat** (TBS), provide micro-economic advice to cabinet pertaining to all internal government expenditure and personnel management (Dyck and Cochrane 2014, 543). It is a department headed by a cabinet minister, who is the president of the Treasury Board. The TB includes other cabinet ministers, such as the minister of finance, but its secretariat, the TBS, is its operational heart.

Staffed by 1,761 public servants in 2015, the TBS reviews and analyzes the annual budgets of all departments in detail to ensure that they fall within the spending parameters set by Finance. Departmental budgets are screened for compliance with government priorities and spending targets and have to receive TBS approval prior to ratification. As the guardian of the public purse, the TBS stays

DISPATCH BOX

TREASURY BOARD SECRETARIAT RESPONSIBILITIES

- Management of public service
- Financial management support to departments
- Accountability oversight for departments
- Human resources management support to departments
- Staff training and development support to the public
- Official employer of the public service

in close touch with senior department managers, seeking to contain current and future department spending. And of course those managers typically seek as much latitude as possible over spending in order to expand department goals and activities.

The second major responsibility of the TBS is to oversee the general management of federal public personnel policy. As of 1967, the TB became the official "employer" of government personnel, representing the employer in all matters of collective bargaining and grievances. The TB also manages salaries, salary scales, job classifications, employee training, and long-range recruitment within the public service, as well as promoting the merit principle.

MAKING A MESH OF THINGS

In Paul Thomas's wry assessment of the institutionalized cabinet system, the phrase "making a mesh of things" carries with it both descriptive and analytical insight (Thomas 1999). During the Pierre Trudeau and Brian Mulroney years, the institutionalized cabinet system created a mesh of interrelating roles and responsibilities held by quite a range of political and bureaucratic decision makers, all bringing distinct ideas and professional viewpoints (see Figure 4.5). It clearly made the working of the federal government at the most senior levels much more layered and pluralistic than anything that had gone before.

Such complexity brought with it other, less desirable dynamics, however, as Thomas's pun indicates. While the institutionalized cabinet system was never intended to make decision making simpler, serious concerns began to arise in the 1970s and 80s over whether all the competing advisers, institutions, rules, and responsibilities had made the process too complex and time consuming, and thus too problematic. And had it in fact enhanced the policy-making role of elected ministers and diminished the political influence and power of their deputies?

THE FORMAL VIEW OF DECISION MAKING

It is difficult to encapsulate the nature of cabinet decision making from the late 1960s through to the early 1990s as all governments fine-tuned the institutionalized system. The Pierre Trudeau government was not averse to modifying the decision-making process, and the Brian Mulroney government likewise made a variety of changes during its nine-year tenure, increasing the number of ministers to 40 and expanding the number of cabinet committees to 11. Even the short-lived governments of Joe Clark and Kim Campbell wrought some significant alterations (Kernaghan and Siegel 1999, 396–98; Barker 2008, 181–85; Jackson and Jackson 2009, 288–91), but

certain basic elements remained common throughout these years.

The P&P Sets the Agenda

At the heart of the system, the P&P, chaired by the prime minister, established government policies and priorities and oversaw all other cabinet committees. P&P set the broad agenda, settling on three to five major issues as the defining objectives during a term of office. P&P was closely assisted by the PCO and the Department of Finance, with the latter providing detailed economic forecasts and multiyear revenue and expenditure assessments. And of course, the prime minister was in daily contact with his senior advisers in the PMO throughout the process.

Once the prime minister and P&P had agreed on an agenda for the government and on multiyear revenue and expenditure projections, the information was relayed—with the assistance of the PCO through the communication channels of the senior executive—to cabinet committees, other central agencies, all departments, and their political and administrative heads. With this information in hand, operational policy and program decision making began, or more precisely, continued, now largely centred in the departments.

The Department Sets It in Motion

Each department was responsible for initiating policies and programs within its sphere of jurisdiction and managing undertakings already in play. As a department developed initiatives that would require legislative enactment or amendment and the expenditure of "new" monies, its deputy minister and other senior officials were expected to confer widely and liberally with those concerned

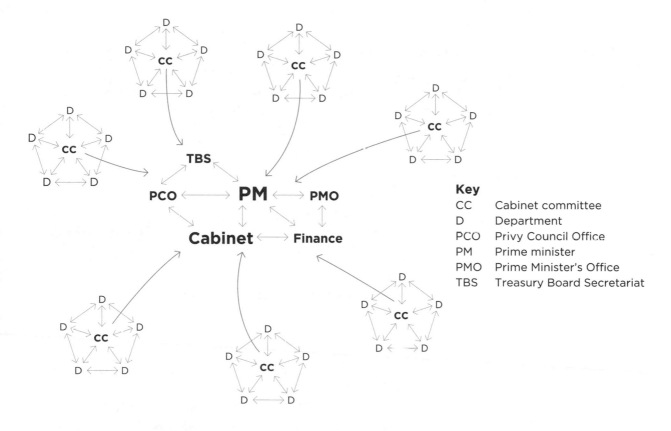

Figure 4.5 **Institutionalized Cabinet Relationship Mesh**

Key

CC	Cabinet committee
D	Department
PCO	Privy Council Office
PM	Prime minister
PMO	Prime Minister's Office
TBS	Treasury Board Secretariat

or affected. Thus, senior department managers routinely communicated with officials from sister departments (deputy ministers remaining in very close contact), as well as with officials in the PCO, Finance, TBS, and even the PMO if needed. This, of course, was in addition to all the department communications and consultations with client groups, interest groups, and the public.

The Officials Produce the Memorandum
Once senior department officials had resolved on a particular course of action, having received sufficient support (or at least non-obstruction),

they produced a **memorandum to cabinet** that would become the focal point of the minister's liaison with cabinet colleagues and officials from central agencies (see Figure 4.6). Each memorandum contained a *Ministerial Recommendation*, an *Analysis* section, and a *Communications Plan*.

The *Recommendation* was normally a short summation of the policy issue and the cabinet decision expected by the sponsoring minister.

The *Analysis* provided the relevant background: the nature of the problem and the ways in which the new policy and related programs would address it. It assessed the strengths and weaknesses of the

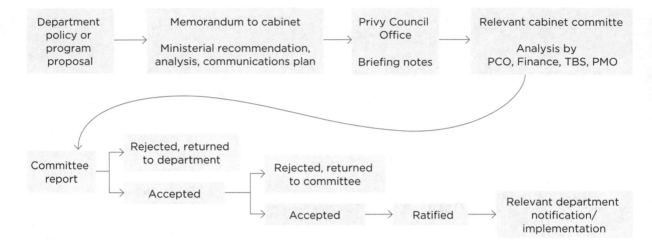

Figure 4.6 **Memorandum to Cabinet (MC) Flow Chart**

proposal, along with other options and the impact each would have on targeted groups in particular, society overall, and directly affected provinces or regions. The analysis examined the direct and indirect political implications—for example, how well the proposal matched general policy priorities set by P&P, existing government commitments, and past party promises—and projected costs, sources of funding, and personnel requirements. It then emphasized either the new initiative's conformity to pre-established spending guidelines set by Finance and the TB or strong reasons for revising the guidelines to allow the initiative to proceed. The analysis also delineated the positions taken by other departments and central agencies over the proposal.

The *Communications Plan* outlined how the minister intended to present the new policy to the public, how the department would implement it, and the structure of ongoing consultations with affected individuals, corporations, interest groups, and the media.

In short, the memorandum to cabinet was designed to "provide ministers with a full range of realistic options, the advantages and disadvantages of each, and their financial and policy implications" (Dyck and Cochrane 2014, 538–39; Jackson and Jackson 2009, 290).

The Committee Reviews It

Once produced and approved by the minister, the memorandum was transmitted to the PCO for distribution to the members of the relevant cabinet committee. The PCO also drew up briefing notes on the proposal for the committee, the PM, and the PMO. These contained a detailed assessment by PCO, Finance, and TBS officials. The cabinet committee then met to discuss the matter and make a decision.

At this meeting the sponsoring minister advanced and defended the memorandum. Such meetings could become testy affairs as ministers debated the theoretical, practical, administrative, and political value of a proposal. And, as Jackson and Jackson (2009, 290–91) have observed, any minister's chance of getting a memorandum through cabinet committee was contingent on gaining central agency support and demonstrating to committee colleagues that the initiative would not threaten funding for their own initiatives.

The Committee Report Is Produced

Following the discussion, which could extend over several meetings, the committee decision would be written up by staff provided by the PCO, in the form of a *Committee Report*. If the proposal was rejected, the report explained why, and the proposal was sent back down to the sponsoring department with a suggestion that it rework its plans in accordance to the analysis.

The Proposal Is Sent to Full Cabinet

If the proposal was accepted, the report was sent to full cabinet for ratification. The report recorded whether the committee vote in favour had been unanimous, and usually in such cases full cabinet would endorse it without discussion. During the Mulroney administration, in fact, P&P routinely endorsed such committee reports without referral to full cabinet.

But a report that was not unanimously endorsed would be subject to full cabinet debate, with PCO and PMO briefings for the prime minister. In these meetings the objections of Finance and the TBS were well represented by their respective ministers.

Once cabinet had resolved a matter to the satisfaction of the prime minister, the outcome was drafted as a *Record of Decision* and transmitted to the relevant department.

THE PRIME MINISTERIAL PREROGATIVE

This outline of the formal process from the 1960s to the early 1990s remains a good description of routine decision making within the Chrétien, Martin, and Harper cabinets in the early years of this century, with some modifications mentioned below. However, a shadow decision-making process has always operated alongside, and in competition to, the formal process. This is prime ministerial direction, or what Tom Axworthy (1988), a former principal secretary to Pierre Trudeau, has called the **strategic prime ministership**.

Just as a minister must choose his or her policy focus strategically, so a prime minister selects policies for the government's agenda. According to Bakvis and MacDonald (1993, 64–65), that strategic focus usually encompasses three to five main issues over a four-year term of office. The prime minister and most senior ministers and advisers (P&P, PMO, PCO, Finance, TBS) devote most of their attention to these priorities, delegating everything else to individual ministers and departments. Once again, senior department officials are expected to manage routine activities, keeping their ministers and thus the government out of trouble and thereby enabling the prime minister and the inner circle to devote themselves to major initiatives. During the Pierre Trudeau years, that meant bilingualism and biculturalism, wage and price controls, constitutional reform, national unity, and the National Energy Policy. Under Mulroney, it was regional development, free trade, privatization and deregulation, constitutional policy, tax reform, and deficit reduction.

Moreover, when a prime minister becomes personally interested in an issue, he or she can assume control above any minister or department and fast-track the policy through P&P and full cabinet, as the minister and senior department officials concerned assume supporting roles. In such circumstances the prime minister is invariably backed by officials from the PCO and PMO, in close consultation with the minister of finance and senior officials. Policy handled in this manner is far from routine, usually touching on political and socio-economic issues viewed by the prime minister and senior advisers as of great national importance.

WEIGHING THE PROS AND CONS

The institutionalized system of cabinet decision making that evolved over the Trudeau and Mulroney years did achieve a number of its goals. The web of organizational relationships created by the system was much more structured and rationalistic than the departmentalized system had allowed. It demanded, and received, a great deal of bureaucratic networking and much greater input from analysts and advisers. Trudeau wanted to create a cabinet system marked by multiple viewpoints from his senior bureaucratic advisers, and this he achieved. The vital role played by central agencies also clearly altered the bureaucratic power relations that had dominated Ottawa prior to the 1960s, as deputy ministers witnessed a relative decline of their power and influence.

Cabinet ministers, at least those on P&P, sharpened their policy-planning role, and the cabinet committee system provided all ministers with a venue to hash out policy and program development. The system institutionalized a much higher degree of interdepartmental and interministerial coordination, giving individual ministers the right to become involved in policies and programs affecting the entire field into which their individual portfolios fell.

Fostering Competition

Yet the institutionalized cabinet system brought with it grave deficiencies. While it was more structured, it was also more time-consuming and bureaucratic. With so many more people involved, there were more opportunities for conflict, and the potential for rationality was not necessarily realized. The convoluted process of review, assessment, and approval was simply unwieldy (Clark 1985; Aucoin 1986; Thomas 1999).

Departments had always competed with one another for scarce financial and personnel resources, but the new structure threw them into competition with the central agencies from which they also needed support. And agencies such as Finance and TBS, in their roles as guardians of the public purse, increasingly attempted to constrain spending or direct it along lines that they, rather than the departments, desired. In subjecting all departmental initiatives to scrutiny from and endorsement by the central agencies prior to cabinet ratification, the institutionalized system created a series of roadblocks.

The rationalist "mesh" involved critical scrutiny not only by the central agencies but also by other departments, ministers, and committees, any of which could offer objections. And bureaucrats can be very parochial and self-serving, jealously guarding their own interests at the expense of the policies and programs favoured by others. As Hartle (1976) has written, the power relations between competitive interests can be viewed as a game, with each player advancing its power and financial and personnel resources over those of the other players. All the players are acutely aware of the constraints imposed upon them by the structured relationships of the institutionalized system. Successful policy and program development— winning the game—requires a department to navigate the webs of competing interests, defend its initiatives, and build the political, ministerial, and bureaucratic allegiances it needs to obtain the obligatory approvals.

Reining in the Deputies?

Although the ability of the institutionalized cabinet to rationalize decision making was hopelessly overblown by early advocates, what of the other great claim: that it would diminish the influence of unelected bureaucratic mandarins and thus enhance the policy decision-making role of elected ministers? Results were decidedly mixed. Ministers did have greater opportunity to make collective policy and program decisions through the work of cabinet committees. And much more detailed information and expert advice were available to them. A minister could become much better informed and generally have a larger impact on policy making than under the old, departmentalized system.

But as Van Loon and Whittington (1987, 494–95), among others, have argued, although the institutionalized system diminished the relative influence and power of individual deputy ministers, the central agencies (except the PMO)

are themselves staffed by career public servants. Thus, the historic influence of one set of senior officials—the deputy ministers—has simply been checked by and balanced against that of another set—the "guardians" in the central agencies. One can argue that the overall authority of deputies has been lessened, but not that senior public servants *in general* are any less influential. The change has been in the number of competing bureaucratic influences.

Senior officials, and especially deputy ministers, remain the kingpins of the departments, and the departments remain the primary developers and implementers of policies and programs. Ministers still need to work closely with their senior departmental staff, and officials from central agencies must work effectively with their departmental counterparts.

THE CHRÉTIEN COMMAND MODE

In the 1990s, changes to cabinet decision making were so radical that although most of the fundamentals of the institutionalized system are intact, we should now refer, as Aucoin (1999) and Savoie (1999) do, to a **command mode** of decision making. Governing is all about the exercise of power, and over the past two decades we have witnessed an ever increasing centralization of power in Ottawa into fewer and fewer hands, with all of these hands serving the prime minister, and with the prime minister being the ultimate decision maker. The command mode of decision making has a number of key characteristics:

- Routine matters of policy development and program administration are left to line departments.
- Strategic matters of policy development and program management are subject to the overriding control of the forces of the centre—the PM, the PMO, the PCO, and, in relation to financial matters, Finance.
- In relation to strategic matters, cabinet is no longer an effective decision-making body, having been superseded by the forces of the centre.
- The Prime Minister and his key advisers in the PMO and PCO determine which matters will be considered strategic and which are merely routine, not needing their close attention and control.

THE CENTRE OF POWER

In addressing the role of the prime minister in Chrétien's system of power politics, Savoie wrote, "There is one individual, however, who can at any time upset the collective versus individual responsibilities and, with no advance notice, take an issue that would properly belong to a minister and her department and bring it to the centre. The Prime Minister can intervene in any issue—big or small—if he feels that his judgment is required.... The important point here ... is that the Prime Minister can intervene in a departmental matter when and where he pleases" (1999, 57). In deciding to bring an issue under centralized oversight, any prime minister will be motivated by strategic considerations. Once the decision is made, however, the PM more or less always prevails.

Savoie considers that by the late 1990s the dynamics of the federal government had become troubling, in particular the relative decline of cabinet as an effective strategic decision-making body. Whereas it had functioned as one under Pearson and somewhat as a university seminar under Pierre Trudeau, he asserts, under Mulroney and Chrétien it degenerated into a prime ministerial focus group (Savoie 1999, 3). While this somewhat cynical attitude fails to recognize the important business cabinet takes care of in routine administration and policy, Savoie is undoubtedly correct about the growing importance of strategic prime ministership. In the most significant policy and program issues confronting his government, Chrétien repeatedly demonstrated that he was *le boss*, and that he would brook little dissent. And the government of Stephen Harper only accentuated this centralization of power. As Michael Harris (2014, 7) wryly noted, even Conservative cabinet ministers came to refer to Harper as "the Chairman."

The practical extent of prime ministerial control over core government decision making will be canvassed in greater detail with respect to financial management and budgetary politics, but it is fair to say that the centralization of authority has been unprecedented among most Western democracies. Savoie (1999, 362) could find few factors to mitigate prime ministerial strength. And since then the power of the centre has simply grown.

THE HARPER COMMAND MODE

Stephen Harper first came to power in January 2006, having defeated the short-lived Liberal government of Paul Martin. It's important to remember that in this election Harper promised the Canadian people that a new Conservative government would promote greater democratization in the functioning of government, greater participation in policy making by MPs, and greater transparency in the way the executive worked. After just a few years of watching the Harper government in practice, many Canadians came to feel cheated with respect to these commitments.

USING LEADERSHIP TO GET THINGS DONE

Harper's government proved to be one of the most controversial in Canadian history, leaving few Canadians neutral. According to Conservatives, one of Harper's great traits was strong leadership. In contrast to the perceived dithering of Paul Martin and the ineptitude of Stéphane Dion, federal Liberal leader between 2006 and 2009, and Justin Trudeau's being "just not ready," Conservatives pointed to the vision and decisive actions of Stephen Harper as prime minister. The designated web page for Prime Minister Harper stressed that the key priorities of the prime minister were to support Canadian families and communities; to cut taxes; to stimulate the economy; to restrain the growth of government; to promote balanced budgets; to rebuild the Canadian Forces; to keep Canadians safe by cracking down on gun, gang, and drug crime; and to promote Canadian sovereignty in the Arctic. And Conservatives would stress that significant progress was made on all these priorities through the years of the Harper government, with a decisive leader capable of getting things done.

ASSESSING THE LEGACY

While opponents would grudgingly admit that Stephen Harper proved remarkably able in turning many of his policy ideas into reality, especially in cutting taxes, diminishing the role and stature of the federal public service, deregulating the economy, promoting the oil and gas industry, increasing the funding to and role of the Canadian military, and establishing much tougher anti-crime legislation, he did so through a very tightly controlled command approach to prime ministerial leadership that critics consider excessive, abusive, close-minded, or worse. The charges against both the style and substance of Stephen Harper's approach to governing are legion. Critics such as Lawrence Martin (2010), Michael Harris (2014), Donald Savoie (2015), and Bob Rae (2015), to name just a few, accused this prime minister of

- concentrating excessive power in his own hands and in that of his PMO;

- rendering cabinet government next to meaningless;
- stripping ministers and caucus members of their independent voices;
- being, in Michael Harris's words, "a party of one";
- being hyper-partisan and intolerant of criticism;
- attacking all those who questioned his policy positions;
- being distrustful and demeaning to the federal public service;
- stripping the federal public service of its important role in the policy process;
- basing policy decisions more on ideological beliefs than on evidenced-based research;
- using distortion, deceit, manipulation, and outright lies to support his policy actions;
- being contemptuous of parliament;
- overturning a half-century of balanced Canadian diplomacy; and
- being a threat to Canadian democracy.

In his critical biography of Stephen Harper, Michael Harris (2014) accuses Harper of being a "rogue prime minister," one who is authoritarian, manipulative, cynical in his hyper-partisanship, secretive, contemptuous of those who disagree with him, and, perhaps worst of all, a direct threat to Canadian democracy. In a similar vein, Lawrence Martin (2010, 272) stressed that Harper, in power, had "circumvented the conventions of democracy so much" that academics were beginning to say that Harper's "abuse of executive power is tilting toward totalitarian government and away from the foundations of democracy and the rule of law, on which this country was founded." Bob Rae (2015),

admittedly a political opponent of Prime Minister Harper, attacked his leadership for being contemptuous of parliamentary democracy. Rae noted the Harper government's serial use of massive omnibus budget bills as a means of passing large numbers of unrelated legislative matters with limited parliamentary review and debate leading to a single Yes or No vote. "A 2012 budget bill," Rae charged, "changed seventy laws, gutted environmental protection, killed off a multitude of agencies, and raised the age of retirement from sixty-five to sixty-seven. Shortly after introducing the bill, the government limited debate and this massive, four-hundred page monstrosity headed to committee for a pro forma discussion" (109). Canadians, Rae stressed, should have been outraged by the Harper government's increasing streak of authoritarianism and disrespect for Canadian democratic traditions. In summing up his assessment of nine years of Stephen Harper's leadership of this country, Rae concluded that "[w]e're now living in a democracy with dictatorial tendencies, and Canadians should not see their democratic institutions diluted and muzzled because of political timidity" (110).

But in his biographical study of this prime minister, John Ibbitson (2015), a more sympathetic conservative analyst, found Stephen Harper to be a man of various shades of grey. His character, according to Ibbitson is authoritarian, cold, and Machiavellian, "the most controlling prime minister in Canadian history" (251), and he is a man committed to the support of core conservative ideas. Stephen Harper has been the most ideological of all Canadian prime ministers, and to Ibbitson, this is what made Harper such a lightning rod of discontent to Canadians who do not share his ideological vision. "One of

Prime minister
Full cabinet

Supported by
Finance, PMO,
PCO, TBS

Agenda and Results Committee (formerly P&P)

Treasury Board

Parliamentary Affairs Committee

Inclusive Growth, Opportunities and Innovation Committee

Diversity and Inclusion Committee

Canada in the World and Public Security Committee

Sub-Committee on Canada-United States Relations

Intelligence and Emergency Management Committee

Open and Transparent Government Committee

Environment, Climate Change and Energy Committee

Figure 4.7 **Trudeau Cabinet System, 2015**

the fundamental priorities of the Harper government," writes Ibbitson, "is to shrink the size of the state. Permanently. Shrinking the size of the state is Harper's greatest imperative. It is what makes him a genuinely conservative prime minister.... It is perfectly reasonable to object to all of these measures. But it is not reasonable to expect a conservative government not to act like a conservative government" (262).

THE TRUDEAU COMMAND MODE

Justin Trudeau officially came to power in November 2015 promising to be very different from his predecessor. He would be a liberal prime minister leading a Liberal government. In his winning election campaign he stressed that his government would be far more open and transparent than that of Stephen Harper, and that the Liberals would restore a culture of professionalism and accountability to Ottawa, where evidence-based policy making would triumph over narrow-minded and divisive ideology, and where collegial and responsive decision making would return to the fore, superseding the rule of one man.

The diversity of the Trudeau cabinet was a reflection of this new approach, as was the soon-noted openness of Liberal cabinet ministers and the prime minister in holding press conferences and in encouraging media scrutiny of their actions. As a sign of the new openness in Ottawa, Trudeau accomplished a first by publishing the Mandate Letters sent to all of his ministers, highlighting the expectations and policy directions the prime minister expected of them. The cabinet committee structure inaugurated by the new prime minister also hinted at the change in focus of the new government and how the more traditional ways of seeing the federal policy and program universe were evolving to a more conceptual and thematic approach to policy values and outcomes.

The reform of cabinet structure and committee terminology, however, in no way changes the fundamental power relations between a prime minister and his or her ministers and senior officials. While Justin Trudeau promised to be more open and collegial in his decision making, he, and he alone, is the prime minister, the head of government, and the leader of his party. On his shoulders rests the ultimate fate of his government, a truth all prime ministers in the past have known, and his exercise of executive leadership will determine whether his government is successful or not, meriting re-election or defeat in 2019.

In keeping with the logic of the strategic prime ministership, a select number of policy matters were front and centre on Trudeau's agenda immediately upon his assuming office:

- Kickstarting a sluggish Canadian economy through needed infrastructure spending that would have the effect of creating many new jobs, especially for young Canadians.
- Providing middle-class tax relief while raising personal income taxes on the wealthiest Canadians, ensuring that they pay their fair share of taxation.
- Getting serious with global climate change by working with the provinces in promoting greenhouse gas emission reductions and

in strengthening Canadian environmental regulations.
- Re-establishing Canada as a moderate and thoughtful voice in global affairs with a foreign policy emphasis on multilateralism, social and economic development, and peacekeeping over more belligerent approaches to global tensions.
- Improving the quality of Canadian democracy and its representative institutions, especially in relation to the Senate, electoral reform, and governmental accountability.

This was always understood as being an ambitious agenda and one that would consume the time and energy of the prime minister. Other less strategic or immediately pressing matters—criminal law reform, the promotion of Charter rights in anti-terrorism legislation, the investigation into missing and murdered Indigenous women, military procurement issues for ships and jet fighters, long-term funding commitments for health care, public pension plans, postsecondary education, and a host of others—would be devolved to responsible ministers, all working under the watchful eyes and guidance of central agencies, including the PMO and the PCO.

Only time will tell if Trudeau`s commitment to openness, transparency, and responsiveness will long survive the harsh reality of exercising power. Many prime ministers entered office making similar pledges, only to see these commitments wither as the discipline of power forces them to make decisions in more closed, opaque, and selective manners, where certain interests are served better than others. What is unlikely to change, however, is the central role of the prime minister in the governmental universe found in Ottawa. There are many stars in this universe, but only one sun.

COURT GOVERNMENT

Donald Savoie has gone so far as to write that the style of governance we now have in Ottawa is best characterized as a court government: "By *court government* I do not mean the rise of judicial power. Rather, I mean that effective political power now rests with the prime minister and a small group of carefully selected courtiers. I also mean a shift from formal decision-making processes in cabinet and, as a consequence, in the civil service, to informal processes involving only a handful of actors. We now make policy by announcements, and we manage government operations by adjusting administrative and financial requirements to the circumstances of the day. Court government has its advantages but also its disadvantages" (2008, 16).

As Savoie notes, some disadvantages of this style of government are that decision making becomes centralized in the hands of a few powerful actors; parliament, cabinet, and the public service become secondary or even tertiary to the power of these few; the roles of senior politicians and public servants become blurred; government operations and leadership come to be viewed in terms of discipline and success, the benchmarks of the private sector; and overall accountability to parliament and the public is diminished, if not lost altogether.

But court government certainly produces efficient decision making. A strong prime minister who knows what he or she wants is in complete command of the vast apparatus of the federal government. As Stephen Harper has himself said, "It is necessary for the government to speak with one voice and ministers to know the announcements of other ministers before reading them in the paper" (*Toronto Star*, July 31, 2007). Whether such decision making is effective and desirable, however, remains a point of ideological debate.

The key focus of this chapter has been power. Who has it? Why do they have it? And how do they use it? By the 1950s concern that senior public servants, especially deputy ministers, were usurping the decision-making role of elected ministers led the Pearson government to move away from a departmentalized cabinet to an institutionalized form. Marked by complex interaction between cabinet committees and central agencies, the institutionalized style came to fruition during the early Trudeau years and has remained the dominant organizational principle of power dynamics, administration, and politics ever since.

From its inception, this system was intended to elevate the role of elected ministers over their deputies. Cabinet committees were to be key decision-making bodies, setting policies and establishing programs with the help of advisory bodies, mainly other departments and central agencies. No single department or deputy minister could wield the influence of the mandarins of old. Although the system did strengthen the role of ministers, however, it did not lessen the influence of unelected senior public servants on policy making and program development. Moreover, policy development and execution became ever more convoluted and time-consuming as the larger numbers of people involved increased the likelihood of disagreement.

In light of the growing complexity of cabinet decision making over the past 40 years, we have also seen greater use of prime ministerial prerogative, or the command mode of decision making. Every prime minister since John A. Macdonald has exercised this type of authority, but power has grown more concentrated at the executive centre since the days of Pierre Trudeau.

Is the decades-long trend toward the centralization of power in Ottawa inevitable? Has Canada become, in the tongue-in-cheek words of Jeffrey Simpson, a "friendly dictatorship"? (And note that Simpson was referring to the Chrétien government when he made that point.) Is the quality of accountability in this country weakening? Savoie's analysis of power relations in contemporary Ottawa is sobering, and there is no evidence that any enhancement of routine accountability mechanisms will make a dent in the strategic powers of the prime minister. He is *le boss*.

REFERENCES AND SUGGESTED READING

Adie, Robert F., and Paul G. Thomas. 1987. *Canadian Public Administration: Problematical Perspectives*. 2nd ed. Scarborough, ON: Prentice Hall Canada.

Anderson, G. 1996. "The New Focus on the Policy Capacity of the Federal Government." *Canadian Public Administration* 39: 469–88.

Archer, Keith, Roger Gibbins, Rainer Knopff, and Leslie A. Pal. 1999. *Parameters of Power: Canada's Political Institutions*. 2nd ed. Toronto: Nelson.

Aucoin, Peter. 1986. "Organizational Change in the Machinery of Canadian Government: From Rational Management to Brokerage Politics." *Canadian Journal of Political Science* 19 (March): 3–27.

———. 1995. "The Prime Minister and Cabinet." In *Introductory Readings in Canadian Government and Politics*, 2nd ed., edited by Robert M. Krause and R.H. Wagenberg, 169–92. Toronto: Copp Clark.

———. 1999. "Prime Minister and Cabinet: Power at the Apex." In *Canadian Politics*, 3rd ed., edited by James Bickerton and Alain-G. Gagnon, 109–28. Toronto: University of Toronto Press.

Axworthy, Tom. 1988. "Of Secretaries to Princes." *Canadian Public Administration* 31: 247–64.

Bakvis, Herman, and David MacDonald. 1993. "The Canadian Cabinet: Organization, Decision-Making Rules, and Policy Impact." In *Governing Canada: Institutions and Public Policy*, edited by Michael M. Atkinson, 47–80. Toronto: Harcourt Brace.

Barker, Paul. 2008. *Public Administration in Canada: Brief Edition*. Toronto: Nelson.

Bourgault, Jacques. 2002. "The Role of Deputy Ministers in Canadian Government." In *The Handbook of Canadian Public Administration*, edited by Christopher Dunn, 430–49. Toronto: Oxford University Press.

———. 2003. *The Contemporary Role and Challenges of Deputy Ministers in the Government of Canada*. Ottawa: Canadian Centre for Management Development.

Bricker, Darrell, and John Ibbitson. 2013. *The Big Shift: The Seismic Change in Canadian Politics, Business, and Culture and What It Means for Our Future*. Toronto: HarperCollins.

Brooks, Stephen. 1993. *Public Policy in Canada: An Introduction*. 2nd ed. Toronto: McClelland and Stewart.

Campbell, Colin. 1983. *Governments under Stress: Political Executives and Key Bureaucrats in Washington, London and Ottawa*. Toronto: University of Toronto Press.

Campbell, Colin, and George Szablowski. 1979. *The Superbureaucrats: Structure and Behaviour in Central Agencies*. Toronto: Macmillan Canada.

Clark, Ian D. 1985. "Recent Changes in the Cabinet Decision-Making System in Ottawa." *Canadian Public Administration* 28: 185–201.

Delacourt, Susan. 2003. *Juggernaut: Paul Martin's Campaign for Chrétien's Crown*. Toronto: McClelland and Stewart.

Doern, G. Bruce, and Richard W. Phidd. 1992. *Canadian Public Policy*. 2nd ed. Toronto: Methuen.

Dunn, Christopher. 2002. "The Central Executive in Canadian Government: Searching for the Holy Grail." In *The Handbook of Canadian Public Administration*, edited by Christopher Dunn, 305–40. Toronto: Oxford University Press.

Dupré, J. Stefan. 1987. "The Workability of Executive Federalism in Canada." In *Federalism and the Role of the State*, edited by H. Bakvis and W. Chandler, 236–57. Toronto: University of Toronto Press.

Dyck, Rand. 1996. *Provincial Politics in Canada: Towards the Turn of the Century*. 3rd ed. Scarborough, ON: Prentice Hall Canada.

———, Rand, and Christopher Cochrane. 2014. *Canadian Politics: Critical Approaches*. 7th ed. Toronto: Nelson.

French, Richard. 1984. *How Ottawa Decides: Planning and Industrial Policy Making, 1968–1984*. 2nd ed. Toronto: James Lorimer.

Gray, John. 2003. *Paul Martin: The Power of Ambition*. Toronto: Key Porter Books.

Harris, Michael. 2014. *Party of One: Stephen Harper and Canada's Radical Makeover*. Toronto: Viking.

Hartle, Douglas G. 1976. *A Theory of the Expenditure Budgetary Process*. Toronto: University of Toronto Press.

Ibbitson, John. 2015. *Stephen Harper*. Toronto: Signal/McClelland and Stewart.

Inwood, Gregory J. 2011. *Understanding Canadian Public Administration: An Introduction to Theory and Practice*. 4th ed. Toronto: Pearson Canada.

Jackson, Robert J., and Doreen Jackson. 2009. *Politics in Canada: Culture, Institutions, Behaviour and Public Policy*. 7th ed. Toronto: Pearson Prentice Hall Canada.

Kernaghan, Kenneth, and David Siegel. 1999. *Public Administration in Canada: A Text*. 4th ed. Toronto: Nelson.

Martin, Lawrence. 2010. *Harperland: The Politics of Control*. Toronto: Viking Canada.

McGregor, Glen. 2014. "Number of Staffers Working for PM, Cabinet Ministers Ballooned under Harper Government." *National Post*, December 10, http://news.nationalpost.com/news/canada/canadian-politics/number-of-staffers-working-for-PM-cabinet-ministers-ballooned-under-Harper-government.

Monahan, Patrick. 1997. *Constitutional Law*. Toronto: Irwin Law.

Rae, Bob. 2015. *What's Happened to Politics?* Toronto: Simon and Schuster.

Radwanski, Adam. 2016. "All Pearson, No Pierre: Inside Trudeau's Inner Circle." *The Globe and Mail*, January 9, pp. F6–F7.

Savoie, Donald J. 1990. *The Politics of Public Spending in Canada*. Toronto: University of Toronto Press.

———. 1999. *Governing from the Centre: The Concentration of Power in Canadian Politics*. Toronto: University of Toronto Press.

———. 2003. *Breaking the Bargain: Public Servants, Ministers, and Parliament*. Toronto: University of Toronto Press.

———. 2008. *Court Government and the Collapse of Accountability in Canada and the United Kingdom*. Toronto: University of Toronto Press.

———. 2010. *Power: Where Is It?* Montreal: McGill-Queen's University Press

———. 2015. *What Is Government Good at? A Canadian Answer*. Montreal: McGill-Queen's University Press.

Thomas, Paul G. 1999. "The Role of Central Agencies: Making a Mesh of Things." In *Canadian Politics*, 2nd ed., edited by James Bickerton and Alain-G. Gagnon, 129–48. Toronto: University of Toronto Press.

Treasury Board Secretariat. 2015. *Population of Federal Public Service by Department*. http://www.tbs-sct.gc.ca/psm-fpfm/modernizing-modernisation/stats/ssa-pop-eng.asp.

Van Loon, Richard J., and Michael S. Whittington, eds. 1987. *The Canadian Political System: Environment, Structure and Process*. 4th ed. Toronto: McGraw-Hill Ryerson.

Whitaker, Reginald A. 1995. "Politicians and Bureaucrats in the Policy Process." In *Canadian Politics in the 1990s*, 4th ed., edited by Michael S. Whittington and Glen Williams, 424–40. Toronto: Nelson.

Whittington, Michael S. 2000. "The Prime Minister, Cabinet, and the Executive Power in Canada." In *Canadian Politics in the 21st Century*, edited by Michael S. Whittington and Glen Williams, 31–54. Toronto: Nelson.

RELATED WEBSITES

Department of Finance Canada. www.fin.gc.ca

Government Electronic Directory Services. http://sage-geds.tpsgc-pwgsc.gc.ca/en/GEDS

Government of Canada. www.canada.ca

Prime Minister of Canada. www.pm.gc.ca

Privy Council Office. www.pco-bcp.gc.ca/premier.asp

Treasury Board of Canada Secretariat. www.tbs-sct.gc.ca

CHAPTER 5

Organizational Design and Management Decision Making

It is common sense to take a method and try it. If it fails, admit it frankly and try another. But above all, try something.

–Franklin Delano Roosevelt, 1932

After reading this chapter and its related web pages you will be able to

- identify ten key management functions;
- explain six major differences between the public and private sectors;
- discuss the pros and cons of two classic models for understanding organizational theory;
- describe Max Weber's theory of bureaucracy;
- assess why the organic-humanistic model of organizational theory dominates the modern workforce;
- debate the merits of incrementalism and rationalism; and
- identify and explain five other approaches to managerial decision making.

5   Organizational Design and Management Decision Making

No government can exist without bureaucracy, and no bureaucracy can function without management. Governments that set expansive public policy objectives need large numbers of educated, trained, and directed public servants, organized into numerous institutions, to execute the will of elected ministers and, in the largest sense, to promote the interests of society. Such a vast undertaking demands effective organization, human and material resources, and legal expertise, all channelled into meeting the needs and goals of the government.

The remainder of this text concentrates on the management function in government, with particular focus on its history, evolution, and current dynamics at the federal level. As an introduction, this chapter undertakes a theoretical review of the schools of thought about organizational design and managerial decision making, especially in relation to the public sector. In doing so it explores the two dominant broad conceptual models of organizational structure and the ideal flow of bureaucratic influence and power. We also look at theories of decision making and the techniques associated with them and assess the motivations of those who apply them.

An emerging theme in any examination of public sector management is the significant difference between its values and operational dynamics and those of the private sector. The public sector is the more demanding environment, but this conclusion often seems counterintuitive to people brought up with a rather cynical view of government, and so the underlying reasons need to be explored.

We also consider the elastic nature of the terms *political* and *administrative* in relation to public policy. At the highest level of public sector management, administrative and political considerations are intrinsically related (Whitaker 1995). Although some organizational theorists insist there should be a clear division between politics and administration, we can see already that such a demarcation is impossible, especially at the most strategically important level of managerial decision making. We do not live in a simple world where political leaders design policies and the public service implements them. Senior managers play an important role in the development, review, analysis, and reform of policies and programs, working closely with ministers.

Another theme is the tension between structural-mechanistic and organic-humanistic models, both of which strongly influence how we think about public administration and the working of governments. The structural-mechanistic approach once dominated the field but has waned in the past half-century under pressure from the organic-humanistic approach. We assess the strengths and weaknesses of this ascendant model, concluding that in fact the structural-mechanistic approach remains very useful to an understanding of the levers and pulleys of management.

The final theme is the tension between rationalist and incrementalist forms of management. Despite a long-standing managerial drive to promote rationalism over incrementalism, we identify the problems associated with both models and the pervasiveness of incrementalism as an important and viable way to conduct management.

Many of the theoretical concepts addressed here will be encountered again in subsequent chapters as we turn from theory to practice.

THE FUNCTIONS OF MANAGEMENT

What does management do? Many analysts have used this question as a starting point for studies of organizational theory and practice, and regardless of whether one is looking at public or private sector bureaucracy, certain management functions are common. In his studies of French management in the early twentieth century, Henri Fayol (1971) documented five functions common to managers in all organizations:

1 planning
2 organizing
3 commanding
4 coordinating
5 controlling

GULICK'S FUNCTIONS OF MANAGEMENT

American organizational theorist Luther Gulick (1937) later expanded this list into seven categories in his own study of management within the American federal government:

1 **p**lanning
2 **o**rganizing
3 **s**taffing
4 **d**irecting
5 **co**ordinating
6 **r**eporting
7 **b**udgeting

These activities, known collectively as **POSDCORB**, delineated not only government management but administrative responsibilities essential to the success of any bureaucratic organization. As Robert B. Denhardt has noted, these elements provide a checklist to managers "about what they should be doing" (1999, 286).

Gulick's list of management functions quickly became a classic within the field of organizational theory, and POSDCORB the thumbnail explication of management roles and responsibilities (see Table 5.1). While the list is instructive, it is not definitive, and numerous other organizational theorists have reformulated or elaborated on it, using Gulick's taxonomic technique to search for more precise interpretations of management functions.

MINTZBERG'S FUNCTIONS OF MANAGEMENT

Garry Yukl (2012, chap. 2) highlights several reinterpretations of Gulick in his work on organizational leadership, devoting special attention to the analysis of Henry Mintzberg. Mintzberg's review of management roles (1973, 92–93) identifies ten concepts that echo Gulick's findings, but he also emphasizes the importance of leadership and crisis management. In this taxonomy, Mintzberg divides management functions into three fields:

1 *Information-processing roles*: monitoring information, disseminating information, and acting as a spokesperson for the organization
2 *Decision-making roles*: being involved in policy and program development and administration, resource allocation, negotiation between interested actors, and conflict resolution
3 *Interpersonal roles*: performing as a figurehead for the organization, making connections with other bodies in its broad

operational environment, and providing leadership

Mintzberg sees the leadership role as pervading all others. Leadership unites all other management functions in a coherent direction, coordinating and focusing responsibilities and actions toward the realization of basic organizational goals. It is *the* most important managerial function because the success or failure of an organization is contingent on the quality of its managerial leadership.

Among the leadership qualities Mintzberg highlights is skill in handling crises, the "disturbance handler role" (Yukl 2012, 28). Managers are called on to deal with unforeseen threats to the effectiveness of the organization in pursuing its given tasks. All organizations face such problems sooner or later, and the ability of the manager to resolve them is paramount. Mintzberg suggests, furthermore, that crises should be seen as learning opportunities, providing the impetus to rethink operational behaviour, redesign the organizational methods in use, and even to re-evaluate and renew the purposes and goals of the organization itself. To be successful over the long term, institutions need to adapt constantly to the operational environment as it evolves. Successful adaptation requires the manager to seize opportunities for creative action to resolve difficulties while maintaining the best of the organization's operational and managerial heritage.

PUBLIC VERSUS PRIVATE SECTOR MANAGEMENT

Organizations of any considerable size become intricate, comprising many human, material, and

intellectual components with a multiplicity of interests and power dynamics that may not always be directed to the same organizational goals. A fundamental objective of management is to define, coordinate, and direct those elements toward the realization of established organizational ends. This is an involved task in any institution, but consider the heightened complexity of management within the public sector (Inwood 2004, 9–14).

Public sector managers confront a Byzantine policy and program environment in which organizations routinely possess several goals, often attached to sweeping concepts of socio-economic, cultural, and political well-being. These

TABLE 5.1

Gulick's Functions of Management

	WHAT?	HOW?	WHY?	EXAMPLE
Planning	The assessment of an organization's current condition, direction, and goals—in modern terms the SWOT analysis of strengths, weaknesses, opportunities, and threats—and its future aims.	Understanding the organization's *raison d'être*, effectiveness in its organizational goals, and operational environment.	Enables the organization to respond to changes in its environment, to address weaknesses in its operational behaviour, and to develop new and better policies and programs that will also promote its interests into the future. An organization that neglects planning will devote too much attention to routine administration and not enough to overall objectives and ways to achieve them.	The Canadian Armed Forces have long planned for the acquisition of a modern jet fighter to replace the aging CF-18. This planning process has been going on for over a decade within the Department of National Defence. But such a lengthy period is justified on the grounds that the replacement aircraft will possess an operational lifespan of some 30 years.
Organizing	A collection of activities related to the structure of the bureaucratic entity, establishing an organizational design and defining the roles and responsibilities of management and staff.	Deciding whether the organizational hierarchy should be steep or shallow, centralized or decentralized; whether the flow of information, authority, and influence should be top down, bottom up, or some balance of the two; and whether power relations between management and staff and within management itself should be more authoritarian or egalitarian.	Thinking about the fundamental goals and responsibilities of the organization and creating the bureaucratic structure to fulfill them in the most economical, efficient, and effective ways is an integral aspect of smooth functioning.	National Defence established a specialized new jet fighter procurement and assessment project team within the department, tasked with finding the appropriate aircraft and its industrial support package.
Staffing	"Acquiring, training and developing of personnel to conduct the organization's activities" (Denhardt 1999, 286), including hiring, promotion, discipline, demotion, and firing.	Managing personnel using communication, motivation, resolution of interpersonal conflict, and promotion of sound management–workforce interaction.	Human wants and needs, likes and dislikes, attitudes, and expectations—with all the potential for disagreement and conflict that human interaction implies—require management and negotiation for effective organizational functioning.	The department staffed this jet fighter project team with a range of experts, from Air Force pilots to strategic analysts and military procurement and industrial development officials.

	WHAT?	HOW?	WHY?	EXAMPLE
Directing	Directing staff toward the realization of institutional goals and the application of material, financial, and legal resources toward the same end.	Making decisions and undertaking "the three critical management activities: leading, motivating and changing things when necessary" (Denhardt 1999, 286).	One of the natural outcomes of managerial–workforce interaction and a vital component of good leadership, directing is "often the most dynamic and most visible management function" (Denhardt 1999, 286).	The jet fighter project team was under the direction of a senior Air Force officer charged with staffing the team, giving it direction, and overseeing its research and deliberations.
Coordinating	Bringing things together, or "making a mesh of things," in Paul Thomas's (1999) phrase, to ensure that personnel and resources are connected in a timely and productive manner to facilitate organizational ends.	Networking by bringing together people and offices with shared or related interests and responsibilities. Coordination is rooted to joint planning, sharing information, and institutionalized systems of meetings.	The resources and functions of the entity—along with the interests, responsibilities, and needs of personnel—must be recognized and integrated into the development and implementation of organizational objectives.	The team coordinated its work with officials from the departments of Industry, Foreign Affairs and International Trade, and Public Works and Government Services, as well as regional development agencies. Coordination also extended to Air Force and Defence counterparts in the United States and NATO.
Reporting	Communicating information throughout the organization and beyond.	Turning information into organizational intelligence and then disseminating it to everyone who needs it. The process can flow internally, either downward to subordinate managers and staff or upward to managers and political leaders; or externally and laterally to other organizations and parties.	Sound information management is central to effective management in general and crucially important in helping a bureaucratic entity to understand its current operational strengths, weaknesses, opportunities, and threats and its future needs, goals, and options.	The project reported regularly to National Defence senior officials, the minister, and PCO/PMO senior officials. Ultimately the department reported regularly, through the minister, to parliament.
Budgeting	Securing, planning for, and managing organizational funds.	Raising, handling, and distributing money within and beyond the organization.	All organizations run on money, and budgeting may develop overarching organizational significance, dominating even the leadership of the bureaucratic entity.	National Defence financed the activities of the project team. And the team was charged with determining the final cost of the entire operational package to replace the CF-18s.

organizations have convoluted reporting relationships with innumerable "superiors," not all of whom agree about even the fundamental policy purpose. Managers serve a range of interests and responsibilities that may at times compete because of the omnipresent political manoeuvring. In fact, achievement or failure are as likely to be assessed in political terms as in administrative ones. That great managerial challenges are found within the public sector is readily discerned through a comparison with the operational environment of the private sector.

THE PROFIT MOTIVE

The private sector is always geared to the demands of profitability. All the activities of the staff and management of a private organization are directed toward making a profitable return on investment. This focus is the ultimate test of the private organization's worthiness: is it making money? This fundamental business goal is easily verifiable through a review of budget, balance sheets, and financial statements. Acceptable profit margins indicate overall organizational, and hence managerial, success, while losses are a clear indication of managerial failure leading to organizational decline. The profit margin thus constitutes an acid test of private sector managerial capability. Organizations that pass the test will continue to prosper, and their management will remain relatively secure; for those that fail, owners and boards of directors will find new managers; if business success remains elusive, the organization will sooner or later die.

Government organizations (with the exception of most Crown corporations) simply do not possess the same bottom line focus. The primary purpose of most is not to realize a profit but to provide a public service to meet public needs and interests, as defined by an elected and accountable government. One role of public sector organizations is to provide operational form to the plans and vision of a prime minister or premier and cabinet. An equally important purpose, however, is to serve the long-term interests of the public through the fair, competent, and professional implementation and administration of government policies and programs (see Table 5.2).

In fulfilling these roles, profitability is rarely, if ever, a factor, nor would most Canadians want commercial considerations to come into play. For example, the administration of justice, the enforcement of law, and the operation of the courts cannot be measured in terms of profitability, and the same generally holds true for other public services such as health care, education, social assistance, environmental protection, cultural promotion, and national defence. While most people expect programs to be administered efficiently, they do not assume that the state should be generating profits and its managers approaching their duties with that perspective.

The provision of publicly administered education and health care policy, for example, has come to be perceived as a collective good, an entitlement held by all citizens and designed to enhance individual and collective security, just as environmental and defence policies are seen as serving the well-being of the entire society. Of course, there is much current debate over the commercialization of health care and educational policy, and the potential for two-tiered systems in which those who could afford it would be entitled to purchase arguably superior forms of services. The vehemence of the debate

TABLE 5.2

Private Sector/Public Sector Differences

	PRIVATE SECTOR	PUBLIC SECTOR
Purpose	Provision of private goods and services through commercial activity	Provision of public services
Goals	Simple, economic	Complex, economic, social, political
Service recipients	Customers, clients	Citizens
Criteria of success	Profitability	Effective implementation of services
Evaluation of success	Financial, objective	Political, subjective
Accountable to	Owners/shareholders	Elected leaders/citizens
Operational environment	Marketplace, business realm, private	Government, political realm, public
Focus of Management	One-dimension	Multidimensional
Skills of Management	Business oriented	Program and policy oriented

reveals the degree to which most Canadians hold these policy fields to be essential public services divorced from the commercial realm.

MEASURING OPERATIONAL SUCCESS

In the absence of a clear profit-and-loss method for measuring operational success, the public sector nonetheless provides a vital managerial motive: to allocate finite financial and human resources in order to get the most desirable results. Political and administrative judgements of success or failure take into account not only quantitative issues such as resources deployed and the numbers of goods and services produced or delivered but also the qualitative benefits that ensue.

How can the success of a government program be determined? How can we measure the merit or quality of a program that provides a necessary public service but doesn't make any money? In this environment, the ends, means, and evaluation are all subject to differences of opinion.

Let's look at the administration of the Canada Health Act. Do we take into account the amount of money currently spent on health care and the medical facilities, staff, and patient care that such spending supports? Or at the pattern of spending support over the past decade, comparing the responses of appropriately sampled staff and patients against the decline in funding over the mid-1990s? Do we look at the new and developing medical procedures available to Canadians and at their increasing life spans? Or at their quality of life? And how does one measure quality of life? Evaluation of a government policy might also be made from beyond the system. For example, how does Canadian medical coverage compare with that of the United States, Britain, or the Scandinavian countries? Where in the spectrum of publicly and privately administered health care in North America do Canadian health services fall? Should we focus on the right of all citizens in this country to advanced standards of medical care regardless of ability to pay, or on lengthening waiting lists and the number of physicians relocating to the United States?

The answer to each of these questions—indeed, the wish to answer them at all—depends greatly on political and ideological orientation. And how a public sector manager within the health care system would answer depends on the leadership of senior management, the minister, the cabinet, and the prime minister. All managerial actions are evaluated in light of the policy objectives of the particular government, whatever the policy field.

Rather than possessing a single, essential form of evaluation—the profit motive in the private sector—the public sector has many, some primarily quantitative and some principally qualitative. Performance evaluation can be more or less comprehensive, more or less detailed, more or less oriented to policy or to administration. Future chapters devote greater attention to program evaluation and government efforts to improve their evaluation methodologies, but a basic truth remains: organizational performance evaluation within the public sector is at heart a political act.

DISPATCH BOX

THE OBLIGATIONS OF THE PUBLIC SERVICE

- To deal with people as citizens
- To respect the rights of citizens
- To treat all citizens equally
- To implement and administer public policy professionally
- To serve the political executive in developing public policy
- To uphold the law
- To serve and promote the interests and traditions of the public service
- To serve and promote the public interest

PRIVACY VERSUS ACCOUNTABILITY

Within the private sector, and without any legal requirement for openness or public disclosure of decision making, managers operate in a largely confidential environment. Their workplaces are private property, and they usually insist on their rights to conduct management functions behind closed doors.

Contrast this with the public sector, where management is accountable to senior departmental officials, who are accountable to elected ministers, a cabinet, and the prime minister or premier, in turn accountable to a parliament or legislature, which is accountable to the public. This system of public service, founded on public policies and funded by public monies, naturally engages public interest. And as public sector management is the outgrowth of public policies developed by an elected government and enshrined in law, it is administratively and legally obligated to be open. The accountability relationships extend to central agencies and the auditor general in relation to financial management; to the Public Service Commission of Canada, the Public Service Labour Relations Board (PSLRB), the Office of the Commissioner of Official Languages, and the Canadian Human Rights Commission with respect to personnel policy; and the Canadian courts in regard to all matters of administrative law.

Furthermore, government decision making carried out in the public interest is subject to freedom of information legislation that allows members of the public, usually media employees, to gain access to government files and reports. The logic behind such openness and reporting relationships is that the public service is *public* and its actions therefore subject to scrutiny, comment, and oversight.

CONSUMERISM VERSUS RIGHTS AND ENTITLEMENTS

Think of the differences between **consumers/ clients** and **citizens**. The private sector deals with people who are consumers or clients in a strictly commercial setting. Transactions between a private organization and its consumers/clients involve the provision of goods or services in exchange for payment. If the would-be consumer or client cannot afford the fee, he or she has no right to the product and the organization will refuse to engage in the transaction. Now, although some

Crown corporations such as Canada Post and VIA Rail engage in commercial relationships with consumers/clients, most government organizations—departments, regulatory agencies, and other Crown corporations—deal with people as citizens.

As citizens, we are equal members of society. We bear, simply by virtue of citizenship, rights or entitlements to government services such as

- elementary and secondary education;
- medical care as provided by federal and provincial health care legislation;
- legal protections as enshrined in the Criminal Code and human rights legislation;
- occupational health and safety protections under federal and provincial product standards and labour codes; and
- environmental protection, social welfare, border security, and national defence as outlined in public policies.

Specific groups of Canadians—children, parents, or pensioners; farm producers, fishers, or forestry workers; the unemployed, those seeking job skills retraining, or students seeking loans—may also be entitled to particular federal or provincial program assistance.

The government has a legal obligation to treat all citizens equally, whether as individuals or as a group. It must provide for the legitimate needs and interests of all citizens as mandated by law and refrain from illegally discriminating against individuals. For example, a bureaucratic decision to refuse a citizen necessary medical care, law enforcement protection, or public education because he or she could not otherwise afford the service would constitute blatant discrimination and a breach of the law. Whereas the private sector deals solely with transactions between sellers and buyers, the public sector deals with a much broader array of policy concerns, ranging from rights and duties as defined by law to the regulation and promotion of "peace, order, and good government."

THE CHAIN OF COMMAND

Managers in the private sector face a range of actors and forces among the customers/clients of the enterprise, along with certain legal obligations, but their essential duty is to render service to their superiors. These superiors in turn are part of a generally straightforward chain of command leading to either an owner or a board of directors. Public sector managers, in contrast, confront several different superiors. They have formal reporting and accountability relationships with their immediate departmental or agency superiors, and these officials report up the chain of command to a deputy minister, and beyond to the minister and eventually the prime minister. But managers simultaneously serve their organization, its senior management, and their minister in a relationship that becomes more intricate and sophisticated the higher up the organizational pyramid one moves in a blend of broad political and administrative duties. Senior departmental managers are often closely involved with ministers in formulating policy and resolving program implementation difficulties, and the most senior among them— assistant deputy ministers, associate deputy ministers, and deputy ministers—interact closely and continuously with their ministers. Deputy ministers, as administrative heads of departments, are in daily contact with their ministers, briefing them on departmental developments, helping them to deal with issues emerging from the portfolio, and working with them on new project undertakings. Deputy ministers also work with ministers to determine the best ways to defend and promote departmental and ministerial interests within the broader context of the government bureaucracy, the operations of cabinet, the interests of the prime minister, and the requirement to deal with parliament and the media. From this perspective, deputy ministers are as closely involved in the political life of their ministers as they are in the operation of their departments, and the general understanding is that these are two sides of the same bureaucratic coin. Just as managers possess a duty to serve their minister, they must also report to and serve other administrative actors: the central agencies, parliamentary committees, and the various commissions noted above. Deputy ministers likewise serve both their minister and the prime minister through their management of departmental responsibilities, possessing two masters while also maintaining a close operational liaison with the clerk of the Privy Council.

THE DUTY OF PUBLIC SERVANTS

All members of the public service have a further three duties: to uphold the law, to promote the interests and traditions of the public service, and to serve the public interest.

The actions and powers of the public service are prescribed by law, policy and program activities are mandated by law, and public servants bear a duty to preserve and promote the law in all their undertakings. Public servants thus have a duty to the law, and under no circumstances are they to counsel a subordinate or a superior to violate the law.

Public servants also have a duty to abide by and promote the interests and traditions of the public service as a profession with its own principles and expectations. Members of the public service, and especially its managerial leadership, are expected to embody these values and put them into practice through their work. Thus they must always undertake their duties in a manner that brings credit to the profession of public service.

Finally, public servants have a duty to serve the public interest, as defined by law and understood through the professional judgement of public managers themselves. The basic rationale for public service is to affirm the legal rights of citizens and to improve the quality of life within society. Far from the materialistic self-interest that lies at the heart of the private sector, public service has at its core the noble aspirations of collective duty and assistance to others.

ORGANIZATIONAL DESIGN

Management functions are crucially important to the success of any organization. The complexity of the public sector environment, moreover, heightens the difficulty of the management role. To appreciate the nature of management and its work, however, it is necessary to understand the organization being managed. All bureaucracies, whether public or private, are founded on organizational principles designed and practised in one of various different ways.

Over the past century two broad models of organizational design have emerged from the theory and practice of bureaucratic activity. Both models have proven highly influential in the structural and operational characteristics of public sector management in this country. The **structural-mechanistic model** of organization supports a hierarchical, authoritarian, centralized, top-down command-and-control approach to management. The **organic-humanistic model** focuses on the importance of people over structure and promotes a more egalitarian, decentralized, top-down and bottom-up participatory approach to management in which managers and employees work together to achieve organizational goals.

THE STRUCTURAL-MECHANISTIC MODEL

MAX WEBER

Organizational theory has its origins in the late nineteenth and early twentieth centuries, when ways of thinking about bureaucracies were explored by such authors as Max Weber (1946), Frederick W. Taylor (1967), and Luther Gulick and Lyndall Urwick (1969). Among these classical theorists Weber (1864–1920), a German sociologist and political economist, contributed the most to our modern understanding of bureaucracy.

According to Weber, **bureaucracy,** a composite of the French word for *office* and the Greek word for *power*, should be seen as a strictly neutral noun. Bureaucracy is a system of organization in which power and influence is held by officials in offices assigned specific roles in order to achieve ends set by the overseers of the organization. The work of all offices is orchestrated by these leaders to serve the broader goals and interests of the organization in total. A bureaucracy is found in any complex private or public organization of an appreciable size. A properly constituted bureaucracy within any organization, Weber contended, embodies eight principles:

1 a hierarchical structure
2 a unity of command
3 specialization of labour
4 employment and promotion based on merit
5 positions based on full-time employment
6 decisions founded on impersonal rules
7 work recorded and maintained in written files
8 a clear distinction between bureaucratic work responsibilities and the private interests of employees

The first five are organizational principles designed to create a professional bureaucracy capable of the efficient and effective administration of organizational goals. To obtain these ends, Weber added three principles of ideal bureaucracy.

Hierarchical Structure

Weber suggested that the structure of any bureaucracy must be hierarchical, its components arranged in a series of superior–subordinate relationships based on a formal chain of command between managers and employees. Each component within the **hierarchy** has its head official, who reports directly to the head of the next most superior office, and so on up the chain of command to the very top of the organization and its most superior officer.

Unity of Command

The chain of command allows directions to be transmitted speedily and effectively from top management down through the hierarchy, and

information, reports, and advice to be similarly passed upward from the lower echelons of the organization. The chain of command maintains strict control and managerial leadership over administration and policy direction while facilitating communication and accountability throughout the organization.

Along the chain, subordinate managers know precisely what their duties are, and they receive all the necessary instructions and directives from their immediate superiors. They know what they are responsible for, to whom they owe responsibility, and the consequences of failure to perform those duties. If this understanding of bureaucracy sounds highly militaristic, that's because it is—Weber was greatly influenced by the structure and organization of the Imperial German Army.

Specialization of Labour

Within an organizational hierarchy labour is specialized: broken into particular jobs with clearly defined roles, responsibilities, and requirements. Once work duties have been determined, managers or employees are assigned to them according to their education, training, skills, experience, and abilities. They then devote all their labour to their assigned tasks, becoming specialized in their roles and therefore performing their work as efficiently as possible. Specialization produces the most effective results.

Employment and Promotion Based on Merit

Closely associated with the specialization of labour is the principle of merit. Management and staff gain and keep their positions solely on the basis of objective professional merit. Appointment to particular duties is based on education, training, skills, or experience. Retention of a position or promotion to a higher one within the hierarchy is then contingent on demonstrated merit: improving upon education and training and undertaking given duties and responsibilities successfully.

Positions Based on Full-Time Employment

Officials in a bureaucracy should not be subject to other occupational or professional obligations or factors that could affect or interfere with the performance of their duties. They are expected to devote all their occupational attention to their jobs, and their service belongs to the organization as a whole. This principle serves the organization rather than the individual.

Decisions Founded on Impersonal Rules

The first of Weber's three principles of ideal bureaucracy is that decisions must be founded on impersonal rules. They cannot be based on personal likes and dislikes, whims, bias, or self-interest. By adhering to established rules based on the long-term goals of the organization, officials use their bureaucratic power and influence in the interests of the organization.

Furthermore, reliance on rules enhances objectivity, consistency, regularity, and uniformity in decision making. It ensures that like cases are treated in a like manner, and therefore that everyone who deals with the bureaucracy receives equal, fair, and objective treatment. It also signals to management that its aims are being consistently implemented across the organization—that the actions of the bureaucracy and its officials reflect the professional policy and program objectives

rather than the arbitrary and subjective interests of subordinates.

The Use of Written Records

Closely related to the principle of impersonal rules is that of maintaining written records. The rules on which bureaucratic decision making is founded need to be formally delineated in all official decisions. They require codification and promulgation so that all interested parties understand which rules apply to a given situation and are able to track precedents. Written records can be useful to the organization in a number of ways:

- Records permit field-level officials to document their actions, demonstrating that they have applied the rules properly and fairly to a given case. This verification is an important aspect of organizational accountability.
- Records can be used to identify when officials have misapplied or misunderstood the rules through either misconduct or interpretive errors.
- Records provide the opportunity for review and analysis as part of the accountability function, enabling senior management to maintain oversight, correct faulty decisions, and determine when officials need further education, training, advice, supervision, or discipline.
- Records provide senior managers with an overview of operational decision making, the types and volume of cases with which the organization deals, and the nature of the ensuing bureaucratic decisions.

- Records enable senior managers to review the achievements of the organization and to identify the need for staffing and job growth, for employee training, for redesign or fine-tuning of rules, and for wholly new policies and rules.
- Records explain how and why decisions were made and why alternatives were not considered or pursued. If a person or group wishes to challenge a bureaucratic decision over violation of established rules, unfair or improper application of rules, or inadequacy in the rules themselves, the written record is vital to launching a specific appeal or a broader policy protest.

The Position versus the Person

The power, responsibilities, and privileges associated with a bureaucracy are understood to reside in its positions and not in the people who hold them. A position is held by the organization, and its leadership decides who will occupy it. Bureaucratic employment is thus a form of professional service: management and staff are organized within a system of full-time, permanent employment that provides them with job security while ensuring that they are dedicated to the work of the institution and not under obligation to other occupational forces.

In keeping with this logic, employees should be well remunerated for their work, and it is further understood that no employee will use the powers and responsibilities of an office for private gain. An official cannot pass a position along to a chosen successor. Influence peddling (selling access to the decision-making power inherent in a position), bribery, and conflicts of interest constitute improper behaviour that corrupts the professionalism, efficiency, effectiveness, and rationality of the organization.

WEBERIAN BUREAUCRACY

Weber elucidated what bureaucracy is and how and why organizations are bureaucratically structured. But he also asserted that bureaucracy in its ideal form is the best means of achieving the organizational ends of professionalism: efficiency, effectiveness, and rationality. According to Weber, these are the most important considerations of any organization, regardless of whether its goals are commercial, philanthropic, or governmental:

> Experience tends to universally show that the purely bureaucratic type of administration ... is ... capable of attaining the highest degree of efficiency and is in this sense formally the most rational known means of carrying out imperative control over human beings. It is superior to any other form in precision, in stability, in the stringency of its discipline, and in its reliability. It thus makes possible a particularly high degree of calculability of results for the heads of organization and for those acting in relation to it. It is finally superior both in its intensive efficiency and in the scope of its operations, and is formally capable of application to all kinds of administrative tasks. (Weber 1947, 337)

The impact of the Weberian approach to bureaucracy on the evolution of organizational thought and practice, especially in relation to public sector management, merits consideration. The bureaucratic features and principles that Weber describes are clearly discernible in the structure of organizations. As a rule, government organizations are hierarchical, with formal managerial and accountability systems based on linear chains of command. Specialization of labour and the merit principle have become the essential organizing principles of personnel management. And record keeping has become a fundamental component of bureaucracy, especially important for the legal dimensions of rule application and dispute resolution. Bureaucratic professionalism—the clear differentiation of bureaucratic obligations and private interests—has also always been a topic of concern for those interested in the well-ordered functioning of organizations.

Weber's assessment of bureaucracy identifies components of organizational design and function that are as significant now as they were a century ago.

Problems of Bureaucracy

Weber's interpretation helps us as well to understand how the pejorative connotation of the term *bureaucracy* emerged. Although his use of the word was neutral, the establishment of large bureaucracies designed to work along Weberian lines has led to organizational systems that many people find difficult to deal with and easy to criticize.

Large and complex hierarchies can be hard to comprehend and intimidating to those affected by or forced to cope with bureaucratic decision making. Their size can cause people to view them as populated by nameless, faceless bureaucrats whose real life is far removed from those whom their decisions affect.

The requirement for established rules can cause the nuances of a real case to be lost or ignored by decision makers. People who believe their cases to be special and unique—either because the situation is genuinely unusual or simply because the rules apply uniquely to it—find their needs treated routinely and like any other case. The bureaucratic ideals of consistency, uniformity, and fairness can leave affected individuals feeling that rule-bound officials have applied ill-designed and rigid approaches in a thoughtless and regimented manner that subverts the individual characteristics of a particular case.

The bureaucratic ideal of written documentation can lead to an organization awash in paper, whose decision making becomes bogged down in paperwork. This criticism holds that documents come to matter more than people and that excessive reliance on formal records prevents officials seeing the human side of the case before them.

Finally, the Weberian principle that decision making be efficient, fair, and rational can lead to criticisms that an organization is remote, intimidating, rule bound, confusing, short-sighted, stupid, delay ridden, or obsessed with red tape—in other words, *bureaucratic* in the pejorative sense.

Bureaucracy as Machine

Final reflections on Weber must be directed toward his analytical focus. His approach was highly structural and systematic. He conceptualized bureaucracy as a hierarchical organization subject to the will of a centralized and decisive managerial authority, exercised through a clear chain of command. The fundamental purpose of bureaucracy, moreover, was instrumental, rational administration: the creation of a system through which the organization could achieve its goals in the most economical, efficient, and effective manner conceivable. The realization of operational and instrumental competence was viewed as the hallmark of rationality—organizational ends conceptually and systematically correlated to the most carefully crafted and efficiently implemented means of achieving them.

From this perspective, a bureaucracy is analogous to an elaborate machine, or a military organization, designed and controlled by managers and their superiors to exercise some form of power in society and, by so doing, to serve the ends of those superiors. The machine is a structured system of means–ends relationships, subject to the will of a unified managerial presence, and, when effectively led, it can produce phenomenal organizational results.

The actual ends of the machine and their moral worth, however, were subjects that Weber refrained from exploring, asserting that these were subjective matters more suited to political and philosophical analysis.

FREDERICK W. TAYLOR

While Weber's work offered a classic statement of the mechanistic approach to organizations and the importance of formal, hierarchical structures, Frederick W. Taylor (1856–1915) presented a systematic analysis of desirable operating practices *within* an organization (Taylor 1967). Whereas Weber focused on macro-institutional dynamics, Taylor was interested in the micro-management of industrial employees and the ways by which their work could be made more efficient, and therefore more productive and more profitable. Taylor's approach complements Weber's in that both sought organizational rationality through the development of structures and operating procedures calculated to realize managerial and organizational ends.

Like Weber, Taylor adopted a mechanistic view of organizations, seeing them as equivalent to machines and employees as the components of and adjuncts to these machines. According to Taylor, the role of management was to ensure that the organizational machine ran as smoothly as possible and that individual workers were used as productively as possible. This approach was called **scientific management**: the reduction of management to clearly defined, objective, and systematic principles and practices through which organizational behaviour could be rendered most rational—**rationality** conceived in terms of means–ends relationships à la Weber.

As a part of the quest for rationality, Taylor placed great stress on the duty of management to review every job performed by an employee. Using the techniques of scientific management, a manager could break down the functions of every job into component elements to determine how each was undertaken and how it could be improved upon and made more rational, which would lead to the discovery of the "one best way" by which the employee should perform the task. This technique invited managers to analyze the entire work process for which they were responsible; to devise ways to make the process better and speedier; and to decide how to evaluate each worker's performance in light of established rational expectations. Employees who exceeded expectations could be financially rewarded, while those who fell short could be better trained, or warned, or otherwise disciplined.

Taylor viewed all employees as essentially poorly educated, lazy, and uninterested in the organization that employed them, seeking at best to get the most pay for the least amount of work. The role of management was to study and supervise employees closely, selecting them for particular jobs based on their physical or mental attributes and then working them like machines to gain the maximum productivity while paying them accordingly. He saw management personnel as the enlightened members of any organization, those who were to practise the principles of scientific management in organizing and running the institution along eminently rational lines.

LUTHER GULICK AND LYNDALL URWICK

In the 1930s and 40s, American public administration analysts Luther Gulick (1892–1993) and Lyndall Urwick (1891–1983) redirected attention to broad institutional dynamics, seeking to establish a "science of administration" by identifying, analyzing, and defining administrative truths common to the design and working of all organizations (Gulick and Urwick 1969). They were most concerned with developing systemic knowledge about managerial issues such as institutional design, span of control, the effectiveness of command systems, the nature of departmentalization, the functioning of management, and the politics/administration dichotomy.

Gulick and Urwick stressed the importance of hierarchical organization but noted that a bureaucracy could be organized into various forms, based on the desired span of control of superiors. **Span of control** determines the pattern of reporting relationships between a superior and his or her immediate subordinates. It can be narrower or wider, with each articulation causing strengths and weaknesses in the organization as well as defining its structure, as shown in Figures 5.1 and 5.2. More detailed coverage of the issues surrounding span of control can be found on the Thinking Government website.

Departmentalization

Systematic attention to management problems also led Gulick and Urwick to address the issue of **departmentalization**. How should government departments and sub-units be organized, and by what defining principles of organization?

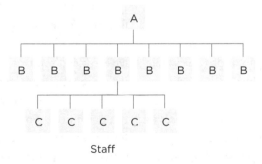

Figure 5.1 **Broad Span of Control**

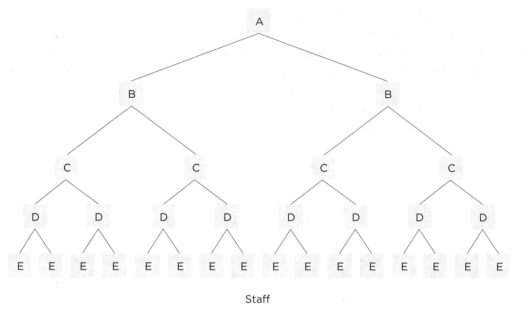

Staff

Figure 5.2 **Narrow Span of Control**

They identified four concepts of departmental organization:

1 purpose
2 process
3 persons or things served
4 place

Purpose refers to the function that department or sub-unit is conceived to do or provide, while *process* refers to the means by which it achieves that end. Thus departments or sub-units can be organized, for example, around the *purposes* of "furnishing water, controlling crime, or conducting education," or around the *processes* of "engineering, medicine, carpentry, stenography, statistics, or accounting." Or they can be organized around the *persons or things served*, such as "immigrants, veterans, Indians, forests, mines, parks, orphans, farmers, automobiles or the poor," or around the *place* of service, such as "Hawaii, Boston, Washington, the Dust Bowl, Alabama, or Central High School" (Gulick and Urwick 1969, 15).

Gulick and Urwick found that there was no firm rule for selecting the appropriate method of departmentalization. Moreover, a department may have to blend some or all of these features through its sub-units, especially large departments of a federal government with geographically dispersed responsibilities. For example, the Department of National Defence is based on purpose—the provision of military services for national defence and the promotion of strategic interests—but has functional sub-units based on process, such as land, air, and naval services; specialized equipment procurement; legal and medical services; and officer training systems. These departments, furthermore, are highly influenced by considerations of place, as operational elements of each are largely decentralized across the country and abroad.

In determining the appropriate form of departmentalization and the desired blend of organizational requirements for a single institution, Gulick and Urwick emphasized the importance of administrative and managerial judgement based on organizational functions and attributes and the desired role of the institution.

Line and Staff Functions

Concern for departmentalization also led Gulick and Urwick to devote attention to the concepts of line and staff functions as considerations in organizational design:

- A line function is one in which officials provide a service directly to the public or to a client group within the public.
- A staff function is one in which officials possessing a specialized skill or mandate provide services either to officials engaged in line functions or to the government as a whole.

Classic examples of staff functions are legal support, personnel and financial management support, and policy and planning support to those engaged in line functions.

This distinction between line and staff functions is common, and most government departments possess sub-offices devoted to the staff support functions just listed. In fact, departments themselves can be classified as either line or staff, depending on the nature of their activities and whether they provide services directly to the public or to specialized client groups or to the government as a whole. The organizational feature explained in Chapter 3, whereby federal departments have either *service* or *support* roles, is a classic line/staff function distinction.

As Gulick and Urwick sought to develop a science of administration, Gulick devoted special consideration to the essential functions of management, eventually delineating them with his now-famous taxonomy of POSDCORB, as outlined at the beginning of this chapter.

The Politics/Administration Dichotomy

Gulick and Urwick also noted the importance of the politics/administration dichotomy, which had emerged from the writings of Woodrow Wilson. Wilson argued that matters of a purely political and partisan nature should be clearly separated from matters of management and administration. The former is the focus of passionate political and ideological debate over leadership and policy ends, while the latter is the preserve of systematic rationality to develop the means to those policy ends. The logic of the dichotomy, as understood by Gulick and Urwick, was that matters of policy definitely shaped the purposes of state action, but that the actual design and implementation of policy and the operationalization of government activity were subject to the dispassionate, reasoned, and professional wisdom emerging from the science of administration.

As we have already noticed, however, the politics/administration dichotomy cannot withstand critical scrutiny as either a description of or a prescription for bureaucratic activity. And, as we will see, much of the work of Gulick and Urwick was subjected to serious criticism. Even Gulick and Urwick themselves came to realize that they had been privileging systematic analysis of organizational phenomena and considered managerial judgement over scientific truth in the making of decisions.

But this does not diminish the importance of their contribution to the study of organizations. In speaking of their intellectual legacy, Kernaghan and Siegel wrote that "Gulick and Urwick contributed to the theory of organizational behaviour by synthesizing and disseminating other people's ideas. Nevertheless, these two men made a valuable

contribution both by forcing people to think about management in a systematic manner, and in beginning to set out certain principles—many of which are still seen as beneficial guides to action today" (1999, 54).

THE ORGANIC-HUMANISTIC MODEL

MARY PARKER FOLLETT

Even as the structural-mechanistic model dominated organizational thought and practice in the early decades of the twentieth century, it became the subject of criticism by analysts seeking a more accurate approach. One of the first of these was Mary Parker Follett (1868–1933), whose studies of organizations led her to question the command-and-control approach to power (Follett 1951, 1965).

Follett argued that instead of viewing power as operating through the organizational hierarchy in a linear and downward-flowing fashion it was better to understand it as flowing in a circular manner, like a current. Power, according to Follett, can be exercised downward upon subordinates, but their reactions, both positive and negative, will flow back up the hierarchy and influence those who wield formal power. Hostile employee reactions to the exercise of managerial authority will weaken an organization's ability to realize its goals, while supportive reactions will enhance it.

Thus, Follett recognized a distinction between the formal power held by management and the informal power held by employees through their reactions to formal power. The sound exercise of management power, so Follett believed, is to be found in management making decisions in a manner that motivates employees and elicits positive reactions. From this perspective, the exercise of power is part of a human and interactive process, with the reaction of subordinates being just as important as the objectives and methods of superiors who initiate executive decisions.

THE HAWTHORNE STUDIES

Interest in the sociological and psychological aspects of organizational life was heightened by the Hawthorne Studies of the 1920s (Mayo 1960; Roethlisberger and Dickson 1964). The studies got their name from the Hawthorne Works, a Western Electric factory outside Chicago that initially commissioned a study to see if worker productivity would change in higher or lower levels of light. Productivity seemed to improve when changes were made but slumped again when the study was over. It seemed that workers became more productive not so much because of the change in light levels but because they were motivated by the interest in their lives that the study demonstrated. Other changes, such as moving obstacles away from the path of workers or keeping work stations clean, also changed productivity levels. Later on, the term *Hawthorne effect* came to be used for any short-term increase in worker productivity.

These experiments into worker behaviour, undertaken in the spirit of scientific management, led researchers such as Elton Mayo to argue that organizational behaviour could not be understood in simplistic terms of incentive and power. Employee reaction to management efficiency initiatives was nuanced, but the main factor was the existence of informal groups of employees and their attitudes to work.

The Hawthorne Studies broke ground in identifying factors of organizational life outside the formal parameters of the structural-mechanistic model. The discovery of informal groupings within organizations—that is, the tendency of employees, and even managers, to band together with similarly situated and like-minded colleagues for mutual comradeship, socialization, and support—fundamentally challenged assumptions about organizational behaviour and called into question the relevance and effectiveness of many "truths" of scientific management.

The discovery of informal groups led a new wave of organizational theorists to devote attention to informal interpersonal relations, especially between superiors and subordinates. If such group relations were the dominant factor in explaining employee activity, as the Hawthorne Studies indicated, then the whole realm of informal organizational dynamics merited closer attention.

CHESTER BARNARD

One early writer on the subject was Chester Barnard (1886–1961), who said that effective management and organizational success depended on clear and open communication between employees and management and on managers recognizing and progressively responding to the complex nature of employee attitudes (Barnard 1962). The role of management, he thought, was to encourage employees to identify psychologically with the basic goals of the organization, thus ensuring that they supported its interests and encouraged others to do so. Employee loyalty could be induced not only through monetary reward but through such newly emerging concepts as providing good working conditions, encouraging employees' pride in their work, and promoting organizational unity.

By promoting a sense of shared purpose, managers convey the idea that the organization comprises both management and workers and that all have a necessary place in the organization. The success of the whole is contingent upon working together toward the common goals of the organization. As these organizational objectives are met, so too are the interests of those who make up the organization, whether management or workers.

Barnard's work, first published in 1938, was a "how to" managerial approach to employee motivation and marked a divergence from the views of Taylor and his disciples of scientific management. The emphasis on employer–employee cooperation and the need for management to respond to both the material and the psychological needs of workers set the stage for Abraham Maslow's famous work on motivation.

ABRAHAM MASLOW

Abraham Maslow (1908–70) was interested in the nature of motivation in the workplace, believing that it was much more complex than the structural-mechanistic model suggested. He thought that financial reward or fear of discipline or job loss were not the only motivational factors affecting workers. Through his studies, Maslow (1970) developed a hierarchy of human needs (Figure 5.3), asserting that all workers, and indeed all people, are motivated by five successive types of need, ranging from the most basic and material to the most sophisticated and intangible:

1 food, shelter, clothing, sex, and sleep
2 security, stability, and freedom from fear
3 belonging and love, friendship, and membership and involvement in a community

Self-actualization

Esteem needs: achievement, prestige, status

Human needs: belonging and love, friendship, community

Safety needs: security, stability, freedom from fear

Physiological needs: food, shelter, clothing, sex, sleep

Figure 5.3 **Maslow's Hierarchy of Needs**

4 esteem through achievement, competence, independence, prestige, and status
5 self-actualization, self-fulfillment, and the attainment of fundamental goals

Maslow argued that these needs are inherent in human beings; that many aspects of them occupy the thoughts of employees within a workplace; and that, as the more basic needs are attended to, individuals then attempt to satisfy the higher order needs. This approach presented a more intricate explanation of employee expectations than anything devised by Taylor. Maslow averred that all five needs come into play within the workplace, that individual employees have differing needs, and that the same person can have different needs at different times.

The ways in which management must address employee motivation is therefore very complicated; one-dimensional approaches will always fail to respond to the range of human needs. The more that management can meet not only basic needs but also more advanced ones, the greater the likelihood of employee satisfaction, and thus of harmony between labour and management and of greater productivity.

Attaining such levels of satisfaction, however, required a fundamental shift in the way that management traditionally viewed employees. Maslow emphasized that rather than viewing workers merely as adjuncts to machines, as cogs in wheels, enlightened managers should perceive them as complex human beings with a fundamental desire to work, to be active participants in their workplace, and to be valued for their contribution to the organization. The question for management, then, becomes how to satisfy these needs

and reap the rewards of a contented and productive workforce.

DOUGLAS MCGREGOR

Maslow's ideas inspired Douglas McGregor (1906–64) to develop a two-pronged typology of management styles, which he termed *Theory X* and *Theory Y* (McGregor 1960). Theory X refers to the traditional structural-mechanistic approach. In Theory X, employees are assumed to be lazy, with limited education and interests, disinclined to work, and motivated solely to gain as much income for as little work as possible. All workers must therefore be coerced to work, closely supervised and controlled, and disciplined when they misbehave—as certainly they will. It follows that most employees will be passive and irresponsible, uninterested in organizational life, and in need of strong managerial leadership if they are to achieve anything of productive worth to the organization. The psychological profile emerging from Theory X is that employees are like poorly brought up children, and the manager is like a military-style parent who brings order, discipline, and purpose to their lives.

Theory Y is the growing organic-humanistic approach to organizations and management. It suggests that work is natural to human beings; that we are inquisitive and creative creatures who want to be engaged in productive and rewarding labour; and that, under the right circumstances and conditions, work can be very satisfying. Workers should not need to be coerced to work if management makes the workplace and the work process fulfilling and progressive. If workers are engaged in meaningful work, and if management interacts with them as skilled colleagues rather than as lazy children expected to behave as machines, employees will respond with enthusiasm and creativity.

As McGregor argued, most workers subject to traditional mechanistic approaches possess unrecognized and unused skills, and enormous knowledge, experience, and potential. This is a human resource going to waste, and it should be identified and developed by intelligent management to the advantage of the organization. One of the vital skills for management, according to McGregor, is therefore to understand its workforce as a pool of talent and to encourage employees to participate in the development and operation of the workplace.

Through the writing of McGregor, as with Maslow before him, we observe the concept of participatory management as a new, progressive, and exciting method of organizing workplaces in a way that affirms the talents of employees, employer–employee respect and recognition, and the productive potential of cooperative work.

HERBERT SIMON

While Follett, Mayo, Barnard, Maslow, and McGregor, among others, were challenging traditional attitudes toward the formal organization and the nature of employees and their motivations, Herbert Simon (1916–2001) was vigorously criticizing much of the work of Gulick and Urwick and other structuralist writers who sought to develop a science of administration. Simon (1957) attacked the belief that administration could be reduced to scientific rules, stressing that organizations were inherently human creations and, as such, far more subjective than objective in the way they worked. Rather than demonstrating a science, writers such as Gulick and Urwick had advanced principles that were often simplistic, contradictory, and in no way scientific in the sense of relating to objective, verifiable, and repeatable truths. Simon referred to these as the "proverbs of administration." The classic example, so Simon argued, was Gulick and Urwick's notion that administrative efficiency and effective command can be enhanced through a narrow span of control. This ran directly counter to their other principle that flattening the organizational hierarchy and minimizing middle management improves administrative efficiency and command.

As Simon vigorously asserted, it is impossible for a narrow and a broad span of control to coexist. Management has to choose the better form of control in relation to the organization being managed. Even Gulick and Urwick came to admit that such an exercise of judgement was required, but Simon then countered that a true science of administration would not allow such an issue to emerge in the first place. That the necessity for human judgement should arise—rather than a universal and unequivocal application of a hard scientific rule—was proof that the so-called science was at best an elaborate listing of principles, all of which required further human interpretation.

This conclusion, according to Simon, did not belittle the work of Gulick and Urwick with respect to their systematic study of organizational design but simply affirmed the importance of devoting critical social scientific interpretational techniques to the evaluation of organizations and the functions of management. These are at heart human creations and activities and must be subjected to humanistic, rather than mechanistic, forms of analysis.

CHRIS ARGYRIS

Chris Argyris (1923–) asserted that formal organizational structures and traditional management practices were inconsistent with human nature and thus counteracted the long-term interests of organizations. Individual human development from infancy to adulthood routinely passes through several stages, moving from simpler to more involved forms of understanding and behaviour (Argyris 1957, 1964). These stages flow from passivity to activity, from dependence to independence, from a limited to a greater range of interests and behaviour, from shorter- to longer-term perspectives, from smaller to larger individual endeavours, from subordination to equality or superordination, and from lack of awareness to greater awareness. Moving along each dimension contributes to what Argyris believed to be a healthy adult personality.

Normal development, however, is spurned by traditional management theory. Rather than expecting employees to grow with their work and to develop more involvement in, and responsibility for, their actions, the scientific form of leadership expected workers to be unmotivated, passive, submissive, and limited. This approach to management, Argyris suggested, failed to understand human nature and thus to recognize the potential of workers to help build an organization. Moreover, it was likely to result in labour–management conflict, as employees either challenged managerial control or resorted to subterfuge to oppose management goals through passive resistance informed, communicated, and supported through informal group dynamics.

A far better approach to management, Argyris argued, was to recognize the human potential for growth and creative action and to fuse these

DISPATCH BOX

THE ORGANIC-HUMANISTIC APPROACH

1 Organizations are complex, living entities populated by human beings.
2 Organizations possess formal and informal lines of communication.
3 Organizations always possess informal groupings of people.
4 People in an organization possess complex motivations.
5 Employees are an organization's best resource.
6 Management should structure its actions to maximize the innate potential of its human resources.
7 Hierarchies within an organization should be shallow, allowing for ease of communication.
8 Power and influence within an organization should flow from both the top down and the bottom up.
9 Participatory management is the ideal form of organizational managerial behaviour.

qualities with the objectives of the organization. Enlightened management should view employees as human assets that will bring operational vigour and intellectual dynamism to the organization if properly encouraged and allowed to participate in its operational life. From this perspective, the role of management is to recognize that its human resources are just as valuable, if not more so, than its material and financial resources, and to be progressively mobilized in the service of the long-term interests of the organization. With Argyris, as with McGregor, we observe the beginning of the concept of participatory management.

PETER DRUCKER

Much of the analytical thrust of the organic-humanistic model leads to support for the concept of **participatory management**. Two pioneering studies on the theory and practice of participatory modes of decision making and goal achievement within organizations are "Patterns of Aggressive Behaviour in Experimentally Created Social Climates," written by Kurt Lewin, Ronald Lippitt, and Ralph K. White in 1939, and "Overcoming Resistance to Change," produced by Lester Coch and John R.P. French in 1948. The best-known and most influential advocate of participatory management, however, is Peter Drucker (1909–2005).

Drucker (1954) challenged some of the most basic suppositions of Weber and the structuralists. Rather than viewing hierarchy and specialization as necessary and desirable features of organizations, Drucker claimed that they led to problems and failures. As we have already observed, if organizations employ a narrow span of control between superiors and subordinates, they become increasingly hierarchical, weakening communication flows, putting distance between field-level workers and top management, reducing the ability of senior management to stay abreast of organizational actions, and creating a structure that becomes increasingly difficult to understand and direct.

An overemphasis on specialization, moreover, can cause sub-units to become excessively focused on their own work and interests to the detriment of the overall needs and interests of the organization. Specialization can threaten organizational unity, leading sub-units to think and act in highly individualistic ways. It can also threaten managerial unity when generalist managers come to believe that a sub-unit is so specialized that only its own managers can effectively supervise its actions. The organization thus loses managerial direction and common purpose.

Drucker argued that management constantly needs to direct attention to the life and operations of the whole organization and, in doing so, promote the highest degree of communication both downward and upward. This practice makes use of personnel resources to assess organizational strengths, weaknesses, opportunities, and threats and to set goals and oversee operations. In keeping with authors such as Mayo, McGregor, and Argyris, Drucker stressed that management should actively embrace its employees, decentralizing the exercise of power by involving them in decision making related to their work and thereby enabling management to benefit from their experience.

Management can gain a wealth of knowledge from employees about

- how the organization operates both formally and, more important, informally;
- how operations can be improved and streamlined;
- how field-level actions, service delivery, and rapport with consumers, clients, and other external actors can be enhanced; and
- how products or services can be improved.

Involving staff in the decision-making process, Drucker asserted, also makes employees more likely to accept and support operational decisions. They will buy into new operational approaches and goals, giving them far greater formal and informal support than they do when decisions are made in a top-down manner. This form of participatory decision making

THE ROLE OF MANAGEMENT

• Structural-Mechanistic Model

The chief proponents of this model, in historical order, are Max Weber, Frederick W. Taylor, and Luther Gulick and Lyndall Urwick.

- **Weber:** The chief concern of management is instrumental rational administration: a system through which the organization can achieve its goals in the most economical, efficient, and effective ways possible.
- **Taylor:** The role of management is to ensure that the organizational machine runs as smoothly as it can and that individual workers are employed in the most efficient and productive ways possible.
- **Gulick and Urwick:** The functions of management are planning, organizing, staffing, directing, coordinating, reporting, and budgeting (POSDCORB) in the most efficient way possible, based on the narrow or broad span of control within the organization.

• Organic-Humanistic Model

The chief proponents of this model, in historical order, are Mary Parker Follett, Chester Barnard, Abraham Maslow, Douglas McGregor, Chris Argyris, and Peter Drucker.

- **Follett:** Management exercises its power soundly by using its authority and making decisions that motivate employees and elicit positive reactions.
- **Barnard:** The role of management is to encourage employees to identify with the fundamental goals of the organization, ensuring that, through informal communication patterns, employees sympathize with and support the interests of the organization and encourage others to do so.
- **Maslow:** The more that management is able to satisfy not only basic but also more advanced human needs, the greater the likelihood of employee satisfaction and harmony between labour and management, and the greater the productivity of workers.
- **McGregor:** Management requires several vital skills: to understand the organization's employees; to recognize the workforce as a pool of talent ready and willing to be used in the service of organizational goals; to be willing to interact with the workforce more as partners and colleagues than as masters and servants; and to encourage the participation of employees in the development and operation of the workplace.
- **Argyris:** The role of management is to recognize that the organization's human resources are just as valuable as its material and financial resources, if not more so, and that employees deserve involvement in the development and operational life of the organization. This attitude will result in the progressive mobilization of employee talent in the service of the long-term interests of the organization.
- **Drucker:** Management should decentralize the exercise of power within the organization by involving employees in decision making related to their work, thereby enabling management to learn and benefit from their workplace experience.

- educates employees in the operational working and overall strategic direction of the organization;
- enhances the problem-solving and analytical skills of employees and middle managers;
- furthers the abilities of middle managers because they have to master a more complicated yet rewarding form of decision making; and
- facilitates conflict resolution and team building.

Drucker argued that effective participation would reduce problems because better decision making leads to better communications and operations, resulting in a more efficient, effective, rational, and ultimately happier organization. The exercise of decentralized power through participatory modes of decision making was thus, to Drucker, the key to organizational success.

THE CHALLENGE TO PARTICIPATORY MANAGEMENT

That view has not gone unchallenged. As Inwood (2004, 67–69) has argued, participatory forms of consultation and decision making can be very disruptive to the routine operations of an organization and may raise expectations among employees that cannot be realized. Participatory management is meant to devolve and decentralize managerial decision making, but is the central motivation to enhance the workplace experience and role of employees or to promote the interests of management by enhancing employee productivity? While these two purposes may not always be mutually exclusive, they certainly can be.

This raises the question whether the interests of employees can be merged with those of management in a viable form of co-management. But is that what management truly wants? Is it prepared to relinquish its role to a significant degree? In other words, does participatory management dilute command and control authority? And if it is instead a simple form of consultation between staff and management, in which managers retain the full right to make decisions, will it gain the active support of employees?

The tension between power and authority is central to any analysis of participatory management. It is particularly relevant to public sector organizations because of the additional issue of accountability. Simply put, if public sector organizations are to facilitate public policy, as promoted by accountable politicians, is participatory management a threat to democratically elected government? Is accountability compromised if some of the decision makers—namely the unelected employees—are not accountable for their actions in a chain of command? If ministers and senior managers must always be accountable, is there any justification for devolving decision-making authority to subordinates, even if it appears to be operationally effective? These questions are central to participatory management initiatives within the public sector.

TECHNIQUE AND MOTIVATION IN MANAGERIAL DECISION MAKING

This chapter thus far has devoted attention to managerial functions and organizational theory.

We have reviewed the major roles and responsibilities of management and the two main models of organizational design and operation that have emerged from the extensive literature.

A related field of study involves analysis of the various approaches to managerial decision making. Regardless of the organizational nature of an institution—steeply hierarchical or not; centralized or decentralized; rooted in a top-down, authoritarian, command-and-control model or in an egalitarian, participative form of management—the techniques and motivations by which management addresses its policy and program environment vary. Some approaches to the subject of managerial decision making are normative, explaining how it *should* be exercised. Others are descriptive, suggesting how decision making *actually* occurs. Thus, some approaches deal with the *techniques* of making decisions, while others focus on the *motivations* behind the process. In all instances, however, decision-making approaches involve such factors as

- how management understands and organizes information and knowledge
- how management interprets its own interests and aims in decision making
- what management views as the most effective and viable means to established ends

Managers choose to organize their policy and program decision making in various ways, and a range of approaches helps us to understand those choices. The rest of this chapter describes the major decision-making techniques that organizational theory identifies—incrementalism, rationalism, bounded rationalism, and mixed scanning—and then the major analytical frameworks for them: **public choice theory, bureaucratic politics theory,** and **policy network theory**.

INCREMENTALISM

Charles E. Lindblom (1917–) is one of the earliest proponents of **incrementalism,** which he saw as the oldest and most traditional form of managerial decision making (1959, 1968). The essential logic of incrementalism is that managers inherit most of their policy and program responsibilities from past decisions and that their natural inclination, and also their duty, is to maintain the smooth implementation of these institutional initiatives.

Thus, most of the work of management involves maintaining the status quo and managing current issues in order to provide institutional consistency. Even when difficulties arise, as they inevitably do, the incrementalist technique dominates. When managers are confronted with problems, Lindblom said, they should find the easiest and quickest solution at hand, expending the least time and effort and maintaining the greatest fidelity to existing

---

DISPATCH BOX

INCREMENTALISM

- Current decisions should be rooted in past decisions.
- Decision making should be as simple and easy as possible.
- Management should look for easy, achievable solutions to problems.
- Reform works best in small, successive stages.
- Management should base proposed reforms on past successful reforms.

operations and accumulated institutional wisdom. Managers should deal with operational problems as they present themselves, in as evolutionary and elementary a manner as possible.

Lindblom suggested two kinds of mutually reinforcing reform: simple reforms that improve immediate organizational action, and marginal, incremental reforms to policies. Reform is a necessary feature of managerial action if an organization is to successfully adapt to its own changing environment, but, for Lindblom, the key to its success is that reform be

- easily understood by management and staff;
- achievable without significant time and resources or new and complex skills; and
- institutionally viable, meeting defined goals.

As has often been said of incrementalism, it is at best the science of muddling through.

Lindblom, however, asserted that the technique is both descriptive and normative:

- descriptive in that it illustrates how most managers in organizations actually make decisions, and
- normative in that it defines how decisions ought to be made.

He argued that incrementalist techniques of decision making are found in all organizations and that when they are ignored in favour of more rationalistic ones, they nonetheless tend to reappear. The strength of incrementalism, both descriptively and prescriptively, is that its simplicity makes it effective. Rather than managers having to engage in highly complex forms of intellectual analysis and problem solving, or to reinvent and re-engineer the entire policy and program structure, they have more time to do what they arguably do best: manage and maintain the work of the organization.

But in these strengths, some critics see the major flaws of incrementalism. Amitai Etzioni (1967) contends that operational simplicity can ignore thornier problems and sophisticated solutions in the quest for the easiest fix. The logic of incrementalism militates against giving new or elaborate policy and program options serious consideration. In this sense, incrementalism can be seen as a succession of essentially unplanned decisions. It makes management reactive instead of proactive and bypasses creative ways to forestall problems before they arise.

Incrementalism's stress on past practices is also a subject of criticism. Such an approach, by its very logic, moves away from or even counter to progressive thought and action, while it benefits interests that have already been well served, whether in government or in society. Social groups seeking reform of government policy or action in order to redress injustices, for example, will find little comfort when government takes an incrementalist approach.

Lindblom's validation of marginal policy and program reforms within the life of any organization is also open to serious dispute. As Kernaghan and Siegel (1999, 132–33) assert, while he is correct that most organizational decisions effect simple variations on previous actions, some of the most important institutional decisions cannot be explained by this logic. For example, the creation of the CBC, the National Film Board, and Petro-Canada as federal Crown corporations, or the establishment of workers' compensation, labour relations, collective bargaining, publicly funded medical insurance, or official bilingualism could not have occurred incrementally. Decisions of this sort may not be the most common ones, but they are among the most significant that any organization makes, as it develops innovative ways to address difficulties and opportunities.

If incrementalism fails to explain decision making in these circumstances effectively, as Kernaghan and Siegel suggest, the interpretative value of the technique is seriously called into question.

RATIONALISM

Rationalism emerged in the United States in the 1950s, primarily centred on the American defence establishment, as a comprehensively logical and systematic alternative to incremental decision making. At its core is the belief that the main focus of management should be to develop policies and programs that maximize organizational goals with the minimum cost, effort, and other drawbacks, always looking toward the future.

Rationalist decision making, as expounded by James R. Anderson (1984), begins with planning. Rather than basing current and future actions on past practices, managers are encouraged to

- analyze their organization, and
- conceptualize its values and objectives and prioritize all organizational objectives.

After determining and ranking organizational ends, managers must identify and analyze all possible operational means to reach them. In government this involves systematically assessing each and every policy and program for strengths and weaknesses, costs and benefits, potential and limitations. The logical result of this ranking process is the identification of the best option. Once a policy option has been implemented, however, the rationalist process involves constant review. Regularly measuring how closely a program is meeting its goals provides a steady flow of information that enables managers either to fine-tune it or to revisit the entire issue.

This technique of decision making was much applauded by policy analysts when it first appeared. Future chapters examine the influence of rational planning within Canadian federal and

DISPATCH BOX

RATIONALISM

- Decision making should be based on planning, analysis, and critical thinking.
- Planning requires clear objectives.
- Objectives must be prioritized according to need.
- All means to achieve desired ends must be identified and analyzed.
- Ends-means analysis necessitates cost-benefit analysis.
- The programs (means) to achieve the chosen policy (ends) must be prioritized according to the likelihood of success.
- Programs best able to maximize results are preferred.
- Program implementation must be monitored and assessed to determine whether the means are achieving policy ends or means-ends refinement is needed.

provincial governments and the practical problems it encountered, but some of its limitations can be summarized here.

Planning necessitates the setting of goals—but how can they be agreed upon? What if an organization has multiple, opposing goals, each with its own supporters? What happens when managers set different priorities within the same organization? And what is the first priority of a government? Economic development? Social development? The preservation of law and order? National unity? Health care? What's more important, for example: making sure that elderly people have adequate food and shelter or that mothers have access to hospitals for childbirth, or perhaps that we preserve our national boundaries? Is it possible for a government to prioritize these broad issues, and, if so, how? Would those decisions be based on objectively rational considerations, or do they in fact lie in the realm of subjective judgement?

These questions foreshadow the problems associated with government policy and program analysis. Is rational cost–benefit analysis possible when the activities involved have broad socioeconomic, cultural, and political overtones? And does one really have to assess all government activities and options? What about those that run counter to prevailing ideology or sound and moral policy? Sinking foreign fishing vessels, for example, might help preserve Canadian fish stocks, but surely it isn't worth considering. On a practical level, the work involved in thorough analytical effort, even for serious options, would be enormously complicated and time-consuming.

Conceptually, too, rationalism poses difficulties: how do you quantify qualitative conditions? A clean environment, for example, affects quality of life as well as economic activity. How can they both be meaningfully measured? If we embrace the importance of value judgements in decision making, we can no longer call the process purely rational. What happens when analysts produce differing cost–benefit analyses because they have applied different value judgements to the same issue? Perhaps instead of a recipe for sound and beneficial decision making, pure rationalism is more liable to produce rancour and discord, tearing at the fabric of management.

And finally, how can we accurately measure the costs and benefits of policies and programs that don't yet exist? In the 1950s, for example, the Canadian government commissioned the development of the Avro Arrow fighter plane, designed to intercept Soviet bombers. It seemed an eminently sound defence policy, and the result was an aircraft universally recognized as ahead of its time. However, by the time it became a reality, the Soviets and others were putting nuclear warheads on missiles, and the whole idea of defending against bomber aircraft had become obsolete.

Critics of rationalism, such as Lindblom, have asserted that despite the superficial appeal of its logic, the promise of systematic thought, rational planning, and policy and program prioritization is hopelessly compromised by the complex nature of organizations. Their inability to gain consensus on goals or on cost–benefit analyses of policy and program options, and the sheer difficulty of trying to plan rationally in the real world, profoundly circumscribe the chances of success. Instead, Lindblom suggests, rationalism leads to confusion, disagreement, and much time-consuming analysis that detracts from the decision-making capacity of the organization—in other words, to "analysis paralysis."

'ISMS AND 'OLOGIES

• Incrementalism

Incrementalism holds that management involves doing what management has done in the past. Management is about maintaining established, ongoing organizational responsibilities and programs in keeping with existing policies and set goals. When problems arise, management must undertake reform in a simple, incremental, considered fashion.

• Rationalism

The main focus of management should be the development of policies and programs to maximize organizational goals with the minimum cost, effort, and other institutional drawbacks. Management identifies all the options that the organization either confronts or possesses. It then systematically and logically analyzes each one in terms of strengths, weaknesses, costs, benefits, potential, and limitations in order to choose the most appropriate policy or program to meet the defined end.

• Bounded Rationalism

While management should strive for the basic ideals of rationalism—careful planning, goal identification, systematic analysis of ends and means, and prioritization—all such actions must be understood as circumscribed by reality. Rather than seeking the best, most rational solution derived from all possible options, bounded rationality calls for management to determine the most satisfactory option in light of the operational constraints under which the organization and its management function.

• Mixed Scanning

Management directs systematic and highly detailed attention to a single policy or program in question, leaving all other matters to be managed incrementally. For the subject under review, decision makers take a broadly rationalistic approach, reviewing objectives; assessing reasonable and viable options given ideological and practical constraints; and determining the strengths, weaknesses, costs, and benefits.

Thinking about Decision Making

Think about the following government decisions:

- The federal government endorses the Trans Pacific Partnership free trade agreement in 2015.
- The Department of Veterans Affairs cuts the number of regional facilities providing services for veterans.
- The federal government amends the Criminal Code to impose mandatory minimum sentences for specified violent crimes.
- The federal Department of Transport imposes stricter regulations on airport security following the terrorist attacks of 9/11.
- The federal government sends Canadian troops to help fight a war in Iraq and Syria in 2014.

Which theory of decision making best explains each real-life decision? Why?

Are some of these decisions easier to explain than others? Why or why not?

WHITE PAPER

BOUNDED RATIONALISM

As rationalism came under attack for its theoretical and practical limitations, other techniques were advanced to synthesize some of the best elements of both rationalism and incrementalism. Herbert Simon argued in favour of what he termed **bounded rationalism** (1957). In this technique of decision making, although management strives for careful planning, goal identification, systematic analysis of ends and means, and prioritization, those rationalist actions are understood as realistically circumscribed. Their "bounds," or "givens," are determined by

- the history of the organization;
- the political and socio-economic; environment within which the organization functions;
- legal and constitutional frameworks;
- limits to financial and personnel resources; and
- the amount of time available for policy making.

All these givens establish a framework within which a public sector organization must operate, meaning that no bureaucracy has perfect freedom to engage in the type of unrestricted policy analysis suggested by rationalism in its purest form.

Government bodies must function according to established legal and constitutional orders, tradition, and finite financial and personnel resources and time. They must also recognize that certain options are simply non-starters. It is highly unlikely, for example, that a department of industry or economic development would devote any significant attention to wholesale nationalization.

That course would be ideologically unacceptable to a Canadian government of any stripe and thus unworthy of consideration. For similar reasons, it is unlikely that the current federal Department of Intergovernmental Relations would spend time assessing the merits of Quebec separation. Simon, like Lindblom, was very clear that managerial decision making has to occur within the bounds of reason and practicability, in light of real-world constraints.

Rather than seeking the best, most rational solution derived from all possible options, bounded rationality calls for decision makers to determine the most satisfactory option in light of organizational and operational constraints. To do so, managers have to engage in thoughtful policy analysis in keeping with the basic principles of rationalist inquiry. Their aim is still to plan, to set priorities, and to assess means–ends relationships through cost–benefit analyses and other methods of modern management, but the scope of the task is greatly reduced from the depth of analysis required by a purely rationalistic approach.

MIXED SCANNING

Amitai Etzioni (1929–) produced a different analysis of decision-making techniques (1967). He stressed that organizations and governments generally make two types of decisions: fundamental and incremental. Etzioni agreed with Lindblom that the vast majority of organizational and government decisions are incremental, constituting marginal, successive changes to ongoing policies and programs without wholesale reform of existing priorities or practices. But at times, Etzioni suggested, governments and organizations make fundamental reforms to achieve newly established

DECISION MAKING AND THE CHARTER OF RIGHTS

The 1982 Charter of Rights and Freedoms is often lauded as the single most important development in Canadian politics, government, and law in the past 50 years. How can its development be understood in terms of management theory?

Incrementalism

It can be argued that most of the rights and freedoms enshrined in the Charter were pre-existing, such as freedom of expression, the right to vote, trial rights, and bilingualism, such that the Charter was really only an incremental compilation of political and legal rights already found in Canada.

There is much truth to this, but it fails to acknowledge that the Charter really did break new ground in enshrining equality rights in the constitution and in making all laws and actions subject to the Charter.

Rationalism

It can be argued that the Charter developed after years of careful study by federal and provincial governments on how to systematically improve human rights protection in Canada.

This position is undermined by the fact that the Charter was developed piecemeal, based upon sporadic assessments of the current state of rights and laws in Canada in the late 1970s and early 1980s. The drafters of the Charter did not analyze all existing laws to identify all possibilities of rights reform. Economic and environmental rights, for example, were not on the table.

Bounded Rationalism

It can be argued that the Charter was the result of careful selection of certain political and legal rights for enhanced protection. The drafters opted for a narrow set of viable propositions on which they could get a reasonable degree of consensus.

There is a lot to be said for this explanation. The Charter was a child of political compromise, and the drafters needed to focus on a small but important number of issues.

Public Choice Theory

It can be said that the Charter was the result of the prime minister and the premiers advancing their own electoral interests by appealing to voters concerned with rights. In this view, bureaucrats in justice and other departments used the Charter and its implementation as a means to secure their own positions and to get a steady diet of administrative work for years to come.

There may be some truth to this position, but remember that the federal Liberals were badly damaged in the election that followed. And although the Charter has certainly created much work for public servants, that cannot be identified as a motivation for its drafters.

Bureaucratic Politics Theory

It can be said that federal and provincial departments of justice used the Charter to enhance their role and power in future intragovernmental budget battles.

There may be some truth to this in that the Charter does enhance the role of these departments and their officials, but it is highly problematic to draw a connection between motivation and effect in this context.

Policy Network Theory

It can be argued that the Charter emerged out of a political environment populated by a host of interest groups involved in human rights promotion, the elaboration of law reform within Canada, and the impact of these rights in the society and economy.

There is much truth to this position. The lead-up to the drafting of the Charter was marked by much discussion among interest groups and the submission of many reports on the pros and cons. Interest groups across the political spectrum, business and labour, feminist, and anti-feminist groups, for example, were actively involved in this networking.

Thinking about Theories

All these theories are helpful in thinking through the reasons for the development of a policy, though some apply to the given case more closely than others. And approaches may need to be combined to fully explain why a policy has come into existence. That's the case with the Charter.

objectives and priorities. At other times, as Mintzberg has noted, they must quickly develop new approaches in order to manage crises.

New initiatives such as these cannot be explained in incrementalist terms but instead emerge from a highly defined yet circumscribed form of rationalism. At such times, decision makers direct systematic and detailed attention to the issue in question, but they manage all other matters in the traditional and easier incremental fashion. For the subject that demands rationalistic review, decision makers will

- study the problems confronted by existing policy and programs
- review desired policy and program objectives
- assess the options in terms of ideological and practical constraints
- review the strengths, weaknesses, costs, and benefits of the options under scrutiny

Etzioni recognized that all such decision making would be both complicated and contentious for governments, affected organizations, and interested observers. Debate and controversy are endemic in any form of rationalism, as we have observed, but when institutions apply rationalist techniques to a narrow range of important matters, they do so on the grounds that on a limited scale, such decision making will result in superior program reform.

Governments generally, and commercial organizations consistently, seek the best of incrementalism and rationalism, scanning their environments, activities, needs, and objectives to determine which approach suits the task at hand. Examples of mixed scanning in the chapters that follow indicate the practicality of this method.

THEORETICAL APPROACHES TO DECISION MAKING

Incrementalism, rationalism, bounded rationalism, and mixed scanning represent methods of decision making widely found in practice or strongly advocated and promoted in policy-making theory. Each technique has its advocates, all of whom emphasize that their preferred method offers a normative foundation for managerial decision making. Each is *prescriptive*, claiming to be an ideal form of decision making, but supporters also argue that their particular technique is *descriptive* of how much decision making is actually performed in government.

These techniques, however, do not stand alone within management theory. Other approaches offer more analytical appraisals of how and why governments, management, and bureaucracies act as they do, especially the underlying motivations of decision makers. Among them are public choice theory, bureaucratic politics theory, and policy network theory, which identify the motivations behind decision making as, respectively, individual self-interest, institutional self-interest, and group self-interest. For detailed coverage on these theoretical approaches to understanding organizations, please see the Thinking Government website.

There are a number of ways of thinking about how organizations should be structured and how management should approach its operational and leadership responsibilities. The structural-mechanistic and organic-humanistic models have significantly influenced management theory and practice in this country, and their interplay can be seen in the centralized, command-and-control approach to federal executive power versus the initiatives of recent decades to make management systems more open and participatory. The operational history and degree of success or failure of these initiatives reveals not only the strong formal interest in an organic-humanistic model but also the continuing strength of the older elements of the structural-mechanistic model, at least in terms of the *realpolitik* of government decision making.

The management techniques of incrementalism, rationalism, bounded rationalism, and mixed scanning each provide a framework for thinking about how governments make policy, how managers make decisions, and how they set priorities and determine what actions are needed. All four techniques help to explain the actions of governments, though the push for policy and program rationalism has always experienced great problems of legitimacy as rationalistic initiatives confront major practical obstacles. Thus, incrementalism continues to be a fundamental aspect of managerial decision making, and mixed scanning is both a viable technique and a helpful explanation for real-world government and managerial action.

Similarly public choice theory, bureaucratic politics theory, and policy network theory probe aspects of decision-making motivation: individual self-interest, institutional self-interest, and group self-interest. Taken together they offer a picture of bureaucratic motivation at different times and under different circumstances.

We have at our disposal a complex array of theoretical models, techniques, and approaches for understanding government and managerial decision making. The four techniques of management apply equally under either of the two models of organizational design. Managers operating in a hierarchical environment may pursue their goals through either incrementalist or rationalist techniques, for example, just as those with a participative orientation may use bounded rationalism or mixed scanning. Each of the approaches to managerial motivation, moreover, can explain decision making within either of the two organizational models and all four decision-making techniques.

Given the vast scale of government action, no single explanation of its bureaucracy can be comprehensive, but these theories and techniques help to explain how and why governments and their managers act as they do.

REFERENCES AND SUGGESTED READING

Allison, Graham. 1971. *Essence of Decision: Explaining the Cuban Missile Crisis*. Boston: Little, Brown.

Anderson, James R. 1984. *Public Policy-Making*. New York: Holt, Rinehart and Winston.

Argyris, Chris. 1957. *Personality and Organization: The Conflict between System and the Individual*. New York: Harper and Row.

———. 1964. *Integrating the Individual and the Organization*. New York: John Wiley and Sons.

Barnard, Chester. 1962. *The Functions of the Executive*. Cambridge, MA: Harvard University Press.

Breton, Albert. 1974. *The Economic Theory of Representative Government*. Chicago: Aldine.

Coch, L., and J.R.P. French Jr. 1948. "Overcoming Resistance to Change." *Human Relations* 1: 512–32.

Denhardt, Robert B., with Joseph W. Grubbs. 1999. *Public Administration: An Action Orientation*. 3rd ed. Fort Worth, TX: Harcourt Brace College.

Downs, Anthony. 1957. *An Economic Theory of Democracy*. New York: Harper and Row.

Drucker, Peter F. 1954. *The Practice of Management*. New York: Harper and Row.

Etzioni, Amitai. 1967. "Mixed-Scanning: A 'Third' Approach to Decision-Making." *Public Administration Review* 27: 385–92.

Fayol, Henri. 1971. *General and Industrial Management*. Translated by Constance Storrs. London: Pitman.

Follett, Mary Parker. 1951. *Creative Experience*. New York: Peter Smith.

———. 1965. *The New State*. Gloucester, MA: Peter Smith.

Gulick, Luther. 1937. "Notes on the Theory of Organization." In *Papers on the Science of Administration*, edited by Luther Gulick and Lyndall Urwick, 1–46. New York: Institute of Public Administration.

———, and Lyndall Urwick, eds. 1969. *Papers on the Science of Administration*. New York: Augustus M. Kelley.

Hartle, Douglas G. 1976. *A Theory of the Expenditure Budgetary Process*. Toronto: University of Toronto Press.

Inwood, Gregory J. 2004. *Understanding Canadian Public Administration: An Introduction to Theory and Practice*. 2nd ed. Scarborough, ON: Prentice Hall Allyn and Bacon.

Kernaghan, Kenneth, and David Siegel. 1999. *Public Administration in Canada: A Text*. 4th ed. Toronto: Nelson.

Lewin, K., R. Lippitt, and R.K. White. 1939. "Patterns of Aggressive Behaviour in Experimentally Created Social Climates." *Journal of Social Psychology* 10: 271–301.

Lindblom, Charles E. 1959. "The Science of Muddling-Through." *Public Administration Review* 19: 79–88.

———. 1968. *The Policy-Making Process*. Englewood Cliffs, NJ: Prentice Hall.

Maslow, Abraham H. 1970. *Motivation and Personality*. New York: Harper and Row.

Mayo, Elton. 1960. *The Human Problems of an Industrial Civilization*. New York: Viking Press.

McGregor, Douglas. 1960. *The Human Side of Enterprise*. New York: McGraw-Hill.

Mintzberg, Henry. 1973. *The Nature of Managerial Work*. New York: Harper and Row.

Pross, A. Paul. 1986. *Group Politics and Public Policy*. Toronto: Oxford University Press.

Roethlisberger, F.J., and William J. Dickson. 1964. *Management and the Worker*. Cambridge, MA: Harvard University Press.

Simon, Herbert. 1957. *Administrative Behaviour*. 2nd ed. New York: Free Press.

Taylor, Frederick Winslow. 1967. *The Principles of Scientific Management*. New York: Norton.

Thomas, Paul G. 1999. "The Role of Central Agencies: Making a Mesh of Things." In *Canadian Politics*, 2nd ed., edited by James Bickerton and Alain-G. Gagnon, 129–48. Toronto: University of Toronto Press.

Weber, Max. 1946. *Max Weber: Essays in Sociology*. Edited and translated by H.H. Gerth and C. Wright Mills. New York: Oxford University Press.

———. 1947. *The Theory of Social and Economic Organization*. Translated by A.M. Henderson and Talcott Parsons. New York: Oxford University Press.

Whitaker, Reginald A. 1995. "Politicians and Bureaucrats in the Policy Process." In *Canadian Politics in the 1990s*, 4th ed., edited by Michael S. Whittington and Glen Williams, 424–40. Toronto: Nelson.

Yukl, Garry. 2012. *Leadership in Organizations*. 8th ed. Upper Saddle River, NJ: Prentice Hall.

RELATED WEBSITES

Keith Rollag's Website (Organizational Theory). http://faculty.babson.edu/krollag/org_theory.html

Organization and Management Theory Web. www.omtweb.org

CHAPTER 6

Financial Management

Business requires understanding financial matters, but management is different from running the financial aspects of the business—it requires understanding complex systems, how they operate, the nature of organizations, what happens when people interact in groups and how to motivate and guide people.

–Rosabeth Moss Kanter, 2016

After reading this chapter and its related web pages you will be able to

- discuss current trends in federal budgeting;
- explain the difference between a revenue and an expenditure budget;
- debate the merits of budgetary incrementalism and rationalism;
- trace the evolution of federal financial management from PPBS to EMIS;
- highlight the weaknesses of rationalist systems of financial management;
- outline budget-making tactics from the viewpoints of spenders and guardians;
- explain the audit function in government; and
- assess the strengths and weaknesses of the roles of auditor general, the parliamentary budget officer, and parliament itself.

6   Financial Management

Governments live on money—huge amounts of cash, income, securities, and credit. They couldn't function without hundreds of billions of dollars to sustain their policy and program activities, so revenue generation and expenditure are among the most important and controversial aspects of public sector management.

For the better part of four decades, macro-financial management has dominated the Canadian political landscape as federal and provincial governments wrestle with the implications of budgetary deficits, surpluses, or balance. From around 1980 to 2000, governments became more conscious of the need to live within their means. By the 1990s all governments, regardless of political affiliation, had come to subordinate their activities to the overarching policy objective of deficit reduction and eventual elimination. The politics and administration of fiscal restraint resulted in

- public sector budget cuts
- public sector employment cuts
- program and service reductions
- privatization
- deregulation
- downloading and offloading of government services
- greater use of consumption taxes
- user fees for many government services

Through these initiatives most Canadian governments (and especially, for our purposes, the federal government) have shown that deficits can be reduced and even eliminated and that with

sufficient political will progress can be made on public debt reduction. Indeed, the government of Alberta in 2005 established a debt retirement account, the assets of which were used *only* to pay down the provincial debt. On March 1, 2013, the Government of Alberta announced that the province was debt free, having paid off the last millions of a fiscal liability that stood at $23 billion in 1994. Managing money, especially government budgets, however, is not for the faint of heart. Later that same year the Alberta government reported in their latest budget that, due to sluggish economic growth attributed to the slow international recovery from the 2008 global financial crisis, the province's books were back in the red, with a deficit of $6.3 billion. By July 2015, and following a decline of more than 50 per cent in international oil and gas prices in 2014, the Alberta budget reported another deficit of $5 billion, with the provincial debt standing at $11.9 billion. While governments can become much leaner and more efficient than they have been, and have proven themselves financially adaptable and, some would say, creative in coping with fiscal and political pressures pointing toward a reduced state presence in society, public sector financial management always exists in a highly political and ideological world.

Governments operate in a world of economic interdependence and uncertainty, where the actions of other governments, private businesses, and stock markets can drastically affect what they do. The worldwide recession of 2008–09, precipitated by failures in American mortgage and lending businesses, had adverse effects on all Canadian governments, leading the federal Conservative government to engage in major spending initiatives to stimulate the Canadian economy and employment and to aid the private sector, even at the expense of running renewed deficits until 2014–15. And note the irony here: that a Conservative government and leader long pledged to balanced budgets and a smaller role for the state came to support Keynesian economic policy.

Policy choices of course bear program consequences. Stimulus spending may provide short-term relief for a troubled economy, but it will not necessarily improve the economic fundamentals, especially when a recession has international origins. And the renewed federal budget deficits that resulted led this country back into debates about how to rebalance our finances.

There's more than one way to eliminate a deficit and balance a budget and, as the federal election of 2015 illustrated, the major political parties had some sharp policy differences respecting the management of public finances. The Conservative Party led by Stephen Harper remained true to their Conservative beliefs in supporting low taxes, balanced budgets, and limited program spending. For the first time in almost two decades, however, the issue of tax increases came to be a matter of debate and choice, with both the New Democrats and the Liberals promising to raise taxation levels if they were to be elected. The NDP promised to increase the corporate tax rate by two percentage points while the Liberals stressed they would increase individual tax rates on the wealthiest Canadians, those earning over $250,000 per year. Both of these parties also promised billions of dollars in new spending on everything from child care programs and tax cuts for the middle class to needed infrastructure

spending, enhanced environmental regulations, improved funding for Indigenous Canadians, industrial support for Canadian industries, greater spending for Canadian seniors, and more money for national defence and Canada's veterans. But all the NDP promises were premised on the assertion that a New Democratic government would always run a budgetary surplus while the Liberals stressed that they would fulfill their campaign promises by running modest deficits of some $30 billion over three years. Commentators quickly picked up on the interesting policy shift noted here, with Thomas Mulcair and the NDP coming to align themselves more with the balanced budget orthodoxy of the Stephen Harper Conservatives while the Liberals led by Justin Trudeau occupied the economic terrain of the progressive left.

With victory for the Liberals, the Trudeau government faced the tough reality of turning campaign promises into reality, all in light of a sluggish economy, a depressed price for oil, and many demands for new spending on a host of policies and programs that would challenge the government's ability to keep its planned deficits to just $10 billion per year between 2015 and 2018, let alone moving to a balanced budget by 2019, in time for the next federal election. While the Trudeau government came into power with high expectations, the discipline of power has a way of quickly taking the shine off new administrations.

FINANCIAL POLICIES AND POLITICS

This chapter explores the many issues of federal budgetary politics and administration. We focus first on the politics and management of deficits: the lessons of the 1990s, the policy and administrative choices in an era of budgetary surpluses in the decade that followed, the start of another prolonged period of deficits in 2008–09, and the financial management decisions ahead as the Liberal government of Justin Trudeau strives to stimulate the economy and create jobs via deficit financing and balance the budget by 2019—a tall order. This chapter also assesses the many aspects of routine financial management across government organizations, devoting particular attention to the historical development of contemporary financial management systems.

All governments face criticism over their management of public monies. They are tarred with a reputation for wasting—through sheer bloated inefficiency—hundreds of millions, if not billions, of hard-earned dollars taken from taxpayers. If a government were put in charge of the Sahara Desert, said American economist Milton Friedman, within five years they'd have a shortage of sand. While this image is much more myth than reality, it remains potent. Financial mismanagement *causes célèbres* attract the media and, hence, public attention. The debate over the seemingly ever-increasing costs of new jet fighters to replace the Canadian military's CF-18s remains a notable case in point. The annual report of the auditor general always reveals numerous examples of questionable government and managerial behaviour—ranging from sloppy accounting practices to weak managerial oversight and poorly designed and administered programs—and urges the government in general, and senior management in particular, to devote greater care to accountability. In response, government has tried a variety of initiatives, such as establishing the position of the **parliamentary budget officer** (PBO) to provide independent financial analysis—with mixed results.

Accountability, the public duty to perform government duties with due regard for prudence, law, social responsiveness, and the managerial concepts of economy, efficiency, and effectiveness, has become one of the organizing principles of modern democratic government. It has important financial management implications as well. Departments and agencies and their managers have a duty to handle public monies in accountable and responsible ways. Public sector financial management is thus best viewed as a form of trusteeship.

As we study the financial management of the public service, notice the programmatic tension between incrementalist and rationalist approaches. The influence of rationalist methods of financial administration continues despite their many limitations. The dynamics of budgeting are inherently political, and the best-laid plans of "rational" budgeting will often founder in the complex public sector environment.

THE NATURE OF GOVERNMENT SPENDING

Every year the Department of Finance publishes what it calls Fiscal Reference Tables. These tables, found on the department's website, are a treasure trove of information about the financial health of the federal government and its history of budgetary management. For the fiscal year 2014–15, total federal expenditures amounted to $280.4 billion and total revenue was $282.3 billion, resulting in

THE PARLIAMENTARY BUDGET OFFICER

• The Mandate

The office of the parliamentary budget officer was established in 2006 by an act of parliament. The PBO has the responsibility to provide independent analysis to the House of Commons and the Senate with respect to federal budget planning, the state of the Canadian economy, trends in federal finances, and the accuracy of the estimates and predictions used by the government in making budgetary decisions.

• The Controversy

The Harper government created the PBO on the strength of a promise made during the 2006 election to bring greater clarity, transparency, and accuracy to federal budget making by giving MPs greater access to current information on the nation's finances.

Soon after its inception, however, the PBO faced increasing criticism from the Harper government. The PBO challenged the government on the accuracy of its financial estimates and, following the recession of 2009, asserted that the country was facing a structural deficit due to excessive tax cuts. In 2012 the PBO also requested that all departments provide information to it respecting how many job cuts and service reductions would occur in each department, as these organizations were mandated to trim their budgets by 5 to 10 per cent as part of a government-wide cost-cutting program review exercise. Many departments refused to comply with the PBO's request for information, stressing that the PBO was exceeding its general mandate by delving into future operational details of departmental management. The then-parliamentary budget officer, Kevin Page, brought legal action against the government in the Federal Court of Canada, asking this court to clarify whether his office's mandate included being able to ask for and obtain the type of information he was seeking in this case. In 2013 the court ruled that the PBO does have the right to ask for such information in future and such requests must be honoured by the government.

Leading figures in the Conservative government, including Stephen Harper himself, came to increasingly reject PBO reports, most notably the study on cost overruns with respect to the F-35 jet fighter acquisition plan. This study asserted that the Harper government's estimate that this military procurement initiative would cost only $9 billion was inaccurate and that the likely cost of purchasing and maintaining 65 F-35 aircraft would likely be in the $30 billion range. The federal auditor general later confirmed the PBO numbers, but this did not stop the Harper government from questioning the independence and impartiality of Kevin Page. This government then announced plans to reduce funding for the office.

Opposition parties rallied to the defence of the PBO, noting that Page was simply doing his job, that his analyses were professional and balanced, and that his predictions about the fiscal state of the country were more accurate than those coming from the Department of Finance.

THE FUTURE

Kevin Page announced in 2010 that he would not seek reappointment at the end of his term in 2013. In that year Jean-Denis Fréchette was appointed as the new parliamentary budget officer and continued his work in the traditions set by his predecessor. Just a month after the Justin Trudeau government came to power, the PBO issued a report questioning the likelihood of the new government being able to balance its budget by its planned timeline of 2019. While the Liberals, when in opposition, cheered such critical commentary of the Harper government's planned financial management, whether they will continue to be enamoured of the PBO's commentary remains to be seen.

TABLE 6.1

Federal Revenues, 1979–2015 ($ millions)

	INCOME TAX			OTHER TAXES AND DUTIES				OTHER		
	PERSONAL	CORPORATE	NON-RESIDENT	GST/SALES TAX	CUSTOMS IMPORT DUTIES	ENERGY TAXES	EMPLOY-MENT INSURANCE	PREMIUMS	REVENUE	TOTAL
1979–80	16,808	6,951	883	4,651	2,996	1,171	1,397	2,778	5,675	43,310
1984–85	28,455	9,234	1,021	7,592	3,794	4,479	2,312	7,676	7,436	71,999
1989–90	50,584	12,820	1,361	17,672	4,587	2,471	3,425	10,727	12,240	115,887
1994–95	60,648	10,969	1,700	17,062	3,575	3,824	2,996	18,293	11,724	130,791
1999–2000	85,070	22,115	2,646	23,121	2,105	4,757	3,315	18,628	14,651	176,408
2004–05	98,620	31,422	3,560	29,758	3,091	5,054	4,954	17,307	20,471	214,237
2009–10	105,040	32,247	5,293	26,947	3,490	5,178	4,958	16,761	22,189	222,103
2014–15	135,743	39,447	6,216	31,349	4,581	5,528	5,724	22,564	31,194	282,346

Note: Due to a break in the series following the introduction of full accrual accounting, data from 1984 onward are not directly comparable with earlier years.

Source: Data from Canada, Department of Finance 2015.

a narrow budgetary surplus of $1.9 billion. This surplus was the first in seven years, dating back to 2007–08. In the following year, 2008–09, the worldwide recession hit and the federal government led by Stephen Harper engaged in deficit spending to stimulate the economy. Between 2009 and 2015, these federal deficits added an additional $144.6 billion to the national debt. This current period of deficit financing, however, came after 11 years of budgetary surpluses dating back to 1997–98, when the Liberal government of Jean Chrétien finally slew a pattern of deficits that began in 1970–71. Between 1997–98 and 2007–08, total federal surpluses amounted to $104.7 billion, and all of this money went to pay down the accumulated national debt. The national debt, referred to as the "accumulated deficit" by the Department of Finance, is the total of all deficits ever run by the federal government. In 1970 it stood at $20.3 billion. Then came 27 years of uninterrupted deficits, racked up by both Liberal (Trudeau and Chrétien) and Conservative (Mulroney) governments. All these deficits created a national debt burden the country still bears, as the federal government must pay debt servicing charges. By 1980 the debt was at $91.9 billion, by 1990 it stood at $377.6 billion, and in 1996 it hit a then all-time high of $562.8 billion. After a decade in which the government chipped away to bring the figure below the half-trillion mark again, as of 2014–15—following six years of renewed deficit spending—it had soared to $612.3 billion, the new high-water mark.

On the revenue side, as of 2014–15, 56.1 per cent of total federal revenues came through personal taxes, including employment insurance premiums;

TABLE 6.2
Federal Expenses, 1979–2015 ($ millions)

	TRANSFERS TO CITIZENS (BENEFITS)			TRANSFERS TO OTHER LEVELS OF GOVERNMENT							
	OLD AGE SECURITY	FAMILY ALLOWANCE/ CHILD TAX CREDIT	EMPLOYMENT INSURANCE	CANADA HEALTH AND SOCIAL TRANSFER/ OTHER	FISCAL TRANSFERS	OTHER	ALTERNATIVE PAYMENTS FOR STANDING PROGRAMS	NATIONAL DEFENCE	OTHER PROGRAM EXPENSES	PUBLIC DEBT CHARGES	TOTAL
1979–80	6,320	1,725	3,922	7,026	3,575			4,588	19,627	8,494	55,277
1984–85	11,418	2,418	10,052	12,340	6,208			7,900	33,943	24,887	109,166
1989–90	16,154	2,653	11,694	13,835	9,582			10,982	38,884	41,246	145,030
1994–95	20,143	5,322	14,815	17,443	8,870			10,580	46,065	44,185	167,423
1999–2000	22,856	6,000	11,301	14,891	10,721	56	-2,425	10,113	45,253	43,384	162,150
2004–05	27,871	8,688	14,748	28,031	13,467	3,779	-3350	14,318	71,104	34,118	212,774
2009–10	34,653	12,340	21,586	35,678	16,789	7,772	-3,299	20,863	101,905	29,414	277,701
2014–15	44,103	14,303	18,052	44,696	20,505	2,142	-4,234	23,669	90,605	26,594	280,435

Notes: Due to a break in the series following the introduction of full accrual accounting, data from 1984 onward are not directly comparable with earlier years.

a In 1996 the Canada Health and Social Transfer became law, replacing three federal-provincial social welfare transfer programs: insurance and medical care, education support, and the Canada Assistance Plan. Figures prior to 1996 reflect the funding of these older programs.

b Alternative payments for standing programs are recoveries from Quebec of an additional tax point transfer above and beyond the tax point transfer under the Canada Health Transfer and the Canada Social Transfer.

Source: Data from Canada, Department of Finance 2015.

16.7 per cent from indirect taxation and the GST; and 14.0 per cent from corporate tax. By contrast, in 1992–93, the last full year of the Mulroney government, personal taxation accounted for 61.0 per cent of total revenues, indirect taxation provided 21.5 per cent, and corporate taxation 5.7 per cent (see Table 6.1).

The Fiscal Reference Tables for 2015 show that the single largest form of expenditure, consuming 40.7 per cent of the total, was on direct programs including national defence. Close behind, with 32.0 per cent, came all the mandatory expenditures such as debt financing and social policy funding transfers to the provinces for health, social assistance, and postsecondary education. Public debt charges alone accounted for 9.5 per cent of all federal spending. Transfers to individual citizens in the form of old age security, family allowance, and employment insurance benefits accounted for 27.3 per cent. (see Table 6.2).

TRENDS AND PERSPECTIVES

Certain longitudinal dynamics can be discerned in these figures (see Table 6.3, Figure 6.1). The proportion of total revenue accounted for by

TABLE 6.3

Federal Budget and National Debt, 1979–2015 ($ millions)

	REVENUES	PROGRAM EXPENSES	OPERATING SURPLUS/DEFICIT	PUBLIC DEBT CHARGES	BUDGETARY SURPLUS/DEFICIT	NATIONAL DEBT
1979–80	43,310	46,783	–3,473	8,494	–11,967	77,392
1984–85	71,999	84,279	–12,280	24,887	–37,167	194,419
1989–90	115,887	103,784	12,103	41,246	–29,143	343,757
1994–95	130,791	123,238	7,553	44,185	–36,632	524,156
1999–2000	176,408	118,766	57,642	43,384	14,258	539,885
2004–05	214,237	178,656	35,581	34,118	1,463	494,717
2009–10	222,103	248,287	–26,184	29,414	–55,598	519,097
2014–15	282,346	253,841	28,505	26,594	1,911	612,330

Note: Due to a break in the series following the introduction of full accrual accounting, data from 1984 onward are not directly comparable with earlier years.

Source: Data from Canada, Department of Finance 2015.

personal taxation (income tax and employment insurance premiums) increased through the early 1990s, reaching a peak of 61 per cent in 1992–93. Since then the figure has declined marginally to 56.1 per cent in 2014–15. Over the same period, the proportion of total federal revenues deriving from corporate taxation has more than doubled, from 5.7 per cent of the total in 1992–93 to 14.0 per cent in 2014–15.

These figures, however, reflect surging national economic growth and increasing business and commercial activity more than they do actual increases in corporate tax rates. In fact, the rates have been declining in recent years, as evidenced by the drop in corporate tax revenues between 2007–08 from 17.2 to 14.0 per cent of the figure for 2014–15. Also, while both total revenues and expenditures have tended to increase since the 1970s—the latter outpacing the former, thus leading to annual deficits and a growing federal debt—dramatic fiscal swings have occurred over the past 20 years or so. In the early 1990s, federal revenues actually declined as a result of recession, while total expenditures grew and then hovered around the $120 billion range. In the mid-1990s, federal revenue climbed to the $160 billion range, mainly due to a growing national economy, while total program expenditures were reduced to a low of $111.3 billion in 1996–97.

The result of all these developments, however, was the elimination of the federal deficit by 1997–98 and the beginning of a gradual paying down of the accumulated national debt. As we entered the new century, program spending increased as the government reaped the rewards of balanced budgets. In 2000–01, total federal spending on all

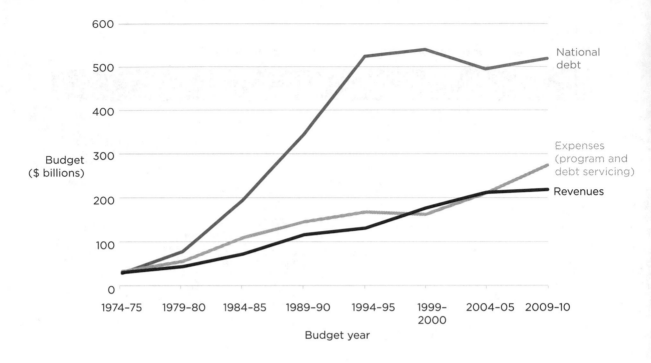

Figure 6.1 **Federal Budget and National Debt, 1974–2010**

programs amounted to $136.2 billion. By 2005–06, the last year of the Martin Liberal government, this figure stood at $177.3 billion, and even under the Harper Conservatives, program spending increased in every year, hitting a high of $253.8 billion in 2014–15.

But note a different way of looking at these figures. Viewed as a percentage of gross domestic product, the growth of federal spending has been relatively flat for some 20 years, averaging around 12–13 per cent of GDP since the mid-1990s. Looking back, that makes the quantity of federal program spending roughly equivalent to that of the early 1960s and even the 1950s, the era before the great boom in the social welfare state. In this sense, have we gone back to the future? Has the

presence of the state declined in Canadian socio-economic life compared to what it was in the 1960s and 1970s and, if so, has this decline been for the better, or has it hurt the quality of public services and what Canadians should expect of the federal government?

Or to put this another way, over the decade of federal surpluses from 1997 to 2008, were we being overtaxed? Or should we have seen new programs such as a national day care plan, or pharmacare, or major new green environmental programs, or the abolition of university tuition? Once again, Canadians are divided on these questions. The Harper Conservative government always stressed that Canadian tax rates were too high and needed to be reduced, putting more money back in the pockets of hard-working Canadians. And for the better part of his time in power, this Harper mantra dominated the way most Canadians thought about federal tax policy. Only in the 2015 federal election did the New Democrats and the Liberals begin suggesting that taxes should be marginally increased, but only in special and limited ways. New Democrats favoured an increase of two percentage points on the corporate tax rate, while the Liberals promised to increase individual income taxes on the wealthiest Canadians, those earning over $250,000 per year, while reducing taxes on the "middle class." Each party was cautious not to be seen as advocating for tax increases that would be felt by most "ordinary" Canadians. But will the modest tax increases promised by the Liberal Party bring in sufficient revenue to pay for all the ambitious economic, social, and environmental plans the Justin Trudeau government has for the country? Or are we at a point where our needs—for new national infrastructure, improved health care, a national pharmacare system, a national child care system, an improved postsecondary education system with greatly reduced or eliminated tuition fees, and enhanced climate change initiatives to create a greener economy while weaning us off fossil fuels—necessitate that we increase taxes on almost everyone? Would we be better off as a society if we had a national tax on carbon fuels, with revenues reinvested into the creation of new, green energy alternatives, and increased individual, corporate, and consumption taxes centred on the GST, with revenues going to a range of needed social programs? This debate, one rooted as much in politics and ideology as it is in economics and financial management concerns, is still in its infancy in this country, and the Trudeau government has the opportunity to chart a new course for Canada in line with more liberal as opposed to conservative values.

Two general lessons, however, can be derived from all of these figures and dynamics:

1 The scope of federal financial management is truly enormous. The federal government is the single largest economic actor in the country, and the impact of its financial decision making is felt by each and every Canadian.
2 Government decisions about financial management result in discernible changes in budgetary policy, with a demonstrable impact on the entire society.

Current political concerns—such as the impact of stimulus spending, deficit reduction, the social and economic consequences of cutbacks, the fraying of the social safety net, the perceived declining relevance of government, fiscal choices confronting governments over budget deficits, and the role of the state in a renewed post-deficit era—reflect the ongoing importance of government financial management and the policy trade-offs and options it embodies.

THE TRADITIONAL ELEMENTS OF FINANCIAL MANAGEMENT

Government financial management, indeed any financial management, involves two separate but related processes: revenue and expenditure.

THE REVENUE PROCESS

How is money raised to sustain the operations of governments? Individual and corporate taxation, service charges, fees and duties, and borrowing are among the sources, and the particulars are the concern of the revenue process, as laid out in the **revenue budget**.

The preparation of the federal annual revenue budget is the foremost responsibility of the prime minister and the minister of finance. In Chapter 4, we noted that these two have always been the dominant figures in government budgetary planning, and with the command approach to leadership exhibited by Chrétien, Martin, and Harper and their finance ministers, the authority and influence of these leaders has become even more elevated within official Ottawa. The Trudeau government elected in the fall of 2015 will likely be no different and, while cabinet committees may be given a greater role in shaping this budget, the key architects will remain the minister of finance and, ultimately, the prime minister. Assisting these officials are the Departments of Finance and Customs and Revenue. Officials in these institutions, under the close leadership of their ministers, develop a government-wide economic policy outlook, a fiscal plan, and specific revenue-raising proposals to facilitate government functions while staying true to broad government economic and fiscal objectives. The officials develop these plans in close consultation with the prime minister and the minister of finance, the full cabinet and cabinet committees, and the leading central agencies: the Treasury Board of Canada Secretariat (TBS), the Privy Council Office (PCO), and the Prime Minister's Office (PMO). Consultations also extend to senior officials from other departments and even other provincial governments, and it is now common for the Department of Finance to hold pre-budget hearings with leading groups representing business, labour, and social interests. The focal point of this work is the presentation of the annual budget by the minister of finance to the House of Commons, usually in late February or early March (Treasury Board Secretariat 2010b, 1–5).

The revenue budget attracts great popular and media attention because its taxation component has a direct impact on almost everybody and also because the budget speech is a highly theatrical presentation. But despite the notice the revenue budget draws, the aspect of financial management of greatest importance to those either working within or interested in governments is the expenditure process.

THE EXPENDITURE PROCESS

The development of the **expenditure budget** involves officials from every department and agency as institutional goals and financial requirements are established. In turn, cabinet committees assess these requests, assisted by further studies, reviews, and financial management plans and evaluations prepared by Finance, the PCO, and the TBS. The annual federal expenditure budget, presented to parliament in the form of massive **Main Estimates** (the Blue Book), is awesome in its breadth and complexity and terribly important for its impact upon government.

The Main Estimates directly outline the levels, purposes, and objectives of public spending within each department and agency, thereby providing a reference both for measuring total government and department spending and for assessing specific spending priorities. The Main Estimates are the starting point in the chain of accountability for the quantity and quality of government spending activities great and small.

Accountability has historically been tied to parliament as the ultimate guardian of the public purse, but it now extends far beyond the floor of the House of Commons. Parliamentary debates on the revenue and expenditure budgets have always tended to be more symbolic than substantive, given the influence of the governing party. Indeed, in 2011, then-Conservative Senator Lowell Murray argued that parliamentary oversight of federal budgets had become so slight and ineffectual, with most elements of huge budget bills never being scrutinized by MPs at all, that parliament had lost effective control of the public purse (May, 2015). We will spend more time on this devastating critique of parliament's accountability function toward the end of this chapter. The main actors in the financial management accountability process are in fact departments, cabinet committees, and central agencies; the auditor general; the Public Accounts Committee of parliament; and political parties, interest groups, and the media. Their respective roles are considered in more detail below.

APPROACHES TO EXPENDITURE BUDGETING

Expenditure budgets have several purposes. On a fundamental level they are guidelines for how, when, where, and why a government will spend revenue, and how much (Adie and Thomas 1987, 252–53). In this respect, a budget acts as a statement of financial intent, allowing administrative and political superiors to exercise some control over departments and agencies by insisting that set expenditure levels not be exceeded.

On a deeper level, a budget is a management tool, allowing senior managers to evaluate the degree of economy, efficiency, and effectiveness within an organization. By relating changes in expenditure to quantitative and qualitative phenomena such as greater output, better service delivery, or enhanced client or citizen satisfaction, managers can gain important knowledge about how well their organization is meeting its objectives. Good budgetary analysis identifies procedures that enhance employee efficiency and program effectiveness and reveals activities that are less economical and efficient. It helps managers and their political superiors determine whether any practices can be modified, improved, or eliminated to free monetary resources for new priorities and initiatives. In this respect a budget acts as an ongoing form of organizational intelligence for the leaders of a bureaucracy.

The ideal budget contains aspects of three elements: control, provision of management information, and planning. In practice, however, the ideal is often not realized. Canadian governments practised two major forms of budgeting until the mid-1990s: budgetary incrementalism and budgetary rationalism, and only rationalism consciously sought to achieve the ideal—with limited success. It is important to study these forms because they constitute the heritage of financial management through which current budgetary policies, interpretations, and practices have evolved. Much of what follows looks at failed or weak financial management initiatives, especially in relation

TABLE 6.4

Hypothetical Line-Item Budget, Federal Court of Canada Regional Office

ITEM	2016 ACTUAL ($000s)	2017 BUDGET ($000s)
Salaries (regular)	404.0	415.0
Salaries (overtime)	20.5	24.0
Employee Benefits	65.0	67.0
Office Equipment	28.7	33.5
Office Supplies	12.5	15.1
Facility Rent	87.7	90.9
Cleaning Services	36.0	38.0
Security Services	49.0	51.0
Travel	5.0	5.0
Library	33.6	35.0
Miscellaneous	5.0	5.0
Total	**747.0**	**779.5**

to budgetary rationalism. These offer important lessons about which financial management practices work well in the real world of decision making and which do not.

BUDGETARY INCREMENTALISM

The traditional expenditure budget process in Canadian governments until the 1960s was **incremental budgeting**, or line-item budgeting (Kernaghan and Siegel 1999, 621–24). This approach is so named because the budget document that results is a line-by-line list of expenditures to be paid for by a given department or agency or office over a specific year (see Table 6.4). As you can see, the budget lists items such as salaries, benefits, equipment, rent, travel, and vehicles and determines expenditure for them in the context of the year before. This form of budget is quite rudimentary. A budget manager need only take the previous year's figures and marginally adjust them to take account of inflation, contractual obligations, change in service levels, and alterations in populations served. Such adjustments to an established base cause only incremental change to the overall budget, and the basic activities of the organization are accepted as given. The only question is the degree to which funding for established objects of expenditure will increase or decrease.

A line-item budget tends to develop from the bottom up rather than the top down within the organization. The detailed concern for items of expenditure, changing costs, and service level alterations make this a type of budget most easily prepared by middle managers, as they are the ones most familiar with the financial and operational routines of their organizations and their changing incremental needs. This system is inherently decentralized, placing the bulk of the decision-making power in the hands of middle managers who establish budgetary requests and submit them up the bureaucratic hierarchy. It is unsurprising that incremental budgeting has been highly praised by these same officials.

THE PLUS SIDE

Incremental budgeting has the benefits and problems associated with simplicity. On the positive side are several factors:

- Managers have the stability of knowing that the shape and form and content of next year's budget will simply be a revision of this year's budget.
- Managers do not have to justify the purposes and interests of their organization within the broader spectrum of government activities.
- Established organizational actors are guaranteed that the fundamentals of their programs and policies will persist. They do not have to negotiate trade-offs in broad government policy and spending priorities.
- The process is not abnormally difficult or time-consuming. Middle-level managers with

a solid understanding of their branches can easily draft a budget, and senior managers and their political superiors can readily understand them. (Henry 1995, 210–11)

THE MINUS SIDE

On the negative side, simplicity brings certain drawbacks:

- The rudimentary nature of the line-item budget makes it of limited value as a planning tool. Senior managers cannot fine-tune organizational operations or systematically plan policy and program improvements on that basis.
- It provides limited information for senior managers and political superiors to evaluate the quality of the work being undertaken. It says only how much money is being spent, on which items, and how much the figure has increased or decreased from the previous year.
- The budget does not contain data to support studies of how efficiently resources are being used or the effectiveness of programs over time or across program fields.
- The line-item budget is essentially a backward-looking document.

At best, the line-item budget allows senior officials to exert some control over the spending habits of middle managers, as overspending can be readily observed. But its bottom-up, incremental simplicity guarantees that it is of limited value for centralized program evaluation and policy development either within an organization or across the government in general. Of course, that limitation enhances the influence and power of middle managers (Brown-John, LeBlond, and Marson 1988).

PERFORMANCE BUDGETING

A variation on the line-item budget, developed in the late 1960s and designed to provide greater planning information to senior officials, is the **performance budget** (Henry 1995, 211–12). Efficiency evaluations are built into the process by determining a relationship between financial inputs and service outputs. Middle managers are asked to provide not only a line-item list of annual expenditures but also, where possible, a quantitative list of services provided.

Thus, a performance budget connects money spent and services rendered. How many documents were prepared or phone calls answered per secretary? How many workers' compensation claims were handled per claims officer? How many restaurant investigations were conducted per board of health officer?

THE PLUS SIDE

Through this approach, the limited nature of the line-item budget can be overcome to a degree. Performance budgeting permits efficiency evaluations, since the efficiency of a single operation can be measured over time, and the efficiency of different operations can be compared.

Senior managers, policy analysts, and political leaders can also evaluate the claims for budgetary support from different organizations. The more

efficient organizations can be rewarded and the less efficient can be informed that their operational performance needs to be improved before funding will be increased.

Similarly, performance budgeting techniques enable senior managers to pinpoint middle managers who are adept at gaining efficiency improvements and those who are not. Higher performers can be rewarded accordingly.

THE MINUS SIDE

Despite these benefits, performance budgeting has weaknesses. It is still essentially an incrementalist device and can be applied only to services that are easily quantifiable: letters written, calls answered, investigations undertaken. But not all public services are easily quantifiable. International diplomacy or intelligence gathering or policy analysis is ongoing, part of a web of activities, any part of which may be unimportant in isolation but all of which are necessary components of the whole.

A related point is that quantitative analysis of administrative processes such as documents, phone calls, and meetings reveals nothing about quality. Are they good documents? Do callers receive sound, helpful information? Do meetings help to promote communication and solve problems? These are qualitative considerations that require careful analysis in which people may reasonably debate the merits of a given undertaking.

Quantitative analysis provides certain crude efficiency indicators, which may be narrowly valuable, but as a general management tool and planning device, performance budgeting results in more frustration than satisfaction. By the late 1960s management and policy analysts in this country and abroad were looking toward radically new methods of public sector expenditure budgeting that would bring such concerns to the fore.

BUDGETARY RATIONALISM

The development of program budgeting systems can be traced to the US Department of Defense in the 1950s and 60s. The weaknesses of incremental line-item and performance budgeting prompted a concerted effort to develop a new system that would systematically link monetary inputs to policy and program outputs. The aim was to establish an organizationally holistic and rational form of budgeting that would allow senior administrative and political leaders to comprehend the operations of any organization fully while facilitating comprehensive, rational policy prioritization and planning at the level of both the individual organization and the government overall (Henry 1995, 212–13).

By the mid-1960s program budgeting swept through public administration circles in the Western world as the new, rational way to do public sector expenditure budgeting. Within Canada, **budgetary rationalism** was first embraced by the federal Liberal government of Pierre Trudeau. In 1969 his government introduced the **planning-programming-budgeting system** (PPBS), which was to dominate federal financial management thinking for the better part of a decade (French 1984, 34–37). Since then, governments have struggled to operationalize the system, and several versions have been propagated, implemented, and either discarded or modified.

The history of federal financial management over the past five decades is a story of successive federal governments, both Liberal and Conservative, seeking to demonstrate that their plans for raising and spending public monies were grounded in sound, forward-looking, comprehensive rational thinking where all budgetary decisions are rooted in the systematic rigour of ends–means relationships and hard-headed cost-benefit analysis. In the intellectual contest between budgetary incrementalism and rationalism, it always sounds so much better to claim that you're being "rational" rather than merely "incremental," and that you're basing your actions on systematic planning rather than simply doing next year what you more or less did last year. So, from the late 1960s until the current day, the federal government has operated under a variety of rationalistic financial management systems and sub-systems. Please see the Thinking Government website for a critical overview of the leading approaches that dominated federal budget making over these decades. What you'll find there is a veritable alphabet soup of system acronyms that tell a tale of successive governments tinkering with the rationalist model of financial management, budget making, and budget implementation, always searching for a better, more rational way to do financial management. PPBS was first implemented during the Pierre Trudeau years, augmented with Management by Objectives (MBO) and Operational Performance Measurement Systems (OPMS). Those were followed by the Policy and Expenditure Management System (PEMS) and Zero-Based Budgeting systems (ZBB) of the Mulroney years, the Expenditure Management System (EMS) of the Chrétien years, and the revised Expenditure Management Information System (EMIS) and Managing for Results (MFR) of the Harper government. It is this EMIS process, now once again referred to simply as EMS, that we will focus on here, as it is the most recent iteration in a long string of rational budgeting systems and it is this system that the Justin Trudeau government inherited in 2015. As with all of its antecedents, the current EMS process possesses a significant number of tensions and difficulties common to all rationalistic forms of budgeting and financial management that undercut their claims to rational and systematic decision making. These problems also highlight the continuing importance of incremental decision making and the superior authority of the prime minister in setting governmental priorities and deciding what gets done immediately and with how much money.

THE EXPENDITURE MANAGEMENT SYSTEM, 2015

The Liberal government of Justin Trudeau that came to power in November 2015 inherited the Expenditure Management System designed by the previous Harper Conservative government and first implemented in 2007. This Harper system, however, was a revamped version of the original EMS process that had been inaugurated by the Chrétien Liberal government in 1995. As of 2015 the EMS existed as a comprehensive budgetary and financial management policy and program framework designed to "provide the information necessary to support the development of spending plans, the government's priority-setting process, fiscal and budget decisions, and the translation of those decisions into resource allocations for government programs" (Treasury Board Secretariat

2015). As with its earlier rational planning forebears, EMS was designed to provide a financial management system to cabinet ministers, cabinet committees, central agencies, and senior departmental leaders to structure their decision making respecting

- setting government-wide priorities
- setting departmental priorities
- establishing and maintaining sound programs designed to meet set priorities
- determining appropriate program funding levels to meet priorities
- measuring the ability of departments to achieve set priorities with given funding
- measuring all program spending in relation to the concepts of economy, efficiency, and effectiveness
- identifying lowest-priority and lowest-performing programs within departments so as to eliminate these programs and reallocate financial resources to higher priority programs or to budget reduction efforts
- providing central agency and departmental management with the information necessary to continuously improve the government's capability, efficiency, and effectiveness in all of its policies and programs (Treasury Board Secretariat 2014)

Central to EMS were strategic reviews. All federal organizations—including departments, Crown agencies, and Crown corporations receiving appropriations from parliament, such as the CBC and Canada Post—were required to undertake a strategic review of their direct program spending and the operating costs of their major statutory

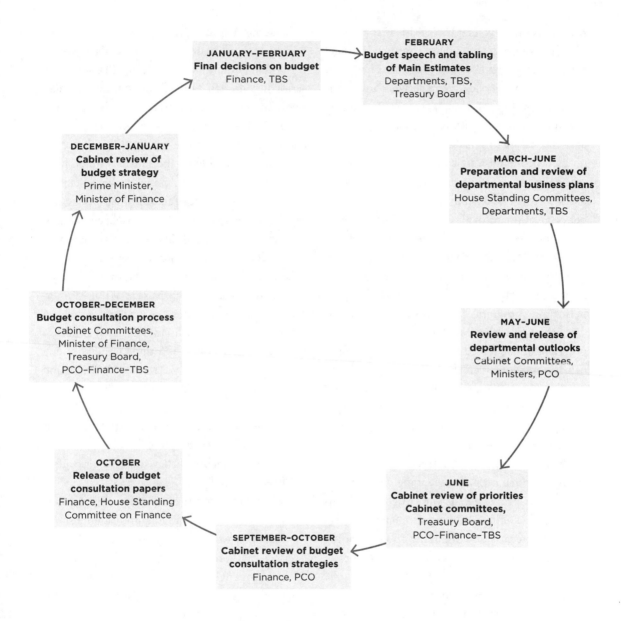

Figure 6.2 **The Expenditure Management System**

programs on a cyclical basis. This meant that a department or agency would routinely conduct such a strategic review of its programs once every four years. These reviews were designed to provide information to senior managers within affected institutions as well as senior officials in central agencies, cabinet ministers, and the prime minister as to how these institutions could enhance efficiency and effectiveness, how they could better focus on core responsibilities, and how they could better meet the priorities of Canadians. Through these reviews, according to the Treasury Board Secretariat, target institutions were "required to identify a total of five per cent of their program spending from their lowest-priority and lowest-performing programs" (TBS 2011, 3). These funds were then to be reallocated to higher priority programs or budget reduction efforts. As part of its deficit elimination plan, in 2011 the Harper government announced a special one-year "strategic and operating review" calling upon all departments and agencies, covering approximately $75 billion in direct program spending, to engage in this review process for that year. Departments were asked to reduce planned program spending by 7 per cent from levels projected forward to 2016–17. This had the effect of flat-lining departmental program spending in 2011 and reducing such spending by about $3 billion from 2009–10 levels (Lester 2012, 3).

As the Liberal government of Justin Trudeau moves forward with its approaches to financial management, it will likely revise and reform this Expenditure Management System to meet its needs. (Changes occurring to this system will be covered on the Thinking Government website.) If the past half-century of federal financial

management systems dating back to that of his father is any indication of future trends, however, it is unlikely that Justin Trudeau will completely scrap the rationalist models of financial management that have dominated the federal public service since the late 1960s. All of these models and methods of financial management, however, share similar problems and tensions inherent in rationalist approaches to money management. It's important to be aware of these limitations, as they highlight why federal financial management, as it is experienced in real life in departments and agencies and Crown corporations, is never as neat and rational as the TBS flowcharts and EMS planning documents suggest. Full coverage of these limitations as experienced over the past five decades of rationalist systems of financial management in the federal government is found on the Thinking Government website. But certain key tensions and challenges can be readily enumerated:

- Can departments easily define and rank their policy priorities in order?
- What if departments have multiple priorities of equal value?
- What if the process of priority ranking results in bitter divisions and infighting amongst managers working within departments? Is such division a sign of healthy debate or a symptom of organizational dysfunction?
- Can and should a government be required to rank its policy priorities?
- Can all policy and program outcomes be measured objectively?
- Can the quality of public policies and program administration be measured quantitatively and, if not, how can policy

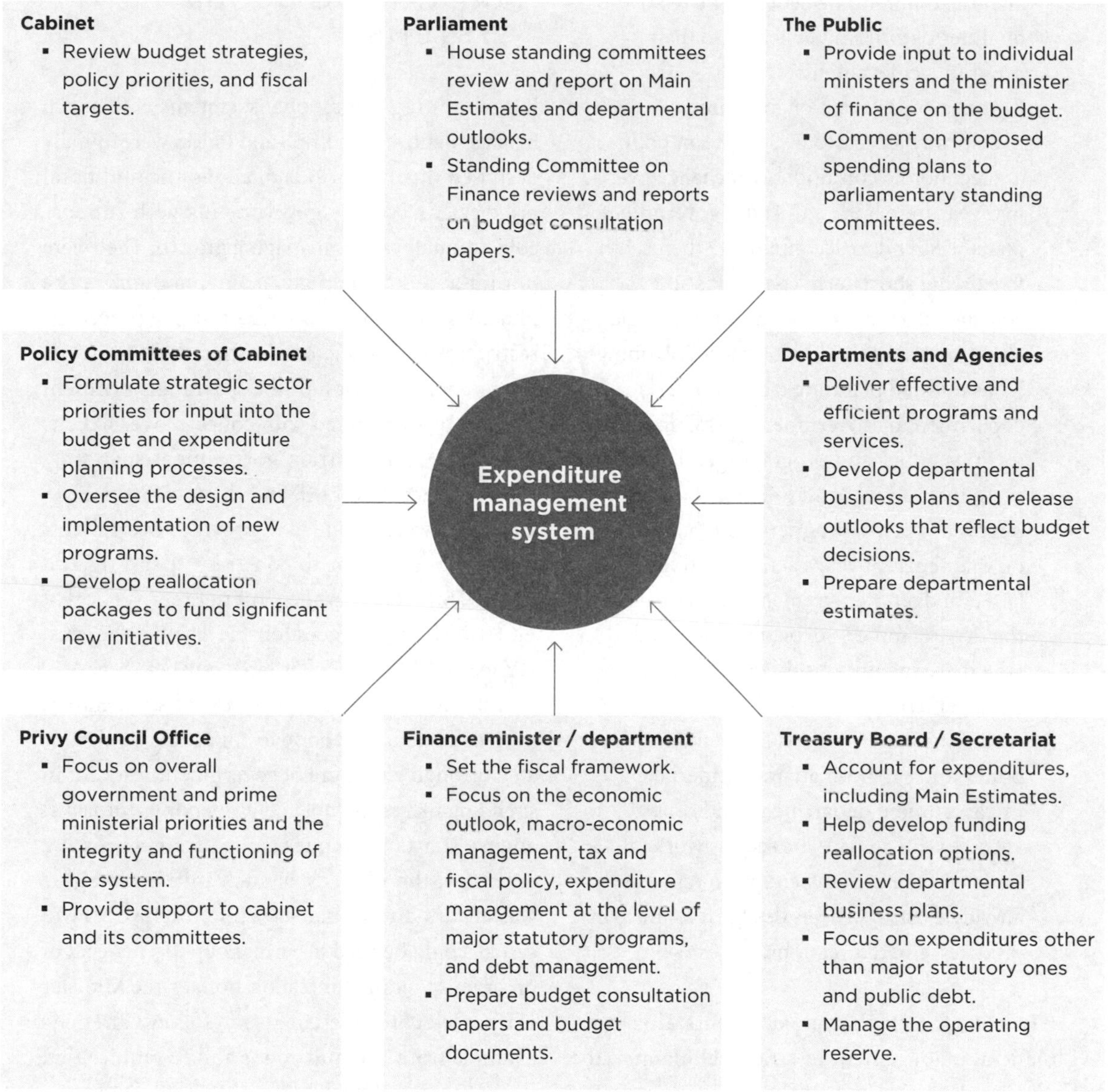

Cabinet

- Review budget strategies, policy priorities, and fiscal targets.

Parliament

- House standing committees review and report on Main Estimates and departmental outlooks.
- Standing Committee on Finance reviews and reports on budget consultation papers.

The Public

- Provide input to individual ministers and the minister of finance on the budget.
- Comment on proposed spending plans to parliamentary standing committees.

Policy Committees of Cabinet

- Formulate strategic sector priorities for input into the budget and expenditure planning processes.
- Oversee the design and implementation of new programs.
- Develop reallocation packages to fund significant new initiatives.

Expenditure management system

Departments and Agencies

- Deliver effective and efficient programs and services.
- Develop departmental business plans and release outlooks that reflect budget decisions.
- Prepare departmental estimates.

Privy Council Office

- Focus on overall government and prime ministerial priorities and the integrity and functioning of the system.
- Provide support to cabinet and its committees.

Finance minister / department

- Set the fiscal framework.
- Focus on the economic outlook, macro-economic management, tax and fiscal policy, expenditure management at the level of major statutory programs, and debt management.
- Prepare budget consultation papers and budget documents.

Treasury Board / Secretariat

- Account for expenditures, including Main Estimates.
- Help develop funding reallocation options.
- Review departmental business plans.
- Focus on expenditures other than major statutory ones and public debt.
- Manage the operating reserve.

Source: Treasury Board of Canada 1995, 10.

Figure 6.3 **Roles in the Expenditure Management System**

analysts differentiate between the relative qualities of differing policies and their program achievements?

- Can any department or government realistically forecast how long-term political and economic conditions will change over a five-year time horizon? And if government plans will tend to accommodate themselves to existing short-term conditions and contingencies, should significant time and attention be devoted to long-term planning?
- Does rational planning truly assist a department or government overall in setting forth its policy and program agenda, or do these institutions tend to simply base their next year's plans, programs, and budgets on their current year's activities? If the latter, budgetary incrementalism remains the driving force in explaining how and why these institutions do their financial management.
- And if this latter point is true, much of the policy and program analysis undertaken in government departments and central agencies can come to be seen as work of limited value, tending simply to reinvent already existing wheels designed to move in predetermined directions.

In fact, for all that governments aim to do financial management in a rational manner, the old, simple, and much maligned incrementalist approach to budget making still has great explanatory value in highlighting how any given federal institution creates its annual budget.

APPRAISING BUDGET SYSTEMS

It is interesting that rationalist systems of financial management such as PPBS and PEMS were initially designed during periods of economic and fiscal prosperity to supply governments with supposedly rational ways of managing growth. They were not intended to help governments manage the difficult and painful tasks of restraining programs, restricting spending, and cutting deficits. Yet as the financial position of the federal government came to be dominated with concern over deficits and the need to restrain government spending, PEMS gave way to EMS and then to EMIS. EMS and EMIS were intended to provide governments with rational means to constrain spending and balance budgets. But the Chrétien-era version of EMS failed, and it is questionable whether the latest version of EMIS/EMS has fared any better.

Although the Harper government stressed that the federal deficits of 2009 to 2014 could be eliminated through a mixture of government restraint in spending increases (not actual spending cutbacks) and greater tax revenues gained from a growing economy, the efficacy of such initiatives alone was always questionable. While the EMIS/EMS system could be used to earmark up to 5 per cent of program spending for reallocation, Prime Minister Harper felt compelled in 2011 to follow Chrétien's example from the mid-1990s and to require that the entire federal public service be subjected to a system of program review tasked with eliminating $30 billion from the total federal budget by 2014 (Savoie 2015, 201). This reinauguration of program review was an explicit acceptance by Prime Minister Harper that the existing EMIS/EMS system of financial management was not up to the tasks of controlling government expenditures or of achieving the budget cuts deemed necessary to balance the budget by the 2015 election. In the spring of 2015 the Harper government released what was to be its last budget, with then-Finance Minister Joe Oliver reporting that the federal budget would have a slim $1.9 billion surplus. After the defeat of the Harper government in October, the new Liberal minister of finance, Bill Morneau delivered a fiscal update in late autumn indicating that the federal budget had slipped back into a deficit position due to weakness in the Canadian economy associated with sluggish growth in the world economy and the decline in the price of oil. The federal budget was predicted to be in a deficit position for years to come, even without planned deficit spending promised by the Liberal Party in the 2015 election as a means to stimulate the Canadian economy and generate new economic growth and needed jobs. In the 2015 election Justin Trudeau had promised a return to a balanced budget by 2019 and the next federal election. Given the difficulties faced by the Canadian economy and the volatility of the global economy, this may be a difficult promise to keep. And whether the EMS system inherited by the Liberal government will be capable of providing the means to achieve a balanced budget through its own processes is an open question. If recent history is any guide, the answer will be no.

It is also instructive that despite some five decades of concerted efforts to develop a viable system of rational financial management, none so far has clearly succeeded. In practice much of the routine development and operation of organizational budgets remains essentially incremental, notwithstanding the formally rationalistic framework within which such decision making is structured. While departments and agencies supposedly use rationalistic methods of budget making, in practice these methods tend to collapse under their own weight. Middle and senior managers have had to muddle through as best they can, using the previous year's budget as a guide and assuming that the A budget is sacrosanct and alterations to it, for better or worse, only incremental.

The persistence of this approach to budget making in the real world of bureaucratic politics, despite its many apparent limitations, gives one pause. Apparently, the importance to bureaucratic decision making of simplicity, comprehensibility, and manageability should not be underestimated. Furthermore, it seems that abstract rationalism cannot cope with the inherently political nature of government budgeting: its competing visions, vested interests, institutional actors, and traditional assumptions about what is just and necessary. These lessons should not be lost on those interested in the theory and practice of government.

BUDGET-MAKING TACTICS

Before leaving this study of financial management systems it is worth briefly considering another analytical perspective on expenditure budget making. So far, this chapter has adopted a macro-analytical perspective. An equally interesting approach is a micro-analytical review of budget-making tactics of bureaucratic actors.

As French (1984) and Hartle (1976), among others, have explicitly argued, public sector budget making can be viewed as a game. In this extended analogy, the players assume various roles as they compete for the big stakes of money, power, position, and prestige within the world of government policies, programs, and bureaucratic interests. American political scientist Aaron Wildavsky (1964, 1992) applied this approach to the American bureaucracy, devoting much attention to the relationships between budgetary actors. The following borrows from his work to give a sense of the game tactics within the senior managerial ranks of government when budget making is underway (Wildavsky 1992, chap. 3).

According to Wildavsky, on one side of the government budget process are the **spenders**: departments and agencies intent on developing and running programs to serve citizen and client needs while enhancing the power and prestige of the enacting institution, its senior management, and its minister. On the other side are the **guardians**: central agencies such as Finance, the TBS, and the PCO, tasked with controlling spending and ensuring that it follows government priorities and achieves its ends efficiently. In the ongoing struggle between the spenders and the guardians, each side employs various tactics to achieve its ends.

SPENDER TACTICS

Inflate the Budget

This tactic is quite universal. Since spenders know that guardians will be scrutinizing their budget in a hunt for "fat," they build in fat in the hope that not all the surplus requests will be trimmed. They also hope that in focusing attention on more obvious fat, they will cause guardians to overlook less obvious funding enhancements. In essence they ask for more than they want in order to get what they believe they need by incorporating something that will satisfy the guardians' imperative to cut the budget.

Spend Now, Save Later

This is an ingenious tactic that is not necessarily a deception. Spenders argue that certain new programs requiring funding support now will eventually improve savings in other fields later. For example, more money in nursing and preventative health care now can reduce the amount spent on physicians' services and hospitalization later; more spent on regional development now may mean less spent on unemployment and welfare later.

Mobilize Interest Groups

If spenders know that a new program will be difficult to fund, they can alert the interest groups that will benefit from it. These groups can lobby for the new program, at once placing pressure on the government to take action and enhancing the profile and perceived political awareness of the spending department. This tactic is extremely common, especially in relation to business groups.

Drive the Thin Edge of the Wedge

This is another classic tactic. When spenders realize that it will be difficult to get a new program funded it may be advantageous to get at least an initial part of it started. Once a program has begun, the department can encourage clients to make use of it and, as public demand grows, can return to the guardians in later years to ask for additional funding to support an established and successful initiative.

Take Advantage of Crisis

It's an ill wind that blows no one good. Spenders know that crises, real or perceived, can become the catalysts for new programs and more money—crisis initiatives. The 9/11 terrorist attacks against the United States resulted in greater funding for the Canadian military and enhanced security at Canadian airports and border checkpoints, for example. Similarly, concern over global climate change presents a funding advantage to any initiative that can be seen as promoting a greener energy future.

Attack Popular Programs

If spenders are confronted with the absolute necessity to cut programs, it may be in their long-term interest to cut one of their most desirable ones. By slashing a popular program, the spending department angers its own clients and then suggests to them that to save the program they need to lobby the government. In confronting cutbacks in Ontario in 1992, for example, the provincial Ministry of the Attorney General announced that the number of Crown attorneys would have to be reduced, resulting in longer delays in criminal proceedings and the likelihood that more cases would be dismissed for excessive delay. Needless to say, this proposal elicited public outrage and demands for more funding for the courts.

Make an End Run

A final tactic, rarely used but brazen when seen, is for the spender to simply ignore the financial management rules of process, promise a new program, and start spending money on it. The department and minister then confront their colleagues with a fait accompli in the hope that public support for the initiative will prevent the guardians, and the cabinet and prime minister, from killing it.

Minister of Indian Affairs and Northern Development Ron Irwin took such action in 1994, when he promised major new funding to improve water and sewage services on northern Manitoba Indian reserves without prior central agency approvals. In making this announcement, he was gambling that he would gain the endorsement of Indigenous communities, generally favourable public opinion and media support, and, most important, prime ministerial backing for what he perceived as a needed and politically desirable social policy action. His suppositions were borne out, and his commitment was accepted as government policy.

Such unilateral actions are very risky, however. The cost of failure can extend from repudiation and public embarrassment to demotion or dismissal from cabinet.

GUARDIAN TACTICS

Set the Rules

Officials in central agencies can seek to thwart department overspending by establishing systemic rules and procedures for all funding requests. The history of rational financial management is a reflection, in part, of senior guardians seeking to establish systems that militate against end runs, crisis initiatives, or cases of special pleading. Indeed, according to a somewhat perverse logic, the slower and more complex the process of budgetary approval the better, as it may wear down the enthusiasm of spenders.

Demand Documentation

Guardians traditionally slow down and even stop spenders by requiring studies and analyses for all their plans. When a spender claims that a program can save money in the long run, a guardian can demand to see the studies and statistics to bear that out. If such documentation is forthcoming, it can be subjected to rigorous analysis and, if guardians are unconvinced, can use its deficiency as a justification for denying the requested funds.

Confer and Investigate

Just as spenders can manipulate groups to advance their interests so, too, can central agencies. When guardians are confronted with policy analysis from influential groups that they do not wish to support, they can seek the contrary opinion from other affected groups and departments. No program will ever have unanimous support, and if central agencies doubt the merits of an initiative, broad consultation is likely to elicit enough opposition to form the basis for a rejection of the proposed policy.

Know Thy Opponent

As central agencies must deal regularly with departments, it is in their interest to recruit analysts who are former departmental employees. In this way, guardians receive intelligence from those who used to be spenders and become closely aware of departmental tactics. Of course this is a two-way street. Departments recruit former central agency officials for the same purposes.

Just Say No

A final tactic available to guardians is simply to reject department requests for additional funding and to confront spenders with budget reductions that they must absorb. This has become an increasingly popular tactic in recent years for guardians, the prime minister, and the minister of finance.

THE AUDIT FUNCTION

All the foregoing macro- and micro-policy analysis has devoted attention to the creation of the expenditure budget. But this is only one part of the budgetary process. An equally important element, and a vitally important component of the accountability process in government, deals with the review of budgetary decision making and program performance once the budget has been established. When an expenditure budget has been approved by cabinet and passed through parliament in the form of the Main Estimates for all departments and agencies, the institutions receive their appropriations for the upcoming year. These monies fund established programs and new initiatives for which the department or agency has received authorization.

Once funds have been allocated and expended, we enter the second and lesser known stage of public sector financial management—the audit function. A number of institutions have significant auditing roles, but the most important are operating departments and agencies, the Office of the Auditor General, and the Public Accounts Committee of parliament.

Auditing is a management process in which expenses incurred are measured and evaluated in light of established criteria. Public sector audits are usually conducted annually for each department and agency and traditionally provide a

THE AUDITOR GENERAL OF CANADA

The auditor general has the following responsibilities:

- auditing the public accounts of all federal departments and most federal Crown corporations and regulatory agencies
- auditing the public accounts of the federal territories of Nunavut, the Northwest Territories, and Yukon
- reporting to parliament on the effectiveness of federal programs
- providing advice to federal departments and agencies about how to improve their efficiency and operational managerial capacity
- providing empirical information about the financial management of policies and programs to enable MPs to hold the government to account
- promoting best practices with respect to the financial management of departments and agencies
- bringing the state of federal government financial management to the attention of the Canadian public
- acting as a watchdog for parliament, and by extension the media and the public, regarding the quality and control of public spending

rather narrow financial accounting of monies spent. They offer

- a detailed listing of expenditures;
- the legal authority for such spending;
- a comparison of incurred and planned expenses; and
- findings of irregularities.

This is known as **attest and compliance auditing**. It is designed to allow any interested party—manager, politician, citizen—to understand the financial position and recent financial history of the given institution, and whether it has conformed to the financial mandate planned for it by government and approved by parliament (Kernaghan and Siegel 1999, 651).

In the past 30 years this traditional approach to auditing has been augmented by additional managerial concerns (Sutherland 1980). As interest in sound management and financial restraint has grown, the audit process has been expanded. On the supposition that all government spending is simply a means to a policy end, public sector audits should measure not only dollars and cents but also whether expenditures are as *economical* as possible, whether they make *efficient* use of government resources, and whether programs *effectively* meet the goals they were established to achieve. With its constant reference to the "three E's" of economy, efficiency, and effectiveness, this is known as **comprehensive auditing**, and it has become the dominant, although controversial, approach to auditing in governments across Canada.

THE DEPARTMENTAL AUDIT PROCESS

As departments and agencies have most of the responsibility for spending money, they also have a primary duty to conduct audits of their financial activities. Departments must keep accurate records of all their financial transactions and collect data on their achievement of departmental objectives. All such information is integral to the management process, not simply in order to exercise financial control over middle managers but to enable them to undertake departmental responsibilities in an optimal fashion.

THE OFFICE OF THE AUDITOR GENERAL

Although departments and agencies play a large part in the audit process, the most important institutional actors in this field are the **auditor general of Canada** and provincial auditors general (Sinclair 1979). Federal and provincial auditors general act as parliamentary watchdogs, carefully scrutinizing all financial activities and providing advice and criticism about their findings. The federal auditor general is an officer of parliament. He or she is nominated by the prime minister but officially appointed by parliament to a fixed term of ten years or until the appointee reaches the age of 65. The auditor general possesses the same quality of tenure as a federal judge, with the extraordinary independence required by someone who must oversee audits of the government itself.

The Office of the Auditor General is responsible for auditing

- most federal institutions, including all departments and agencies;

- 50 Crown corporations;
- the public accounts of Yukon, the Northwest Territories, and Nunavut; and
- government-wide financial policies such as centralized purchasing, communications, and payroll management.

In fulfilling these duties the auditor general issues several reports to parliament each year, usually tabled quarterly, about the quality of financial management for the financial year just past—that is, the previous year's accounts. The reports recommend improvements to financial management practices and list the responses of departments and agencies to these recommendations.

All such documentation becomes important not only to the government but also to the opposition parties and to the national media. Opposition MPs make the reports the subject of parliamentary questions and debate, and the media typically highlight examples of wasteful government spending. But it is always important to read the reports themselves to gain a sense of the broad dynamics of the quality of such management.

Contrary to popular opinion, federal audit reports generally reveal a high calibre of financial management and spending control and oversight. All government programs are subject to close audit scrutiny, and, as a general rule, most spending in any given year meets the requirements of the auditor general. Of course, with federal spending approaching $300 billion, there will always be exceptions, and these do of course elicit criticism from the auditor general. And it is these cases—as illustrated in 2010 by reports of cost overruns in military purchases for helicopters and armoured personnel carriers—that attract media and parliamentary attention.

The Onset of Comprehensive Auditing

In fulfilling their responsibilities, auditors general traditionally undertook only the basic attest and compliance audit; they reported on whether or not the government's financial books were in order and whether all transactions were undertaken with proper authority. By the 1970s, however, the worth of this type of audit was being questioned by public policy and management analysts, who stressed that critical analysis should also become a part of the auditing function. In 1977, under the leadership of federal Auditor General James J. Macdonell, and following a series of damning indictments of federal financial mismanagement, the Office of the Auditor General was given legal authority to engage in comprehensive auditing. This approach is officially defined as

> an examination that provides an objective and constructive assessment of the extent to which financial, human, and physical resources are managed with due regard to economy, efficiency and effectiveness, and, accountability relationships are served.
>
> The comprehensive audit examines both financial and management controls, including information systems and reporting practices, and recommends improvements where appropriate. (Canadian Comprehensive Auditing Foundation 1985, 8)

The Problem of Assessment

As the federal and provincial auditors general have implemented comprehensive auditing, they have become embroiled in operational and political controversies that stem from the nature of the concept itself. First, though measuring economy can be fairly straightforward, the same cannot be said for measuring efficiency or effectiveness. As Kernaghan and Siegel (1999, 651) have said, "Efficiency and effectiveness, like beauty, are frequently in the eye of the beholder."

Federal regional development programs, for example, have routinely been attacked by the more conservative for being wasteful and inefficient and for failing to solve the problems of regional underdevelopment. But such programs have been defended just as strongly by others of all political stripes for a variety of reasons. They may prove themselves effective over the short term in creating jobs and over the long term in generating industrial and commercial activity in economically depressed parts of the country. The results can be needed economic development, industrial diversification, employment opportunity, and greater wealth. Such long-run policy outcomes, in turn, justify spending on the program as an efficient use of resources in the support of broad government objectives. Evaluation thus becomes contingent on time. Does one measure efficiency and effectiveness over a year? Or five? Or ten years or more? Conclusions can be diametrically opposed over time.

In the 1880s Sir John A. Macdonald was viciously attacked for building the Canadian Pacific Railway at great public expense, almost bankrupting the young country. At the time, many viewed the prime minister's National Dream as an act of stupidity, proof of his poor leadership and wanton disregard for financial prudence. Ten years after his death in 1891, the railway had become instrumental in binding the country across the continent and was an integral part of Canada's growing economy. Since then its construction has been recognized as one of the greatest examples of political leadership in Canadian history.

Also, the effectiveness issue raises the old problem of program objectives. What is the objective of increasing spending on employment equity policy and the Canadian Human Rights Commission? Is it to enhance human rights in general? Or the rights of groups previously discriminated against? Does it promote certain jobs and a certain federal institution? Or perhaps a symbolic "feel good" sense among Canadians? Does it make the government look good leading up to an election? Analysts and auditors could approach this issue from any one of these perspectives and interpret program effectiveness and desirability accordingly. Whose opinion should then prevail? That of an unelected senior bureaucrat or that of the elected government?

The Problem of Confidentiality

A second problem arises from these operational difficulties. The Office of the Auditor General has tended to find itself in political disputes with governments over its role in evaluating programs, especially in past decades and often over the integrity of regional development programs. That said, the single greatest controversy erupted in relation to a Pierre Trudeau government decision to allow Petro-Canada to purchase Petrofina in the early 1980s with public funds of $1.7 billion. The federal government maintained that this undertaking was a sound investment, necessary to strengthen Petro-Canada and secure Canadian influence in the petroleum industry.

But the Office of the Auditor General questioned whether due regard for economy and efficiency had been followed by the government and Petro-Canada in this initiative. The auditor general requested access to all documents pertaining to the sale, only to be told that the core planning and operational papers were cabinet documents protected by the rule of cabinet confidentiality.

As this dispute dragged on, the Mulroney government came to power. Despite their loathing of the old Trudeau government, the new leaders refused to hand over the documents on the grounds that cabinet decisions on matters of national policy should be free from scrutiny by the auditor general. The auditor general, in turn, brought a legal challenge to the government, claiming that he had the legal right to review all relevant documentation pertaining to any investigation by his office. The government still contested this claim, and the case eventually proceeded to the Supreme Court of Canada.

In 1988 the court ruled in favour of the government, asserting that the auditor general had no legal right to scrutinize confidential cabinet documents. The court held that the appropriate course of action in such cases is for the auditor general to mention the denial of access in the annual report and to let parliament decide the appropriate response. The government was quite satisfied with this decision, but the Office of the Auditor General viewed it as a serious setback to its ability to carry out audits of significant undertakings (Canada, Auditor General 1989, 23–27).

This case was very important in drawing to public attention the controversies that comprehensive auditing can generate between governments and the auditors general. By seeking to evaluate the three E's, auditors general can move into direct conflict with the government of the day.

Such conflicts pose a dilemma: what body should ultimately assess the economy, efficiency, and effectiveness of governments? The government itself? The auditor general? Or parliament? All three institutions have important roles in the auditing process, and an appropriate balance must be struck between them. That is easier said than done.

THE PUBLIC ACCOUNTS COMMITTEE

The work of the **Public Accounts Committee** (PAC) closes the financial management accountability loop. A permanent committee of the House of Commons, the PAC reviews and analyzes the annual reports of the auditor general and recommends reforms to the government. The PAC is unique among parliamentary committees in that, by tradition, it is chaired by a member of the Official Opposition, ensuring that its agenda is not under the control of the governing party. The committee's actual independence is limited, however, because as with any parliamentary committee, membership is based on party standing in the House of Commons. Under a majority government, the committee will therefore be dominated by members of the governing party. When party discipline is factored into the mix, it is clear that the PAC is far from an independent watchdog. That is its greatest disability, but it nevertheless has a significant role (Kernaghan and Siegel 1999, 656).

As an official conduit through which the auditor general's report must pass, the PAC provides the Office of the Auditor General with a platform from which to publicize its findings and provoke discussion. Likewise, the committee's proceedings and its report to parliament give the chair and opposition members an opportunity to scrutinize and criticize government financial management, often calling senior managers to appear before it to answer questions about their operational undertakings. Such events garner media attention if a story is considered juicy enough, and prolonged coverage of the auditor general's report and related PAC hearings can cause great discomfiture for those deemed responsible for administrative problems.

The Human Resources Development Canada transitional jobs funding and accounting scandal of 2000 proves the point (Geddes 2000). The department was severely criticized by the auditor general, the media, and the opposition parties for devoting hundreds of millions of dollars to job-training initiatives but limited supervision and accounting for the money spent. Jane Stewart, the minister responsible, and her senior department staff had to endure scathing criticism and ridicule, and, as the minister repeatedly proclaimed to the PAC, the House of Commons, and the media, her department would never again allow such sloppy managerial and auditing practices.

The eventual report of the PAC to parliament stands as an official appraisal of government management, to be referred to later in debate and election campaigning. Thus, even though the governing party knows that with a majority it can control the decisions of the PAC, it must treat the process with care. And senior officials need to demonstrate respect as well. No one wants to be castigated by the PAC as incompetent or uncooperative.

Once the final report of the PAC is tabled in parliament, the accountability loop is closed, and parliament is at liberty to do with the report and its recommendations as it pleases. The ability of parliament to effectively oversee government spending, however, has long been questioned by outside observers such as Free and Radcliffe (2009) and even by some distinguished insiders such as the Parliamentary Budget Office and former Senators Lowell Murray and Tommy Banks (May 2015). With a majority government, any prime minister knows that the House of Commons will eventually approve any and all of his or her budget policies and related audits. And given the sheer size and scope of federal budgetary documents, inclusive of omnibus budget bills during the Harper years running to the hundreds of pages, parliamentary insiders have warned that MPs are increasingly unwilling and incapable of scrutinizing all these documents in depth and reviewing their related audits. Former Senators Murray and Banks complained that the nearly 400-page 2007 omnibus budget bill eliminated parliament's ability to maintain ongoing scrutiny over the federal government's borrowing and the funding of the national debt. These commentators also suggested that the steady decline in parliament's ability to

COPING WITH DEFICITS, AGAIN

After 12 years of surpluses the federal government slipped back into deficits in 2009 due to the worldwide recession beginning in 2008. Between 2009 and 2011 the Harper government pumped some $60 billion into the economy through stimulus projects associated with their Economic Action Plan. This deficit spending was supported by all the parties then in opposition. After 2011, the Conservatives slowly laboured to pull the government out of deficit through government downsizing and spending cuts. In the lead-up to the 2015 federal election the Harper government announced that it was back in surplus by some $3 billion. On a budget of almost $300 billion this was a thin margin.

In the 2015 election the Liberal Party promised to stimulate the economy and promote necessary infrastructure development (all designed to promote job growth) by agreeing to use deficits of no more than $10 billion a year for three years. This would mean that the Liberals would balance the budget by 2019, just in time for the next election. This campaign promise helped make Justin Trudeau prime minister, but it was also a promise that quickly became awkward. Soon after taking power, the new Minister of Finance, Bill Morneau,

announced that the federal books were in worse shape than expected due to the sluggish world economy: the federal government was now looking at a deficit of $3 billion in 2015, rising to $3.9 billion in 2016. And this did not include any new stimulus spending by the Liberal government.

The Trudeau government's first budget was delivered on March 22, 2016, and it blew past Liberal projections out of the water. Given Liberal commitments to promote stimulus spending to aid the economy, including $120 billion over 10 years on national infrastructure projects as well as revamping child and family tax benefits while also spending an additional $8.4 billion on Indigenous peoples, the federal deficit for 2016/17 soared to $29.4 billion, with a projected deficit of another $29 billion for 2017/18. As of 2016, the government still aims for a balanced budget in 2019, just in time for the next election. A growing national economy should ease the government's path to this objective, and the government's debt-to-GDP ratio is expected to remain mostly flat at around 32 per cent (CBC 2016).

Check the Thinking Government website for periodic updates on current federal government financial management issues and national budgets.

WHITE PAPER

maintain effective oversight of the public purse could be traced to 1968 and the introduction of the "deeming rule," whereby federal Estimates sent to various parliamentary committees for detailed study would be "deemed" to have been approved and adopted by set timelines whether they had been reviewed or not. Parliamentary control over federal spending, while enormous in theory, is highly questionable in practice.

AUDITING THE AUDIT SYSTEM

The auditing process leaves many people feeling uneasy. Effective auditing is an essential requirement of any financial management system, yet the manner in which it works holds many problems. The whole concept of comprehensive auditing is problematic, as auditors general become enmeshed in controversial and political issues of evaluation and interpretation. The Office of the Auditor General nevertheless has wide and independent power to audit the financial activities of the government and to assess the degree to which government spending upholds the principles of economy, efficiency, and effectiveness.

But the auditor general has only the power to review and to report to parliament, not the executive authority to order that reforms be made. Only the government can reform itself, and it is formally answerable only to parliament. And the impact of the auditor general's reporting to parliament via the PAC is diminished because this body, and the broader institution of parliament itself, is politicized, subject to the influence of party discipline and, most of the time, to the political realities of a majority government.

It is a common complaint that the audit process constitutes much sound and fury, signifying very little: reports by auditors general are duly presented to parliament and just as duly talked about and then shelved, to collect dust. This attitude, however, fails to appreciate the real significance of the auditing process and the institutions of the Office of the Auditor General and the PAC. Because they exist and all governments must submit themselves to the auditing process, their political and administrative leaders must necessarily devote attention to financial management. Governments must be concerned with the economy, efficiency, and effectiveness of their operations because these will be the focus of auditing attention.

An auditor general's greatest power is publicity. No government wants to be the subject of intense and critical opposition and media scrutiny over its ability to manage public finances. And most of the time, as auditors general report, most government financial activities therefore uphold the principle of accountability. Notwithstanding the difficulties of conducting comprehensive audits, the most important fact is that they are done.

In the enduring interplay between spenders and guardians, no one dominates all the time (though the prime minister and minister of finance always lead the game). The power of these respective forces ebbs and flows with changing economic conditions, interest group pressure and media interest, the quality of ministerial and bureaucratic leadership, and the prevailing political climate. Micro-level budgetary tactics and activities also affect the long-term development and success of macro-level financial management planning.

The ideas and practices of incrementalism and rationalism in macro-level federal budgetary politics have had a tense coexistence over the past 50 years. Incrementalist approaches have long been dismissed by the Department of Finance and the TBS as outmoded and undesirable. Since the late 1960s Ottawa has been firmly in the rationalist camp. Budgets are to be developed within frameworks of systematic planning, policy and program prioritization, cost–benefit analysis, program development based upon multiyear planning, and program and policy evaluation against set policy standards. Every federal government, from Pierre Trudeau's to Harper's to Justin Trudeau's, would stress that its system of budgeting was based on the most rational approach. And no government over this period would admit that it based financial management decisions on incremental adjustments to the previous year's budget. Yet it is hard to see a clear and consistent rationalism flowing through their financial practices.

During the Trudeau and Mulroney years, PPBS and PEMS failed to stop ballooning deficits and debt. Between 1970 and 1997 the federal government ran a deficit budget every single year. In 1970 the national debt stood at $20.2 billion; by 1997 it totalled $562.8 billion. And through these years the federal government was officially practising rational financial management. But if that failed to stop deficits, incrementalism offered nothing better. Rather, one can see a long steady incrementalist slide into the deficit and debt problem of the mid-1990s. By 1994 the Chrétien government was fast confronting a deficit crisis that required extraordinary measures to bring the country back to fiscal stability. EMS and program review preached a rationalistic method of budget control to do so, but in reality program review was an incrementalist exercise in command-and-control budget cutting from the centre of the government: the prime minister and his finance minister, along with the Department of Finance.

Under Harper's Conservative government, EMS gave way to EMIS, the latest rational system, now known as EMS once again. But even with this new system, the Harper government had to resort to an incrementalist form of program review from 2011 to 2014, seeking to eliminate the deficit that had piled up following the recession of 2008–09. Whether the government of Justin Trudeau can promote budget making with greater rationalism than its predecessors remains an open question. If the overview of budget setting provided in this chapter has taught anything, the key lesson should be this: never underestimate the practical influence of incrementalism, and never overestimate the capabilities of rationalism. In the reality of managing complex organizations and mediating conflicting interests, incrementalist decisions often become cloaked in rationalist systems.

REFERENCES AND SUGGESTED READING

Adie, Robert F., and Paul G. Thomas. 1987. *Canadian Public Administration: Problematical Perspectives.* 2nd ed. Scarborough, ON: Prentice Hall Canada.

Armit, Armelita, and Jacques Bourgault, eds. 1996. *Hard Choices or No Choices: Assessing Program Review.* Toronto: Institute of Public Administration of Canada.

Bakvis, Herman, and David MacDonald. 1993. "The Canadian Cabinet: Organization, Decision-Rules, and Policy Impact." In *Governing Canada: Institutions and Public Policy*, edited by Michael M. Atkinson, 47–80. Toronto: Harcourt Brace.

Brown-John, C. Lloyd, André LeBlond, and D. Brian Marson. 1988. *Public Financial Management: A Canadian Text.* Scarborough, ON: Nelson.

Canada, Auditor General. 1989. *Report of the Auditor General of Canada to the House of Commons, Fiscal Year Ended 31 March 1989.* Ottawa: Supply and Services.

Canada, Department of Finance. 2011. *Canada's Economic Action Plan: A Seventh Report to Canadians.* January 31. www.fin.gc.ca/pub/report-rapport/2011-7/index-eng.asp.

———. 2015. *Fiscal Reference Tables.* Ottawa: Department of Finance.

Canadian Comprehensive Auditing Foundation. 1985. *Comprehensive Auditing in Canada: The Provincial Legislative Audit Perspective.* Ottawa: CCAF.

Carmichael, Edward A. 1988. "The Mulroney Government and the Deficit." In *Canada under Mulroney: An End of Term Report*, edited by Andrew B. Gollner and Daniel Salée, 221–45. Montreal: Véhicule Press.

CBC. 2016. "Federal Budget 2016: Highlights of Bill Morneau's First Budget." www.cbc.ca/news/politics/federal-budget-2016-highlights-1.3501803.

Doern, G. Bruce, Allan M. Maslove, and Michael J. Prince. 1988. *Public Budgeting in Canada.* Ottawa: Carleton University Press.

Dunn, Christopher. 2010. *The Handbook of Canadian Public Administration.* 2nd ed. Toronto: Oxford University Press.

Free, Clinton, and Vaughan Radcliffe. 2009. "Accountability in Crisis: The Sponsorship Scandal and the Office of the Comptroller General in Canada." *Journal of Business Ethics* 84: 189–208.

French, Richard D. 1984. *How Ottawa Decides: Planning and Industrial Policy Making 1968–1984.* 2nd ed. Toronto: James Lorimer.

Geddes, John. 2000. "Saving Ms. Stewart." *Maclean's*, 14 February, 17–21.

Hartle, Douglas G. 1976. *A Theory of the Expenditure Budgetary Process.* Toronto: University of Toronto Press.

Henry, Nicholas. 1995. *Public Administration and Public Affairs.* 6th ed. Englewood Cliffs, NJ: Prentice Hall.

Inwood, Gregory J. 2012. *Understanding Canadian Public Administration: An Introduction to Theory and Practice*. 4th ed. Toronto: Pearson Canada.

Kernaghan, Kenneth, and David Siegel. 1999. *Public Administration in Canada: A Text*. 4th ed. Toronto: Nelson.

Lester, John. 2012. *Managing Tax Expenditures and Government Program Spending; Proposals for Reform*. SPP Research Papers, vol. 5, issue 35, December 2012. Calgary: University of Calgary School of Public Policy.

Maslove, Allen M., and Kevin Moore. 1998. "From Red Books to Blue Books: Repairing Ottawa's Fiscal House." In *How Ottawa Spends 1997–1998: Seeing Red: A Liberal Report Card*, edited by Gene Swimmer, 23–50. Ottawa: Carleton University Press.

May, Katherine. 2015. "Parliament Lost Control of Borrowing in Omnibus Budget Bill." *Ottawa Citizen*, March 16, 1.

McQuaig, Linda. 1995. *Shooting the Hippo: Death by Deficit and Other Canadian Myths*. Toronto: Penguin Books.

Pacquet, Gilles, and Robert Sheppard. 1996. "The Program Review Process: A Deconstruction." In *How Ottawa Spends 1996–1997: Life under the Knife*, edited by Gene Swimmer, 39–72. Ottawa: Carleton University Press.

Savoie, Donald J. 1999. *Governing from the Centre: The Concentration of Power in Canadian Politics*. Toronto: University of Toronto Press.

———. 2015. *What Is Government Good at? A Canadian Answer*. Montreal: McGill-Queen's University Press.

Sinclair, Sonya. 1979. *Cordial but Not Cosy*. Toronto: McClelland and Stewart.

Strick, John C. 1999. *The Public Sector in Canada: Programs, Finance and Policy*. Toronto: Thompson Educational.

Sutherland, Sharon. 1980. "On the Audit Trail of the Auditor General: Parliament's Servant, 1973–1980." *Canadian Public Administration* 23: 616–44.

———. 1986. "The Politics of Audit: The Federal Office of the Auditor General in Comparative Perspective." *Canadian Public Administration* 29: 118–48.

Treasury Board of Canada Secretariat. 1969. *Planning, Programming, Budgeting Guide*. Ottawa: Queen's Printer.

———. 1995. *The Expenditure Management System of the Government of Canada*. Ottawa: Supply and Services.

———. 2000. *Managing for Results*. Ottawa: Supply and Services.

———. 2006. *The Expenditure Management Information System*. Ottawa: Supply and Services.

———. 2010a. *Frequently Asked Questions: What Is the Expenditure Management System?* May 3. www.tbs-sct.gc.ca/sr-es/faq-eng.asp.

———. 2010b. *The Reporting Cycle for Government Expenditures.* www.tbs-sct.gc.ca/hgw-cgf/finances/pgs-pdg/em-gd/rc-cr-eng.asp.

———. 2011. *What Is the Expenditure Management System?* www.tbs-sct.gc.ca/sr-es/faq-eng.asp.

———. 2014. *Management Accountability Framework.* www.tbs-sct.gc.ca/maf-crg/index-e.asp.

———. 2015. *Expenditure Management System.* www.tbs-sct.gc.ca/hgw-cgf/finances/pgs-pdg/em-gd/index-eng.asp.

Westmacott, Martin W., and Hugh P. Mellon, eds. 1999. *Public Administration and Policy: Governing in Challenging Times.* Scarborough, ON: Prentice Hall Allyn and Bacon.

Wildavsky, Aaron. 1964. *The Politics of the Budgetary Process.* Boston: Little, Brown.

———. 1992. *The New Politics of the Budgetary Process.* 2nd ed. New York: Harper Collins.

RELATED WEBSITES

Department of Finance Canada. www.fin.gc.ca

Office of the Auditor General of Canada. www.oag-bvg.gc.ca

Treasury Board of Canada Secretariat. www.tbs-sct.gc.ca

CHAPTER 7

Human Resources Management

Let each man pass his days in that wherein

his skill is greatest.

–Sextus Propertius, c. 10 BCE

THE PLATFORM

After reading this chapter and its related web pages you will be able to

- trace the history of the merit principle in the federal government;
- debate the pros and cons of partisan appointments to the public service;
- describe the role of the Public Service Commission;
- highlight the ever-lasting interest in public service reform and renewal;
- identify the goals of the Public Service Modernization Act;
- highlight the goals of Blueprint 2020;
- assess whether the federal public service reflects Canadian societal diversity; and
- debate the merits of public service unionization and collective bargaining.

7 Human Resources Management

Canadian governments employ hundreds of thousands of workers to provide myriad public services. CF-18 pilots, national park wardens, nurses and teachers, fire fighters and customs guards, policy analysts, economists, scientists, secretaries, regulatory inspectors, diplomats, historians, social workers, lawyers, and managers—the list goes on and on. Just as no part of life is unaffected by the state, so, too, the servants of the state—public servants—are all around us. This chapter explores the nature of public sector human resources management: the size of government, employment shifts, the **representativeness of the public service**, and public sector pay levels. We examine the concept and problems of patronage, the development of the merit principle, and its enactment at the federal level through the work of the **Public Service Commission of Canada**. And we assess contemporary federal personnel initiatives to revitalize the public service following years of downsizing and budget cutbacks.

As we move deeper into a new century, the issue of public service recruitment is fast becoming one of the most important topics within federal and provincial governments. Years of cutbacks have left governments understaffed, and now, with projected budgetary deficits and renewed demands for improved services, they are coming to realize that initiatives to enhance policy and program capacity will require them to rebuild their human resources.

PUBLIC SECTOR EMPLOYMENT STATISTICS

The federal government is the single largest employer in Canada. The public sector, as defined by Statistics Canada, is divided into two components: governments and government business enterprises.

1 The government component comprises the three levels of government—federal, provincial, and municipal—and all their departments, agencies, boards, and commissions. Also included are health and social service institutions: hospitals, public school systems, postsecondary educational institutions, cultural facilities, and federal and provincial regulatory agencies.

2 The government business enterprise component consists of public enterprises— Crown corporations—controlled by governments and engaged in the provision and sale of commercial goods and services. Such bodies include, for example, the CBC, Canada Post, the National Film Board, Hydro-Québec, and SaskEnergy.

THE SIZE OF THE PUBLIC SERVICE

As Table 7.1 shows, as of 2015, total public sector employment within Canada accounted for roughly 3.6 million people—almost 10 per cent of the total population. This figure includes everyone working within the public sector at the federal, provincial, and municipal level and everyone working in government departments and agencies; the foreign service; the military, coast guard, and police services; health and social service institutions; the publicly funded educational sector; and federal and provincial Crown corporations. The figures reveal the substantial presence of the public sector in this country and the importance of governments both as providers of public services and as employers offering an enormous range of job opportunities here and abroad. Table 7.1 also shows the slow but steady growth in public sector employment from 2005 to 2015. Despite the existence of tough economic times over the past decade and even the election of federal and provincial governments committed to reducing the role of the state in society, public sectors have continued to expand in this country, testament both to the importance of the function of public services in this society and to the difficulties of cutting public service jobs and corresponding programs and services once people and businesses get used to them.

There are many ways, however, to count the size of public services in terms of persons employed. Table 7.1 offers the grand overview of everyone employed in some form of public duty and receiving a pay cheque ultimately deriving from Canadian taxpayers. Table 7.2 offers a

TABLE 7.1

Canadian Total Public Sector Employment, 2005–15 (in 000s)

2015	3,629.3
2014	3,545.7
2013	3,545.5
2012	3,503.7
2011	3,473.1
2010	3,426.9
2009	3,561.0
2008	3,493.5
2007	3,383.8
2006	3,310.5
2005	3,240.9

Notes: Employment data are not in full-time equivalent and do not distinguish between full- and part-time employees. Includes employment both in and outside of Canada.

Source: Data from Statistics Canada 2005–15.

TABLE 7.2

Core Public Administration Employment by Level of Government, 2010–14 (in 000s)

	2010	2011	2012	2013	2014
All public administration	1,043.3	1,052.4	1,041.6	1,036.3	1,039.8
Federal administration*	295.6	300.7	287.8	276.5	275.2
Provincial and territorial administration	279.4	281.9	283.7	284.9	285.7
Local government administration	423.6	424.9	421.8	423.5	426.0

*Excluding the military

Source: Statistics Canada, CANSIM Tables 281-0024, 281-0027, 2015.

narrower focus on those public servants employed by federal, provincial and territorial, and local governments in more traditional forms of public administration, typically employed in traditional governmental departments, agencies, and offices. Note that this "core" public service is some 2.5 million persons smaller than the total public sector number found in Table 7.1. Omitted from Table 7.2 are all those persons employed nationwide by Crown corporations, hospitals and health boards, school boards, postsecondary educational institutions, social service agencies, police forces, and the military. Even without these people, the "core" public service nationwide is still huge, numbering more than 1 million Canadians. Of these, as of 2014, federal public servants make up the smallest cohort at 275,200 employees, compared to the 285,700 persons employed by provincial and territorial governments. And, not surprisingly given their vast number, the largest number of public servants working in this country are employed by local governments, with a total employment figure of 426,000.

Table 7.3 shows some intriguing dynamics in the federal public service. The Treasury Board of Canada Secretariat (TBS) put the total public service in March 2014 at 181,356, but their way of calculating is different from that of Statistics Canada; it omits members of the military, RCMP officers, and members of some special agencies. The TBS figures capture the segment of public service employees traditionally understood as bureaucrats, working for departments, agencies, boards, and commissions.

As Table 7.3 indicates, total employment in the federal public service declined over the 1990s, falling from a high of 224,640 in 1994 to 141,253

TABLE 7.3

Federal Public Service Employees, 1993–2014

Year	Employees
2014	181,356
2013	188,342
2012	198,793
2011	202,631
2010	202,386
2009	195,667
2008	186,754
2007	179,540
2006	176,630
2005	165,856
2004	165,976
2003	163,314
2002	157,510
2001	149,339
2000	141,253
1999	178,340
1998	179,831
1997	186,378
1996	201,009
1995	217,784
1994	224,640
1993	221,114

Note: Revenue Canada became a separate employer, the Canada Customs and Revenue Agency, on November 1, 1999, causing a significant drop.

Source: Data from Treasury Board of Canada Secretariat, Annual Reports on Employment Equity in the Public Service of Canada, 2009–14.

in 2000. The year 1995 was pivotal: that year the program review exercise of the Chrétien Liberal government announced a planned reduction of the federal public service by 45,000 full-time positions. In reality, between 1995 and 1999 a total of 39,444 seasonal and indeterminate positions (those with no contractually specified length of employment, i.e., full-time permanent jobs) were eliminated, an 18.1 per cent decrease in such positions, though some 3,000 term and casual positions were added over the same period.

In 1999 Revenue Canada was replaced by the Canada Customs and Revenue Agency (CCRA), which was not defined as a regular department or agency for the purposes of federal employment statistics. The roughly 37,000 employees of the old Revenue Canada who found themselves employed by the CCRA were no longer officially employed by the TBS, meaning that they were no longer contained in board statistics, thus allowing the government to record a seemingly large drop in the official size of the federal public service in 1999. This drop was more apparent than real. CCRA employees were still government employees in the broader sense: they remained public servants working within a very important arm of the federal government, and their salaries were still funded from general tax revenues. (In 2003, in a context of concern for heightened border security in the aftermath of 9/11 terrorist attacks, the CCRA was modified once again. It was split into the Canada Revenue Agency and the Canada Border Services Agency.)

It is also noteworthy that in 2001, employment in the public service actually increased compared to the previous year, a development not witnessed since 1994. Between 2001 and 2006, covering the last year of the Liberal government of Paul Martin, employment in the federal public service increased by 27,291, or 18.2 per cent. This upswing indicates both that the federal government possessed a balanced budget and that senior management recognized that the service was in need of reinvestment in terms of both funding and staffing. A Conservative government led by Stephen Harper was elected in 2006 and, notwithstanding its ideological rhetoric respecting the need to curtail the role and size of the state in Canada, over the first five years of Harper's rule the number of persons employed in the federal public service went up, not down. Prime Minister Harper inherited a public service numbering just over 176,000 employees, but by 2011 it had grown to 202,631. While it is true that during the first five years of his government he governed with a minority parliament, meaning that he was constrained in his ability to make deep cuts to the public service, it's also true that it is bureaucratically easier and generally more politically appealing to be seen to be increasing public services and new programs than to be cutting those services and their corresponding jobs. Only after Harper had won his first and only majority government in 2011 did this prime minister begin to trim the size of the federal public service through his own version of program review. Between 2011 and 2014, total employment in the federal government fell by 21,275, or 10.5 per cent. But the roughly 181,000 persons working for the federal public service in 2014, the last full year of the Harper government, was still more than the 176,000 employees he had started with in 2006. This is a fact that sympathetic commentators such as John Ibbitson (2015, 257–64) have used to argue that Stephen Harper was never really as conservative as many of his critics would have us believe.

TABLE 7.4

Federal Public Service by Occupational Category and Age, 2013–14

	EXECUTIVE	SCIENTIFIC AND PROFESSIONAL	ADMINISTRATIVE AND FOREIGN SERVICE	TECHNICAL SERVICES	ADMINISTRATIVE SUPPORT	OPERATIONAL	ALL CATEGORIES
16–19	0	0	1	10	7	7	25
20–24	0	128	566	165	325	406	1,590
25–29	0	1,974	4,987	615	1,528	2,234	11,340
30–34	38	3,974	9,806	1,068	2,222	3,762	20,875
35–39	338	5,300	12,791	1,364	2,361	4,172	26,338
40–44	880	5,310	12,913	1,444	2,404	4,066	27,032
45–49	1,253	4,811	13,650	1,957	2,928	4,315	28,931
50–54	1,448	4,702	15,029	2,934	3,710	4,865	32,710
55–59	936	3,350	8,796	2,070	2,692	3,364	21,154
60–64	317	1,610	3,306	768	1,265	1,364	8,633
65–69	39	555	742	220	363	345	2,264
70+	3	140	123	41	86	71	464
Total	5,252	31,854	82,710	12,656	19,891	28,971	181,356

Source: Data from Treasury Board of Canada Secretariat 2014a, Table 10. Note that there were 85 positions that could not be categorized.

OCCUPATIONAL CATEGORIES AND REPRESENTATIVENESS

As Table 7.4 highlights, the federal public service in 2009 was composed of six occupational categories: executive, scientific and professional, administrative and foreign service, technical services, administrative support, and operational. The executive category had the smallest population, with a total of 5,252, while the largest category was that of administrative and foreign service at 82,710.

It is interesting to note in Table 7.5 the gender and age variations both between and within all six categories. Over the past two decades the federal government has taken concerted efforts to promote gender equity in the public service of Canada, and we can now see this laudable goal coming to fruition. Although women came to account for more than half of all federal public servants by 1998 thanks to their own professional credentials, talent, and the assistance of employment equity programs, most of these jobs were overwhelmingly concentrated in rather traditionally female-dominated occupational categories associated with administrative support, secretarial, and clerical work. Even as of 2014, 78.7 per cent of all federal public servants classified as administrative

TABLE 7.5

Federal Public Service Employees by Occupation, Group, and Age, 2014 (%)

OCCUPATION	AGE	WOMEN	INDIGENOUS PEOPLE	PEOPLE WITH DISABILITIES	PEOPLE BELONGING TO A VISIBLE MINORITY
Executive	25–29	0.0	0.0	0.0	0.0
	30–34	42.1	4.7	2.4	10.4
	40–44	48.6	4.0	2.6	11.6
	45–49	49.5	4.9	5.3	9.1
	50–54	47.5	3.2	6.0	6.4
	55–59	43.9	2.4	8.0	7.6
	60–64	33.8	3.2	5.7	6.6
	65–69	23.1	0.0	0.0	0.0
	70+	0.0	0.0	0.0	0.0
Total		46.1	3.7	5.4	8.5
Scientific and Professional	20–24	58.6	0.0	0.0	18.8
	25–29	60.1	3.1	2.0	20.2
	30–34	55.9	2.8	2.8	18.4
	40–44	56.4	2.9	3.5	16.8
	45–49	55.7	2.9	3.5	16.8
	50–54	46.8	3.0	5.7	16.1
	55–59	43.1	2.8	6.7	14.4
	60–64	38.4	3.4	7.1	14.0
	65–69	27.9	2.9	7.6	20.4
	70+	24.3	0.0	0.0	24.3
Total		51.3	3.1	4.5	17.2
Administrative and Foreign Service	16–19	0.0	0.0	0.0	0.0
	20–24	65.2	3.7	2.7	18.6
	25–29	63.3	4.1	1.9	19.4
	30–34	60.9	4.7	3.1	17.8
	35–39	61.2	5.2	4.0	17.2
	40–44	62.1	6.1	5.6	15.6
	45–49	64.0	6.4	6.9	13.4
	50–54	65.9	5.3	8.4	9.4
	55–59	63.4	4.9	9.8	9.4
	60–64	60.3	4.9	10.9	11.4
	65–69	56.1	4.9	11.7	16.0
	70+	41.5	0.0	0.0	0.0
Total		62.9	5.4	6.2	14.1

OCCUPATION	AGE	WOMEN	INDIGENOUS PEOPLE	PEOPLE WITH DISABILITIES	PEOPLE BELONGING TO A VISIBLE MINORITY
Technical Services	16–19	20.0	0.0	0.0	0.0
	20–24	29.1	0.0	0.0	0.0
	25–29	35.6	3.6	0.0	9.8
	30–34	36.2	4.9	3.2	8.1
	35–39	36.7	4.0	2.9	9.8
	40–44	31.9	6.3	3.7	7.9
	45–49	25.4	4.2	3.9	8.0
	50–54	19.4	3.6	6.1	5.4
	55–59	16.9	4.1	6.9	7.2
	60–64	12.1	3.8	8.2	9.1
	65–69	9.1	2.7	6.8	14.1
	70+	9.8	0.0	0.0	29.3
Total		24.9	4.2	4.8	7.7
Administrative Support	16–19	85.7	0.0	0.0	0.0
	20–24	77.2	6.8	0.0	16.6
	25–29	71.8	5.9	2.5	20.3
	30–34	72.2	5.8	4.0	19.3
	35–39	76.1	7.6	5.8	19.0
	40–44	80.7	8.3	7.3	15.3
	45–49	80.1	7.8	8.0	12.9
	50–54	82.5	6.1	9.5	9.9
	55–59	81.1	4.9	9.8	10.0
	60–64	79.8	5.8	13.0	14.2
	65–69	77.7	5.8	17.1	16.3
	70+	84.9	0.0	7.0	0.0
Total		78.7	6.5	7.7	14.5
Operational	16–19	0.0	0.0	0.0	0.0
	20–24	28.6	5.9	2.2	6.9
	25–29	33.5	5.1	1.5	11.0
	30–34	34.0	5.3	2.4	10.7
	35–39	35.4	6.8	2.9	12.1
	40–44	29.9	8.1	3.5	9.4
	45–49	30.0	7.9	4.6	8.1
	50–54	26.4	4.9	6.7	5.5

OCCUPATION	AGE	WOMEN	INDIGENOUS PEOPLE	PEOPLE WITH DISABILITIES	PEOPLE BELONGING TO A VISIBLE MINORITY
Operational (continued)	55–59	21.5	4.8	8.5	5.0
	60–64	18.1	5.4	8.9	6.1
	65–69	16.5	4.3	8.7	11.3
	70+	15.5	0.0	0.0	0.0
Total		29.2	6.1	4.7	8.5
All Categories	16–19	32.0	0.0	0.0	0.0
	20–24	54.0	4.5	0.0	13.9
	25–29	56.5	4.3	1.9	17.5
	30–34	55.0	4.6	3.0	16.3
	35–39	56.0	5.2	3.8	16.0
	40–44	55.6	6.1	4.9	14.6
	45–49	55.2	6.0	6.1	12.8
	50–54	54.2	4.8	7.6	9.4
	55–59	50.5	4.4	8.7	9.3
	60–64	47.1	4.7	9.7	11.1
	65–69	41.5	4.2	10.6	16.1
	70+	37.3	0.0	7.5	0.0
Total		54.1	5.1	5.7	13.2

Source: Data from Treasury Board of Canada Secretariat 2014a, Table 10. Note there were 85 positions that could not be categorized due to respondents not reporting their demographic identity.

support workers are female. Women now constitute 54.1 per cent of the entire public service, and they are increasing their presence in all occupational categories. Women account for 62.9 per cent of all persons employed in the administrative and foreign service function and 51.3 per cent of all employees engaged in scientific and professional work. While women are still a minority in the more male-dominated fields of technical and operational support, even here their numbers are increasing, especially when one looks at the younger age bands. But most importantly, women are coming close to achieving gender parity in the all-important executive category, where the formal leaders of the public service are found. We can see the contours of the next generation of senior executives in Ottawa amongst those women currently in their thirties and forties.

The promotion of employment equity within the federal public service has been a key goal of the federal government since the 1980s, and its successful implementation with respect to women, Indigenous Canadians, persons with disabilities, and visible minority Canadians is proof that governments can effect positive change and that public policy can improve the lives of Canadians. How this is being achieved is assessed more fully below.

TABLE 7.6

Federal Public Service Employees by Salary Range, 2013–14

SALARY RANGE$	NUMBER OF ALL EMPLOYEES	% OF ALL EMPLOYEES	NUMBER OF WOMEN	% OF WOMEN IN THIS SALARY RANGE
Under 5,000	41	2.3	15	36.6
5,000–9,999	141	0.1	35	24.8
10,000–14,999	67	0.0	35	52.2
15,000–19,999	149	0.1	103	69.1
20,000–24,999	260	0.1	191	73.5
25,000–29,999	393	0.2	319	81.2
30,000–34,999	382	0.2	332	86.9
35,000–39,000	1,567	0.9	1,194	76.2
40,000–44,999	4,017	2.2	2,817	70.1
45,000–49,999	14,809	8.2	10,383	70.1
50,000–54,999	19,791	10.9	13,691	69.2
55,000–59,000	16,869	9.3	10,939	64.8
60,000–64,999	14,840	8.2	8,484	57.2
65,000–69,999	18,827	10.4	9,275	49.3
70,000–74,999	14,716	8.1	5,711	38.8
75,000–79,999	9,265	5.1	4,689	50.6
80,000–84,999	16,917	9.3	8,098	47.9
85,000–89,999	7,448	4.1	3,929	52.8
90,000–94,000	7,499	4.1	3,583	47.8
95,000–99,000	8,252	4.6	3,372	40.9
100,000 and over	25,106	13.8	10,883	43.3
Total	**181,356**	**100.0**	**98,078**	**54.1**

Note: Total does not sum to 100 per cent due to rounding.

Source: Data from Treasury Board of Canada Secretariat, 2014a, Table 4.

Table 7.6 shows the annual salaries of public servants broken down into salary ranges. These figures deserve careful attention, as the Treasury Board does not make it easy to see the broader contours of pay narratives. You need to do some cumulative reckoning of all employees in these salary bands to see patterns of pay while also looking carefully at the salary ranges dominated by women. Contrary to popular opinion, most public servants do not make great bags of money. Some 22.9 per cent of those with term appointments of three months or more, seasonal employees, and full-time (indeterminate) employees earned less than $55,000 per year in 2013–14. Slightly more than half of all these employees (50.8 per cent) earned less than $70,000, with only 10.4 per cent of all employees earning between $65,000 and $69,000 per year. Three-quarters (71.7 per cent) of them earned less than $85,000 per year, with only 9.3 per cent of employees earning between $80,000 and $84,999 per year. Only 13.8 per cent earned more than $100,000 per year. The public and the media tend to think of public sector salaries as overly generous, and although senior officials do make handsome incomes, most public servants earn merely ordinary incomes, and their management salaries pale in comparison to those found in the private sector. As US President Harry Truman once said in reference to working in the American public service, "If you're honest, you'll never become rich working for the government."

The gender difference in salary scales is still significant, although this is a dynamic that the Treasury Board now seeks to obscure. It no longer provides a cumulative tally of female salary levels as one moves through the salary ranges, as can be found in renditions of this table in earlier editions of *Thinking Government*. But one can still discern gender inequality in income levels. It is common knowledge that women generally earn less than men. You can see this when looking carefully at certain salary ranges. Women account for more than 80 per cent of all employees earning between $25,000 and $35,000 per year; men account for less than 20 per cent of employees in this salary range. Likewise, women make up 70 per cent of all employees earning between $40,000 and $50,000 per year, and 61 per cent of employees making between $55,000 and $65,000 were women. Conversely, women tend to represent a minority of all employees in the upper income salary ranges. Only 43 per cent of those public servants earning over $100,000 per year were women, even though 54.1 per cent of the entire membership of the federal public service was female. Both occupational and age dynamics come into play in this issue. Women tend to be congregated in administrative support roles—secretaries, clerks, cleaners—and thus in lower paid occupations, while older men dominate the higher paid executive, professional, and technical occupations and so generally get paid more. But once again, these dynamics are changing. As more women move into more senior positions within the public service, wage discrepancies will become more muted.

REGIONAL DISTRIBUTION

Table 7.7 categorizes the federal public service by region of work. As with the Statistics Canada figures, these TBS figures demonstrate how the population distribution of federal public servants tends to mirror that of the general population with one obvious exception: roughly 44 per cent of all

TABLE 7.7

Federal Public Service Employees by Group and Region, 2013–14

	WOMEN	INDIGENOUS PEOPLE	PEOPLE WITH DISABILITIES	PEOPLE BELONG TO A VISIBLE MINORITY	ALL EMPLOYEES NUMBER	%
BC	48.6	6.0	5.6	20.4	15,774	8.7
AB	56.0	8.7	6.9	11.9	9,083	5.0
SK	57.4	16.7	5.8	6.3	4,464	2.5
MB	56.3	14.6	6.6	9.3	6,442	3.5
ON (without NCR)	54.8	5.2	6.9	17.5	23,340	12.8
NCR	56.2	3.9	5.7	14.5	80,358	44.3
NCR (ON)	55.7	3.2	5.9	15.2	56,025	30.8
NCR (QC)	57.2	5.2	5.4	13.0	24,333	13.4
QC without NCR	53.1	1.7	3.5	6.8	20,427	11.2
NB	55.9	3.6	5.2	2.4	6,387	3.5
PE	63.1	2.8	7.2	2.5	1,554	0.9
NS	42.7	4.9	7.1	5.9	8,349	4.6
NL	42.3	6.2	5.5	1.9	2,784	1.5
NU	55.4	34.2	4.8	8.7	231	0.1
NT	60.4	20.8	6.0	6.5	385	0.2
YT	63.1	16.6	8.6	6.6	290	0.1
Outside Canada	45.8	1.5	3.4	13.7	1,489	0.8
Total	54.1	5.1	5.7	13.2	181,356	100.0

Note: NCR = National Capital Region, includes Gatineau (Quebec) and Ottawa (Ontario). Total does not sum to 100 per cent due to rounding.
Source: Treasury Board of Canada Secretariat 2014a, Table 2.

federal public servants work within the **National Capital Region** of Ottawa-Gatineau. (And nearly 70 per cent of all those in executive positions work in the region, an even more disproportionate finding.) Two conclusions can be drawn from this information.

First, about 56 per cent of federal public servants live and work *outside* of the country's capital. For all the talk of the federal government being out of touch with the regions, most policies and programs are administered by employees working throughout the country. Regional offices, in turn, are in direct and steady contact with their head offices in Ottawa-Gatineau, meaning that the senior leadership of departments and agencies located in the National Capital Region maintain a close liaison with their field offices.

Second, however, Ottawa-Gatineau is the political and administrative heart of the country, where the executive leadership of the federal government is found. Here one finds deputy ministers, associate and assistant deputy ministers, senior managers, and advisers responsible for the policy and administrative operations of the government's departments and agencies. Though the federal public service has roots in every part of the country, executive power is firmly attached to the centre.

STAFFING SIZE

In Table 7.8, the distribution of the federal public service across departments, agencies, boards, and commissions shows the great range in size of various federal institutions. Some offices and boards—such as the Copyright Board of Canada and the registry of the Competition Tribunal—are tiny. National Defence, Employment and Social Development, Correctional Services, the Canada Border Services Agency, Public Works and Government Services, and Fisheries and Oceans, on the other hand, are vast. Even departments can vary greatly in terms of numbers of employees. The ones just mentioned stand in high relief compared to Justice, Veterans Affairs, Canadian Heritage, and Finance.

But staff size does not correlate with importance and political influence. As we have seen, the single most powerful department in the government is Finance because of its central role in budgetary policy and financial management. Likewise, although the Departments of Justice and Foreign Affairs, Trade and Development Canada (now Global Affairs Canada) are comparatively small, their policy subjects are of great importance because they are essential to the domestic and international policy agenda, a significance recognized by most Canadians. These departments have influence greater than other small departments such as Veterans Affairs and Heritage simply on the basis of what they do.

The list is a reflection of what the current federal government believes to be worthy of consideration, management, and development. The range of activities is expansive, extending from the regulation of fisheries and oceans to the administration of multiculturalism and citizenship, health and welfare, and human resources. Table 7.8, in short, is as much a listing of government priorities as it is of federal public servants. Another point is that the organizational structure of the government evolves. The current list of departments, agencies, and offices is significantly different from the structure of the Pierre Trudeau and Mulroney ministries, for example, and the government of Justin Trudeau has altered the scope of departments and agencies in contrast to the Harper government.

TRADITIONAL ISSUES IN HUMAN RESOURCES MANAGEMENT

Many of the great historical and contemporary debates about how to improve government services and accountability have involved the public sector personnel system. Patronage and meritocracy, staffing and hiring policy, and personnel training and renewal are all contentious aspects of

TABLE 7.8

Federal Public Service Employees by Department or Agency, 2013–14

DEPARTMENT OR AGENCY	NUMBER OF EMPLOYEES
National Defence[a]	22,112
Employment and Social Development Canada	19,802
Correctional Services Canada	17,834
Canada Border Services Agency	13,391
Public Works and Government Services Canada	11,352
Fisheries and Oceans Canada[b]	9,097
Health Canada	8,761
Environment Canada	5,852
Royal Canadian Mounted Police (Civilian Staff)	5,830
Foreign Affairs, Trade and Development Canada	5,607
Shared Services Canada	5,158
Citizenship and Immigration Canada	4,918
Agriculture and Agri-Food Canada[c]	4,572
Industry Canada	4,541
Transport Canada	4,500
Statistics Canada	4,433
Department of Justice Canada	4,410
Aboriginal Affairs and Northern Development Canada	4,405
Natural Resources Canada	3,782
Veterans Affairs Canada	2,939
Public Health Agency of Canada	1,943
Treasury Board of Canada Secretariat	1,648
Canadian Heritage	1,640
Public Safety Canada	962
Public Prosecution Service of Canada	952
Library and Archives Canada	889
Immigration and Refugee Board of Canada	798
Department of Finance Canada	719

DEPARTMENT OR AGENCY	NUMBER OF EMPLOYEES
Public Service Commission of Canada	713
Privy Council Office	665
Canadian Space Agency	587
Canada School of Public Service	565
Atlantic Canada Opportunities Agency	555
Court Administration Services	550
Office of the Chief Electoral Officer	434
Canadian Radio-television and Telecommunications Commission	402
Canadian Grain Commission	393
Parole Board of Canada	393
Canada Economic Development for Quebec Regions	288
Western Economic Diversification Canada	286
Infrastructure Canada	271
Offices of the Information and Privacy Commissioners of Canada	241
Canadian Transportation Agency	206
Federal Economic Development Agency for Southern Ontario	201
Canadian Environmental Assessment Agency	199
Office of the Registrar of the Supreme Court of Canada	196
Transportation Safety Board of Canada	192
Canadian Human Rights Commission	182
Office of the Commissioner of Official Languages	157
Office of the Secretary to the Governor General	141
Canada Industrial Relations Board	76
Canadian International Trade Tribunal	61
Commission for Public Complaints Against the Royal Canadian Mounted Police	56
Office of the Commissioner for Federal Judicial Affairs Canada	54
Prices Review Board Canada	51
Canadian Dairy Commission	48
Military Grievances External Review Committee	35
Office of the Public Sector Integrity Commissioner of Canada	27

DEPARTMENT OR AGENCY	NUMBER OF EMPLOYEES
Public Service Staffing Tribunal	26
International Joint Commission	25
Office of the Commissioner of Lobbying of Canada	25
Canadian Intergovernmental Conference Secretariat	21
Human Rights Tribunal of Canada	17
Farm Products Council of Canada	16
Indian Residential Schools Truth and Reconciliation Commission	13
Military Police Complaints Commission of Canada	12
Copyright Board of Canada	12
Registry of the Specific Claims Tribunal of Canada	9
Transportation Appeal Tribunal of Canada	8
Disclosure Protection Tribunal of Canada	7
Registry of the Competition Tribunal	6
RCMP External Review Committee	4
Total	**181,356**

a. Civilian staff only (data for members of the Canadian Armed Forces are not included because the Treasury Board is not the employer).
b. Fisheries and Oceans data include data for the Canadian Coast Guard.
c. Agriculture and Agri-Food Canada data include data from the Prairie Farm Rehabilitation Administration.

Source: Treasury Board of Canada Secretariat 2014a, Table 1.

public human resources management, and they are explored in the remainder of this chapter. We also look at public sector representativeness, bilingualism and multiculturalism, the impact of human rights policy, gender equity, employment equity, collective bargaining, and the right to strike.

THE PATRONAGE SYSTEM

In 1867 the federal and provincial public services were of course far smaller than they are today, and their dominant organizational principle was **political patronage** (Simpson 1988, 7–16). Appointments and government contracts and licences were grounded in the political affiliations of prospective employees or grantees and in the partisan interests of the government of the day. In the half-century following Confederation, it was commonplace for newly elected governments to fire the vast majority of the public servants they had inherited from the previous administration in order to give the jobs to their own relatives, friends, and supporters.

This approach to public service management, also known as the "spoils system" (from American president Andrew Jackson's famous rationalization, "To the victors go the spoils of the battle"), sent clear signals to those directly involved as well as to the public about the nature of the public service:

- Employment and government contracts depended on partisan support for the governing party.
- Education, experience, and personal attributes—merit—were usually insufficient to gain and keep employment, contracts, or licences.
- The public service was the refuge of political hacks and those with connections. It was not what you knew but who you knew that mattered.
- Public service was not a professional career, with professional standards and qualifications. It was instead the property of the government of the day, to be manipulated for its own ends.
- The public service had no identity because it could not promote professionalism, it had no control over its own appointment process and was thus inherently transitory, and it had no political independence.

Individual political activity during this period was therefore influenced by direct material considerations. Many people supported and worked for a political party not out of ideological convictions but because of what they hoped to gain. A patronage connection existed between parties and their supporters. The latter offered their loyalty, money, or labour in return for material benefits—jobs, contracts, licences—once the former gained power. Party leaders created and nurtured these expectations, and understood that they had to be satisfied if they were to retain support (Simpson 1988, chaps. 3, 4).

The patronage system was not without its detractors, and it came under increasing disapproval in the late Victorian era. Patronage was attacked as both immoral and inefficient. Critics from universities, churches, and social reform movements, including early feminist leaders such as Nellie McClung, challenged its morality on the grounds that the bureaucracy was used and abused for political advantage rather than for the benefit of the entire society. By the turn of the century, detractors argued that favouritism, nepotism, and partisan manipulation had produced grossly inefficient bureaucracies across the country.

In this sense, the push for a merit-based system of personnel administration was one of the first examples of a demand for a rationalist approach to public sector management.

THE MERIT PRINCIPLE

It was at the federal level that this patronage system first came under sustained attack and the organizing principle of meritocracy first became established in Canadian public sector management. The earliest, half-hearted attempts at public service reform occurred in the 1880s when the Macdonald government, responding to public opinion, established the Board of Civil Service Examiners to help ministers and deputies select public servants. The impact of this institution was minimal, however, as ministers retained full control over criteria for employment and hiring decisions. By the first decade of the twentieth century, though, public criticism of patronage had reached such a level that the Laurier government passed the Civil Service Act, 1908, which recognized for the first time the importance of merit in the management of the federal public service (Kernaghan and Siegel 1999, 557; Juillet and Rasmussen 2008, 40–43).

The **merit principle** contains two related considerations:

1 All Canadian citizens "should have a reasonable opportunity to be considered for employment in the public service."
2 All employment decisions must be based "exclusively on merit or fitness to do the job." (Jackson and Jackson 2001, 347)

Under the new legislation, decisions about hiring, promotion, demotion, and dismissal were to be based on a rational assessment of education, experience, competence, and professionalism, rather than on political or personal affiliations. In order to implement this new approach to personnel management, the Civil Service Act also created a new institution, the Civil Service Commission. The commission was to enforce the merit principle within Ottawa by posting jobs; establishing classifications and criteria; conducting examinations, interviews, assessments, and evaluations; and making hiring decisions based on those criteria.

While this reform is significant in the history of the merit principle, it was flawed. At this time the federal public service was divided into two categories: the Inside Service, comprising employees situated in Ottawa; and the Outside Service, comprising those employed elsewhere in the country. The provisions of the Civil Service Act were applicable only to the Inside Service. Given that five-sixths of all federal employees were in the Outside Service, the vast majority of the federal public service still was subject to the rules of the old game. But times were changing.

World War I finally brought the application of the merit principle across the full federal public sector. During the war numerous government scandals erupted over the management of the war effort and how the Canadian forces were financed and equipped. Bureaucratic foul-ups caused by a combination of administrative incompetence, graft, self-interest, and corruption resulted in troops being provided with substandard clothing and food, flawed and hazardous munitions, and unreliable rifles. In peacetime such snafus would have been embarrassing, the stuff of political finger pointing and debate. During the war they meant the difference between life and death.

News of the avoidable hardships, wounds, and loss of life enraged those on the home front, including patriotic group leaders, social reformers, church leaders, the media, opposition party spokesmen, and large numbers of the general public. Demand for an end to patronage and the introduction of rationalist meritocracy throughout federal public service became a common refrain. Thus, in 1918, the Union government of Robert Borden brought forth a new Civil Service Act, extending the application of the merit principle through the entire federal government and strengthening the enforcement powers of the Civil Service Commission (Simpson 1988, 123–32; Kernaghan and Siegel 1999, 557; Juillet and Rasmussen 2008, 48–51).

PROFESSIONALIZING THE PUBLIC SERVICE

Since 1918, the task of the Civil Service Commission—renamed the Public Service Commission (PSC) in 1967—has been to nurture a professional public service free from partisan interference, insulated from the evils of patronage, and capable of providing meritorious service to the

Canadian public. To accomplish these objectives, the PSC established a complex and rationalistic merit system to replace patronage. Merit-based personnel relations required highly codified rules and procedures for staffing, and rationalism thus came at the expense of simplicity and expedience in decision making (Juillet and Rasmussen 2008, 57–65).

If everyone is to be treated equally, employment decisions must be open and subject to relatively objective standards of evaluation. The benefit is that the system is fair and perceived as fair. The drawback is that it becomes highly bureaucratized and cumbersome and, correspondingly, more expensive and time-consuming to operate. As is commonly known, to hire or fire anyone in the federal public service is a complex and slow process—much less efficient than in the private sector. It is always important to bear in mind, however, that such bureaucratic rules have developed from the goal of eliminating the worst features of patronage, and that "efficient" decision making may not be fair decision making.

Through its responsibility for the implementation of the merit principle, the PSC and its predecessor established a complex system of personnel management consisting of certain managerial processes:

- job classification
- human resources planning
- performance evaluation

Human resources planning comprises all aspects of personnel recruitment, training, retention, mobilization, and promotion. These matters are central to the role of the PSC, yet they are fraught with difficulties.

MERIT IN PERSPECTIVE

Merit is the first great organizing principle of the modern, professional public service. After merit became entrenched in federal law in 1918, the Civil Service Commission was able to eliminate the worst excesses of political patronage, and the federal government has developed a public service noted for its professionalism and freedom from partisan bias. Indeed, from the reform of 1918 the Civil Service Commission and leading prime ministers (Mackenzie King, St. Laurent, and Pearson) and public servants (O.D. Skelton, Robert Bryce, Mitchell Sharp, and Gordon Robertson) transformed the service into a meritocracy. The leadership and vision they displayed helped to make the federal government the dominant governmental actor within this country through most of the twentieth century, and its attributes were subsequently emulated by the provincial governments.

CHOOSING AMONG CANDIDATES

But development of the principle has neither guaranteed that merit will always guide personnel management nor eliminated political patronage altogether. The goal of objective analysis confronts the subjective nature of decision making when human beings are involved. It is possible to establish coherent job requirements and conduct fair evaluations, rigorously overseen and subject to a right of appeal to independent and knowledgeable superiors. It is possible to discount political favouritism and distinguish weak applicants and employees from strong ones.

But what do personnel managers do when, say, 400 people apply for one policy analyst position, and the top 30 applicants possess equally excellent qualifications? Does the principle necessitate identifying the best candidate, or simply a qualified candidate?

The Best Person for the Job

If the first view prevails, it leads to a demonstrable inflation in job requirements and credentials in the public service. Administrative positions that three decades ago would have required a high school diploma as an educational minimum will now normally require a university degree or college diploma; policy positions that a generation ago required only a BA may now require an MA or a PhD. And even then, personnel managers often find the selection process difficult, as numerous candidates for the same position will possess such credentials.

The thrust to find distinguishing characteristics of merit thus heightens the quest for credentials and experience on all sides, leaving personnel managers confronting the same problem they had at the outset: how to distinguish between comparably well-qualified candidates? To resolve this dilemma managers have tended to find recourse to the criteria that the merit principle was intended to replace: individual connections, bureaucratic patronage, and conformity to an established administrative culture.

A Good Person for the Job

If the second view prevails, an overabundance of qualified candidates forces some other selection criteria into play. And again, personnel managers clearly favour those they know over those they do not, and those who share the values of the given organization over those who do not. But other forms of subjective preference have caused groups such as women, ethnic minorities, Indigenous people, and disabled people to be historically over-looked as job candidates, and stringent efforts have been underway for over a decade to eliminate such systemic bias.

Discrimination based on innate characteristics is actively prohibited by human rights law (Howe and Johnson 2000), but selection based on conformity to institutional needs and practices is perfectly legitimate. It is important for an organization to hire, retain, and promote those who fit the corporate culture, in order to maintain the long-term stability and effectiveness of the organization. Thus, those who fit will be advantaged: those currently doing well in public service or possessing attitudes shared within the organization. Such candidates benefit from their connections because they are among the first to hear about upcoming job opportunities, and they can be schooled in the interests and predispositions of decision makers on selection committees.

If all this sounds rather informal and subjective—personnel selection tied to personal contacts and inclinations—it is. And it is this way because simply being educationally or technically qualified is insufficient.

MAKING SENIOR POLITICAL APPOINTMENTS

Another issue is that the merit principle still does not apply to all federal public service positions. PSC jurisdiction extends only to the public servants employed by departments and certain major agencies. It does not cover personnel management in Crown corporations and regulatory agencies. Although these institutions normally follow the merit principle in their routine staffing decisions, the appointment of senior executives remains a prerogative of the government of the day. This is also true of all appointments to the Senate, the federally appointed judiciary, ambassadorships and missions abroad, and all those appointed under orders-in-council.

That means thousands of positions, from the significant to the obscure, remain subject to patronage. Also, many contracts—from legal and accounting services to advertising and management consulting services—are subject to the preference of the government of the day. While the federal government now advertises much of its contract work via the MERX electronic tendering service, which lists tenders for upcoming contracts and outlines a systematic bid process for private service providers, the awards remain subject to political oversight. It is common, for example, for Liberal governments to favour professional firms with Liberal connections and Conservative governments to favour those with Conservative credentials.

The traditional form of patronage can still be found when governments bestow positions or benefits on party loyalists of dubious merit, a charge often brought against both the Chrétien and Harper governments over appointments to regulatory agencies such as the Canadian Immigration and Refugee Board and the National Energy Board. This old style of patronage is waning, though, the victim of media scrutiny, public anger, professional need, and political sensitivity. Governments now seldom retain people simply because they are party loyalists if they are also unqualified. Such hiring, when it does occur, arouses professional, media, and public criticism, as Harper learned from the scathing response to many of his appointments to both government agencies and the Senate (Martin 2010, 120–37; Harris 2014, chap. 7). The Harper government hired a number of senior officials for agencies, boards, and commissions noted as much for their ideological and partisan conformity to the prime minister's worldview as for their professional experience, and such hirings eventually came to give Stephen Harper a reputation for being a one-dimensional "control freak" who was intolerant of diverse opinions. Such a reputation eventually came to haunt him and his party in the election of 2015.

Critics of patronage, however, cannot deny governments the right to hire those qualified to perform senior managerial tasks who are also supporters. As Jeffrey Simpson (1988) has long argued, some may consider this patronage, but it is not illegitimate patronage. It ensures that important governing institutions are subject to the direction of good managers who also share the same ideological orientation and policy perspective of the government and therefore have no motivation to sabotage its work. Why should a Conservative government, for example, pass over qualified professionals who are Conservative supporters in favour of other qualified professionals who are Liberals or New Democrats or Blocistes or strictly neutral? The provincial governments of Bernard Landry and Pauline Marois (Parti Québécois), John Hamm (Conservative), Brad Wall (Saskatchewan Party), and Greg Selinger and Rachel Notley (NDP) all favoured their own qualified loyalists over all others as they sought to create senior agency leaderships loyal and trustworthy to their governments.

Governments tend to refrain from hiring loyalists who are not competent for two reasons. First, to do so exposes them to public criticism and places important institutions in the hands of substandard management, a condition that may return to haunt the governing party. Second, with an increasingly well-educated and experienced workforce it is not difficult to find loyalists who are also well qualified.

REFORM AND RENEWAL

While application of the merit principle has been the signature dynamic in the federal public service over the past century, other important human resource issues have also attracted attention. Just as there have been many rationalistic attempts to redesign financial management, so too has the federal public service been the focus of repeated reform and renewal initiatives, all aimed at fundamentally improving the quality of government services, the work of its personnel, and managerial relationships between departments and agencies.

REFORM INITIATIVES FROM THE 1980S TO THE 2000S

The success of most of these initiatives, which are covered in greater detail on the Thinking Government website, has been limited at best, for reasons we will explore in the next chapter. Donald Savoie (2015) has noted that the federal public service has witnessed a cavalcade of rationalistic programs of human resources development and management reform over the past three decades. During the Mulroney years, the Increased Ministerial Authority and Accountability initiative led into the Public Service 2000 initiative designed to make government more accountable and effective for the dawn of the new millennium. But during the Chrétien

PUBLIC SERVICE COMMISSION OF CANADA

The Public Service Commission of Canada oversees staffing decisions affecting the federal public service. The PSC assists federal departments and agencies with the recruitment and hiring of employees and plays an advisory role with respect to promotions, lateral transfers, demotions, and dismissals.

University students interested in a career in the federal public service should check the PSC website, www.psc-cfp.gc.ca, as it offers a huge amount of information on the work of the commission and has links to federal job ads, www.jobs-emplois.gc.ca, and to the three main hiring programs designed to attract university grads into the public service:

1 Federal Student Work Experience Program
2 Research Affiliate Program
3 Post-Secondary Co-operative Education and Internship Program

There are also a variety of specialized recruitment programs run by individual departments.

The Public Service Commission website also has important information on how to apply for posted jobs, and what to expect in the mandatory public service entrance exam.

If you're looking for a career in the federal public service, this is the place to start.

years of the mid-1990s, the Program Review exercise of 1995–98, designed to eliminate the federal deficit, left the federal public service battered and demoralized. In 1997 the Clerk of the Privy Council launched La Relève, yet another program to renew the public service, promote hiring of new public servants—the New Professionals who would lead the public service forward— and make the public service more energetic and effective. In particular, La Relève was designed to promote leadership skills and professional behaviour throughout the entire government. By the mid-2000s, however, the federal sponsorship scandal was acting like a cancer on the Chrétien and Martin governments, all the while weakening the reputation of the federal public service. In 2003 the Martin government passed the **Public Service Modernization Act**, aimed at improving

accountability, streamlining public sector labour relations, and improving leadership training in the public service. But none of this was enough to save that Liberal government. Stephen Harper came to power on the back of the sponsorship scandal, promising to clean up Ottawa and make the federal public service more accountable. To this end he passed the Federal Accountability Act in 2006, bringing in a wide variety of new accountability measures and controls, designed to increase oversight of bureaucratic behaviour and to tighten the control of senior officials and cabinet ministers over the actions of their departments. The most recent incarnation of these federal reform initiatives is Blueprint 2020, a program championed by the PCO under both the Harper and subsequent Trudeau governments to help envision a better public service by the year 2020.

Donald Savoie, one of Canada's leading authorities on the history and current practice of the federal public service, is jaundiced by all such programs and initiatives. "If history is a guide," writes Savoie (2015, 126), "the clerk's vision exercise will lead to countless meetings, numerous position papers and reviews, and lucrative contracts for some consultants, but, in the end, its impact will be hardly visible." The cynicism found here is understandable to one who has documented all of these reform undertakings over past decades, while noting the rather limited effect of these renewal initiatives. It can be argued that the federal public service always seems to be in a state of renewal, seeking to rebuild itself so as to be more open, responsive, and accountable while also promoting better service delivery, stronger policy development, and heightened public service leadership.

A less cynical, more sympathetic view of public service renewal efforts, however, is that they are beneficial and necessary visioning exercises designed to remind all public servants, from new hires to the most senior of leaders, of the need to be ever focused on core public service values and behaviours while fulfilling all the routine work of government and public administration. In this sense, far from being critical of public service renewal initiatives, we should recognize the value of these undertakings. It is all too easy for the members of any large organization to be swamped with the demands and obligations of routine work. It is important to be reminded every five years or so of the fundamental purposes of the organization for which you work, what its key goals are, and the ways and means by which those objectives can be better attained. Self-reflection, critical analysis, and forward thinking are never bad things in life.

BLUEPRINT 2020

This latest federal public service reform initiative was launched in 2013 by Wayne Wouters, then-Clerk of the Privy Council, with the aim of preparing the employees of the government of Canada to be ready to meet the challenges of providing effective policy development and program implementation and management for the year 2020 and the decades beyond. **Blueprint 2020** sets out an ambitious vision of what the federal public service should be by the turn of the decade:

> A world-class Public Service equipped to serve Canada and Canadians now and into the future. We will be recognized as having the best people working together with citizens, making smart use of new technologies and achieving the best possible outcomes with efficient, interconnected and nimble processes, structures and systems. Our core objective is to improve the lives of our citizens and secure a strong future for our country. (Privy Council Office 2013a, 4)

To achieve this vision, Blueprint 2020 has four guiding principles designed to shape the design of the public service to come:

1 "An open and networked environment that engages citizens and partners for the public good. We will support responsive, adaptable, open and networked approaches, services, processes and structures."

2 "A whole-of-government approach that enhances service delivery and value for money. We will focus on efficient and— where they make sense—consolidated

operations to increase flexibility, drawing on innovative and proven approaches to complex problems."

3 "A modern workplace that makes smart use of new technologies to improve networking, access to data and customer service. We will pursue affordable, interoperable tools and systems, and emphasize a tech-savvy and responsible culture that puts citizens first, making investments that are appropriate to sound public finances and the concrete needs of Canadians."

4 "A capable, confident and high performing workforce that embraces new ways of working and mobilizing the diversity of talent to serve the country's evolving needs. We will stress the importance of competent, engaged and productive leaders, managers and employees. We will also focus on the value of knowledge as well as learning from the collective experience in developing evidence-based options for decision-makers." (Privy Council Office, 2013a, p. 4)

As with all public service renewal initiatives of the past, Blueprint 2020 sets out ambitious goals and cherished principles. But as with all such projects, the key is how well the public service is able to breathe life into these ideals. In a subsequent 2013 update report on the roll-out of Blueprint 2020, the PCO noted that when asked their opinion on this initiative, many public servants were insistent that if it was to leave a lasting legacy, certain realities would have to be achieved, demonstrating that lofty rhetoric would be met with concrete results. Key findings from this study indicated that many public servants wanted to see

- innovative practices and networking resulting in improved information-sharing, better collaboration across the public service, enhanced public access to information, and greater engagement with external partners;
- improved processes and empowerment leading to reduced red tape in their day-to-day work, much more streamlined approaches to planning and reporting, greater empowerment of individual employees to show and be rewarded for initiative, and reduced emphasis on hierarchy and power relations in the routine working of their organizations;
- with respect to technology, greater use of online tools, the use of social media as a means of communication and information sharing, and the utilization of smart technologies for gathering, assessing, and disseminating ideas and actions;
- better "people management" through better employee training and professional development, the building of core competencies and skills enhancement for staff, improved opportunities for staff networking, collaboration in policy design and program implementation, staff involvement in critical assessment and feedback sessions on how well programs are working, greater opportunities for on-the-job learning and professional and career development, and better recruitment for and staffing of all government organizations; and

BLUEPRINT 2020—MAKING IT REAL

According to the PCO (2014, 4), Blueprint 2020 "articulates a vision for a world-class Public Service equipped to serve Canada and Canadians now and into the future.... We are collectively focused on transforming the Public Service."

Blueprint 2020 marks the latest in a long number of reform initiatives aimed at modernizing and improving the federal public service, making it more responsive to the needs of Canadians and effective in serving them. Blueprint 2020 was the largest engagement exercise ever undertaken in the public service, with more than 110,000 federal public servants participating in Blueprint 2020 engagement activities, meetings, focus groups, and studies.

To assist in attaining the lofty goals of Blueprint 2020, the PCO has set out the following criteria: Deputy heads need to

- lead by embodying the change they want to see in others;
- set the tone by ensuring that engagement governs their approach to change management;
- set the direction by nurturing and sustaining dialogue among public servants; and
- ensure follow-through and clear accountability.

Managers need to

- establish a culture where employees bring their hearts and minds to their jobs;
- learn to thrive outside their comfort zone by finding the courage to challenge their assumptions and abandon usual management preferences;
- foster innovation and a culture of openness;
- adopt a networking style of leadership by engaging employees at every stage of change implementation; and
- support employees as they take action to improve their own units and to implement ideas that have a larger application.

Employees need to

- embrace their role as agents of change by adopting a positive attitude, keeping an open mind, and remaining steadfast and committed;
- take ownership of the process by identifying and proposing areas of change and improvement;
- implement changes by collaborating with colleagues and by positively contributing to the change process; and
- seize the opportunity to shape the public service in a way that helps them deliver service excellence now and into the future. (Privy Council Office 2014, 30)

Do you believe these goals are realistic and doable? Or are they more wishful thinking, noble ideals that quickly get forgotten in the routine life of any organization? What does organizational theory teach us about such goals? And where is power found in Blueprint 2020? Are employees really the agents of change? Or are they ultimately being called upon to "adopt a positive attitude" while "remaining steadfast and committed"?

- a fundamental commitment to diversity in the public service, the promotion of official bilingualism, and the adherence, by all officials and political leaders, to the core public service values and ethics of non-partisanship, professionalism, evidence-based research and policy development, respect for the role of the public service in society as well as respect for the role of elected leaders. (Privy Council Office 2013b)

The concerns and aspirations expressed here emerge from a public service bruised by a tempestuous and often acrimonious relationship with the Conservative government of Stephen Harper. As noted in the first three chapters of *Thinking Government*, the Harper government was noted for its ideological and often authoritarian approach to decision making, and a style of governing that was often dismissive of and openly hostile to the role of public servants and the idea of a critical, nonpartisan approach to policy development and program evaluation. In working to mend the relationship between the government and the public service while seeking to build a better public service attuned to the needs of both citizens and political leaders, Blueprint 2020 has its work cut out. It has, as all renewal initiatives must have, an ambitious agenda. It seeks to make the federal public service more open, integrated, innovative, and effective. And the senior leadership of the PCO asserts that all of this can be achieved and that the process of getting to these goals is a part of the reform dynamic (Privy Council Office 2014, 4–5). The election of a Liberal government led by Justin Trudeau in the fall of 2015, one committed to government reform and the re-establishment of a better relationship between elected politicians and public servants, bodes well for Blueprint 2020. But again, rhetoric is easy, and the building of a truly better public service committed to matching public sector ideals with better programs and services for Canadians is the acid test of effective reform. And as Donald Savoie (2015, 126) reminds us, we should always be sceptical of the ability of these reform initiatives to live up to their hype. It is important, nonetheless, that governments periodically focus on their ideals, and how they should always strive to be better.

A REPRESENTATIVE AND EQUITABLE PUBLIC SERVICE

If the first great administrative reform to modernize federal human resources management was the push for the merit principle, the second has been the drive for a public service that is representative of the society it serves and equitable in its relationships with citizens and employees. But whereas the objective of entrenching the merit principle has ceased to be a point of debate, the aim of creating a representative and equitable bureaucracy still elicits sharp divisions of opinion.

Though most Canadians will not quarrel with the idea that the modern federal and provincial governments should reflect the society they serve and should deal equitably with those they serve or employ, many question the ways in which governments reach these ends. Substantive policy initiatives such as official bilingualism, multiculturalism, the recognition and promotion of human rights, **employment equity**, public service unionization, **collective bargaining**, and the right of public servants to strike have been contentious, and some remain so.

BILINGUALISM AND BICULTURALISM

From Confederation until the 1960s the composition of the federal public service was overwhelmingly English Canadian and the common language of work in Ottawa was English. As Jean Chrétien mentions in his autobiography (1986, 16–18), the Ottawa of the early 1960s was far from a national capital in which French Canadians could feel at home. Though francophones constituted roughly 25 per cent of the total population, they represented only 12 per cent of the federal public service. They were even more poorly represented in senior management. Immediately following World War II, for example, the number of francophone deputy ministers was precisely zero (Kernaghan and Siegel 1999, 584–85).

Such underrepresentation was not perceived as a national problem until the Quiet Revolution of the 1960s and the resurgence of French-Canadian nationalism and cultural reawakening. During these years the French-Canadian media and intelligentsia grew increasingly critical of the discriminatory environment within the federal public service, arguing that it could not hope to serve the interests of French Canadians if it did not represent them. At this time, the public service was viewed by most French Canadians as a foreign entity, staffed primarily by, and essentially for, English-speaking Canadians. In short, it was an organization in which few French Canadians could or would want to build a career.

The criticism cut deeply against the liberal vision of the modern state. If the state were to represent the society it served, and roughly one-quarter of that society was francophone, then one-quarter of the federal public workforce should also be francophone, across all occupational levels. Anything less was not only discriminatory but also implied that the federal government could not adequately understand the needs and interests of French Canadians and therefore could not effectively develop and administer policies and programs for them.

The Glassco Royal Commission on Government Organization, undertaken in the early 1960s, went far in endorsing this way of thinking, recognizing that francophones were greatly underrepresented in the federal public service and that "a career at the centre of government should be as attractive and congenial to French-speaking as to English-speaking Canadians" (Canada, Royal Commission on Government Organization 1962, 29).

A NEW POLICY

By the mid-1960s the Liberal government of Lester Pearson had committed itself to the policy of promoting **bilingualism and biculturalism** across the country generally and within the public service in particular. As the Royal Commission on Bilingualism and Biculturalism was studying these concepts and planning ways by which the federal government could be more inclusive of French Canadians, Pearson stated, in 1966, that "the linguistic and cultural values of the English-speaking and French-speaking Canadians will be reflected through civil service recruitment and training" (Canada, House of Commons 1966, 3915). In inheriting and defending this policy,

Prime Minister Pierre Trudeau pronounced that "the atmosphere of the public service should represent the linguistic and cultural duality of Canadian society, and ... Canadians whose mother tongue is French should be adequately represented in the public service—both in terms of numbers and in levels of responsibility" (Canada, House of Commons 1970, 84–87). Bilingualism and biculturalism were fully entrenched into the federal public service by the **Official Languages Act, 1969** and the Official Languages Program of the TBS, which was developed the same year. These initiatives stipulated the following:

- The federal government was committed to operating in both official languages.
- Citizens had the right to be served in either official language when dealing with federal government offices.
- Public servants should be able to work in the official language of their choice.
- The federal public service should become broadly representative of Canada's cultural and linguistic identity.

THE RESULTS

Since 1969, these goals have largely been met. Indeed, as of 1982, official federal bilingualism has been constitutionally entrenched in the Charter of Rights and Freedoms. Federal institutions pride themselves on their ability to provide services in both official languages, and the government has been able to bring the level of francophone representation in the public service up to its proportion of the overall national population.

Table 7.9 highlights the current participation of anglophones and francophones in the federal public service by province, territory, or region. The proportion of anglophones has declined to 68.1 per cent as of 2014, while the proportion of francophones has increased to 31.9 per cent. These numbers reveal that francophones are actually *overrepresented* in the federal government by 9.9 percentage points. (As of the 2011 census, French Canadians accounted for 22 per cent of the Canadian population.)

The disproportion is usually explained by the greater degree of bilingualism among French Canadians than among their English-Canadian compatriots, meaning that they can more effectively compete for bilingual public service positions. It is interesting to note the impact of official bilingualism on the federal public service in both the National Capital Region and New Brunswick, reflecting the substantial proportion of francophones who now work in the nation's capital and the strength of the Acadian population in the Maritime province. Ottawa is far different from what it was in the early 1960s, illustrating the type of social changes that can be wrought by the consistent application of policy over time. While elected ministers and senior public servants trumpet the extent to which the public service has come to support bilingualism, these same officials refrain from drawing attention to the degree of francophone overrepresentation. In all likelihood they fear a backlash from English Canada. Table 7.10 shows the changing linguistic requirements for positions in the federal public service nationwide from 1978 to 2014. It reveals a steady increase in the proportion of federal positions that are classified as bilingual. As of 2014 fully 43.3 per cent of all such

TABLE 7.9

Anglophones and Francophones in the Core Public Administration by Region, 2013–14

	ANGLOPHONES (%)	FRANCOPHONES (%)	ALL EMPLOYEES
BC	98.2	1.8	15,972
AB	97.1	2.9	9,151
SK	98.4	1.6	4,509
MB	96.3	3.7	6,477
ON (without NCR)	94.7	5.3	23,369
NCR	58.8	41.2	81,763
QC (without NCR)	9.7	90.3	20,478
NB	55.1	44.9	6,466
PE	88.7	11.3	1,637
NS	94.1	5.9	8,205
NL	98.4	1.6	2,845
NU	90.0	10.0	229
NT	96.9	3.1	389
YT	96.8	3.2	308
Outside Canada	67.6	32.4	1,403
Total	**68.1**	**31.9**	**183,201**

Note: NCR = National Capital Region, includes Gatineau (Quebec) and Ottawa (Ontario).

Source: Data from Treasury Board of Canada Secretariat 2014b, 24.

positions required a working facility in both official languages. This figure, however, can be interpreted in two ways. One is to welcome the growing degree of bilingualism within the federal government. The other is to note that the remaining approximately 56 per cent of positions are unilingual, and the vast majority of those are "English essential": 49.6 per cent of all positions, versus just 3.6 per cent of the total for "French essential" positions. These figures reflect the more unilingual status of federal government services outside the National Capital Region and New Brunswick.

In light of this finding, the information in Table 7.11 bears scrutiny. It highlights language requirements by region. As of 2014 some 67.5 per cent of federal positions in the National Capital Region were classified as bilingual. This figure illustrates the unmistakable importance of bilingualism

TABLE 7.10

Language Requirements of Core Public Administration Positions, 1978–2014

	BILINGUAL (%)	UNILINGUAL (%)			INCOMPLETE RECORDS (%)	ALL EMPLOYEES
		ENGLISH ESSENTIAL	FRENCH ESSENTIAL	ENGLISH OR FRENCH ESSENTIAL		
2014	43.4	49.6	3.6	3.2	0.3	183,201
2013	42.8	49.9	3.7	3.3	0.3	187,105
2008	40.5	51.0	3.9	4.4	0.3	187,580
2000	35.3	52.8	5.8	5.0	1.0	143,052
1978	24.7	60.5	8.1	5.7	0.0	211,885

Source: Data from Treasury Board of Canada Secretariat 2014b, 20.

within the headquarters of government departments, Crown agencies, and central agencies, strongly suggesting that anyone who wants a career in the federal public service and the potential to rise through the ranks of bureaucratic power is well advised to become proficient in both official languages. The table also highlights the importance of bilingual positions in both Quebec and New Brunswick.

The tables reveal that the federal public service has become increasingly bilingual, especially within the National Capital Region and, most importantly, abroad, as well as in the provinces of Quebec and New Brunswick. In this sense, the policy aims of bilingualism and biculturalism, at least with respect to the federal public service, have largely been fulfilled. French Canadians have come to be well represented, even overrepresented at times and in certain occupational categories, including the influential management level.

AN ASSESSMENT

The shift in francophone representation, however, elicits some troubling questions about the practice and theory of public service representativeness. Has the change made the federal government more responsive to the needs and interests of French Canadians since 1969? And do French Canadians view it as being so? Does the relative overrepresentation of francophones cause problems for non-francophones? Are the needs of all citizens being effectively served by such federal policy?

These, of course, are very difficult questions. Any answer is likely to depend on the respondent's linguistic background and views on Quebec nationalism, federalism, the role of the federal government within Quebec, and whether the requirements of official bilingualism impose an unfair burden on unilingual anglophones seeking federal employment.

TABLE 7.11

Language Requirements of Core Public Administration Positions by Region, 2013–14

	BILINGUAL (%)	UNILINGUAL (%)			INCOMPLETE RECORDS (%)	ALL EMPLOYEES
		ENGLISH ESSENTIAL	FRENCH ESSENTIAL	ENGLISH OR FRENCH ESSENTIAL		
BC	3.2	96.4	0.0	0.2	0.2	15,972
AB	4.1	95.3	0.-	0.5	0.1	9,151
SK	3.1	96.7	0.0	0.1	0.0	4,509
MB	8.1	91.5	0.0	0.3	0.1	6,477
ON (without NCR)	10.8	88.5	0.1	0.5	0.1	23,369
NCR	67.5	25.4	0.2	6.6	0.3	81,763
QC (without NCR)	67.1	0.7	31.2	0.7	0.2	20,478
NB	53.7	44.6	0.3	1.2	0.1	6,466
PE	29.4	70.5	0.0	0.1	0.0	1,637
NS	11.0	87.3	0.1	0.5	1.1	8,205
NL	3.9	95.7	0.0	0.4	0.1	2,845
NU	6.1	92.1	0.0	1.7	0.0	229
NT	2.6	97.4	0.0	0.0	0.0	389
YT	5.2	97.4	0.0	0.3	0.0	308
Outside Canada	98.5	0.7	0.0	0.4	0.4	1,403
Total	43.4	49.6	3.6	3.2	0.3	183,201

Note: NCR = National Capital Region, includes Gatineau (Quebec) and Ottawa (Ontario).

Source: Data from Treasury Board of Canada Secretariat 2014b, 21.

Within the Public Service

How do French Canadians working in the government perceive the effectiveness of the language policy? In 2003, the authors of *French to Follow: Revitalizing Official Languages in the Workforce*, a report prepared by the Canadian Centre for Management Development, asserted that although the federal public service professes to offer substantial bilingualism in its working environment, all too often English dominates office routines due to the limited French capabilities of anglophone employees. This is regrettably true even of those English Canadians who have undertaken French-language training.

Francophone employees raise common complaints about official bilingualism in practice:

- the absence of work tools such as manuals, internal memos, working papers, training guides, and telephone messages in their chosen official language
- the absence of computer tools such as software in both official languages
- the frequent mismatch between the linguistic profile of bilingual positions and the tasks to be performed in the second language
- the tendency for information sessions and meetings to be conducted in one language only
- the English unilingualism of supervisors and senior managers
- the unilingualism, usually English, of circulated draft documents
- the necessity to work in English in order to be understood
- the fact that once English speakers complete their language training, they find it hard to consolidate their knowledge of French (CCMD 2003, 7–8)

Grievances such as these highlight the practical difficulties in making official bilingualism work in a society where second-language capabilities are far more prevalent within the French-Canadian community than the English-Canadian one.

Just as many English Canadians complain about the limitations imposed upon entry into and promotion within the federal public service by official bilingual requirements so, too, many French Canadians complain of a hollow bilingual reality and the continuance of English as the dominant language of work. Similar concerns are expressed in Graham Fraser's brilliant study of official language policy in Canada, "Sorry, I Don't Speak French" (2006, chap. 5, 10).

Within National Culture

Regardless of these difficulties, it remains clear that the federal public service is a much more welcoming environment for French Canadians than it used to be. But whether their increased presence in the service has made federal policy more responsive to French-Canadian interests is a point of great debate. On one hand, broad support for Quebec nationalism increased over the first decades of official bilingualism, resulting in its near victory in the 1995 Quebec referendum. On the other hand, support for the federal government and the federal presence in Quebec remains relatively strong, as evinced by two referendum defeats for the sovereignty position and the inability of the Parti Québécois to develop the "winning conditions" for sovereignty. It is an open question whether any of this is related to official bilingualism policy and the status of French Canadians within the federal government.

Official bilingualism has long been a concern for unilingual English Canadians, who see their chances for employment restricted by federal language policy, especially when seeking advanced positions in the Ottawa bureaucracy or the foreign service. As the English-Canadian public becomes ever more conscious of the disproportionate share of federal employment now held by francophones, will they grow disenchanted, believing that the federal government is becoming less responsive and open to them? That line of thinking is not far-fetched when we see so much of Canadian politics being shaped by the politics of group identity.

What happens if English Canadians demand equitable representation within the federal public service? It doesn't need much imagination to see how ugly and divisive that debate could become. But one should not overdramatize this point. The federal public service is legally committed to the practice of official bilingualism and it consistently welcomes unilingual anglophones into its ranks. The inability to speak French does not preclude any Canadian from getting an entry-level position in the Government of Canada. If, however, such a person wishes to rise through the ranks and move into management, then the ability to speak French becomes an increasing requirement for promotion. Fully cognizant of this reality, the Public Service Commission of Canada and the Canada School of Public Service have developed a wide array of language training programs designed to provide employees with the opportunities to become functionally bilingual.

EMPLOYMENT EQUITY

Over the past three decades the impetus to create a representative public service has extended from a focus on language to one embracing the interests of women, Indigenous people, people with disabilities, and visible minorities. Its genesis can be traced to growing Canadian multiculturalism; increasing political awareness, as expressed in federal multicultural policy dating from 1971 and the official recognition of equality rights in the 1982 Charter of Rights and Freedoms; and the level of political consciousness and influence of groups representing people who have suffered discrimination.

As representative institutional groups developed over the 1970s and 80s, they directed much attention to systemic discrimination in the ranks of the federal public service, which they perceived as dominated by white, able-bodied males. These men were considered to have a grip on significant positions and occupations within the public service; women, conversely, were usually found in clerical and administrative support roles—the "pink-collar ghettoes"—and so were among the lowest paid government employees.

The criticisms had much validity. Studies ranging from the works of John Porter (1968), Wallace Clement (1983), Dennis Olsen (1980), and Kernaghan and Siegel (1999, 570) repeatedly demonstrated that a "number of important groups are under-represented in the service, and both the senior and middle echelons are unrepresentative of the general population." These studies agreed that the most underrepresented were those from the four groups listed above—all historically disadvantaged in this society.

In the 1970s and 80s group leaders, as well as certain journalists, academics, and political leaders, began to demand that wrongs be righted and the public service made to represent the entire society (Weiner 2010). The example of official bilingualism policy initiatives suggested that multiculturalism and employment equity might likewise be successful. Analysts rejected criticism of the representational principle and advanced claims for much greater initiatives to alter the composition of the public service fundamentally. The proponents of employment equity policy in particular have persistently maintained the following:

- Major socio-economic and cultural groups should be equitably represented within government.
- Representation is integral to the ability of governments to respond to the needs and interests of particular groups.
- Individual public servants will and should be seen, and should see themselves, as ambassadors of their group.

Moreover, advocates of employment equity asserted that when past discrimination had hindered members of underrepresented groups from getting government employment and being promoted, the state should employ affirmative action policies to rectify such abuses. The practice would produce a clear, public political and social statement:

- Social discrimination had been wrong and hurtful to those individuals and groups affected.
- Society in general and governments in particular had failed to make full use of the wealth of human capital available to them.
- Groups that have suffered from discrimination have valuable contributions to make to society.

Therefore, all governments must now engage in a policy of reconciliation with groups historically discriminated against. Past discrimination must be admitted and condemned, current discrimination prohibited, and the work of governments founded on the principles of equitable representation and responsiveness.

FEDERAL EQUITY POLICIES

Federal government initiatives to address these representational issues began in 1977 with the passage of the Canadian Human Rights Act, which prohibits discrimination within federal institutions and federally regulated industries on the basis of gender, colour, religion, ethnic and national origin, age, or disability.

The D'Avignon Committee

In 1979 the D'Avignon Special Committee on the Review of Personnel Management and the Merit Principle endorsed the concept of employment equity, noting that the federal public service had not been fair in its dealings with women and visible minorities and had not supported true equality of opportunity for all citizens. The committee argued in favour of special programs to open the public service by targeting and recruiting members of previously disadvantaged groups for employment and accelerating their career paths within the federal public service.

Recognizing that programs such as these would be criticized as reverse discrimination against men and non-minorities and counter to the merit principle, the D'Avignon Committee stressed that, at times, merit "can and should be temporarily suspended by parallel provision for special treatment of members of designated groups in support of eventual real equality of opportunity." Indeed,

the committee went further in its efforts to enshrine the new principle of special treatment for the members of certain groups. They recommended amending the Public Service Employment Act to allow preference in appointment for members of designated groups with minimum qualifications, and for the "suspension of certain qualifications" which could later be obtained through training on the job. The merit principle, according to the committee, was to remain, but it was to operate along with other principles such as equality of opportunity, efficiency, effectiveness, sensitivity, responsiveness and equity. (Adie and Thomas 1987, 82)

The Abella Commission

Support for equity policy was further advanced by the 1984 Royal Commission on Equality in Employment, known as the Abella Commission. Its report tackled the complexities inherent in the concept of equality and various ways to counter inequality:

> Sometimes equality means treating people the same, despite their differences and sometimes it means treating them as equals by accommodating their differences....
>
> We now know that to treat everyone the same may be to offend the notion of equality.... Equality means nothing if it does not mean that we are of equal worth regardless of differences in gender, race, ethnicity or disability.... Ignoring differences and refusing to accommodate them is a denial of equal access and opportunity.
>
> It is discrimination. (Canada, Royal Commission on Equality in Employment 1984, 3)

As did the D'Avignon Report, the Abella Commission argued that justice required more than simply a prohibition of future discrimination.

To create the foundations for equality, groups that had suffered from systemic discrimination should be accorded collective support for their future claims to equal treatment, and government should endorse affirmative action programs to remedy past inequity and ensure that members of those groups were now welcomed and encouraged to enter the public service.

The point was not only to redress past discrimination but to send an important message to society in general and minority groups in particular. To the former, the message was that discrimination was wrong and that all groups deserved equal treatment and respect. To the latter, the message was that society now recognized the wrongs that had been perpetrated against them, valued them, and understood that they deserved respect, dignity, and affirmation. That meant actively supporting their full integration into society, including the public service (Weiner 2010, 170–74).

The Charter

Affirmative action programs were given constitutional recognition and protection under the Charter of Rights and Freedom. Section 15(1) reads, in part, "Every individual is equal before and under the law and has the right to the equal protection and benefit of the law without discrimination." But section 15(2) reads, in whole, "Subsection (1) does not preclude any law, program or activity that has as its object the amelioration of conditions of disadvantaged individuals or groups including those that are disadvantaged because of race, national or ethnic origin, colour, religion, sex, age, or mental or physical disability."

Programs of employment equity were thereby exempt from Charter challenge, even if it was argued that in themselves they constituted policies of reverse discrimination.

Mandates and Policies

The federal government adopted equity policies with regard to hiring and promotion in the mid-1980s, formalized in the Employment Equity Act of 1995. Both the PSC and the TBS have responsibilities in the development and implementation of employment equity programs.

The PSC defines employment equity as "employment practices designed to ensure that the regular staffing process is free of attitudinal and systemic barriers in order that the Public Service reflects all groups present in the Canadian labour force, and designed to ensure that corrective measures are applied to redress any historical disadvantage experienced by certain designated groups."

The TBS has the tasks of "eliminating barriers to the employment and advancement of designated groups; establishing positive policies and practices to enable the equitable representation and distribution of the designated groups in the Public Service; providing advice and assistance to departments in developing and implementing their employment equity plans; and, establishing strategies to help departments deal with under-representation" (Treasury Board of Canada Secretariat 1994, 6).

Initiatives and Programs

The PSC and the TBS have undertaken vigorous initiatives to promote employment equity. Candidates from designated groups are actively sought during the hiring process and are accorded special support and standing. Equity initiatives also facilitate training and development, leading to accelerated promotion.

The TBS offers several programs geared to training women and Indigenous people, for example, and has established the Task Force on an Inclusive Public Service and the Task Force on the Participation of Visible Minorities in the Federal Public Service.

The PSC operates offices such as the Women's Career Counselling and Referral Bureau and the Office of Native Employment. It also encourages all departments to establish mentoring programs for members of designated groups, whereby younger employees are taken under the wing of older ones and given support, encouragement, and advice to develop their skills and knowledge.

IS THE PUBLIC SERVICE EQUITABLE?

Equity policies are intended to work in tandem with the merit principle. When decisions are made about hiring and promotion, equity doesn't trump merit but coexists with it. Equity policy in itself does not justify hiring a demonstrably incompetent job applicant, for example, but when several candidates meet the established criteria, equity considerations are taken into account. As merit and equity principles work in tandem, the result should be a public service that both represents society and employs the best talent that society has to offer.

Table 7.12 plots the results of equity undertakings from the early 1990s, showing the gradual increase in female workforce participation. As can be seen, women in 2014 constituted 54.1 per cent

TABLE 7.12

Public Service of Canada Employees by Designated Group

YEAR	ALL EMPLOYEES	WOMEN		INDIGENOUS PEOPLE		PEOPLE WITH DISABILITIES		PEOPLE OF VISIBLE MINORITY	
		#	%	#	%	#	%	#	%
2014	181,356	98,078	54.1	9,239	5.1	10,390	5.7	23,919	13.2
2010	202,386	110,867	54.8	9,307	4.6	11,620	5.7	21,567	10.7
2007	179,540	96,816	53.9	7,610	4.2	10,192	5.7	15,787	8.8
2004	165,976	88,175	53.1	6,723	4.1	9,452	5.7	13,001	7.8
2001*	149,449	77,785	52.1	5,316	3.6	7,621	5.1	9,143	6.1
1998	179,831	90,801	50.5	4,770	2.7	6,943	3.9	9,260	5/1
WORKFORCE AVAILABILITY									
2006 Census & PALS			52.3		3.0		4.0		12.4
2001 Census & PALS			52.2		2.5		3.6		10.4
1996 Census & PALS			48.7		2.6		4.8		8.7

*Including Revenue Canada. The new Canada Customs and Revenue Agency was established on November 1, 1999.

Source: Data from Treasury Board of Canada Secretariat 2014a, Table 7. The estimates on workforce availability are based on information from the Census and Statistics Canada's Participation and Activity Limitation Survey (PALS).

of the federal public service, a figure higher than their presence in the general national workforce, of which they form 52.3 per cent.

People with Indigenous heritage also had greater representation in the public service than in the general workforce. They accounted for 5.1 per cent of the federal public service as of 2014, but 3.0 per cent of the national labour force. Again, we see a marked increase—almost double—in the proportion of Indigenous people in the federal public service since the mid-1990s.

People with disabilities have also exceeded their proportion of the general workforce over the first years of the new century, accounting for 5.7 per cent of the public service in 2014 but 4.0 per cent of the total national workforce.

Visible minorities are now finally equitably represented in the federal public service, holding 13.2 per cent of positions with a workforce availability of 12.4 per cent. As can be seen from Table 7.12, this achievement of equity has been a slow evolution.

OCCUPATIONAL SEGREGATION

Table 7.5 reveals the occupational segregation of women within the public service as of 2014. As already noted, women make up more than half of the public service, but they account for a minority, 46.1 per cent, of the executive category. They account for 62.9 per cent of employees in the administrative and foreign services and 51.3 per cent of the members of the scientific and professional category. But women represent only 29.2 per cent of the operational category and 24.9 per cent of the technical category. Most notable, however, is the vast overrepresentation of women in the administrative support category, at 78.7 per cent. To advocates of employment equity, these figures reveal a historical pattern of discrimination that has consigned women, for too long, to the more menial and poorly paid positions of clerks, secretaries, typists, data processors, and office equipment operators.

It is interesting to note, also in Table 7.5, that the other designated groups follow a roughly parallel trend. They all tend to be underrepresented in most occupational categories and especially the executive group, and Indigenous people are overrepresented in operations and administrative support—again, categories with more jobs requiring lower skills and educational levels, and thereby with lower remuneration. Likewise, people with disabilities achieve their highest representational score in the administrative support category.

People belonging to visible minorities, however, achieve their highest score in the scientific and professional category, making up 17.2 per cent of this category. They are employed in fields such as auditing, chemistry, engineering and land surveying, mathematics, medicine, scientific research, and scientific regulation. This is evidence of the interest that first- and second-generation immigrants show in acquiring professional skills as the key to entry into Canadian middle-class life. Since math and sciences constitute a universal language in which English-language expertise and social knowledge are insignificant, they are a popular choice among new Canadians and a viable career path in the public service.

AGE AND REPRESENTATION

Age is an employment issue, especially in relation to women within the executive category (see Table 7.5). While women represent only 38.8 per cent of senior managers (55 to 65 years old), their underrepresentation is most pronounced in the older age bands, that is, among those who experienced the systemic occupational discrimination of the post-war era up to the 1980s. Of all executives aged 60 to 64, a group that includes the most senior in the government, women account for only 33.8 per cent. But younger women—those who entered the public service in the last two decades and are now benefiting from employment equity programs—account for much larger proportions of the executive ranks in their age bands. Women account for roughly 49 per cent of executives in their forties. Women in their thirties, however, constitute only 42.3 per cent of executives in that age group.

The figures suggest that although much progress has been made in enhancing female participation rates in management, much more work remains to encourage young women to enter management ranks, and to support them once there. The general trend, however, remains positive.

The data suggest two conclusions:

1 The current low representation of older women in senior executive positions will become a thing of the past. As they retire, they will be replaced by those rising through the organization, as the younger age bands are increasingly equitable in gendered representation. Indeed, one can predict that within 20 years gender disparity within the executive ranks of the federal public service will have ceased to exist.

2 Governments will continue to promote employment equity policies for women, notwithstanding the current achievement of gender parity within the public service overall, until women account for half of all executive positions across all age bands.

THE PUBLIC SERVICE AND UNIONIZATION

Many features distinguish the public and private sectors, and one of the most notable is that the vast majority of public sector employees are unionized. This is true across federal, provincial, and municipal levels of government and across all formats of public service organization: traditional departments, regulatory agencies, and Crown corporations. As Inwood (2012, 290) has noted, although public service employees constitute less than one-quarter of the total Canadian labour force, they constitute almost half of all union members. By extension, the three largest unions in Canada represent public servants: the Canadian Union of Public Employees, the National Union of Public and General Employees, and the Public Service Alliance of Canada.

Full unionization and collective bargaining rights were extended to federal public servants employed in traditional departments and related offices in 1967. But many others had long been unionized and able to engage in collective bargaining by virtue of their employment in Crown corporations. These institutions—the CBC, Canada Post, the NFB, and so forth—are free to develop their own approaches to labour relations, and many recognized staff unions and collective bargaining

rights early on under general labour relations legislation. Within the regular federal public service prior to the 1960s, employee initiatives in labour relations decision making took the form of various staff associations formed in the late nineteenth and early twentieth centuries. In 1944, as part of its move to garner the support of organized labour and left-leaning voters, the Liberal government of Mackenzie King agreed to formalize its consultations with staff associations through the creation of the National Joint Council of the Public Service of Canada. This institution promoted communication and consultation between the government and leaders of staff associations, but it was only an advisory body (Inwood 2012, 290–91).

By the early 1950s the staff associations, dissatisfied with this system, began to press for full collective bargaining rights. Public service collective bargaining became an election issue in 1963, as the Pearson Liberals promised that they would unionize the federal public service and extend full collective bargaining rights to its members. Pearson won a minority government that year and had to depend on the NDP to sustain his government. One of the prices of NDP support was fulfilling this election pledge, so in the following years the Pearson government established the Prefatory Committee on Collective Bargaining, which was charged with the task of researching the introduction of unionization and collective bargaining into the federal public service.

This committee's work led to the enactment in 1967 of the Public Service Staff Relations Act (PSSRA), the Public Service Employment Act, and amendments to the Financial Administration Act. These legislative initiatives provided the framework for the system of collective bargaining found today in the federal government (Inwood 2012, 291). More recently, in 2005, the PSSRA was superseded by a new **Public Service Labour Relations Act** (PSLRA), which maintains the core operational structure of the old PSSRA while providing greater opportunities for labour dispute mediation.

THE FEDERAL COLLECTIVE BARGAINING SYSTEM

The federal system of labour relations is unique in that, although it gives employees the right to engage in collective bargaining and to take strike action under certain circumstances, it also imposes many restrictions on the scope and substance of collective bargaining. Although most federal employees are unionized, they do not have the same range of rights and powers as unionized workers in the private sector. This is often overlooked by political actors, media analysts, and citizens.

Overshadowing the entire federal collective bargaining system is the government, through parliament. Because the government is both employer and governor, commanding the will of parliament, it is common for major labour relations disputes to become major political disputes, and the balance of power resides securely in the hands of government.

Although the collective bargaining system is quite complex, its basic structure can be quickly outlined. The PSLRA established the **Public Service Labour Relations Board** (PSLRB), a quasi-judicial regulatory agency that

- establishes bargaining units of employees;
- certifies recognized bargaining agents (unions);
- oversees the settlement of contract negotiations (known as interest disputes) and

of grievances launched during the life of a contract (known as rights disputes); and
- resolves disputes respecting unfair or improper bargaining behaviour or conflicting interpretations of labour relations law.

Who Can Bargain

The legislation stipulates that bargaining units be based on the occupational groups and categories recognized by the TBS and the PSC, meaning that there are some 70 bargaining units covering the federal public service. The TBS is the official employer for the purposes of negotiations, and its officials are assisted in this work by senior management from departments and offices specifically concerned with particular bargaining units.

The PSLRA also excludes certain classes of public servants from collective bargaining: managers in the executive category, legal officers in the Department of Justice, TBS officials, and management advisers with respect to labour relations, staffing, and classification. Such exclusions, in the name of distinguishing management from labour, elicit little criticism, but other restrictions have proven very controversial. The legislation distinctly limits collective bargaining to a much narrower set of matters than that found in private sector labour relations.

What Can Be Bargained

The PSLRA confirms that collective bargaining can be undertaken with respect to "rates of pay, hours of work, leave entitlements, standards of discipline, other directly related terms and conditions of employment, grievance procedures, check-off of union dues, occupational health and safety, and career development." Excluded are all matters

FEDERAL PUBLIC SERVICE COLLECTIVE BARGAINING TRACKS

Collective bargaining in the federal public service is complex and time-consuming. Bargaining units can follow two tracks: arbitration or conciliation/strike.

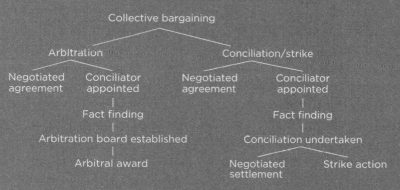

Figure 7.1

Despite the often negative view of public service unions and their collective bargaining rights held by the media and the general public, the federal public service has had a relatively stable history of labour relations with its unionized personnel. Most bargaining units opt for the arbitration track, and the vast majority of negotiations that follow the other track result in a settlement without recourse to strike action.

In fact, strikes in the federal public service are rare. In 1991 the Mulroney Conservative government suspended collective bargaining rights as a means to battle the deficit. The Chrétien Liberal government continued this policy until 1998. The only federal public service strikes in almost two decades took place in 2004, when nearly 5,000 Parks Canada employees struck in August, joined by over 25,000 Canada Revenue Agency employees in September. Both strikes were settled within weeks. And despite great antipathy between the Conservative government of Stephen Harper and federal public service unions, there were no general strikes within the core departmental public service between 2006 and 2015.

THINKING ABOUT COLLECTIVE BARGAINING

1 Do you support the continuation of public sector collective bargaining? If so, are you committed to the right of public servants to strike? Or could this be forsaken in return for a commitment to strengthen the conciliation process? If so, how?

2 If you support the right of public workers to strike, would you place any limits on it? Should firefighters be allowed to strike?

Teachers? Should there be any time limits? Should different sectors of public servants be allowed to strike at the same time, such as border guards and customs and revenue agency employees? Or municipal garbage collectors and public transit drivers?

3 If you aren't in favour of public sector collective bargaining, what would you replace it with?

respecting the organization of the public service, the assignment of duties, the classification of positions, and job evaluation. These are considered management prerogatives.

Also excluded are matters falling within the jurisdiction of the PSC, as denoted by the Public Service Employment Act. This means that recruitment, promotion, transfers, demotion, and firing issues are shut out from collective bargaining. This approach is designed to preserve the special role of the PSC in overseeing the administration of the merit principle. The objective is laudable, but the practice imposes substantial limitations on bargaining units that wish to bring a union perspective to concerns about recruitment, promotion, and transfer.

Governments establish systems designed to meet numerous goals—here, a labour relations system that must adhere to both the merit principle and the rationale of collective bargaining—and those goals can clash. The system has worked tolerably well in recent decades, but the compromises required to establish it remain a source of tension.

COLLECTIVE BARGAINING TRACKS

Bargaining units choose one of two procedures for dealing with the employer: an arbitration track or a conciliation/strike track. The choice is at the discretion of the union, and once chosen it cannot be changed during the course of negotiations.

The first three steps in the two tracks are identical. If negotiations run into difficulties, either party may ask the PSLRB to appoint a conciliator to assess the positions and to advise how to reach an agreement. The conciliator normally provides the board and the parties with a report within 14 days. Fact finding is a further advisory option open to the parties. If it is invoked, it must precede either arbitration or conciliation requests. A third-party fact finder, similar to a conciliator and appointed by the PSLRB, has the duty of communicating with the parties, assessing their positions, and offering advice on how to obtain a settlement. Unlike the conciliator, though, the fact finder has 30 days to report to the board; if the parties fail to reach an agreement within 15 days after submission of the fact finder's report, it is made public. This procedure is designed to promote conciliation, as no party wants to be publicly labelled as unreasonable.

If no agreement has been reached following these steps, the procedure diverges depending on which track has been endorsed. If the arbitration track is followed, the parties are asked to agree on as many issues as possible, and all matters remaining in dispute are handed to an arbitration board acting under the auspices of the PSLRB. These boards are tripartite, consisting of one representative chosen by each of the parties and a third nominee from the PSLRB, selected by the labour and management representatives. The arbitration board then reviews the matters in dispute, hears arguments from each side, and after deciding the merits of the outstanding issues, fashions a collective agreement. This agreement, known as an *arbitral award*, is final and legally binding on both parties for the duration of the contract.

If the conciliation/strike track is followed, either party may request the formation of a conciliation panel. This body, also tripartite in the manner of the arbitration board, gives the parties one last chance to reach an agreement. The conciliation board is mandated to report back to the PSLRB on its work, usually within 14 days. If either party finds the advice of the conciliation board unacceptable,

THE NEW PROFESSIONALS

Between 1997 and 2006 the federal public service went on a hiring spree. Following the lean years of the Chrétien government's program review and the quiet crisis, the senior leadership of the public service knew that the government of Canada had to get re-staffed.

Starting under the leadership of then-Clerk of the Privy Council Jocelyne Bourgon in the late 1990s, the federal public service promoted a policy of institutional renewal to bring new people into the service, improve the working environment, enhance training and development opportunities, and fast-track gifted young employees into management. Between 2003 and 2010, 47,580 new full-time, permanent employees were hired. Those with aspirations for careers in management are known as the new professionals.

The idea is that new professionals bring with them a professionalism defined by certain core values and ideals, such as the desirability of flattening traditional hierarchies. **New Professionalism** is all about greater

- communication
- creativity
- decentralization
- informality
- innovation
- learning
- participation
- teamwork
- variety

The influx of new hires brought with it great opportunities to change the organizational culture, and many of the aspirations and goals of Blueprint 2020 have their genesis in the New Professionals movement.

THINKING ABOUT NEW PROFESSIONALISM

- In your opinion, what are the key values and skills that young Canadians can bring to public service? Enthusiasm? Creativity? Social networking skills? Information management skills? Respect for social diversity?
- What organizational practices and attitudes should be changed by a new generation of employees? Top-down command and control decision making? Hierarchy? Overemphasis on rules and regulations? Overemphasis on job security? Others?
- What values and practices of the federal public service are worth maintaining? Nonpartisanship? Professionalism? Public service ethics? Bilingualism? Respect for authority and tradition? Why?

Sources: Public Service Commission of Canada 2014; New Professionals Organizing Committee 2001.

the bargaining unit has the right to strike following a seven-day cooling-off period after the PSLRB receives the conciliation report.

In the event of a strike, the union and management act out the drama common to any such action: pickets, management continuing to work, protests, press conferences, accusations and counter-accusations, negotiations, mediation, and eventually settlement.

It is important to know how this system operates in practice. While public sector strikes attract a great deal of media attention and public criticism, they are rare. As Morley Gunderson and Robert Hebdon (2010, 195–97) document in a study of collective bargaining across federal, provincial, and municipal public services in Canada, between 1999 and 2007 only 4.8 per cent of contracts were settled following strike action. In contrast, 71.5 per cent were agreed to at the initial bargaining table. A further 6.4 per cent were arrived at through arbitration, and 13.2 per cent through conciliation. A further 2.4 per cent of contracts were the result of legislated impositions and 1.7 per cent by other means.

Despite the fact that there was no love lost between the Conservative government of Stephen Harper and the leadership of federal public service unions, it's also a fact that there were no federal public service-wide strikes during the entirety of Harper's years in power, 2006–15. But this surface calm belied tensions seething below, and certain actions taken by the Harper government likely gave union members reason to question the effectiveness of voting for strike action. A number of legislative acts are noteworthy, illustrating the power that governments hold over their unions:

- In 2007 Bill C-46, the Railway Continuation Act, legislated an end to a CN Rail strike, forcing 2,800 employees back to work and imposing a final offer selection process on outstanding issues.
- In 2009 Bill C-10, an omnibus budget bill including the Expenditure Restraint Act and the Equitable Compensation Act, established salary caps on federal employee raises while prohibiting non-wage increases such as allowances and bonuses. This legislation also stripped public service unions from being able to file pay equity disputes collectively to the Canadian Human Rights Commission.
- In 2011 Bill C-6, the Restoring Mail Delivery for Canadians Act, terminated a postal strike, ordering 48,000 locked-out workers to return to work while also imposing wage raises

lower than those the employer had previously agreed to in collective bargaining.
- In 2012 Bill C-33, the Protecting Air Service Act, pre-empted bargaining between Air Canada and its employees, preventing a strike and imposing a settlement favourable to the employer.
- In 2013 Bill C-60 empowered the federal cabinet to intervene in collective bargaining between Crown corporations and their staff, giving the government the authority to direct the negotiating positions of management.
- Also in 2013 Bill C-4 empowered the federal government to unilaterally define any employee's work as essential, preventing any such employee so defined from taking strike action (Sandborn 2015).

These actions served to tilt the labour relations playing field in favour of the government side in all the affected disputes, while informing union leaders and their membership that if they ever voted for a government-wide strike, the strike would be quickly terminated by legislative fiat and the government would likely dictate a settlement highly favourable to management.

Federal public service union leaders applauded the demise of the Harper government in the fall of 2015, and they hoped the Trudeau Liberal government would be more conciliatory in its approach to federal labour relations. Indeed, Justin Trudeau promised to be so. But the powers that Stephen Harper wielded over the unions still exist. If and when federal public sector collective bargaining leads to impasse and strike votes, the unions will always find themselves at a power disadvantage in comparison to the federal government.

The federal human resources system has become so unwieldy that it is the butt of jokes about the red tape in which almost every action, from hiring to firing, is tied up. But what is insufferable bureaucratese to one person can be fundamental due process to another.

The range of institutions, actors, and policies involved in human resources management is truly staggering. Any significant human resources reform in a single department or agency can involve the institution itself, the TBS, the PSC, the Office of the Commissioner of Official Languages, the PSLRB, the Canadian Human Rights Commission, and public service unions.

The system would clearly be far more efficient if managers could hire and fire at will and use their own judgement in all other personnel decisions as well. But although it would be less prone to formal disputes, would such a laissez-faire, management-oriented approach be desirable? We had such a system prior to World War I, and it came to be universally scorned as patronage ridden and ineffective.

The human resources policies and programs adopted since the early decades of the twentieth century uphold specific values and practical ends deemed important by governments and the public. Thus, we have rules to enforce merit that require open competitions, examinations, interviews, and impartial assessment of candidates, directly circumscribing the personal judgement of managers. Similarly, staffing, deployment, training, and promotion must now take into account official language requirements, anti-discrimination provisions, and employment equity. And managers must also respect the collective bargaining process and contractual obligations. Their work is thus intricate, serving standards far exceeding those of the private sector, and the system we have now has emerged from rationalist considerations. Administrative complexity has been an unfortunate by-product.

The public sector human resources management system *has* to be more open, meritocratic, representative, and equitable than private sector systems. Thus it must also be more institutionally rational. Of course, one can debate the rationalistic merits of systemic elements such as public sector representativeness, responsiveness, employment equity, and the right to strike. And despite claims of rationalist development, the evolution of the system in fact suggests a strongly incremental orientation.

There's always room for improvement in the operationalization of policies and programs, but the principles underlying the public human resources system have evolved over decades and are now well embedded in the nature and working of the Canadian state. If the basic concepts and rules of meritocracy, representativeness and responsiveness, official bilingualism, multiculturalism, human rights policy, employment equity policy, and collective bargaining did not exist, the vast majority of Canadians would probably, once again, invent them.

REFERENCES AND SUGGESTED READING

Adamson, Agar, and Ian Stewart. 1996. "Party Politics in the Not So Mysterious East." In *Party Politics in Canada*, 7th ed., edited by Hugh G. Thorburn, 514–33. Scarborough, ON: Prentice Hall Canada.

Adie, Robert F., and Paul G. Thomas. 1987. *Canadian Public Administration: Problematical Perspectives*. 2nd ed. Scarborough, ON: Prentice Hall Canada.

Agócs, Carol. 1986. "Affirmative Action, Canadian Style: A Reconnaissance." *Canadian Public Policy* 12: 148–62.

———. 1994. "Employment Equity: Is It Needed? Is It Fair?" In *Crosscurrents: Contemporary Political Issues*, 2nd ed., edited by Mark Charlton and Paul Barker, 394–406. Toronto: Nelson.

———, Catherine Burr, and Felicity Somerset. 1992. *Employment Equity: Cooperative Strategies for Organizational Change*. Scarborough, ON: Prentice Hall Canada.

Cameron, Stevie. 1995. *On the Take: Crime, Corruption and Greed in the Mulroney Years*. Toronto: Seal Books.

Canada, House of Commons. 1966. *Debates (Hansard)*. April 6.

———. 1970. *Debates (Hansard)*. June 23.

Canada, Royal Commission on Equality in Employment. 1984. Rosalie S. Abella, Commissioner. *Report*. Ottawa: Supply and Services.

Canada, Royal Commission on Financial Management and Accountability. 1979. The Lambert Commission. *Final Report*. Ottawa: Supply and Services.

Canada, Royal Commission on Government Organization. 1962. The Glassco Commission. *Report*. 5 vols. Ottawa: Queen's Printer.

Canada, Special Committee on the Review of Personnel Management and the Merit Principle. 1979. *Report*. Ottawa: Supply and Services.

Canadian Centre for Management Development Action-Research Roundtable on Official Languages in the Workplace (Canada), Matthieu Leblanc, Patrick Boisvert, and Michael Wernick. 2003. *French to Follow? Revitalizing Official Languages in the Workplace*. Ottawa: CCMD.

Chrétien, Jean. 1986. *Straight from the Heart*. Toronto: Seal Books.

Clement, Wallace. 1983. *Class, Power and Property: Essays on Canadian Society*. Toronto: Methuen.

Drabek, Stan. 1995. "The Federal Public Service: Organizational Structure and Personnel Administration." In *Introductory Readings in Canadian Government and Politics*, 2nd ed., edited by Robert M. Krause and R.H. Wagenberg, 193–210. Toronto: Copp Clark.

Fraser, Graham. 2006. *Sorry, I Don't Speak French*. Toronto: McClelland and Stewart.

Gunderson, Morley, and Robert Hebdon. 2010. "Collective Bargaining and Dispute Resolution in the Public Sector." In *The Handbook of Canadian Public Administration*, 2nd ed., edited by Christopher Dunn, 186–202. Toronto: Oxford University Press.

Harris, Michael. 2014. *Party of One: Stephen Harper and Canada's Radical Makeover*. Toronto: Viking Canada.

Howe, Brian, and Katherine Covell. 1994. "Making Employment Equity Legitimate." *Inroads* 3: 70–79.

———, and David Johnson. 2000. *Restraining Equality: Human Rights Commissions in Canada*. Toronto: University of Toronto Press.

Ibbitson, John. 2015. *Stephen Harper*. Toronto: Signal/McClelland and Stewart.

Inwood, Gregory J. 2012. *Understanding Canadian Public Administration: An Introduction to Theory and Practice*. 4th ed. Toronto: Pearson Canada.

Jackson, Robert J., and Doreen Jackson. 2001. *Politics in Canada: Culture, Institutions, Behaviour and Public Policy*. 5th ed. Toronto: Prentice Hall.

Juillet, Luc, and Ken Rasmussen. 2008. *Defending a Contested Ideal: Merit and the PSC of Canada 1908–2008*. Ottawa: University of Ottawa Press.

Kernaghan, Kenneth, and David Siegel. 1999. *Public Administration in Canada: A Text*. 4th ed. Toronto: Nelson.

Love, J.D. 1979. "Personnel Organization in the Canadian Public Service: Some Observations on the Past." *Canadian Public Administration* 22: 402–14.

Martin, Lawrence. 2010. *Harperland: The Politics of Control*. Toronto: Viking Canada.

McRoberts, Kenneth. 1993. *Quebec: Social Change and Political Crisis*. 3rd ed. Toronto: McClelland and Stewart.

New Professionals Organizing Committee. 2001. *New Professionals Driving a New Public Service: A Report*. Toronto: Institute of Public Administration of Canada.

Olsen, Dennis. 1980. *The State Elite*. Toronto: McClelland and Stewart.

Porter, John. 1958. "Higher Public Servants and the Bureaucratic Elite in Canada." *Canadian Journal of Economics and Political Science* 24: 483–501.

———. 1968. "The Economic Elite and the Social Structure of Canada." In *Canadian Society: Sociological Perspectives*, 3rd ed., edited by B.R. Blishen et al., 754–72. Toronto: Macmillan Canada.

Privy Council Office. 2013a. *BluePrint 2020: Getting Started-Getting Your Views; Building Tomorrow's Public Service Together*. Ottawa; Queen's Printer.

———. 2013b. *What We've Heard: BluePrint 2020 Summary Interim Progress Report*. Ottawa: Queen's Printer.

———. 2014. *Destination 2020: Excellence, Innovation, Service*. Ottawa: Queen's Printer.

Public Service Commission of Canada. 2014. *Public Service Commission 2013–2014 Annual Report*. Ottawa: Queen's Printer.

Roberts, Jack. 1994. "Employment Equity—Unfair." In *Crosscurrents: Contemporary Political Issues*, 2nd ed., edited by Mark Charlton and Paul Barker, 407–16. Toronto: Nelson.

Sandborn, Tom. 2015. "Harper's Conservatives No Friend to the Union Worker." *The Tyee: News, Culture, Solutions*, July 17. http://thetyee.ca/Opinion/2015/07/17/ Harper-No-Friend-to-Union-Workers/.

Savoie, Donald J. 1999. *Governing from the Centre: The Concentration of Power in Canadian Politics*. Toronto: University of Toronto Press.

———. 2015. *What Is Government Good at? A Canadian Answer*. Montreal: McGill-Queen's University Press.

Siegel, David. 1988. "The Changing Shape and Nature of Public Service Employment." *Canadian Public Administration* 31: 159–93.

Simpson, Jeffrey. 1988. *Spoils of Power: The Politics of Patronage*. Toronto: Collins.

Swimmer, Gene, et al. 1994. "Public Service 2000: Dead or Alive?" In *How Ottawa Spends 1994–1995*, edited by Susan Philips, 165–204. Ottawa: Carleton University Press.

Treasury Board of Canada Secretariat. 1994. *Employment Equity in the Public Service of Canada 1993–94. Annual Report to Parliament*. Ottawa: Queen's Printer.

———. 2014a. *Employment Equity in the Public Service of Canada 2013–14. Annual Report to Parliament*. Ottawa: Queen's Printer.

———. 2014b. *Annual Report on Official Languages 2013–14*. Ottawa: Queen's Printer.

Weiner, Nan. 2010. "Workplace Equity: Human Rights, Employment Equity, and Pay Equity." In *The Handbook of Canadian Public Administration*, 2nd ed., edited by Christopher Dunn, 165–85. Toronto: Oxford University Press.

RELATED WEBSITES

Canada School of Public Service. www.csps-efpc.gc.ca

MERX. Canadian Public Tenders: Federal, Provincial, and Municipal. www.merx.com

Office of the Chief Human Resources Officer. www.tbs-sct.gc.ca/ip-pi/mandate-mandat/chro-dprh-eng.asp

Office of the Commissioner of Official Languages. www.ocol-clo.gc.ca

Public Service Alliance of Canada. www.psacunion.ca

Public Service Commission of Canada. www.psc-cfp.gc.ca

Public Service Commission of Canada – Career Recruitment. www.jobs-emploi.gc.ca

Public Service Commission of Canada – Post-secondary Recruitment. http://jobs-emplois.gc.ca/common-commun/redir/psr-rp.htm.

Treasury Board of Canada Secretariat. www.tbs-sct.gc.ca

CHAPTER 8

Issues in Management Reform

Reform, that you may persevere.

–Lord Macaulay, 1831

After reading this chapter and its related web pages you will be able to

- identify the principles of new public management;
- articulate and assess the ten elements of reinventing government;
- debate the pros and cons of reinvention versus reform;
- analyze the degree to which the Harper government transformed the federal public service; and
- assess the future reform options faced by the Trudeau government.

8 Issues in Management Reform

Government and public sector management have undergone a major rethinking and reworking over the past quarter-century, as previous chapters have noted. Governments have had time now to implement new approaches, and with the benefit of hindsight we can look at the merits and shortcomings of the paradigmatic shift to a "leaner and friendlier" public service. New concepts of governance have brought about some changes in the structure and role of government, but they have been more evolutionary than revolutionary, more a reform than a reinvention.

The idea that government can be, or even should be, reinvented to become more like the private sector is highly contested. Even the relatively modest reforms of the federal government have had a significant impact on both governance and society, and the federal public service remains committed to the ideal of "renewal." But in one area reforms have had little effect: in the practical exercise of executive power, the centralized command-and-control mode of decision making remains firmly entrenched. It is doubtful whether the prime ministership of Justin Trudeau will effect any great change here.

This chapter examines the ideas underlying approaches to government and its management that have emerged since the 1980s, the debates those ideas provoke, and the practical impact of new methods on Canadian governments, particularly the federal government. The logical starting point is what is known as New Public Management.

NEW PUBLIC MANAGEMENT

New public management (NPM) is a theory that emerged in the Conservative government of Margaret Thatcher in Britain, and its influence is still felt across the Western world to this day. As Peter Aucoin (1995, 1–2) has outlined, Thatcher came to power in 1979 stressing that three dimensions of British government had to be reformed:

1 The power of the public service had to be diminished to make government more subject and responsive to the will of elected ministers, not career bureaucrats.
2 Public sector management had to incorporate private sector practices to enhance the economy and efficiency of government programs.
3 Public services were to be redesigned to make them more responsive to the needs of individual citizens, ensuring that public officials had as their primary concern service delivery and quality.

As the Thatcher government began implementing these policies through such measures as privatization, deregulation, public sector downsizing, the contracting out of public services, expenditure restraint initiatives, and the introduction of user fees and the commercialization of public services, the media in Britain and abroad sat up and took notice, as did academics around the world. Facing a hailstorm of controversy, Prime

Minister Thatcher held firm in her commitment to reshape and reform the British government, and this she largely achieved (Savoie 1994, 200–13; Aucoin 1995, 3–5).

What many conservatives considered a much-desired and long-awaited neoconservative revolution after decades of social democratic and liberal reform was something to be emulated elsewhere. President Ronald Reagan in the United States and, to a lesser degree, Prime Minister Brian Mulroney in Canada tried to capture the vision and direction of the Iron Lady.

ARTICULATING THE THEORY

As Thatcherite initiatives came to dominate British government and influence other countries, they came under increasing academic scrutiny. Christopher Hood (1991) coined the term *new public management* and described it as centred on some key assumptions about what is important:

- keeping the roles of politicians and public sector managers separate;
- adopting private sector management techniques;
- focusing on objective results; and
- emphasizing participatory management systems.

A common thread running through these themes is the idea that government bureaucracies must be accountable and responsible to both their political masters and the public. The principles and practices of NPM, it is claimed, make the public sector more faithful and subject to the direction of elected politicians while it devotes much greater attention to the quality of the services it delivers to citizens.

Separating Politics and Management

Politicians and public sector managers must keep their roles clearly distinguished. The former take a decisive lead in policy making, while the latter focus almost exclusively on management and program implementation. In the past, this perspective maintains, senior managers exerted too great an influence on policy, thereby distorting and limiting the role of ministers and distracting senior managers from their primary responsibility: the active and effective management of government activities.

Managers are thus expected to devote most of their attention to improving administrative performance. Governments are to set explicit goals, standards, and measures of performance, and managers are to ensure that objectives are met economically, efficiently, and effectively.

Applying Private Sector Techniques

NPM stresses the importance of private sector modes of operation and management. As much as possible, government is to be run as a business, and its bureaucracy is to operate within a competitive environment. Public sector managers are expected to think and act in a similar way to their private sector counterparts.

Achieving Objective Results

Management is admonished to concentrate on, and achieve, objective results. Government "outputs" are to matter much more than "inputs," though the efficient use of resources is always a primary consideration. The focus on output can require a fundamental redesign of government organizations, downsizing of bureaucracies, disaggregation of bureaucratic units, and decentralization of bureaucratic power through participatory management.

Emphasizing Participatory Management

Systems of participatory management are viewed as essential to liberating the productive potential of government organizations, making them progressive and innovative bodies with a much better record of achievement and customer service. This is in keeping with much of the literature on contemporary organizational theory discussed in Chapter 5.

REINVENTING GOVERNMENT

As new public management came to dominate thinking about the structure and process of government in the Western world, it gained academic proponents. Hood was the first to give the concept a coherent theoretical form, but by far the most influential and well-known advocates of NPM have been two Americans, David Osborne and Ted Gaebler. Their *Reinventing Government: How the Entrepreneurial Spirit Is Transforming the Public Sector* became a bestseller in the United States in 1992, no small feat for a book on public sector management. Its success not only disseminated the ideas across a wide popular audience but also legitimized them among government leaders—both politicians and managers—in the United States and beyond.

Osborne and Gaebler contend that governments can be, and are being, "reinvented" through the application of entrepreneurialism to their managerial forms and operations. By becoming more streamlined, flexible, and responsive, government structures—founded on such concepts as empowerment, competition, enterprise, anticipation, and market orientation—can be radically changed and program results fundamentally improved. In advancing these claims, Osborne and Gaebler developed ten principles of **reinventing government** to turn public sector managers into public sector entrepreneurs.

DISPATCH BOX

THE TEN PRINCIPLES OF REINVENTING GOVERNMENT

1. Catalytic government: steering rather than rowing
2. Community-owned government: empowering rather than serving
3. Competitive government: injecting competition into service delivery
4. Mission-driven government: transforming rule-driven government
5. Results-oriented government: funding outcomes, not inputs
6. Customer-driven government: meeting the needs of the customer, not the bureaucracy
7. Enterprising government: earning rather than spending
8. Anticipatory government: preventing rather than curing
9. Decentralized government: encouraging participation and teamwork, not hierarchy
10. Market-oriented government: leveraging change through the market

CATALYTIC GOVERNMENT

Principle no. 1 is the idea of *steering rather than rowing*. Government should be innovative, not reactive and traditional. Rather than dealing with issues as they arise and engaging in standardized, bureaucratic forms of decision making and program delivery—the routine tasks of administrative "rowing"—governments are encouraged to be catalytic. They should delve beneath the surface of issues to find newer and better ways to address them.

Part of this approach involves bringing together the concerned parties—individuals, interest groups, and businesses—to brainstorm and cooperate in developing new approaches, programs, and forms of delivery. These parties may themselves be able to deal with the issue, leaving the state to function as the catalyst for innovation rather than the default source of service delivery.

Governments and their managers thus become leaders and innovators, encouraging alternative policy and program design and facilitating its implementation. Service delivery is vested in either the public service, the private sector, the voluntary sector, or a mixture of public–private partnerships.

The foundation of catalytic government is thus quite simple: government and management must be prepared

- to be innovative
- to break from traditional ways of doing things
- to encourage interested parties to work with government to redesign policies and programs
- to embrace new forms of policy and program development and implementation

We can find a practical example in federal government use of non-governmental organizations—NGOs—to implement Canadian international development assistance.

COMMUNITY-OWNED GOVERNMENT

Principle no. 2 encompasses the idea of *empowering rather than serving*. Government and the communities it serves need to forge deeper links. Inherent in traditional bureaucratic action is the idea that governments have the answers to problems and control the means of addressing them; citizens are passive recipients of state initiatives.

Rather than maintain this state of dependency, governments should empower citizens and communities to claim ownership of public policies and program initiatives. People should come to see themselves as "clients," "customers," or "consumers" of government services, with stakeholder claims and the right to be involved in particular policy fields. The citizen as client views the public sector as a way to enable individuals, social groups, businesses, and the community as a whole to take responsibility for these policy fields and, ultimately, for their own lives. Such partnerships could take the form of cooperation between a government and local non-profit community development groups, for example, in a project to promote heritage conservation or social housing initiatives in local neighbourhoods.

COMPETITIVE GOVERNMENT

Principle no. 3 involves *injecting competition into service delivery*. Public sector managers are counselled to

- recognize the limitations of government;
- understand that attempting to provide every traditional service drains public resources and overextends the operational capabilities of public organizations, reducing service quality and effectiveness; and
- draw on a wide variety of public, private, voluntary or non-profit organizational actors, and combinations thereof, to deliver services.

By breaking their traditional monopoly on public service delivery, public servants can create an entrepreneurial environment in which the right to deliver services to specified program quality standards for a contractually limited period and for a set amount of money becomes the norm, with the lowest bidder receiving the contract. The results, according to Osborne and Gaebler, are greater economy and efficiency, service responsiveness, and innovation. In practice, competitive government initiatives are found mostly at the municipal level, centred on issues such as the privatization of local sanitation services.

MISSION-DRIVEN GOVERNMENT

Principle no. 4 is to *transform rule-driven government*. Public sector organizations should focus their attention on new ways to achieve their mission rather than on rules and standard operating procedures. The *raison d'être* of an organization should become the driving force behind all of its actions, the premise on which public sector entrepreneurs base their financial, personnel, administrative, and legal operations.

The aim is to create intelligent, innovative institutions and a system of government in which directions and vision are the chief characteristics.

On a very broad scale, think of how the Canada Health Act acts as a mission statement for governments in general, and federal and provincial Departments of Health in particular.

RESULTS-ORIENTED GOVERNMENT

Principle no. 5 entails *funding outcomes, not inputs*. The quest for mission-driven government naturally flows into results-oriented government. The priority of the public sector is the successful realization of desired ends—policy and program results—rather than the routine oversight of organizational means.

While careful operational management will always remain an important consideration, Osborne and Gaebler urge managers to place greater stress on performance and results. In this sense, institutional inputs are to be managed in order to accomplish the organizational mission. The degree to which this is achieved is the benchmark of institutional success. Examples include initiatives such as provincial restorative justice programs to help young offenders come to terms with the consequences of their crimes by working on restitution with their victims, or federal and provincial funding for child care and early education programs, in which the money invested is intended to reduce the risk and cost of problem children and youth crime later on.

CUSTOMER-DRIVEN GOVERNMENT

Principle no. 6 is the concept of *meeting the needs of the customer, not the bureaucracy*. In this new system, citizens engage with government bodies as customers, or clients, and their needs are paramount. Osborne and Gaebler argue that large government bureaucracies have traditionally acted on the opposite principle, that their interests and self-preservation come first and that it is their duty to define and deal with the needs of citizens.

Reinvented government thus turns the system on its head, demanding that government organizations and their employees have citizens' needs as their central focus. Growing government awareness of this dynamic can be seen in the use of employee and customer satisfaction surveys by government offices and departments.

ENTERPRISING GOVERNMENT

Principle no. 7 exhorts a focus on *earning rather than spending*. In light of current limitations on financial resources and the reluctance of governments and the public to accept new tax increases, Osborne and Gaebler emphasize that governments and public sector entrepreneurs must "do more with less," borrowing financial concepts from the private sector.

Public sector entrepreneurs are advised to think more about earning than about spending money and to bring the profit motive into the operations of their institutions. User fees are promoted as a way of raising revenues.

Likewise, government organizations should experiment with ways to save as another form of revenue generation. Rather than spending their full annual appropriations by the end of each fiscal year or seeing the unused portion returned to government coffers (in Canada, the Consolidated Revenue Fund), public sector managers should help to save allocated monies for future use. Any savings they realize are to remain with the organization, to be deployed in the service of its mission as its managers deem best. One creative and long-term practice, for example, is to use savings to create a capital pool for investment, on which the organization derives a return that can fund further activities.

In short, bureaucracies are expected to be less traditional and more enterprising in how they use and develop financial resources.

ANTICIPATORY GOVERNMENT

Principle no. 8 is to act by *prevention rather than cure*. Public sector entrepreneurs accomplish this by being

- progressive in their policy and program thinking
- dynamic and anticipatory in their approach to problems
- engaged in close communication and mutual education with all parties in a policy field to enable the government organization to anticipate developments

Leading change, managing need, and preventing problems are specific ways in which managers act on both this principle and the first: steering rather than rowing. Consider how Canadian banking regulations have long been more stringent than those found in the United States. As a result, the Canadian financial sector did not suffer the catastrophic losses that the American sector did in the 2008–09 recession. Canadian governments anticipated the problems that could follow from widespread financial sector deregulation and steered the financial sector in a preventative direction.

DECENTRALIZED GOVERNMENT

Principle no. 9 is to move away *from hierarchy to participation and teamwork*. Osborne and

Gaebler assert that the public sector must recognize how organizations are moving away from traditional command and control models and learning to operate more economically, efficiently, and effectively if they are decentralized and more participatory.

Advances in information technology and communication systems, and improvements in workforce quality and managerial capabilities have made possible a more flexible, productive, team-based approach. Public sector entrepreneurs are challenged to build "smart organizations" that can make full use of the material and human resources available. Decision making can be extended throughout the organization, placed in the hands of those who are most aware of practical realities and how to serve customer needs more successfully.

Thus, tactical decision making can be decentralized to those most knowledgeable, while overall strategic direction can remain firmly in the control of senior management. Senior managerial/entrepreneurial leadership must keep close communication links with middle management and field-level "customer service agents." Such decentralization can be observed in informal staff meetings at which senior executives discuss work processes and improvements with middle managers, junior managers, and other staff, or when governments fund community development groups that work alongside them to promote social and economic programs at the local level.

MARKET-ORIENTED GOVERNMENT

Principle no. 10 is the concept of *leveraging change through the market*. Public sector managers are advised to think of all facets of socio-economic life in holistic terms, divided not into public and private spheres per se but into markets. International, national, regional, and local markets represent a collection of people, interests, and interwoven socio-economic forces beyond the control of any single public or private sector body. According to Osborne and Gaebler, public servants should

- use the logic of market economics to promote social change and ensure economic growth and prosperity, rather than attempting to control markets through conventional policy and programs; and
- structure policies and programs to work with, rather than against, dominant market forces and their underlying assumptions and trends.

Privatization initiatives are examples of market-oriented approaches to government. The privatization of Petro-Canada, Air Canada, CN Rail, and the Canadian Wheat Board were considered by their proponents as means to promote the full market potential of these industries by turning them over to private management.

By being more in tune with market imperatives, governments can dovetail their activities with those of the private sector to achieve desired public policies within the broader social and economic system.

SUMMING UP THE MANIFESTO

These ten principles of reinventing government stand not only as a widely popular manifesto but also as a fundamental challenge to traditional understanding of the nature and role of the public sector. Osborne and Gaebler provide a new conceptual framework for government and public sector management—an analytical checklist for developing a new paradigm.

"What we are describing is nothing less than a shift in the basic model of governance used in America," they assert. "This shift is underway all around us, but because we are not looking for it—because we assume that all governments have to be big, centralized and bureaucratic—we seldom see it. We are blind to the new realities because they do not fit our preconceptions" (Osborne and Gaebler 1992, 321). The imperatives of that shift calls for government to be

- smaller yet more focused
- driven by mission and results
- geared to customer service
- founded on market-oriented ideas of competition, enterprise, entrepreneurialism, anticipatory action, community empowerment, and participatory management

In short, government must be more businesslike, and that will make it more efficient, responsive, and accountable to those it serves.

THE CANADIAN PERSPECTIVE

New public management ideas are not foreign to this country. In Canada, the reinvention thesis came to be supported by various analysts, most notably Sandford Borins (1995a, 1995b) and Bryne Purchase and Ronald Hirshhorn (1994). Proponents of government reinvention have publicized their views over the past three decades sufficiently well that Canadian governments have seized on these ideas as guidelines for restructuring their own institutional structures and managerial operations. Conservative provincial governments in Alberta (under Premier Ralph Klein) and Ontario (under Premier Mike Harris) both sought to promote NPM principles in their initiatives to restructure their public services, and the federal Conservative government of Prime Minister Stephen Harper did likewise with the national government. The Liberal provincial government in Nova Scotia under Premier Stephen McNeil became the latest administration to seek significant reforms to the structures and functioning of public services according to NPM ideals.

SANDFORD BORINS

Borins emphasized that the theory was neither a "simplistic Big Answer" to government problems nor a panacea for fiscal management difficulties. Rather, he saw it simply as a valid way to reconfigure public sector management. In line with Osborne and Gaebler, Borins (1995a, 122–32) contended that a growing body of Canadian evidence suggested government service can be dramatically improved through innovations in delivery, managerial autonomy, administrative empowerment, and the use of performance indicators geared to competitive, entrepreneurial models of program management.

Spurred by public demand for better service and government imperatives to restrain costs, Borins asserted, these new dynamics of innovation now form a fundamental aspect of the organizational environment of all governments in Canada.

BRYNE PURCHASE AND RONALD HIRSHHORN

Purchase and Hirshhorn (1994, 43) agreed that reinvention is part of the "post-bureaucratic paradigm" in public sector management, in which the core concepts of the old framework—public interest, administration, authority, structure, and cost justification—are transcended by stronger principles: results that citizens value, quality, productiveness, and the identification of "missions, services, customers, and outcomes." The means to these ends include

- restructuring organizations;
- reconfiguring public sector managerial orientation;
- redesigning government programs and responsibilities;
- using private sector approaches to policy and program implementation more extensively; and
- encouraging an environment conducive to smaller government with a more market-oriented, entrepreneurial, and businesslike attitude to public service and management.

KENNETH KERNAGHAN, BRIAN MARSON, AND BORINS AGAIN

More recently, Kernaghan, Marson, and Borins (2000, 23–24) have highlighted the breadth of concepts captured under the rubric of NPM within the Canadian context. They were quite sympathetic to its overall goals, which they describe as embracing three strands of public sector reform:

1 reducing the role of the state through such practices as privatization, deregulation, and contracting out
2 restructuring government organizations
3 improving management through participatory decision making and employee empowerment

All three derive from and inform NPM thinking, but as these authors indicated, specific initiatives can be broader or narrower and more or less radical in their implications for government and for citizens.

In typical fashion, most Canadian governments, especially the federal government and even including the Harper Conservative government, have been relatively moderate and centrist in their application of NPM approaches, privileging managerial reforms over the wholesale reinvention of systems. Such restraint stems in part from the many criticisms of NPM that emerged in the 1990s, and in part from a recognition of inherent limitations in the ability to make fundamental changes in government organizations (Lindquist 2010b, 10–13).

CRITICISM OF REINVENTION

The reinvention thesis has not been without its critics in this country. A number of Canadian scholars have articulated highly unfavourable assessments, none more eloquently than Donald Savoie. Michael Trebilcock and Paul Thomas have also explored weaknesses and gaps in new public management theory.

DONALD SAVOIE

Influenced by the work of American critic James Q. Wilson, Savoie contends that NPM is "basically flawed" in that it fails to recognize fundamental and important differences between the public and private sectors. He warns that the ideologically conservative orientation of the reinvention thesis can lead to a paradigm shift in the way we perceive the nature and operation of government (1995, 112–16). While he does assert that governments can make many improvements to become more economical, efficient, effective, socially responsive, and accountable, reforms should not come at the expense of the core traditions and duties of the public service (Savoie 2015, 114–15).

Remembering the Public Good

As Savoie argues, the state and the public service have important roles to play in the socio-economic, cultural, and political life of this country. The public sector has a distinct purpose: it develops and implements public policy to serve the collective interests of society. Conversely, the private sector promotes private interests as defined by the logic of profit-seeking entrepreneurs. That is wholly different from public interests determined through the decision making of democratically elected governments. In other words, the purpose of government is fundamentally different from the purpose of private sector firms, and the core operational assumptions of the latter are therefore ill suited to the former.

Savoie therefore asserts that government must view people first and foremost as citizens with equal rights and interests, not primarily as consumers or clients with individualized wants. And government itself is an important institution that promotes our broad societal goals of democracy, accountability, social responsiveness, equity, due process, the rule of law, and the serving of collective need. Thus, social purpose and the public good matter more than private interest, just as the provision of public services to citizens as a right is more important than profitability and cost effectiveness.

The fear that Savoie and others express is that the ideological values of NPM will weaken governments, making them smaller and less significant in the life of society and thus diminishing the public realm, the public interest, and the public good.

Working within Constraints

Savoie (1995, 117–21) also notes the managerial and political limitations of NPM. In many ways its principles are simplistic. The radical change envisioned by the reinvention thesis is unlikely to occur—or to survive for long—in an environment of political and administrative complexity. Government policies and programs exist within a world of political and legal constraints, among them public expectations of service standards, established practices, the professional assumptions of political and bureaucratic actors, and judicially recognized rights to particular administrative procedures. In this context, practical wisdom, respect for the political and legal trade-offs that have spawned existing policies and programs, and command-and-control power relations are as important as managerial economy and efficiency. And administrative decision making is thus inherently incremental and restrained.

It is unlikely, as Savoie suggests, that public servants will transform the way they manage policies and programs very radically, just as it is unlikely that client groups will seek fundamental changes to programs to which they have become accustomed. Nor will senior managers and their political superiors embrace participatory management and the democratization of decision-making power when they are used to being in charge. Such a substantial transfer of authority seems implausible—despite rhetoric to the contrary.

Savoie's general conclusion is that change within government is naturally incremental, not only because it is practical but because it is desirable: cautious, gradual reform nurtures an accumulated wisdom that is sensitive to political, legal, and administrative contexts. And that tells managers whether a given change is actually viable.

For these reasons, Savoie is very skeptical about the success on any NPM-inspired reform. "Suffice to note," he stated in 2015, "that very few voices still claim that the managerial revolution was a success or that it had the desired impact…. NPM could never duplicate private sector conditions in government. More to the point, no government has been able to reconcile the need to hold government agencies and their bureaucrats accountable, requiring them to be subordinate to politicians while requiring them to be strong, decisive, and efficient, as NPM called for" (114).

MICHAEL TREBILCOCK

This gradualist defence of reform over reinvention is also reflected in the works of Michael Trebilcock. While Trebilcock, like Savoie, is quite supportive of the idea that governments ought to perform their duties more economically and efficiently, he contends that "institutional evolution, rather than revolution in the way governments do their work is all that we can reasonably aspire to" (1994, 6). In addition to the constraints just described, Trebilcock asserts the importance of established administrative culture within bureaucracies and the relation of that culture to the broader political environment within which an institution operates.

It is important to recall the established concepts of public service: public duty, citizen equality, due process, rights to public services, public accountability, and affirmation of the role of the state as distinct from private interest. Since these concepts are embedded in Canada's political environment, radical alteration of any one is doubtful unless it is influenced by change in the others. But as Trebilcock points out, no fundamental shift can be observed in our expectations of democratic politics, public service, and the role of the state. We want our public bureaucracies to be more efficient, but as observed in Chapter 2, there is no social consensus over the need for a commercialized and downsized public sector (Trebilcock 1994, 68–73).

PAUL THOMAS

Paul Thomas (1993, 55; 2010, 124–27) echoes these points, stressing that change within any organization, public or private, depends on a host of factors such as "size, structure, process, leadership and culture." Adaptation to changing concerns and demands is important for any organization, but one should beware the allure of fundamentalist, holistic prescriptions. In Thomas's analysis, substantial organizational change "tends to be disorderly, disjointed and problematic. There is no magic recipe for success" (1993, 57). He, too, sees public sector reconfiguration as emerging incrementally as managers respond to pressures for reform, political and institutional expectations, rules, and conventional wisdom about the role of the state.

As does Trebilcock, Thomas affirms the importance of administrative culture: "Culture has replaced structure as the most popular variable in the organizational change process" (1993, 57). Significant alterations to government organizations thus depend on their meshing with established and respected institutional values, attitudes, and beliefs. As Savoie emphasizes, the culture of the public sector is fundamentally different from that of the private sector, for important and valid reasons.

And as with Trebilcock and Savoie, Thomas sees no real impetus in Canadian society for a fundamental rethinking of governments and their roles. Rather than witnessing the reinvention of government, at most, he suggests, we will observe its reform (2010, 124).

NEW PUBLIC MANAGEMENT IN PRACTICE

Federal Canadian governments, most notably those of the Mulroney Progressive Conservatives, the Chrétien Liberals, and the Harper Conservatives, have undertaken initiatives influenced by these new ways of thinking about government and public sector management. Financial and personnel management reforms during the 1980s and 90s have been considered in previous chapters and their related web pages; here we consider those initiatives as examples of how government has redesigned its policy in keeping with the logic of NPM. But theory and practice are two different things. As we examine how the NPM-inspired initiatives of the past several federal governments have been implemented, we see the incrementalist

approach to change seeping through the reinventionist principle.

The Mulroney government was the first to embrace the ideals of reinvention, and substantial privatization and some deregulation were its primary NPM accomplishments. Also of importance was the initiative known as **PS2000**. This was a major rationalistic reform launched by the PCO in 1989 to "simplify personnel policies, to loosen central agency controls and increase managerial freedom of department managers, and to increase efficiency and program delivery" (Inwood 2012, 306). PS2000 was launched with much fanfare, promising more business-oriented strategies for departmental planning and human resources and program management, but it never fulfilled the vision of its creators. Its call for greater decentralization of decision making—to "let the managers manage"—caused infighting between central agencies and departments, and the Treasury Board never shared the enthusiasm the PCO felt for PS2000.

Proponents of the initiative spoke of greater participatory management, but increasing deficit and debt problems confronted by the government encouraged a top-down, command-and-control style of governance. By 1992, PS2000 was dead in the water.

THE CHRÉTIEN GOVERNMENT AND REINVENTION

As its Progressive Conservative predecessor was, the Chrétien Liberal government was motivated by NPM principles. In the by then common rhetoric of managerial change, it wanted to make government more responsive, participatory, and accountable, and capable of doing more with less.

The major projects it undertook toward these ends were **program review**, discussed in Chapter 6, and **La Relève**, discussed in the website materials for Chapter 7. The Thinking Government website provides a full analysis of these initiatives and how well they stood as examples of NPM restructuring. While both were signature developments of the Chrétien government in the mid-1990s, program review was by far the more influential and controversial.

The program review exercise between 1995 and 1998, designed as a rationalistic approach to "right-sizing" the programs and public service delivery methods of the federal government, was first and foremost a method to assist the government in balancing the federal budget. Through program review the federal government

- eliminated around 39,000 positions from the public service and the military;
- reduced spending by $29 billion between 1995 and 1998;
- downsized the departments of Agriculture, Agri-Food, Environment, Canadian Heritage, Human Resources Development, Industry, National Defence, Natural Resources, and Transportation;
- unilaterally disbanded Established Programs Financing and the Canada Assistance Plan, replacing them with the Canada Health and Social Transfer (CHST);
- reduced fiscal commitment to the CHST by $4.5 billion;

- revamped the unemployment insurance system, renaming it employment insurance, and introduced stricter requirements for making claims and smaller benefit payments;
- privatized the national system of air traffic control;
- offloaded to local authorities responsibility for airports and harbours; and
- downsized federal agencies responsible for environmental protection, food products and consumer protection, and housing development.

Program review, in short, marked the single greatest reduction in the size and scope of the federal government in Canadian history. And it was heralded as the means to control the nation's finances, lower and eventually eliminate the deficit, and build the framework for budgetary surpluses.

La Relève can be seen as a consequence of program review. As discussed in Chapter 7, restructuring and downsizing took their toll on public service morale and operational capabilities. With years of pay freezes and moratoria on new hiring, the public sector had not been renewing itself, and the quality of service and delivery was suffering. La Relève was launched to revitalize the public service, and to do so it borrowed ideas from NPM with regard to organizational efficiency and effectiveness, participatory management, and improved service delivery. While La Relève was initiated with much fanfare in 1997, by the end of the Martin government in 2006 it had run its course, with questionable success. As is often the case with such reform undertakings, high expectations soon come to confront the realities of standard operating procedures, bureaucratic inertia, and the demands of "command and control" executive leadership. See the Thinking Government website for a fuller assessment of the trials and tribulations of La Relève.

THE HARPER GOVERNMENT AND REINVENTION

When Stephen Harper became prime minister in 2006 his government inherited a public service already committed to strengthening its accountability. The focus on reform came from the government of Paul Martin and his attempts to address the fallout of the sponsorship scandal (see Chapter 1). The main NPM features of the Harper years were the Federal Accountability Act and public service renewal.

THE FEDERAL ACCOUNTABILITY ACT

The new prime minister wanted to put his own stamp on federal reform initiatives, and he quickly did so by passing the Federal Accountability Act, 2006, as his first act as head of government. The main provisions of the legislation were to

- reform political party financing
- strengthen the role of the ethics commissioner
- toughen the Lobbyists Registration Act (now the Lobbying Act, 2008)
- establish a parliamentary budget officer
- clean up the procurement of government contracts
- protect public service whistleblowers

- strengthen legislation governing access to information
- strengthen the power of the auditor general
- strengthen auditing and financial accountability within departments
- establish a director of public prosecutions

When the Act was passed into law in December 2006, the prime minister stated, "We promised to stand up for accountability and to change the way government works. Canadians elected this government to deliver on that commitment and today the Federal Accountability Act has received Royal Assent. From this day on, accountability in government is the law and we can all be proud of that fact" (Canada, Prime Minister's Office 2006).

PUBLIC SERVICE RENEWAL

The other primary reform initiative of the Harper government was to reshape the federal public service through a policy known as **public service renewal**. This policy had its origins in the work of a committee established by Prime Minister Harper in 2006 to advise him how to improve the quality of the federal public service. In its first report, in March 2007, the committee articulated seven conclusions:

1 There is a clear requirement for a strong and sustainable Public Service that can be a source of pride and advantage for Canada in today's globalized economy.
2 While today's Public Service has obvious capacity, commitment and ability, it cannot afford to take these strengths for granted.
3 Renewing the Public Service must produce an institution that is truly representative of

Canadians of all backgrounds and from all parts of Canada.

4 There is a need for a strong and positive Public Service "brand" that will support the marketing of the Public Service as an attractive employment option for talented Canadians.

5 To inspire the best performance from employees, it is essential for leaders to model public service values, and to publicly recognize accomplishments that reflect those values. Non-monetary recognition assumes particular importance in the public service context.

6 The business of the Public Service requires strategic planning and integrates human resources management with business goals, and aligns talent with priorities and higher risk endeavours.

7 The Public Service needs more systematic and rigorous programs of leadership development that involve people with a diversity of skills from across the country, and that equip leaders for success in the future. (Canada, Prime Minister's Advisory Committee 2007, 5)

Shaping the Policy

These ideas came to form the core of the public service renewal initiative established in 2007, and reform was geared to four priority areas:

- First, integrated planning. We must understand the current and future business of departments, and ensure we have the people and resources to deliver it. We must ensure that we connect our people requirement to our business plans and align our resources.

- Second, recruitment. We need to renew and sustain our capacity at all levels. 86% of our hiring right now is for short-term purposes, which only emphasizes the need for strategic, integrated planning. We also need to better promote the Public Service as a dynamic and engaging career choice.

- Third, development. We must invest in people, at all levels, not only in terms of skills, but also in the kind of leadership we need for the long term.

- Finally, we must put in place the systems and processes to support efficient, user-friendly planning, recruitment and development.

With the coming into force of the Public Service Modernization Act, parliament gave us the means to improve the way in which we manage HR resources in the Public Service. (Canada, Standing Committee on Government Operations and Estimates 2007, 3; emphasis in original)

These priorities came to dominate policy discussion in the senior ranks of the public service, as the PCO took the lead in explaining government reform ambitions and giving them focus through specific action plans. As then Clerk of the Privy Council Wayne Wouters noted in his 2010 report to the prime minister, the first priority, integrated planning, was the foundation of renewal in that it called upon all departments and agencies to combine their financial and human resources management, operational planning, and policy development initiatives into a comprehensive plan that delineated directions and operational requirements.

"Done well," Wouters wrote, "integrated planning allows us to clearly identify gaps in resources required to deliver on priorities, and then to close these gaps by redesigning the work, developing employee capacity or devoting more staff to the effort. We can improve our ability to provide advice to ministers and service to Canadians, while simultaneously reducing costs" (Privy Council Office 2010, 16). As part of integrated planning, for example, the federal public service promoted enhanced service delivery through its website. Myriad government services are now available online, from applying for passports or accessing seniors and veterans programs to filing income taxes.

Wouters also asserted that recruitment remained a priority as the government replaced retiring public servants from the baby boom generation and tried to reshape the character of the public service with fresh talent: "Recruitment must be grounded in integrated planning. The goal is to match recruits strategically to identified business needs. Future recruitment efforts will be aimed at both postsecondary and mid-career candidates. Recruitment will continue to be a key tool in increased public service diversity and representativeness" (17).

As new employees entered public service, their training and development were now to be based on a centralized policy, in contrast to the ad hoc and departmentalized initiatives of the past. As Wouters informed the prime minister, "Employee development is the responsibility of both the individual and the institution, but it serves a single purpose: to improve effectiveness and productivity in current and future jobs. This requires going beyond coursework and classroom learning. The task is to consciously create learning environments where knowledge management is done well and where employees have ready access to the information they need to do their jobs" (17).

Finally, Wouters noted that public service renewal would be contingent on improving the organizational infrastructure of government workplaces. Here, the clerk focused on the use of information technologies to give public servants access to the very latest in databases and electronic libraries, web links, wikis, interactive communication systems such as email and text messaging, social networking, information management systems, and systems for planning, implementing, and assessing financial and human resources management. The use of such technologies was also connected to the development of enhanced systems of program evaluation such as the **managing for results** (MFR) requirements of the expenditure and management information system discussed in Chapter 6. Departments would be expected to outline program objectives and operational targets explicitly in their business plans and to establish metrics to determine how well program activities meet department goals.

"Responding to the challenges facing Canada today," wrote the clerk, "requires that departments and, frequently, other governments and sectors work together. Within and across our organizations we need to increase collaboration to improve the quality, speed, and efficiency of our work and our service to Canadians. Improving our programs, policy and advice also requires that we do a better job of listening to Canadians and incorporating their views, without presuming on the responsibilities of parliamentarians and ministers. Ultimately, successful collaboration needs to take place at all levels, not just the most senior" (Privy Council Office 2010, 11–13).

Undertaking the Initiatives

Some major initiatives were undertaken by the Harper government in the name of public service renewal during the early years of his administration. Despite steady talk of restraint over the previous two decades, the Harper government oversaw substantial new hiring into the federal public service. As David Zussman (2010, 226) noted, from 2006 to 2009 more than 20,000 new public servants were hired by the federal government. And the total from 1999 to 2009 was more than 100,000. These were serious numbers.

All this new hiring was aided by the Public Service Modernization Act of 2003, which, as Chapter 7 discussed, required departments and agencies, from deputy ministers on down, to integrate human resources management and staff development into their business plans. And as this renewed focus on new hiring and staff development took root it was aided by the establishment, in 2009, of the **Office of the Chief Human Resources Officer** (CHRO). This new institution took over the role of the former Canada Public Service Agency as well as elements of the Treasury Board Secretariat that managed public sector pensions and benefits. As we saw in Chapter 7, the mandate of the CHRO is to provide centralized guidance for human resources planning and program management across the federal public service.

Finally, federal human resources development initiatives were greatly aided by the Canada School of Public Service. This institution, as we have seen, provides training and development courses for public servants at all levels of the federal service.

Assessing the Results

David Zussman (2010) commented extensively on the various public service renewal initiatives of the Harper government, finding them ultimately "precarious." Significant new hiring was accompanied by substantial turnover in middle management and executive staff, leading to discontinuity in departmental and agency leadership. All too often, policy and program development suffered from a constant churn of new people, especially new managers, wanting to impose their mark. The results were delays and convoluted, ever-changing initiatives and dynamics.

Zussman also noted the intensified centralization of decision making at the highest levels in Ottawa over the past 20 years. Executive authority now rests with the prime minister, the minister of finance, and senior officials in the PMO and PCO. And within departments, especially those within the Harper Conservative government, Zussman

observed, ministers have come to rely heavily on their partisan political advisers at the expense of advice coming from the senior ranks of their own departments. This increased the partisanship of ministerial decision making and diminished the status of senior policy advisers (2010, 227–32).

Perhaps the most damning indictment from Zussman came in relation to the creaking apparatus that developed in the wake of the Federal Accountability Act and other efforts to improve transparency. Complex administrative processes, multiple administrative approvals, and ever more onerous reporting requirements hindered public service reform and renewal: "Rather than increasing transparency and accountability, the web of rules has created an even more pronounced culture of risk aversion. Public servants at all levels have lost the ability to take a balanced approach to reasonable risk taking. Too many rules and procedures have had negative implications on timely decision making, productivity, and innovation, ultimately hindering effective service delivery to the public" (2010, 231).

THE HARPER GOVERNMENT AND PROGRAM REVIEW, AGAIN

As we've seen in Chapter 6, the worldwide recession of 2008–09 resulted in the Harper government feeling compelled to engage in massive stimulus spending, known as the Economic Action Plan, designed to spur the economy, generate jobs, promote national infrastructure development, and, hopefully, drag the country out of recession. While the Harper government had inherited a budgetary surplus in 2006, by 2009–10 the federal government was running a $55 billion deficit. After the Conservatives won a majority government in the 2011 election, Prime Minister Harper made the commitment that the government would return to a balanced budget by 2015—just in time for the next election.

The development of the Economic Action Plan and its $55 billion Keynesian approach to fiscal policy was very much the result of crisis management rather than any long-developed rational plan of financial management. And once the prime minister decided to eliminate the deficit in advance of his next election bid, the program to achieve this was in no way rooted in strategic NPM thinking. Rather, the Harper government's program review initiative, much like that of Prime Minister Chrétien's in the mid-1990s, had more to do with incremental, top-down, command and control decision making than rationalistic objective-setting, planning, cost-benefit analysis, programming, and budgeting.

As noted in Chapter 6, the Harper government's program review exercise required the federal government to reduce overall expenditures by $5.5 billion annually between 2011 and 2016. Departments and agencies were informed by the Department of Finance that they were required to present to the Treasury Board two plans for spending cuts—one seeing the organization reduce expenditure by 5 per cent annually, the other witnessing reductions of 10 per cent annually; the Treasury Board would then impose its preferred plan on the given organization. By 2013 the Department of Finance informed departments that cuts in excess of 10 per cent would now be required. In their defence of these measures, both Prime Minister Harper and Jim Flaherty, minister of finance, stressed that these cuts were to "back office" administration and that no front-line services would be affected. As the prime minister argued, program review was designed to eliminate "billions in fat" (Savoie 2015, 201).

Critics of the Harper government, however, ranging from opposition parties to public service unions to members of the general public, did not trust the government's reasoning. Fears were expressed that such budget cuts would necessarily affect the quality of public services, especially when it was announced that this program review exercise would result in the loss of 19,200 public service jobs between 2012 and 2015. Federal public service union leaders were quick to assert that these job cuts were hurting front-line services in everything from waiting times for passport applications, to food safety inspections and environmental assessments, to programming for veterans. Indeed, the closure of seven regional Veterans Affairs offices became a touchstone for those opposed to the Harper government (Thomas 2014, 186–88).

The Harper government forged ahead with program review, dismissing all criticisms as the ill-founded complaints of its political enemies. By the spring of 2015 then Finance Minister Joe Oliver was able to announce that the federal budget had returned to balance, with the government posting a modest $1.9 billion surplus. But by this time many Canadians were questioning the quality of public services the federal government was claiming to deliver, and morale in the federal public service had plummeted, with sick leaves having grown by 68 per cent in the past 10 years (Savoie 2015, 205). It was to address these growing tensions within the public service that in 2013 the clerk of the Privy

Council initiated the Blueprint 2020 exercise, the latest public service renewal initiative within the federal government.

THE TRUDEAU GOVERNMENT, BLUEPRINT 2020, AND PUBLIC SERVICE RENEWAL, AGAIN

In Chapter 7 we looked at Blueprint 2020, yet another ambitious renewal project aimed at transforming the federal public service into an innovative, creative, and collaborative policy-making and service delivery institution for 2020 and beyond. Although initiated during the Harper years, it was inherited by the government of Justin Trudeau in 2015 and became a Liberal modernization undertaking.

In her *Twenty-Second Annual Report to the Prime Minister on the Public Service of Canada*, then-Clerk of the Privy Council Janice Charette informed then Prime Minister Stephen Harper in March 2015 of many renewal activities happening within the public service as part of Blueprint 2020. She reported that the federal public service was promoting "innovation and continuous improvement," that it was becoming more "nimble and agile" while being "open and collaborative," and that federal public servants were becoming ever more "high-performing." As evidence of these reforms, the Clerk mentioned the following undertakings and commitments as exemplars of many more:

- The Public Health Agency of Canada launched The Play Exchange—a first-of-its-kind partnership with the private and not-for-profit sectors that asked Canadians to submit ideas on how we can be more active. More than 400 ideas were submitted, with Canadians determining which innovation would receive $1 million in investment funding from the Government of Canada to implement their idea.
- We are also applying new thinking to policy development. Over the past year, a dozen innovation hubs and labs were created across the government to explore and apply new approaches to policy and service challenges.
- We also strive to anticipate and respond to new trends and developments as they relate to our daily operations. Whether for Environment Canada's up-to-the-minute weather and environmental services or the Canada Food Inspection Agency's over 240 food recall warnings in 2014, Canadians relied on us.
- We need to remove any step of our processes and operations that is not necessary for achieving quality outcomes. This spirit is embodied in Employment and Social Development Canada's Expose and Explain initiative, which allows employees to question internal processes, policies or rules and propose innovative solutions to improve the way they work.
- We are also supporting Canadians so that they themselves have the tools to connect and collaborate. Our country leads the way in Internet connectedness. Thanks to the efforts of Industry Canada, this year brought high-speed network access to another 280,000 Canadian households in rural and remote regions.

- Every public servant needs to have a clear understanding about the expected results of our programs and services, and their role in achieving these results. This is the key to the new Directive on Performance Management… This Directive requires that all employees know what is expected of them; have an opportunity to understand how their performance will be measured; and, at least twice a year, receive formal feedback on their strengths as well as help on areas of improvement.

THE ANNUAL REPORT OF THE CLERK OF THE PRIVY COUNCIL II

In her 2015 report on the state of the federal public service (Privy Council Office 2015), Clerk Janice Charette informed Prime Minister Harper of three priority areas for action in the coming years.

1 She stressed there was a need to reinvigorate recruitment efforts and that the public service would have to work hard to attract, develop, and retain new talent to replace those who will be retiring in future years. In a clear reference to New Professionals and New Professionalism (see Chapter 7), she stated, "We will need to replace those departing with individuals who have the new competencies to manage in the modern world. These new entrants—whether they enter as postsecondary graduates or later in their careers—will bring with them the fresh ideas, diversity, and skills that will allow us to meet our contemporary challenges."

2 She affirmed there was a need to focus on building healthy, engaging, and supportive workplace environments conducive to good mental health for all employees. "We must create the space for open and stigma-free dialogue that allows for honesty and compassion as well as focus on preventing harm, promoting health and resilience, and addressing incidents and concerns."

3 And finally, she spoke of the need to promote stronger policy development capacities, enabling the government to make better policies and programs while giving Canadians the opportunities to be involved in this process. "The challenges to Canada's future prosperity, security, and cohesion are increasingly interconnected and complex, and the Public Service has a responsibility to provide policy advice in all of these areas. There are greater expectations from citizens and stakeholders alike for ongoing engagement as we develop our advice." (18)

THINKING ABOUT IT

- Do you agree with the Clerk's priorities?
- Are there others that should have been mentioned?
- Are New Professionals and New Professionalism really welcomed in the federal public service? Can new hires really change how the public service works, or will these ideals wither in the face of top-down, command and control leadership?
- Is greater public consultation and collaboration in policy making desirable? Or will this just generate more acrimony and division, making decision making more difficult?

WHITE PAPER

- To better meet learning and training needs, The Canada School of Public Service is revitalizing its curriculum, and modernizing its delivery of learning as part of the new enterprise-wide approach to learning (Privy Council Office 2015, 7–15).

Whether these reform initiatives will be proven effective in leading to a substantial transformation of the nature and working of the federal public service for the better remains an open question. And whether some of these stated goals give pause for concern—for example, why such matters as employee involvement in problem solving and employees being given clear directives as to their work expectations are only now being pursued—is up to individual readers of *Thinking Government* to decide.

Blueprint 2020 was launched, as always, with much fanfare. It has noble aims and ambitions. It promises much as it speaks to the promotion of core values and principles of the public service ethos. Anyone interested in the well-being of the federal public service should hope for its success, that it can make a meaningful impact on the life of the Government of Canada and its employees. But we must also remember the teachings of Donald Savoie. The history of the federal public service is littered with such reform initiatives, with most of them noted more for their rhetoric than their ability to deliver significant change.

EVALUATING NEW PUBLIC MANAGEMENT

The substance of program review under both the Chrétien and Harper governments, La Relève, public sector renewal, and Blueprint 2020 is open to question. Have these initiatives, and the policy and program changes they have prompted, heralded the advent of a coherent NPM approach to government? More pointedly, do they represent a reinvention of government along the lines advanced by Osborne and Gaebler?

Program reviews have certainly changed how government operates and what it does—and doesn't do. And the public service renewal initiatives of the Harper and Trudeau governments have promised more modifications down the road. Borins and Purchase and Hirshhorn stress that NPM "is here to stay" (Kernaghan and Siegel 1999, 78); Savoie, Trebilcock, and Thomas, however, note that the change has been gradual and partial, not a wholesale transformation, and not by way of a coherent NPM approach. The values of NPM have been called into play more in micro- and mid-level management practices than in macro-level alterations to the structure of government and its relationship to citizens.

WHAT CHANGE SHOULD LOOK LIKE

New Public Management has been a point of discussion in the world of public administration now for some four decades, and much of its more grandiose claims, especially those of the reinvention thesis, can already be called into question. Recall what a reinvented government would look like:

- Departments and agencies would steer policy development and program implementation by fashioning new ways to provide public services, in cooperation with their client base.
- Privatization, public–private partnerships, deregulation, contracting out, and even volunteer labour would be countenanced as ways to deliver services.
- Departments and agencies would be closely tied to community and business groups.
- Departments and agencies would promote the commercialization and marketing of their activities and generate revenue through user fees, capital pools, investment funds, and other private sector methods.
- Management would be driven by mission and be results oriented, constantly seeking innovative ways to develop policies and deliver services more economically, efficiently, and effectively.
- Departments and agencies would concentrate on people as consumers and clients rather than as citizens.

Enterprising and anticipatory government organizations would thus blend public service with an entrepreneurial mentality. They would be expected to deliver services to defined markets while maintaining financial stability and even profitability. A reinvented government, in short, would be a radically transformed government.

WHAT CHANGE DOES LOOK LIKE

How has the government in fact changed over the past two decades? The federal government has

- increased privatization and deregulation
- downsized its organizations
- offloaded some responsibilities and functions
- contracted out certain services
- introduced more user fees
- developed public–private partnerships in some fields
- developed some new forms of service delivery
- demonstrated greater concern for economy and efficiency
- applied precise and effective forms of program evaluation such as MFR

All these innovations, as Borins (1995a) and Purchase and Hirshhorn (1994) assert, can be seen as evidence of NPM. And with the privatization of federal Crown corporations, it is indeed fair to assert that we have witnessed a reinvention of how the federal government works. If other policy and program fields were to emulate that level and type of change, it would represent the unquestioned triumph of NPM.

Most of the initiatives undertaken to date, however, can be attributed to incrementalism, or bounded rationalism, or mixed scanning, rather than comprehensive rationalism or the pure application of NPM. The *reform thesis* of government change—the idea that, as Thomas (1993) observed, public sector change emerges incrementally and is "disorderly, disjointed, and problematic"—also helps to explain limitations in government attempts to transform itself. The staff and budget cuts and program offloading of the 1990s and from 2012 to 2015, for example, can all be understood as efforts to deal with the specific problem of deficit spending and debt. In this sense they were reactive and reformist, not rational and transformative.

PUBLIC SECTOR SERVICE DELIVERY

The Canadian Centre for Management Development (the forerunner of the Canada School of Public Service) undertook some interesting research in the late 1990s on Canadian attitudes to service delivery and quality in the public and private sectors. Contrary to much conventional wisdom, most Canadians surveyed believed that, on average, public sector service delivery quality was roughly comparable to that of the private sector and in some areas far outranked it. In fact, the three most highly ranked services were delivered by the public sector.

• CITIZEN SATISFACTION WITH PUBLIC AND PRIVATE SECTOR SERVICE DELIVERY

PUBLIC SECTOR		PRIVATE SECTOR	
SERVICE	RANKING	SERVICE	RANKING
Fire departments	86	Supermarkets	74
Libraries	77	Telephone companies	63
Garbage disposal	74	Taxis	57
Provincial parks	71	Insurance agencies	55
Canada Pension/Old Age Pension	69	Banks	51
Passport office	66		
Motor vehicle licensing	66		
Health care	62		
Colleges/universities	58		
Customs	58		
Canada Post	57		
Revenue Canada/taxation*	57		
Hospitals	51		
Road maintenance	45		
Average	62	Average	62

Note: The public sector average is taken from a combination of specific federal, provincial, and municipal services. The private sector average is taken from seven areas of service. Satisfaction is rated on a scale of 0-100, N = 2,900.

Source: Adapted from Canadian Centre for Management Development 1999, 6.

* Revenue Canada has been superseded by the Canada Revenue Agency since this study was conducted. This category includes taxation at other levels of government as well.

THINKING ABOUT PUBLIC SERVICE DELIVERY

1 How would you explain the high rankings for fire, library, and garbage disposal services?
2 Do you think the results would be different if the survey were conducted today? Which categories would have improved and which lost ground?

REINVENTION OR REFORM?

Economy, efficiency, effectiveness; anticipation of issues instead of reaction to problems; more open, participatory forms of management and communication—these ideals pre-date the advent of NPM and the reinvention thesis. Governments and their bureaucracies have long had an interest in realizing these ends. Results-based management founded on mission statements and rigorous systems of performance evaluation is also a long-standing feature of government reform initiatives, just as is interest in better and more up-to-date forms of service delivery.

In all these respects, the reform thesis can explain much of what has transpired within the federal government over the past decade. And it can also explain much of what did not happen.

Sticking to Traditional Management

Has public sector management become more open and collaborative? No, it has in fact become more centralized in the current era of **strategic prime ministership** (see Chapter 4). Participatory management is a signal component of NPM, but it clashes with the principle of accountability based on ministerial responsibility and with the practical realities of power politics. In organizational terms, as outlined in Chapter 5, participatory management challenges the accountability of senior managers and elected ministers by involving more and more people in decision making, making the process and the lines of responsibility more convoluted. In political terms, it challenges the proper exercise of democratic responsibility by elected officials.

All such theoretical considerations become most germane, of course, when things go wrong.

Who bears responsibility for poor decisions and who must right those wrongs? In such a context, demands for participatory management tend to evaporate quickly. Initiatives for administrative change such as PS2000, program reviews, La Relève, public service renewal, and Blueprint 2020 have all had to contend with the practical reality of power relations within government.

Sticking to Traditional Values

Has government become more competitive, using private sector models of service delivery and treating citizens as customers and clients? The answer again is no. Some departments and agencies have undergone deeper changes than others, but little has changed with respect to fundamental public service values. The core social, economic, and cultural policies and programs of previous governments have continued to define the primary responsibilities of the current one, and our national vision of the appropriate role of the state in society remains entrenched.

Much evidence suggests that despite the restrictions on its institutions and activities over the past decade, the federal government has not lost sight of the essential characteristics of public service or of the important distinctions between the public and the private sectors. For example, it still maintains a major and vital presence in health, education, and social welfare, with an essentially unchanged policy role. Even the Conservative government of Stephen Harper felt obligated, for political reasons, to remain committed to the principles of the Canada Health Act and the preservation of public medical care. All the opposition parties, most provincial governments, and widespread public opinion still oppose the establishment of a two-tiered health care system founded on substantial private sector for-profit service delivery, and the results of recent federal elections confirm this. While health policy has clearly been undergoing some major reforms, attributable for the most part to funding reductions, it is hard to sustain the argument that we have been experiencing its reinvention.

A similar conclusion can be advanced with respect to education policy. Despite funding cutbacks, the federal government remains committed to substantial support for the postsecondary education system through block funding of the Canada Health and Social Transfer, and specialized support for colleges and universities comes from programs such as student loans, financial support for arts and science research, and funding for technological innovation.

The federal government also remains committed to social policies and programs such as the Canada Pension Plan, employment insurance, transfers to provincially administered social assistance and welfare programs, and federal–provincial equalization. Employment and Social Development Canada remains a major federal portfolio and has even been given increased responsibilities for preparing workers for the demands of the "new economy." The nature of federal social welfare obligations has not changed, nor has widespread public support diminished. In fact it has grown, as the effects of spending cuts have deepened over the past decade.

At most, the federal government has tried to maintain its core responsibilities while lowering its financial support for them. At worst, it has neglected its responsibilities in the quest for fiscal balance while failing to pluck up the courage to embrace the market logic of reinvention fully. In either case, the government has not consciously engaged in reinvention, and as the 10 principles enunciated by Osborne and Gaebler indicate, such rational and conscious engagement is the hallmark of reinvention.

DÉJÀ VU ALL OVER AGAIN

It is important to remember that no government starts its mandate with a clean slate. Each inherits more or less coherent policy initiatives, dating back years. The Harper government, for example, inherited

- the Canada Health Act and the medicare system
- the Canada Pension Plan
- the system of federal–provincial financing of established programs
- environmental protection policy
- official bilingualism and multiculturalism policy
- regional equalization and regional development policy
- agricultural, fisheries, and industrial development policy
- free trade policy
- national defence policy
- heritage and cultural policy
- human rights policy

It also inherited fully fledged institutions and bureaucratic actors with well-founded notions of their roles, responsibilities, and legal obligations to policy and program development and implementation. Public servants know the procedures and relationships they need to make things work within their policy communities. And their clientele form distinct interest groups—such as business and industry associations or non-governmental organizations—dedicated to maintaining their relations with relevant state organizations.

Thinking back to Chapter 5, we see that public choice theory, bureaucratic politics theory, and the policy networks model of decision making support the idea that public servants therefore try to preserve existing systems of bureaucratic organization and action on the grounds of familiarity, ease of operation, successful past experience, and fear of change. In other words, with an inherited set of policies and entrenched attitudes, the public service is innately constituted to resist transformative change.

Finally, the system of labour relations and collective bargaining constrain the administrative changes possible within any government institution. Substantial alterations to work patterns would involve contractual negotiations with public sector unions, which are of course committed to defending the interests of employees. Reinventionist initiatives such as contracting out public services and using volunteer community-based labour are bound to get a cold shoulder.

It's also noteworthy that all the major policy and program initiatives inherited by the Harper Conservative government in 2006 were, in turn, passed on to the Trudeau Liberal government in 2015. The fundamental policies and practices of any government change but slowly, and incrementally.

New public management arose in the 1980s as a way to develop a leaner, more focused public sector modelled on private sector appraisals of efficiency and effectiveness. It encouraged policy development that was oriented to results rather than process. Advocates asserted that this kind of restructuring carried the promise of fundamentally transforming the public sector into a more dynamic, capable, and cost-efficient service provider. While we can see influences of NPM in government practices over the past 30 years, especially in relation to program reviews initiated by both the Chrétien and Harper governments, La Relève, public service renewal policies, and Blueprint 2020, what we observe in practice is the gradual reform of government rather than its reinvention. And such reform is always rooted in the policy and program environments passed from one government to the next.

At either the micro-managerial or the macro-policy level, change tends to come slowly and incrementally in government. Even a Conservative government that is ideologically averse to a strong state presence is often compelled to accept substantial state involvement in society and the economy simply because it has inherited that position from its predecessors, and wholesale reconfiguration would be administratively unacceptable and politically dangerous. Certainly the Harper government, facing minority parliaments, had to soften its criticisms of "big government" in its attempt to woo Canadian voters. Hence we have witnessed incremental reform in most federal policies and programs, rather than a rationalist reinvention of government.

Even so, the reforms of the past three decades have been important, and they are ongoing. Maintaining broad continuity with past practices and policies, reforms have nevertheless reshaped government by significantly diminishing its size through privatization and reorganization. Many public services are now delivered and administered electronically, and the Harper and Trudeau governments have attempted to improve the capacity of the public service by rebuilding its staff and by integrating financial and human resources planning directly into program and policy development. In the process, the issues of accountability and leadership have come to the fore, and these are the subjects of our final chapters.

REFERENCES AND SUGGESTED READING

Some short passages from this chapter respecting the New Public Management have been adapted from Howe and Johnson (2000).

Asch, Michael, ed. 1997. *Aboriginal and Treaty Rights in Canada: Essays on Law, Equality and Respect for Difference*. Vancouver: UBC Press.

Aucoin, Peter. 1995. *The New Public Management: Canada in Comparative Perspective*. Ottawa: Institute for Research on Public Policy.

Borins, Sandford. 1995a. "The New Public Management Is Here to Stay." *Canadian Public Administration* 38: 122–32.

———. 1995b. "Public Sector Innovation: The Implications of New Forms of Organization and Work." In *Governance in a Changing Environment*, edited by B. Guy Peters and Donald J. Savoie, 260–87. Montreal: McGill-Queen's University Press.

Brock, Kathy, Mathew Burbidge, and John Nator. 2010. "A Resilient State: The Federal Public Service, Challenges, Paradoxes, and a New Vision for the Twenty-First Century." In *The Handbook of Canadian Public Administration*, 2nd ed., edited by Christopher Dunn, 235–49. Toronto: Oxford University Press.

Brooks, Stephen. 1998. *Public Policy in Canada: An Introduction*. 3rd ed. Toronto: Oxford University Press.

Bruce, Christopher J., Ronald D. Kneebone, and Kenneth J. McKenzie, eds. 1997. *A Government Reinvented: A Study of Alberta's Deficit Elimination Program*. Toronto: Oxford University Press.

Canada, Human Resources and Skills Development. 2001. *Risk Assessment of Government On-Line (GOL)*. May. www.edsc.gc.ca/eng/publications_resources/audit/2000/6522/page01.

Canada, Prime Minister's Advisory Committee on the Public Service. 2007. *Report to the Prime Minister*. March. www.tbs-sct.gc.ca/ren/cpmccpm01-eng.asp.

Canada, Prime Minister's Office. 2006. "Federal Accountability Act Becomes Law." December 12. www.pm.gc.ca/eng/media.asp?category=1&id=1455.

Canada, Royal Commission on Aboriginal Peoples. 1996. Paul Chartrand, J. Peter Meekison, Viola Robinson, Mary Sillett, and Bertha Wilson, Commissioners. Co-chaired by George Erasmus and René Dussault. *Report*. 2 vols. Ottawa: Supply and Services.

Canadian Centre for Management Development (CCMD). 1999. *Citizen-Centred Service: Responding to the Needs of Canadians*. www.iccs-isac.org/en/pubs/CCHandbook.pdf.

Dyck, Rand. 2008. *Canadian Politics: Critical Approaches*. 5th ed. Toronto: Nelson.

Hood, Christopher. 1991. "A Public Management for All Seasons?" *Public Administration* 69: 3–19.

Howe, R. Brian, and David Johnson. 2000. *Restraining Equality: Human Rights Commissions in Canada*. Toronto: University of Toronto Press.

Inwood, Gregory J. 2012. *Understanding Canadian Public Administration: An Introduction to Theory and Practice*. 4th ed. Toronto: Pearson Canada.

Isuma. 2007. "About Isuma." www.isuma.tv/en/atanarjuat/about-isuma.

Johnson, Jon R. 1994. *The North American Free Trade Agreement: A Comprehensive Guide*. Aurora, ON: Canada Law Book.

Kernaghan, Kenneth, Brian Marson, and Sandford Borins. 2000. *The New Public Organization*. Toronto: IPAC.

———, and David Siegel. 1999. *Public Administration in Canada: A Text*. 4th ed. Toronto: Nelson.

Lindquist, Evert. 2010a. "Public Administration Research and Organization Theory: Recovering Alternative Perspectives on Public Service Institutions." In *The Handbook of Canadian Public Administration*, 2nd ed., edited by Christopher Dunn, 149–66. Toronto: Oxford University Press.

———. 2010b. "Surveying the Public Administration Landscape: Frameworks, Narratives, and Contours." In *The Handbook of Canadian Public Administration*, 2nd ed., edited by Christopher Dunn, 3–24. Toronto: Oxford University Press.

Long, David, and Olive Dickason. 1996. *Visions of the Heart: Canadian Aboriginal Issues*. Toronto: Harcourt Brace.

Osborne, David, and Ted Gaebler. 1992. *Reinventing Government: How the Entrepreneurial Spirit Is Transforming the Public Sector*. New York: Plume Books.

Paehlke, Robert. 1990. "Environmental Policy in the 1990s." In *Canada at Risk? Canadian Public Policy in the 1990s*, edited by G. Bruce Doern and Bryne B. Purchase, 214–23. Toronto: C.D. Howe Institute.

Privy Council Office. 1994. *Program Review and Getting Government Right*. Ottawa: Department of Finance.

———. 1995. *Third Annual Report to the Prime Minister on the Public Service of Canada*. Ottawa: Supply and Services.

———. 1998. *Fifth Annual Report to the Prime Minister on the Public Service of Canada*. Ottawa: Supply and Services.

———. 2000. *Seventh Annual Report to the Prime Minister on the Public Service of Canada*. Ottawa: Supply and Services.

———. 2010. *Seventeenth Annual Report to the Prime Minister on the Public Service of Canada*. Wayne G. Wouters, Clerk of the Privy Council and Secretary to the Cabinet. http://clerk.gc.ca/eng/feature. asp?featureId=19&pageId=231.

———. 2011. *Public Service Renewal Action Plan, 2010–11*. www.clerk.gc.ca/eng/feature. asp?pageId=165.

———. 2015. *Twenty-Second Annual Report to the Prime Minister on the Public Service of Canada*. Ottawa: Supply and Services.

Purchase, Bryne, and Ronald Hirshhorn. 1994. *Searching for Good Governance*. Kingston: School of Policy Studies, Queen's University/McGill-Queen's University Press.

Savoie, Donald J. 1994. *Thatcher, Reagan, Mulroney: In Search of a New Bureaucracy*. Toronto: University of Toronto Press.

———. 1995. "What Is Wrong with the New Public Management?" *Canadian Public Administration* 38: 112–21.

———. 2015. *What Is Government Good at? A Canadian Answer*. Montreal: McGill-Queen's University Press.

Thomas, Paul G. 1993. "Coping with Change: How Public and Private Organizations Read and Respond to Turbulent Environments." In *Rethinking Government: Reform or Reinvention?* edited by F. Leslie Seidle, 31–62. Montreal: Institute for Research on Public Policy.

———. 2010. "Parliament and the Public Service." In *The Handbook of Canadian Public Administration*, 2nd ed., edited by Christopher Dunn, 106–30. Toronto: Oxford University Press.

———. 2014. "Two Cheers for Bureaucracy: Canada's Public Service." In *Canadian Politics*, 6th ed., edited by James Bickerton and Alain-G. Gagnon, 177–97. Toronto: University of Toronto Press.

Treasury Board of Canada Secretariat. 1997. *Getting Government Right: Governing for Canadians*. Ottawa: Supply and Services.

———. 2000. *A Policy Framework for Service Improvement in the Government of Canada*. Ottawa: Supply and Services.

———. 2005. *Budget 2005: Strengthening and Modernizing Public Sector Management*. Ottawa: Supply and Services.

Trebilcock, Michael J. 1994. *The Prospects for Reinventing Government*. Toronto: C.D. Howe Institute.

Zussman, David. 2010. "The Precarious State of the Federal Public Service: Prospects for Renewal." In *How Ottawa Spends 2010–2011: Recession, Realignment, and the New Deficit Era*, edited by G. Bruce Doern and Christopher Stoney, 219–42. Montreal: McGill-Queen's University Press.

RELATED WEBSITES

CyberCemetery: National Partnership for Reinventing Government. http://govinfo.library.unt.edu/npr

Government of Canada. www.canada.ca

Institute of Public Administration of Canada. www.ipac.ca

Office of the Chief of Human Resources Officer. www.tbs-sct.gc.ca/ip-pi/mandate-mandat/chro-dprh-eng.asp

Privy Council Office. www.pco-bcp.gc.ca/premier.asp.

Treasury Board of Canada Secretariat. www.tbs-sct.gc.ca

CHAPTER 9

Accountability: Responsibility, Responsiveness, and Ethics

Accountability breeds response-ability.

–Stephen Covey, 2009

THE AGENDA

After reading this chapter and its related web pages you will be able to

- debate the merits of objective and subjective codes of ethics;
- analyze accountability in relation to political, legal, and social responsiveness;
- outline the roles of select federal programs and offices promoting accountability;
- describe the origins of the sponsorship scandal and its impact on the federal government; and
- articulate the dilemmas and difficulties of applying ethical rules in the real world.

9 Accountability: Responsibility, Responsiveness, and Ethics

Government exists to advance the socio-economic well-being of its citizens and promote the public interest. It is a human creation, established to meet important needs and provide key goods and services as defined by citizens themselves. But have Canadian governments been doing their job?

We are all aware of the common criticisms levelled against political leaders and public servants: they are wasteful, they are out of touch, they are arrogant and self-serving, they are stupid, they all too often indulge in folly, and at times they are unethical, even criminal. It's disconcerting that each of these criticisms can indeed be supported by some documented evidence:

- The administration of the Montreal 1976 Olympic Games was wasteful.
- The corruption scandals associated with the Mulroney government involved some arrogant and self-serving behaviour.
- The Canadian military was implicated in wrongdoing over the death of a Somali youth during the 1992 mission to Somalia, and faced accusations of the abuse of detainees during the Afghan war.
- The sponsorship scandal of the late 1990s revealed blatant corruption within the federal Liberal government of Jean Chrétien and came to taint and ultimately ruin the government of Paul Martin.
- In the last decade MLAs/MHAs in Nova Scotia and Newfoundland and Labrador have been implicated in expense account frauds.

- The Harper government was accused of muzzling public servants and rubbishing the reputations of public servants who questioned the worthiness and legality of some of their decisions.
- The Harper government was accused of contempt of parliament in 2010 for withholding documents from MPs who were investigating allegations of prisoner abuse in Afghanistan.
- Prime Minister Harper publicly maligned the integrity of Beverly McLachlin, Chief Justice of the Supreme Court of Canada, when this court ruled that a Harper nomination to that court was constitutionally invalid.
- The Harper government was accused of appointing excessively partisan individuals to the Senate of Canada and of tolerating unethical conduct by certain Tory senators.

Public concern over government misbehaviour, real and alleged, tends to be two-pronged. On one hand it is expressed as dismay or disgust over the actual event or decision in question—and anger that a wasteful or stupid or unethical act was committed. On the other it is articulated as a somewhat deeper concern about government malaise—that those in authority are not making proper decisions in the public interest. Sadly, governments, political leaders, and public servants don't always live up to the ideals of democratic government and public service. Public power can be twisted to benefit the few who wield it.

Government scandals therefore catch our attention and lead many, both inside and outside of government, to look for ways to punish government and administrative misbehaviour and to establish accountability systems to prevent further occurrences.

ACCOUNTABILITY CONCEPTS AND ISSUES

In the *Final Report* of the 1979 Royal Commission on Financial Management and Accountability, the commissioners defined **accountability** as

> the essence of our democratic form of government. It is the liability assumed by all those who exercise authority to account for the manner in which they have fulfilled responsibilities entrusted to them, a liability ultimately to the Canadian people owed by Parliament, by the Government and, thus, every government department and agency.
>
> Accountability is the fundamental prerequisite for preventing the abuse of delegated power and for ensuring, instead, that power is directed toward the achievement of broadly accepted national goals with the greatest degree of efficiency, effectiveness, probity and prudence. (21)

The principle that government officials are liable for both the procedural and the substantive merit of their decisions is crucial in any democratic system. Procedurally, are those decisions reached by due process? Are they made efficiently? Substantively, are they effective? Desirable? Just? As can be seen, accountability does indeed go to the essence of democratic government. An assessment of the quality of government accountability is an assessment of the practical and moral worth of that government itself.

TRADITIONAL PERSPECTIVES

There is a vast literature on understanding and assessing accountability in practice. The traditional starting point is a famous exchange of articles in American public administration journals between Herman Finer (1898–1969) and Carl Friedrich (1901–84) between 1935 and 1941. Both were occupied with ways to enhance accountability in liberal democratic governments in order to forestall the abuse of bureaucratic power, but they came to sharply different conclusions.

Herman Finer

Finer (1941) argued that accountability was best achieved by subjecting bureaucratic officials to strict and detailed rules, regulations, controls, and sanctions. In order to avoid discretionary judgement as much as possible, formal rules should cover all possible courses of action, but when discretion is required, it should be exercised by a superior official, in turn responsible to his or her superior.

Thus, government is a hierarchy of authority in which officials owe a duty of responsibility to their immediate superiors, who must account to officials further up the chain of command. The chain culminates in the hands of elected leaders, who are answerable to democratically elected legislatures.

In this system public officials know who their superiors are and what their duties entail, and also that they are subject to direct control and sanction if they fail to fulfill those duties adequately. This all sounds rather militaristic—and it is. Finer's thinking was very much influenced by the Weberian approach to bureaucratic organization, outlined in Chapter 5.

Carl Friedrich

Friedrich (1940) thought Finer's approach was simplistic and inattentive to the overriding importance for public servants of self-direction and self-regulation. Influenced by the organic-humanistic approach to management, he argued that the detailed rules and strict controls advocated by Finer were simply unworkable. Standard operating procedures could not be expected to cover all the contexts in which judgement would be needed, and a rigid application of formal rules to the myriad circumstances of real life could produce ill-designed government responses to difficult problems.

Beyond these operational criticisms, Friedrich also challenged Finer's theoretical assumptions. To Friedrich, the key to accountability was not external control but internal wisdom that would direct public servants—or people in general—to make good decisions as a matter of routine. In short, rather than directing and forcing people to do good, governments need to establish administrative systems that encourage them to exercise insight and good operational behaviour in the first instance.

Finer versus Friedrich

A different perspective on human nature influences the approach to accountability that each scholar advances. Friedrich was a philosophical liberal. In his view, people tended to be inherently good and wise, and an accountability system need only encourage public servants to keep in mind how and whether their actions contribute to the public good. If the public service has an administrative culture in which the objectives of serving the public interest and responding to broad social and economic needs stand at the fore, it will be accountable. Public servants identify with these goals as a matter of inner, moral choice, and their exercise of state power is therefore likely to accord with good governance.

Finer was much more philosophically conservative. In his view, people were generally flawed. An accountability system therefore has to accommodate not the moral public servant but the problematic one, motivated by very narrow self-interest. The prevalent personality was found in the person simply doing the job with as little fuss and in as little time as possible, and perhaps taking advantage of access to perquisites, benefits, and material gain. The only effective control in Finer's opinion, therefore, was enforcement of strict external rules from the top down.

Finer was writing in reference to public servants following rules set by their superiors, the ultimate superiors being the heads of departments, such as ministers and deputy ministers. When one applies the principle to politicians, their superiors are voters, who exercise control through elections, and the courts, which exercise control through the rule of law.

Frederick Mosher

In the 1960s, Frederick Mosher offered a clarification on the subject of accountability by focusing attention on the two concepts that flow through the work of Finer and Friedrich, namely, *objective responsibility* and *subjective responsibility*. Mosher

(1968, 7–10) thought that both were integral to good government but that only the former was directly related to accountability:

- Objective responsibility "connotes the responsibility of a person or an organization to someone else, outside of self, for some thing or some kind of performance. It is closely akin to 'accountability' or 'answerability.' If one fails to carry out legitimate directives, he is judged irresponsible and may be subjected to penalties."
- Subjective responsibility directs attention "not upon to whom and for what one is responsible (according to law and the organization chart) but to whom and for what one 'feels' responsible and 'behaves' responsibly. This meaning, which is sometimes described as 'personal' responsibility, is more nearly synonymous with identification, loyalty, and conscience than it is with accountability and answerability."

Objective responsibility thus entails rules and regulations that directly establish lines of communication, obligation, and control within government. Officials are assigned duties to perform and objectives to achieve, and their performance will be measured. Success will be rewarded and failure criticized or punished. Mosher believed that this management process was best suited to establishing a clear accountability framework, but he did not underestimate the psychological dynamic of subjective responsibility.

All organizations possess a set of common values, ideas, and beliefs that provide its philosophical foundation, establishing why it exists, what its broader social purpose is, why membership in it is important, and what is expected of its members. Within government, this provides a moral framework to guide public servants to make socially desirable decisions. Objective controls function as a fallback mechanism to be brought into play if the dictates of subjective responsibility fail.

Formal and Informal Lines of Control

The concepts of objective and subjective responsibility allow us to frame accountability in terms of formal and informal lines of control and influence. As Finer and Mosher suggest, formal channels of authority and responsibility are important to any accountability system. Officials need to know where they stand with respect to obligations and responsibilities and what will happen if these are not properly fulfilled.

But as Friedrich and Mosher emphasize, informal controls and responsibility are also significant. A shared value system of ideals and standards, accepted by public servants as the foundation for their decision making, is a basic requirement of any public service. Subjective responsibility nurtures and respects informal lines of control and responsibility, as officials develop moral obligations and expectations in relation to other actors and forces in the political system. Public servants develop an informal loyalty to or identification with the media and social interest groups, the concepts of human rights and the rule of law, and the principles of public participation and decision making in the public interest.

TABLE 9.1

The Synthetic Approach to Accountability

	POLITICAL RESPONSIVENESS	LEGAL RESPONSIVENESS	SOCIAL RESPONSIVENESS
Concept	Ministerial responsibility	Rule of law	Public interest
Systems of Implementation	Formal controls Rules and regulations	Formal controls Judicial review	Informal controls Subjective ideals/political action
Actors	Governments Ministers Public servants Political parties Parliament Citizens Media	Governments Ministers Public servants Courts Tribunals Litigants Media	Governments Ministers Public servants Political parties Interest groups Citizens Media
Problems	Evaluation Imposing discipline on parties and governments between elections	Cost and complexity Assessing merit of courts over tribunals	Evaluation Subjectivity
Strengths	Establishing direct political control over the bureaucracy Holding ministers and officials responsible to parliament for their actions	Keeping bureaucratic power subject to the rule of law Ensuring that governments must be responsible and answerable to the public	Facilitating ongoing public assessment of government actions

A SYNTHETIC APPROACH

The theories just described are important and comprise useful insights. But none offers a correct and comprehensive approach to accountability. For that we must blend objective and subjective, formal and informal approaches into a single, inclusive view (see Table 9.1).

Ministerial and Legal Accountability

Clearly government officials, from public servants to political leaders, must be subject to formal, objective expectations by which their performance can be monitored and, if need be, controlled. Within parliamentary systems of government this approach to accountability is given life through the concept of **ministerial responsibility**: a chain of obligations and controls links public servants to their superiors, who are in turn responsible to their superiors, up to and including the political leadership of the government. The cabinet is subject to the authority and control of parliament, which is ultimately subject to the sanction of the people as expressed through regular democratic elections. Ministerial responsibility, examined in Chapters 3 and 4, thus stands as one of the core elements of accountability.

But procedural and substantive requirements must also be met if decisions are to be accorded legitimacy. When legal obligations are in dispute they are subject to judicial review, meaning that the courts have the ultimate authority to determine whether government decisions conform to law. The legal responsiveness of government actors, as expressed through the rule of law and judicial review, is therefore another fundamental element of accountability.

These two elements of accountability essentially reflect the formal objective obligations and controls advocated by Finer and Mosher.

Social Accountability

The ideals of democratic governance are an important part of the theory and practice of accountability as well. The actions of public servants and political leaders must accord with broadly accepted democratic norms and socio-economic goals. Thus, the final significant element of accountability involves responsiveness to fundamental democratic ideals and the socio-economic needs and interests of the public.

FORMS OF RESPONSIVENESS

Government accountability can thus encompass three distinct yet related concepts: political responsiveness, legal responsiveness, and social responsiveness. Each of these is assessed below.

POLITICAL RESPONSIVENESS

Political responsiveness rests in the doctrine of ministerial responsibility. In theory, the cabinet is collectively responsible to parliament for government policy making and administration. If a cabinet loses the confidence of parliament, either in a formal vote of non-confidence or by failing to pass a major monetary bill or the annual budget, constitutional convention dictates that it must resign en masse, usually resulting in an election.

Furthermore, each cabinet minister is generally responsible for the policy and administrative actions of his or her department and answerable to parliament in this regard, as we saw in Chapter 3. A department is thus ultimately subject to the executive leadership of an elected cabinet minister who is, in turn, subject to the authority of the prime minister and cabinet.

Another facet of the accountability relationship is that public servants working within a department or agency are required to support and implement the minister's decisions. Officials from the most senior to the most junior are expected to help the department fulfill its collective obligation to the minister and the cabinet. Failure to meet these obligations can provoke criticism and disciplinary action up to and including demotion or dismissal in accordance with the rules of the Public

Service Commission and the Public Service Labour Relations Board, as outlined in Chapter 7.

Through this administrative aspect of ministerial responsibility, the government is assured that public servants within a department or agency will exercise their duties in accordance with the wishes of the department's political head and subject to managerial oversight. In theory this is a sound method for ensuring political responsiveness within government. As ever, certain practical difficulties arise.

Theory versus Practice

The weak spot in the theory, as recognized by analysts such as Dyck (1996), Jackson and Jackson (2009), and Inwood (2012), is the role and capabilities of the minister. True political responsiveness would compel a minister to function as a superhuman. Departments can have thousands of employees, spread far across the country, making tens of thousands of decisions every year. Ministers can be directly involved in only a small portion of them—around 200 of the most important policy and administrative decisions of their department annually (Jackson and Jackson 2009, 273). The others must be in accordance with broad departmental policy but are made without the knowledge of the minister.

What happens when a decision is a bad one? If the minister was directly involved, the doctrine dictates that he or she must take responsibility. If it involves a serious error or abuse of power, the minister will be asked to resign. Such was the fate of Minister of Fisheries and Oceans John Fraser in the early Mulroney years. He became embroiled in the "tuna-gate scandal" of 1985, in which he overruled health inspectors and knowingly allowed tainted canned tuna to be distributed to consumers. But what if the minister was not directly involved in the decision—in fact, knew nothing about it? Should resignation be demanded?

Indirect Responsibility

Current opinion is that ministers must remain answerable to parliament but not be held directly responsible for actions in which they did not play a direct role. The disciplinary system within the department or agency will deal with those directly responsible and their immediate superiors who allowed a problem to develop.

This was the course of action followed in a Canada Jobs Fund/HRDC scandal that came to a head in 2000. Allegations of wrongdoing and sloppy administrative and financial management resulted in widespread departmental administrative reforms, and senior managers were informed that stricter controls were to be imposed over funding initiatives. Jane Stewart, the minister responsible for the department, did not, however, have to resign, on the grounds that she had not been responsible for the department in the mid-1990s when the problems began and that she was instrumental in beginning a reform process once she assumed the portfolio in 1998.

The point is often made that a minister cannot be expected to double- and triple-check the work of everyone in his or her department but must trust them to produce sound work. If this trust is violated, the argument goes, the fault must lie with the subordinate official and not the beleaguered minister. In fact, ministers are seldom called upon to resign for policy or administrative malpractice, even when strong evidence suggests that they were either aware of it or should have been. This, of course, was the claim against Jane Stewart. Opposition parties argued that she misled the House of Commons with respect to the severity of the problems in her department and that she should have known about them much sooner than she did.

Direct Responsibility

Ministers are still be expected to resign, however, if they are directly implicated in allegations of personal wrongdoing. In April 2010, the minister of state for the status of women, Helena Guergis, was removed from Prime Minister Harper's cabinet. Guergis was implicated in alleged wrongdoing over business relationships with private individuals. Harper fired her from his cabinet and asked the RCMP to investigate her actions. In the summer of 2010 the RCMP dropped the investigation, but Guergis remained out of cabinet and out of the Conservative caucus.

In a related case, in 2011 Minister of International Co-operation Bev Oda became ensnared in opposition criticism that she had doctored policy approval documents and misled parliament as to who had made a decision to cut funding to a human rights development agency. While she initially informed members of parliament that officials in the Canadian International Development Agency were responsible for this action, she later had to admit that she herself had insisted on this cutback to a popular program. After withstanding withering opposition and media attacks on her credibility, being supported all the while by Prime Minister Harper, Oda lost the support of the prime minister over the summer of 2012. At that time it became known that while attending a 2011 international development conference in London,

England, she had insisted on being upgraded to a 6-star hotel at taxpayers' expense. When the bills came in, it also became public knowledge that her expense claims included high-priced meals, including a $16 glass of orange juice. On such details are ministerial careers broken. After another huge uproar in the media and the House of Commons, she resigned from cabinet and from parliament. Members of the parliamentary press gallery speculated that this resignation likely pre-empted the prime minister having to fire her (CBC 2012).

Ministerial versus Administrative Responsibility

As the onus of ministerial responsibility has lightened, one might expect greater accountability to fall to administrative officials within departments and agencies. This is broadly true but not without controversy. There have been calls for deputy ministers to be made officially responsible for the administrative work of departments, but the initiative has not been implemented in legislation for fear of diminishing the tradition of ministerial responsibility and politicizing the role of deputy ministers.

The formal expectations of accountability imposed on administrators remain subject to the traditional interpretation of ministerial responsibility and the discretion of senior officials. Senior officials decide when and how to impose discipline on public servants suspected of poor decision making or administrative malpractice. Because dozens of officials can be involved in a single action, it can often be extremely difficult to determine responsibility. Incompetence therefore finds strength in numbers and administrative complexity.

Consequently, the effectiveness of the doctrine of ministerial responsibility as a means of imposing political responsiveness can be questioned. Some analysts have spoken, over time, of a growing problem in this regard (Denton 1979; Sutherland 1991; Inwood 2012). They argue that ministers should be more responsible for the administrative cultures they either create or tolerate within their departments. Current Canadian practice is now rather lenient, whereas the British, operating on the same principle of ministerial responsibility within a similar parliamentary system, are much more rigorous. We could follow their example, setting much higher standards for ministerial behaviour than we do at present.

With respect to departmental discipline, however, one should not underestimate the effectiveness of internal review, analysis, and correction. It can be difficult and slow, and is often publicly unseen, but if senior officials have the will to act, the process can effectively exonerate or penalize public servants suspected of poor performance. Any public servant who has experienced an investigation can testify to this.

LEGAL RESPONSIVENESS

The concept of **legal responsiveness**—the procedural and substantive requirements of administrative law—forms the second objective standard of formal accountability. Government officials who make administrative decisions bear numerous and important legal obligations. They can be held to account by the courts for the quality of their legal decision making and overruled if those decisions are determined to be unjust.

Administrative law is practised by the specialized, quasi-judicial administrative agencies that regulate particular fields of socio-economic life and adjudicate the claims of individuals and companies with respect to legal entitlements. These agencies include bodies as diverse as federal and provincial human rights commissions; labour relations and workers' compensation boards; and environmental assessment panels. Leading federal agencies are the Canadian Agricultural Review Tribunal, the Canadian Nuclear Safety Commission, the Canadian Radio-television and Telecommunications Commission, the Canadian Transportation Agency, the Competition Tribunal, and the Immigration and Refugee Board of Canada.

Collectively, agencies, boards, and commissions are often referred to as **tribunals**. They are established by governments with mandates to develop policy and administer programs in their respective fields of jurisdiction. They exercise some judicial authority in that they apply law and adjudicate legal disputes through their program administration. But they are only quasi-judicial bodies because their executive members are not judges but senior public servants who have both policy-making and legal adjudicative powers.

In exercising quasi-judicial adjudicative powers, such as deciding whether a human rights complaint is valid, or whether a new television network should be granted a broadcasting licence, or whether a refugee claimant should be granted asylum, the members of tribunals are governed by very elaborate rules of administrative law established through more than a century of jurisprudence, both statutory and common law. Specialized rules determine if a claimant has a right to a hearing, or in administrative law terms, if the claimant's circumstances *pass the threshold*, and they also govern the procedures for hearings and decisions.

Tribunal decisions are subject to the oversight of regular courts through statutory rights of appeal or judicial review, and that can be problematic. How does one determine which body is most capable of making an expert decision on a matter of administrative law: a specialized tribunal or a generalized court? Should a workers' compensation board, for example, render decisions on the definition of an "accident" under compensation law and the financial consequences? Or should those matters be left to judges who are not specialized in compensation law and policy?

The law is a crucial element of the accountability system within which every department and agency operates (Gall 2004; Boyd 2006). Administrative law has not been at the centre of studies in public administration in this country. This oversight is in need of correction, as formal accountability is not fully satisfied by the doctrine of ministerial responsibility; indeed, legal and ministerial answerability are equally important.

Courts versus Tribunals

The pivotal issue in finding the right balance of power between the courts and specialized, quasi-judicial administrative tribunals is accountability. Does legal accountability necessitate rigid adherence to judicial review as exercised by the courts, or can tribunals be trusted to make legally unassailable decisions? Courts, tribunals, and governments have struggled over this issue for the better part of three decades, reaching a rough equilibrium in which the courts maintain the unhindered right to review any actions that pass the threshold of administrative law but may defer to tribunal decisions if they believe them to be procedurally sound and generally reasonable in law. This is known as the doctrine of **judicial deference**.

Tribunal accountability, the extent to which these administrative bodies are responsible both to the law and to the policy and program aims for which they were established, recognizes three important features of legal responsiveness:

- Systems of accountability can be flexible and are subject to interpretation and change.
- Accountability is related to the quality of formal procedures and control systems.
- The way we assess accountability often focuses on the socio-economic and political quality of tribunal decisions.

Legal accountability is thus not just about due process and formal control but about the substance of government action. At the heart of the judicial deference doctrine is the understanding that, at times, regulatory agencies and tribunals rather than the courts are the most effective, economical, expert, and pragmatic bodies to provide legally sound and just decision making.

SOCIAL RESPONSIVENESS

Social responsiveness is at once the broadest and the most controversial element in the accountability equation. In contrast to political and legal responsiveness, it touches on the subjective aspects of accountability that so concerned Friedrich and Mosher.

From a social perspective, a department or agency is considered to be accountable when the substance of its policies and programs is aligned with broadly understood socio-economic interests. When a government decision maker exercises power in a way that serves societal goals understood to be in the public interest, the social responsiveness criterion has been met. In other words, this form of accountability concerns the substantive merit of government decision making in terms of long-term socio-economic development.

That clearly makes the issue subjective, but it is nonetheless valid, and central to the thinking of many both inside and outside of government. The primary advocates of accountability as social responsiveness are political parties, interest groups, and the media. When they deem the government to be appropriately responsive, they consider it accountable, and of course the reverse is true. From this perspective daily media coverage of national and provincial politics is part of an ongoing accountability process through which governments are judged for the quality of public service they offer.

For example, at the outset of the Harper government in 2006, Canadian environmental policy changed from supporting the Kyoto Protocol and being in favour of hard targets for the reduction of greenhouse gas emissions to supporting the elimination of the Protocol in favour of less onerous regulations on carbon dioxide emissions—which in practice favours the continued development of the Alberta oil sands. Canadians on the centre-left disparaged the policy shift as out of touch with the long-term environmental needs of the country, and thus socially unresponsive. Conversely, most conservatives supported the shift, arguing that it responded to the interests of the Canadian economy.

A deep current of subjective analysis runs through this approach. The definition of public interest depends on the ideological perspective of the person thinking about it. Thus, the ideological concepts discussed in Chapter 2 function not only as core political principles but also as ways to frame government accountability. Any evaluation of how well a government responds to societal imperatives is thus directly linked to party politics, interest group standpoints, media scrutiny, academic study, and general public opinion—ultimately becoming the focus of electoral campaigns and outcomes. The election of the Trudeau Liberal government in 2015 simply confirms this reality. Canadians of a centre-left political persuasion have generally applauded the policy and program changes wrought by the Trudeau cabinet, while those of more conservative predispositions lament the new directions taken by this government.

There is ample evidence that public servants share this approach to accountability. Studies indicate that many do perceive themselves as "servants" of the public interest and that senior managers feel loyalty not only to their departments and to the law but also to the ideals of public service and the public good (Canada, Royal Commission on Financial Management and Accountability 1979, 458, 471). These ideals—honesty, fairness, impartiality, justice, economy, efficiency, effectiveness, sensitivity, and compassion—can provide important motivation and guidance to public servants in pursuit of their responsibilities.

The social responsiveness aspect of accountability thus influences both how external parties assess their government and how internal public officials approach their duties. It also reveals the significance of subjective considerations in the evaluation of government action.

A synthetic approach to accountability encompasses the various forces—political, legal, and social—to which (or for which) accountability is owed. With respect to political and legal responsiveness, accountability is owed to either ministerial or political superiors or superior courts. Social responsiveness is owed by public servants and governments to society itself and is evaluated by political parties, interest groups, the media, and citizens.

But this three-part categorization is simply an aid to thinking about accountability. The multifaceted nature of accountability relationships involves objective and subjective, formal and informal patterns of interaction. Some initiatives will bridge the categories and blend the concepts.

OTHER FORMS OF ACCOUNTABILITY

PUBLIC PARTICIPATION

A long-standing criticism of public sector management in particular and democratic government in general is that it is too closed and elitist—too far removed from the citizens ultimately affected by government decisions. Are governments indeed out of touch with popular sentiments and inadequately accountable to the people? Analysts such as David Osborne and Ted Gaebler and political leaders from across the ideological spectrum, such as Tommy Douglas, René Lévesque, Rachel Notley, and Justin Trudeau, have advocated for greater public participation in the process of government decision making.

What does greater participation mean? The form can range from referendums on major public policies, to more frequent public hearings in advance of significant decisions, to state support for social interest groups to put them on par with business groups and enable them to participate more effectively in policy making. This is one of the reinvention principles of Osborne and Gaebler noted in Chapter 8—community-owned government—and it asserts that those directly affected by state actions should be directly involved in the decisions that lead to them. Public participation from this viewpoint can include

- public consultations by government;
- more formal liaisons between governmental decision-making bodies and major interest groups concerned with the work of government; and
- the formal integration of social interest groups into the institutions of government. (Johnson 1993)

Though informal types of public consultation have tended to dominate Canadian practice, we have experimented, mostly at the provincial level, with corporatist systems of formal group integration into government decision-making bodies. A *corporatist system* is one in which interest group representatives closely involved in policy and program decision making of federal and provincial organizations are directly incorporated into the executive membership of the government organization. Bodies such as labour relations and workers' compensation boards and appeal tribunals are examples. Their membership is divided equally among representatives of government, business, and labour on the rationale that institutionalizing the range of interests involved into the decision-making structure will produce better policy and program implementation.

Participatory initiatives have their strengths and weaknesses, but they are all attempts to enhance government responsiveness by bridging the existing categories of accountability. They usually involve social responsiveness, although some have broader implications. Public hearings and interest group funding, for example, directly affect the objective practice of administrative law, as more groups enter the field and have an impact on the legal responsiveness of governments. Likewise, public hearings, referendums, and corporatist forms of policy making can influence the formal practice of ministerial responsibility if decision-making power flows to non-traditional decision-making bodies and processes. Are ministers responsible for policies they have had only a minority influence in shaping? If not, who is? Public participation initiatives can affect the nature of political responsiveness and have implications for accountability.

This subject comes with an important caveat. While there has been, and probably always will be, much rhetoric in favour of enhanced public participation in government decision making, it remains subject to the tight rules of ministerial responsibility and the authority of responsible officials. As we saw in Chapters 5 and 8, significant theoretical and practical problems associated with the participatory model of public sector management militate against its use in most government settings.

It is interesting, then, to reflect on the success of corporatist forms of organization found in certain regulatory agencies, notably those dealing with highly specialized areas of policy and law dominated by a few major and competing interests. This is clearly visible with respect to both labour relations and workers' compensation boards, which are characterized by the presence of long-established business and organized labour interests. In these policy settings, provincial governments have found it advantageous to give competing interests official representation and encourage them to work with government representatives to develop sound and responsive policy.

While there have been initiatives to expand such approaches, they have been few and far between. Rather than being a harbinger of a new and generally applicable participatory approach to government, such corporatist initiatives are likely to remain intriguing counter-examples of the dominant trend of traditional, centralized government decision making.

FREEDOM OF INFORMATION

Another way to boost government accountability is by legislation that gives citizens access to government documents. Many provinces have such legislation, and the federal parliament approved the Access to Information Act in 1983 (Kernaghan and Siegel 1999, 512–17). It gives citizens, groups, businesses, and, most important, the media the right to obtain most government documents and records. The Act specifically provides

a right to access to information in records under the control of a government in accordance with the principles that government information should be available to the public, that necessary exceptions to the right of access should be limited and specific and that decisions on the disclosure of government information should be reviewed independently of government. (Canada, Department of Justice 2010, schedule 1)

It exempts matters that involve

- national security or cabinet confidentiality;
- either personal or business confidentiality; and
- intergovernmental relations either internationally or between the federal government and its provincial counterparts.

The exemptions are intended to maintain the security of communications between governments, between governments and citizens and businesses, and between ministers and their senior aides and advisers. But the vast majority of documents produced in policy making and implementation are now available.

The legislation was explicitly developed to enhance accountability, and it falls within the parameters of social responsiveness. Its operative principles are as follows:

- Government decision making should be public.
- The actions of the bureaucracy should be subject to public scrutiny or, in most cases, to media scrutiny reported in the public forum.
- Better, more socially responsive government will result from openness and scrutiny.

The knowledge that most government actions are subject to public scrutiny acts as an impetus to make decisions that conform to legal and ethical principles.

But again, the impact extends beyond the ambit of social responsiveness. Applying for access to information or invoking its exceptions falls squarely within the field of legal responsiveness. If a request for information is denied, the legislation provides a two-tiered review mechanism. In the first stage the federal information commissioner interviews the parties and assesses the validity of the arguments. Following this investigation the commissioner issues a recommendation, but it is merely advisory; the government is not compelled to release the information. If the government body refuses to do so, in the second stage the complainant, or the commissioner with the complainant's consent, can apply to the Federal Court of Canada for judicial review. The court has the legal power either to compel the release of documents or to accept the opinion of the relevant government body.

The scrutiny involved in this process puts pressure on ministers and public servants to justify their actions. In this respect, freedom of information legislation has a bearing on political responsiveness, too. Once again, a policy initiative can have an impact across several forms of accountability.

OMBUDS OFFICES

Ombuds offices are another multifaceted initiative to promote accountability (Kernaghan and Siegel 1999, 433–34). Nine provinces and one territory have a parliamentary office of the ombudsman. (The term is indeed still generally *ombudsman*, though British Columbia has an office of the *ombudsperson*. Prince Edward Island, the Northwest Territories, and Nunavut do not have such citizens' representatives.)

An ombuds office functions as a complaints bureau to which citizens can bring grievances about how they have been treated by those in the public service. The ombudsman's staff have legislative authority to investigate complaints they deem to have merit, requiring the officials responsible for the decisions under examination to explain their actions and reconsider the consequences. Ombudsmen have no legislative power to quash a questionable decision or to order that a new one be made, so they are not akin to judges. Nor can they choose to make what they believe to be a better decision on their own, as they have no legal authority to make first-order decisions. Rather, the authority of the ombudsman is investigative and reflective. Its services prompt responsible officials to give issues careful second thought—and, if they choose not to change their decisions, then perhaps bring them unwanted media attention.

Despite significant lobbying the federal government has not established a general ombuds office, arguing that other specialized institutions such as the Office of the Commissioner of Official Languages, the Canadian Human Rights Commission, and the Office of the Information Commissioner already address the needs that would be served by an ombudsman. It is interesting to note, however, that the federal government has established an ombudsman's office for the Canadian military with a mandate to hear complaints from service personnel about their treatment at the hands of peers and more senior officers. This may mark the beginning of a larger role for an ombudsman within the federal public service.

Notably, ombudsmen address all forms of responsiveness expected of governments. They assess the substantive merit of administrative decisions in light of their social responsiveness, but they also assess whether due process and/or ministerial responsibility have been exercised. Ombudsmen's reviews can be a shortcut toward ensuring legal responsiveness without having to go through judicial review. And they are a reminder to those in authority that ministerial responsibility, control, and leadership must be appropriately exercised.

SPECIAL OFFICERS

In the federal election of 2006, Stephen Harper promised Canadians that to improve accountability a Conservative government would create two special institutions to uphold clarity, openness, and responsiveness. One would be a new parliamentary budget officer, mandated to provide impartial professional assessments of federal budgetary planning documents and financial management policies and programs. The other would be a public sector integrity commissioner who would provide public servants with a confidential channel through which to make allegations of wrongdoing within the federal government. Within 18 months of taking power, the government did indeed establish these two entities, but they experienced difficult early years.

The Parliamentary Budget Officer

The position of the **parliamentary budget officer** (PBO) was created in December 2006. As of 2014–15, the office—technically the Parliamentary

Budget Officer of the Library of Parliament—had 17 employees and an annual budget of $2.8 million. Its mandate "is to provide independent and objective analysis to Parliament on the state of the nation's finances, the government's estimates and trends in the Canadian economy; and upon request from a committee or parliamentarian, to estimate the financial cost of any proposal for matters over which Parliament has jurisdiction" (Parliamentary Budget Officer 2015a, 3).

Since its inception the PBO has taken a significant role in the accountability system with respect to financial management and budgetary policy analysis. The office produces scores of reports every year in response to queries from MPs and parliamentary committees. A full list of recent publications of the PBO can be found on its website. In recent years, the reports have been highly anticipated by opposition party members and fodder for much media coverage of Canadian politics.

With a mandate to serve all parliamentarians, not just the members of the government, the office of the PBO soon found itself embroiled in political controversy. The first parliamentary budget officer, Kevin Page, began to question some of the budgetary assumptions and cost projections of various government initiatives, in particular federal stimulus spending between 2009 and 2011. Open to question were the accuracy of Department of Finance estimates about how long the government would run a deficit, whether deficit was cyclical, as asserted by the minister, or in fact structural.

These conflicts of opinion should not be minimized. The Conservative government placed immense importance on its centralized leadership and message discipline. When the PBO asserted that the federal deficit from 2009 to 2015–16 was structural, that it stemmed partly from tax cuts in the first decade of the century, and that government plans to balance the budget by 2014–15 were likely to fail, the report was met with scorn by the Harper government (Parliamentary Budget Officer 2010).

Likewise, in 2011 the PBO challenged the projected cost of new F-35 jet fighters. Whereas the Harper government had put the figure at around $17.6 billion, the PBO's assessment, based on analysis from the US Pentagon, pegged it at $29.3 billion over 30 years (Parliamentary Budget Officer 2011; Page 2015, 128–29). The opposition parties took this as confirmation of their fears about the fiscal risk; the government denounced the report as flawed and inaccurate.

Following his planned retirement in 2013 Kevin Page wrote a scathing yet incisive account of his years as the parliamentary budget officer. Provocatively entitled *Unaccountable: Truth and Lies on Parliament Hill* (Page 2015), this book is a must-read for those interested in the theory and practice of accountability in government and the interplay of politics and public administration in Ottawa.

As of 2016, the parliamentary budget officer was Jean-Denis Fréchette, appointed in September 2013. And true to the legacy of Kevin Page, the PBO remains a source of rigorous and impartial analysis on the state of the federal government's finances. Shortly after the election of the Trudeau government in October 2015, the PBO released an assessment of the new government's fiscal outlook. While the government had projected fiscal surpluses by 2019–20, the PBO contended that, in all likelihood, the federal government would be looking at deficits in the range of $4.2 to $4.6 billion (Parliamentary Budget Officer 2015b). Subsequent downturns in the national economy have shown even the PBO numbers to have been overly generous.

Given the clamour that regularly ensues over its hard-hitting reports, it's fair to say that the office of the PBO is doing its job. It gives parliament, the media, and Canadians themselves vital information to hold the government to account.

The Public Sector Integrity Commissioner

The same, unfortunately, could not be said with respect to the **Office of the Public Sector Integrity Commissioner of Canada** during its debut years. This office was also established as an independent agency of parliament in 2007 under the Public Servants Disclosure Protection Act. It has a mandate to provide public servants and members of the public with a safe and confidential means of disclosing potential wrongdoing within the federal government. The office therefore promoted accountability by

- providing information and guidance to those considering making a complaint
- encouraging efforts to make the federal public service a workplace where employees can raise their concerns about ethics openly
- bringing issues to the attention of senior officials and recommending corrective measures
- addressing complaints of reprisals against whistleblowers
- facilitating settlements through conciliation
- reporting to parliament annually

Arguably the integrity commissioner should have developed as much of a reputation for independence as did the PBO. Such was not the case. The first commissioner was Christiane Ouimet, appointed by Prime Minister Harper on June 12, 2007. She resigned from office on October 18, 2010, two days before the auditor general of Canada released a devastating audit into her office. The audit found that Ouimet personally had behaved unprofessionally with staff at the Public Service Integrity Commission (PSIC), had retaliated against those she believed had filed complaints against her, and had failed to perform mandated actions.

Under Ouimet's leadership the PSIC received 228 disclosures of alleged wrongdoing or reprisals between 2007 and 2010. In response, only five investigations were launched, and none found wrongdoing. In assessing this work, the auditor general found that in many cases decisions not to investigate or to dismiss complaints "were not supported by either the nature of work performed, the documentation on file, or both."

The Harper government defended its commissioner, but members of the opposition parties were scathing of both her and the government. NDP leader Jack Layton accused Ouimet of being "short on integrity" herself, while NDP MP Pat Martin remarked that the government had "let whistleblowers down terribly ... by allowing what seems to be a reign of terror in an office run by a despot" (CBC 2010).

In March 2011 Ouimet appeared in front of the Public Accounts Committee of parliament, where she defended her actions and rebutted the accusations of the auditor general. In her testimony she reiterated her belief that none of the complaints had required further action because they were either outside the jurisdiction of her office or unfounded.

At the hearing it was also revealed that at the time of her resignation, Ouimet had received a separation allowance totalling $534,100—representing about 18 months of severance for serving three years of a seven-year term. The agreement also included a confidentiality clause, and as is typical of such clauses it precluded her from discussing the reason for her departure from office. Opposition MPs complained that this was in effect "hush money," alleging that Ouimet had been following government orders not to investigate allegations of whistleblower abuse directed against the Harper government. Harper, of course, flatly rejected this accusation (CBC 2011).

Ouimet was succeeded by Mario Dion, who served as public sector integrity commissioner from 2010 to 2014, and in 2014 Joe Friday became commissioner. Both of these men were career public servants and lawyers, and under their leadership the PSIC began to build its credibility within the federal public service. In 2012–13 the PSIC received 267 disclosures of alleged wrongdoing or reprisals, leading to 63 investigations and three founded cases of violations of ethical rules (Office of the Public Sector Integrity Commissioner 2013, 8). In 2014–15 the office took in 168 complaints and initiated 34 investigations resulting in five cases of ethical violations (Office of the Public Sector Integrity Commissioner 2015, 9). These figures reveal that public servants feel comfortable in bringing allegations of wrongdoing to this commission and that the commission will investigate cases they deem to raise serious questions about possible unethical behaviour. It's

challenging, however, as with most legal disputes, to prove verified wrongdoing on a balance of probabilities. But proven cases of misbehaviour can have major results. In 2014–15, the chief executive officer of Enterprise Cape Breton Corporation, a federal Crown corporation, was found to have violated his organization's code of conduct by appointing four persons with close ties to the federal Conservative Party to senior executive positions in the organization. This hiring was done in contravention of the merit principle and the ideal of political neutrality in the public service. The upshot of this breach was the removal of the CEO from his position and the eventual disestablishment of ECBC as an independent organization. Its functions have now been subsumed by the Atlantic Canada Opportunities Agency.

The recent histories of the PBO and the PSIC reveal a crucial truth. An accountability watchdog is only as good as the dog itself. And core to a good accountability officer are professional ability, institutional independence, commitment to principle, and a clear desire to fulfill the mandate of the institution in the real world of politics.

ACCOUNTABILITY AND GOVERNMENT ETHICS

Any discussion of accountability has to consider government **ethics**. Jackson and Jackson (2009, 298) correctly suggest that although many Canadians distrust the ethics of their government, they have a deep interest in the issue and rightfully demand the exercise of power to be legal, just, proper, and, quite simply, moral. Very few expect *all* politicians and public servants to be immoral or corrupt, and when evidence of wrongdoing or unethical behaviour surfaces, it causes great concern. Most citizens applauded the introduction of the Federal Accountability Act in 2006.

Government ethics encompasses several concepts that are a matter of social consensus. First, those in government should not lie, cheat, steal, embezzle, or otherwise place their private interest ahead of the public interest. Second, they should be law abiding. Third, they should respect and support the dominant Canadian political ideals of democracy, equality, liberty, and individual human rights while responding to the interests of the society as a whole, as expressed through the democratic political process. This is a tall order, but we are not always conscious of our expectations until they are broken.

Codes of Ethics

The most common form of government action to address concerns about misbehaviour in government has been to draft codes of ethics to control conflicts of interest. A conflict arises when a political leader or public servant uses a public position for private wealth or other benefits. Codes of ethics function in several ways:

- They prohibit public servants and their families from receiving money, gifts, property, trips, or other benefits from private or public parties. The aim is to ensure that the professional integrity of the public official is not impugned by bias or the appearance of bias in favour of an interest external to the government or the public interest.
- They require elected officials to make their private financial assets and interests available for public scrutiny and to avoid conflict between those interests and their public responsibilities (Greene and Shugarman 1997, chap. 6). For that reason, politicians will separate themselves from their business interests while they are in office. Paul Martin placed his stake in Canadian Steamship Lines under a "supervisory agreement" while he was finance minister, for example, and sold it to his sons when he was running for Liberal leader.
- They prohibit public officials from engaging in outside employment that might directly affect their ability to undertake their public duties.
- They impose restrictions on employment subsequent to public service. Some senior public servants must refrain for 6 to 12 months, for example, from joining a private firm that is subject to regulation or direct commercial dealing with the official's former department or agency.
- They can regulate contact between government officials. Politicians and other public servants are forbidden to contact judges and quasi-judicial officers serving on regulatory agencies about the merit of cases before them, for example. Any intervention constitutes bias and is grounds for judicial review of the affected decision.

Enforcement of ethics codes varies from one jurisdiction to another (Inwood 2012, 340–44), sometimes falling within the jurisdiction of a specially appointed conflict-of-interest or ethics commissioner. As of 2004, conflict-of-interest rules and regulations are overseen at the federal level by an ethics commissioner who reports directly to parliament.

Applying the Rules

Before 2004 an ethics counsellor appointed by the prime minister was responsible for applying the guidelines. That key official reported solely to the prime minister (Greene and Shugarman 1997, 155–56). As controversy over Prime Minister Chrétien's financial relationship with the Auberge de Grand-Mère and an associated golf course intensified in the spring of 2001, this reporting relationship came sharply into focus. How could the counsellor serve the public interest independently while reporting to, and owing his or her tenure to, the prime minister? Critics demanded reform of ethics laws as they applied to cabinet ministers and the prime minister. Most wanted an independent ethics commissioner to be appointed by, and to report to, parliament.

It should come as no surprise that Chrétien consistently refused these demands for the diminution of his power and authority. Cabinet ministers served at the pleasure of the prime minister, he asserted, who alone should be the final arbiter of their tenure. With respect to his own position, he averred that the ethical propriety of a prime minister was a strictly political matter and therefore subject to the established channels of political accountability—namely, parliamentary Question Period, political debate, media scrutiny, and, ultimately, the judgement of the electorate. Chrétien was clearly reluctant to forgo any of the prerogatives of power centred in his office and once again demonstrated the command mode of authority long noted as a hallmark of prime ministerial government. He survived the criticism.

With the change in power from the Chrétien to the Martin ministry came a change in attitude. The new government felt the pressure to reform as a result of the developing federal sponsorship scandal that led to the Gomery inquiry of 2004–06. In 2004 the Martin government established an Office of the Ethics Commissioner to make rulings over whether any politician or public servant had violated the standards of federal ethics legislation. This new commissioner was an officer of parliament, functionally independent of the government of the day. But the position was to be short-lived, much like the Martin government itself.

The sponsorship scandal had yet to run its course, bringing significant changes in its wake.

THE SPONSORSHIP SCANDAL

Following the near-death experience of the 1995 Quebec referendum, the federal government established a special fund, the sponsorship program, to promote federalism via Quebec-based advertising. This program was placed under the federal Department of Public Works. By October 2000 audits were indicating that the department was not closely supervising a number of the advertising firms that were receiving substantial funding. On March 11, 2002, the *Globe and Mail* published a story by Daniel Leblanc and Campbell Clark entitled "Ottawa Can't Find $550,000 Report." It alleged that large amounts of federal money were either going unaccounted for or ending up in the pockets of advertising companies with very close ties to the Liberal Party in Quebec.

In May 2002 Auditor General Sheila Fraser released a highly critical report and in a follow-up in November 2003 asserted that out of total program spending of $200 million, up to $80 million may have been misappropriated or otherwise wasted. The auditor general used words like "scandalous" and "appalling" to describe what she had uncovered, also noting that senior public servants implicated in unethical and likely illegal behaviour had "broken every rule in the book."

By February 2004 Prime Minister Paul Martin, just three months into his new job, called a special inquiry led by Justice John Gomery of the Quebec Superior Court. Testimony alleged that millions of dollars were funnelled into the advertising agencies, almost all of which had close ties to the Quebec wing of the federal Liberal Party. It was also alleged that substantial sums had been rerouted back to the federal Liberal Party, contrary to the Canada Elections Act (CBC 2006).

In his first report Justice Gomery brought forth a number of findings that shocked the country:

- clear evidence of partisan involvement in the administration of the program;
- an absence of transparency in the contracting process and program administration;
- insufficient oversight at the most senior levels that allowed program managers to circumvent proper contracting procedures and reporting lines;
- reluctance on the part of almost all public servants, for fear of reprisals, to go against the will of managers who were circumventing policies;
- gross overestimation of hours worked and overcharging for goods and services on the part of communications agencies;
- inflated commissions, production costs, and other expenses charged by communications

agencies and their subcontractors, many of which were related businesses;
- a complex web of financial transactions among Public Works and Government Services, Crown corporations, and communications agencies, involving kickbacks and illegal contributions to the Liberal Party in the context of the program;
- five agencies that had received large sponsorship contracts channelling money, via legitimate donations or unrecorded cash gifts, to political fundraising activities in Quebec in the expectation of receiving lucrative government contracts;
- agencies carrying on their payrolls individuals who were, in effect, working on Liberal Party matters;
- a culture of entitlement among political officials and bureaucrats involved in the program, including the expectation and receipt of monetary and non-monetary benefit; and
- the refusal of ministers, senior PMO officials, and other public servants to acknowledge responsibility. (Canada, Commission of Inquiry 2005, 5–7)

In February 2006 Justice Gomery released his second and final report, this time with 19 recommendations to improve federal accountability. Here are the major ones:

1 Increase funding for parliamentary committees.
2 Establish a public service charter.
3 Explicitly acknowledge that deputy ministers and senior officials are accountable before

the Public Accounts Committee for their statutory and delegated responsibilities.

4 Establish formal procedures by which ministers can overrule the objections of deputy ministers to proposed courses of action.

5 Formally establish that deputy ministers are appointed for three- to five-year terms following open and competitive job searches.

6 Rename the clerk of the Privy Council the secretary to the cabinet. Rename the Privy Council Office the Cabinet Secretariat. Give the secretary of the Treasury Board the title and function of head of the public service.

7 Amend the government definition of advertising to conform to industry standards.

8 Adopt legislation requiring public servants to document decisions and recommendations, and make it an offence either to fail to do so or to destroy documentation. (Canada, Commission of Inquiry 2006, 199–204)

But the damage from the sponsorship scandal had already been done before the release of the inquiry recommendations. Chrétien had been eased out of power by the Martin wing of the Liberal Party, and the scandal acted as a cancer on Martin's government despite the Gomery inquiry. The Liberals fell into a minority government in 2004, only to be ousted by the Conservatives under Stephen Harper in 2006. And in that election, Harper ran a campaign based on the need to punish the Liberals for their arrogance and corruption, and to send to Ottawa a new team that would restore accountability, transparency, and respect for democratic processes.

THE FEDERAL ACCOUNTABILITY ACT

When Stephen Harper became prime minister in 2006 his first legislative action was the passage of the Federal Accountability Act. Its main features were the following:

· banning institutional and large personal donations to political parties

· ensuring that positions of public trust cannot be used as stepping stones to private lobbying

· toughening provisions dealing with post-employment by increasing the time that ministers and other public servants have to spend outside of office before they can lobby the federal government

· increasing reporting requirements for public servants who spend public monies

· increasing accountability oversight over public servants

· increasing the auditing powers of the auditor general

· strengthening the role of officers of parliament, including the auditor general, to hold the government to account

· providing better protection for whistle-blowers who report improper or illegal behaviour within the public service

· creating the Parliamentary Budget Officer of the Library of Parliament

· creating the Office of the Public Sector Integrity Commissioner of Canada

· creating the Office of the Conflict of Interest and Ethics Commissioner

· increasing the transparency of appointments, contracts, and auditing within government and Crown corporations (Treasury Board of Canada Secretariat 2006)

Note that even though the Federal Accountability Act arose out of the sponsorship scandal, it bore little resemblance to the recommendations of the Gomery inquiry. In particular, the Harper government in no way followed Justice Gomery's approaches to altering the relationships between the government and parliamentary committees and between ministers and deputies, and didn't alter the role of the clerk of the Privy Council.

It's clear that although Stephen Harper was intent on demonstrating a commitment to accountability reform, he was not at all interested in changing structural relationships between the key positions at the centre of government in Ottawa.

STEPHEN HARPER AND DUFFYGATE

Between 2012 and 2015 Prime Minister Harper found himself and his PMO ensnared in a political narrative that had many people questioning his ethical judgement.

In 2008 he had appointed a number of high-profile Conservative supporters to the Senate of Canada, including TV journalist Mike Duffy. The newly appointed Senator Duffy was listed as a representative for Prince Edward Island even though it was known that he had a home in Ottawa.

By 2012 questions were being raised about whether a number of these senators were abusing their expense accounts, billing the Senate for private travel. Questions were also raised as to whether Senator Duffy could legally sit as a representative for PEI.

In 2013 a Senate audit into certain senators' expense accounts found that Duffy had claimed some $90,000 in inappropriate expenses, including housing allowances, and he was called upon to repay this money. At this point, Senator Duffy claimed he had done nothing wrong and that he should not have to repay anything.

The Harper PMO then became involved. After intense backroom negotiations involving Duffy, Harper, leading Conservatives in the Senate, and Nigel Wright, Harper's chief of staff, it was announced that Senator Duffy had repaid the $90,000.

It was revealed later in 2013, however, that Wright had given Duffy the $90,000 out of his own personal funds, so as to make a growing political embarrassment to the prime minister go away. The new problem that arose was that it's illegal for anyone to give money to a parliamentarian in return for any return action, just as it's illegal for a parliamentarian to ask for and accept any money in return for doing something. Such quid pro quos are the stuff of bribery.

Prime Minister Harper, Nigel Wright, Mike Duffy, and the entire PMO soon found itself embroiled in an ethics scandal. Was the $90,000 a bribe? Had Wright acted with corrupt intent? Or was he just trying to help an old friend in need? Did Duffy corruptly accept the money? And what did the prime minister know?

THINKING ABOUT ETHICAL BEHAVIOUR

Although this scandal and the resulting trial in 2015 and eventual acquittal of Mike Duffy in 2016 did not directly involve members of the federal public service, it focused national attention on questionable ethical behaviour amongst senior officials in Ottawa and right in the PMO. Do such scandals weaken the perceived integrity of the Canadian public service? Can members of the general public easily distinguish between political leaders, their staffs, and public servants? Should they?

WHITE PAPER

What did change, however, was that the Federal Accountability Act imposed ever more rules, regulations, and restrictions on the actions of public servants. What has become known in Ottawa as the "web of rules" descended upon every member of the Government of Canada, even though the sponsorship scandal was the result of a few rogue public servants who were prepared, as the auditor

DISPATCH BOX

THE VALUES AND ETHICS CODE FOR THE PUBLIC SERVICE

The *Values and Ethics Code for the Public Service* is a definitive statement of the core personal and professional ideals expected of all federal public servants. Its primary points are summarized below.

Democratic Values

- Public servants shall give honest and impartial advice and make all information relevant to a decision available to ministers.
- Public servants shall loyally implement ministerial decisions, lawfully taken.
- Public servants shall support both individual and collective ministerial responsibility.

Professional Values

- Public servants must work within the laws of Canada and maintain the tradition of political neutrality.
- Public servants shall endeavour to ensure the proper, effective, and efficient use of public money.
- In the public service, how ends are achieved should be as important as the achievements themselves.
- Public servants should continually improve the quality of service through innovation and improving the efficiency and effectiveness of programs.
- Public servants should strive to ensure transparency in government while respecting their duties of confidentiality under the law.

Ethical Values

- Public servants shall perform their duties so that public trust in the integrity, objectivity, and impartiality of government is enhanced.
- Public servants shall act at all times in a manner that will bear the closest possible public scrutiny, an obligation that is not fully discharged by simply acting within the law.
- Public servants, in fulfilling their official duties, shall make decisions in the public interest.
- If a conflict should arise between the private interests and the public duties of a public servant, the conflict shall be resolved in favour of the public interest.

Human Values

- Respect for human dignity and the value of every person should always inspire the exercise of authority and responsibility.
- Public service organizations should be led through participation, openness, and respect for diversity.
- Appointment decisions in the public service shall be based on merit.
- Public service values should play a role in recruitment, evaluation, and promotion.

Source: Adapted from Treasury Board of Canada Secretariat 2003, 6–10.

general suggested, "to break every rule in the book." If this was the case, does imposing ever more rules on all public servants solve the problem of unethical behaviour of a few, or does it just impose more burden on all public servants? These burdens have the undesired side effect of stifling innovation and creativity amongst public servants, promoting risk-averse behaviour, and encouraging employees to be hidebound in rule application rather than thinking of better ways to provide services to the public. Remember that Blueprint 2020 (see Chapter 8) is all about promoting greater innovation and dynamism in the development and administration of policies and programs. But can these aims be achieved in organizations facing ever more adherence to the strict enforcement of operational rules and regulations? As Jeffrey Simpson (2013) has noted, the Federal Accountability Act has had the effect of punishing the many for the sins of a few.

THE CONFLICT OF INTEREST AND ETHICS COMMISSIONER

The **Office of the Conflict of Interest and Ethics Commissioner** was created in 2007 as part of the reforms mandated by the Federal Accountability Act. This new office, with a commissioner acting as an officer of parliament, replaced the Office of the Ethics Commissioner established by the Martin government in 2004. Under the current legislation the commissioner administers two laws: the Conflict of Interest Code for Members of the House of Commons, and the Conflict of Interest Act. The former establishes the rules and standards of ethics for members of parliament. The latter applies to the approximately 2,800 full- and part-time appointees of the Government of Canada and

thus governs the actions of senior officials, both elected and appointed, and partisan advisers hired by ministers to assist them in communications and message management, constituency work, and policy development.

Full-time senior appointees, about 1,300 of them, are subject to the Act's requirements on disclosure and divestment of controlled assets. These "reporting public office holders" include ministers, parliamentary secretaries, ministerial staff, senior public servants, and full-time **governor-in-council appointees** such as members of the PMO, or appointees to the Immigration and Refugee Board. The legislation requires public office holders to file detailed, confidential declarations of their assets and liabilities. It restricts their outside activities and prohibits them from holding controlled assets such as publicly traded securities. It also sets out post-employment rules that come into effect after they leave office.

THE VALUES AND ETHICS CODE FOR THE PUBLIC SERVICE

When it comes to enforcing ethical standards on the general rank and file of public service employees and managers, jurisdiction is usually given to senior managers within the specified department or agency. At the federal level, they administer the *Values and Ethics Code for the Public Service*, although disciplinary action for violation of the code must also be consistent with Public Service Commission rules that govern the merit principle. The Public Service Labour Relations Board is responsible for enforcement of collective agreements and grievance procedures.

If a manager wants to discipline an employee for a violation of the *Values and Ethics Code*, the disciplinary measures have to be consistent with precedents set by the PSLRB, and the employee has the right to grieve such an action to this board. Also, any move to demote an employee or to prevent a promotion has to be consistent with Public Service Commission policies on the merit principle and has to take into consideration how collective agreements and grievances affect ethics enforcement.

The *Values and Ethics Code* sets out the ethical standards expected of public servants. It is intended to maintain public confidence in the integrity of the public service and sets out a framework informed by the ideals of democratic responsibility, professionalism, ethical behaviour, and respect for values. The code defines conflicts of interest and how to avoid them or resolve them once they arise; it also describes the requirements for disclosure of private assets and liabilities, for divestiture of certain assets, and for post–public employment activities (Treasury Board Secretariat 2003, 5–9).

The Treasury Board Secretariat's Office of the Chief Human Resources Officer coordinates department and agency initiatives on ethics enforcement. It establishes common benchmarks and standards, noting,

> Enhancing and maintaining public trust in the institutions of government is fundamental to the work of the federal Public Service. All employees must ensure their actions and decisions uphold the values of the public service and conform to high ethical standards as expressed in the Values and Ethics Code.
>
> The Office of the Chief Human Resources Officer is the centre of expertise and leadership on values-based management, which includes workplace well-being.... We maintain networks and partnerships dedicated to the promotion and continuation of the highest standards of values and ethics in the Public Service. (Canada, Office of the Chief Human Resources Officer 2011)

ISSUES IN CONFLICT-OF-INTEREST ENFORCEMENT

Conflict of interest has become the dominant issue covered by codes of ethics. Federal, provincial, and municipal governments have expended much effort over the past 20 years to establish objective rules to deal with conflicts rather than leaving them to be governed subjectively by those directly involved. Increasing public concern about the quality of ethics in governments has thus shifted enforcement away from the organic-humanistic approach espoused by Friedrich and commonplace before the 1970s and toward the objective, formalistic approach championed by Finer.

Most analysts, including Kernaghan and Siegel (1999, 374–75), stress the value and effectiveness of written codes in addressing matters of conflict of interest. Today, objective approaches to responsibility and ethical control are a fact of government life. It would be inconceivable for any government to abolish its code of ethics.

In fact, as scandals in Ottawa have shown in recent years, opposition parties, the media, and the public want stronger ethics codes and stricter enforcement. The Gomery recommendations called for more objective controls. The Federal Accountability Act produced more explicit rules and reporting requirements. As we saw in the last chapter, this ever-growing web of rules is responsible for new problems as it inhibits innovation and creative approaches to solving problems. More and more often, public servants are expected to go by the book. One is reminded of economist Lou Winnick's remark that "in government, all of the incentive is in the direction of not making mistakes. You can have 99 successes and nobody notices, and one mistake and you're dead."

This brings us back to the issues raised in the Friedrich–Finer debate. If most public servants are honest, what is the best way to ensure ethical, accountable government? Are stricter and more detailed rules the answer? Or a culture of accountability and professionalism? Many public servants would probably argue that the current fixation on formal controls is far from the best approach.

ETHICS DILEMMAS

Ethics regulations raise many thorny issues with respect to scope and nature as well as to enforcement. Most public service codes note the importance of the rule of law, honesty, integrity, respect for fundamental human rights, and deference to superior political and administrative authority. These values are desirable and necessary, but in the real world it's often difficult to know how to put them into practice. Reasonable people will reasonably disagree over whether a particular administrative action breaches ethical standards or requires discipline. Consider some hypothetical examples derived from real cases.

ACCEPTING MONEY AND GIFTS

Is it ever permissible for public servants to accept money or gifts from interest groups or businesses with which they interact? All federal and provincial ethics codes prohibit the acceptance of any benefits that could influence either professional judgement or performance of official duties or raise an appearance of a conflict of interest. Indeed, the Criminal Code prohibits bribery of public officials, and either offering or accepting a bribe is a criminal act.

But what if a Canadian ambassador abroad is offered a work of art from the host country as a symbol of goodwill between the two countries? To refuse might insult the donor and damage relations. Here, the considered opinion is that the gift should be accepted but in a very public way and understood as a gift to the Canadian people and not to the individual diplomat.

MAKING PERSONAL USE OF GOVERNMENT FACILITIES

Is it ever permissible for a public servant to use government facilities and working hours for personal activities unrelated to the work of the office? For example, what if a public servant assists the private business interests of his or her spouse in this way? Or trades confidential information gained through the work process? Or uses access to public records or professional influence as a favour to family members or friends? Is it acceptable, for example, for an official in the department of Immigration and Citizenship to fast-track a claim for landed immigrant status made by a family friend?

The rule is that a public servant cannot use public office for any type of private gain or favouritism to family and friends. The principle—impartial and equal application of rules and regulations established by law—is derived from the Weberian logic of bureaucracy.

Yet the hard and fast application of rules can become blurred by human behaviour. In many small ways such personal benefits are a routine part of office life. Not all public servants use government phone lines for official business only; they may use the photocopier to copy a personal document from time to time, or take home some coloured pencils for their children. The salient point here is degree. Most managers turn a blind eye to minor infractions but rightfully attack the flagrant misuse of public office and its perquisites.

With respect to the use of influence by public servants, although it is clearly prohibited and rarely found, it can be subject to shades of grey. Is it wrong, for example, for a senior official to coach a particular junior in interview tactics to help a bright young candidate in the quest for promotion? At what point does mentoring end and discrimination against other officials begin?

MISREPRESENTING THE TRUTH

Is it ever permissible for public servants to lie or misrepresent the truth to members of the public and elected officials? It's easy to say no, but what about in times of war or when matters of national security are at stake? For obvious security reasons, the Canadian government routinely lied to or misled the public about the operations of North Atlantic convoys during World War II. Most citizens condone the exception to normal ethical conduct as a necessary response to abnormal circumstances.

Similarly, must police officers or immigration officers always tell the truth to criminal suspects or detainees? Law enforcement officers may tell a lie to a suspect or detainee to see the type of response it will elicit. A standard technique used when two suspected accomplices are being questioned separately by police is for one to be told that the other has confessed and implicated him or her. If the result is a genuine confession or useful information, is the behaviour unethical?

Most Canadians seem willing to accept the breach on the grounds of a greater public interest. But it is crucial to acknowledge that the ethical rule is being relaxed under specific, warrantable circumstances. It can raise problems over the long term if law enforcement officers come to believe that normal ethical standards do not apply to them.

PURSUING UNPOPULAR POLICY

Is the government ever justified in proceeding surreptitiously with a policy it deems in the public interest even when some members of the public will be inconvenienced? Consider the following: a provincial community and social services agency has identified the need for a halfway house for young offenders. The logic of such institutions is that they be located in residential neighbourhoods to allow their residents to reintegrate into the larger society gradually. The authorities realize, from much past experience, that the move will be vehemently opposed by neighbourhood community groups. They may approve of reintegration in principle but not in practice when it comes to their own neighbourhood. The common community reaction in such cases is termed the NIMBY syndrome—Not In My Back Yard!

Are the authorities justified in going ahead, without public notice? If local community members become suspicious and begin asking questions, is it acceptable for these officials to lie or mislead them? Does it make a difference if the questioner is a private citizen or an elected municipal leader? What if the questioner is a member of the provincial or federal legislature or parliament? Reasonable people can reasonably disagree over the proper course of action.

The imperatives of social welfare authorities have frequently clashed with the interests of local communities in this country, and there is no clearly right answer to disputes like these. Your perspective will be coloured by your attitude to social welfare policy and community interests.

VIOLATING CONFIDENTIALITY

Is it ever permissible for a public servant to violate the oath of confidentiality and leak information to opposition parties, interest groups, or the media on the grounds that it should be in the public realm but is being covered up? While such whistleblowing has always been a feature of life for government, public interest in the issue has come to the fore in recent years at the same time that cynicism about the trustworthiness of governments has become widespread.

The issues are thorny. A public servant deliberately breaks the law by releasing confidential information to non-governmental sources without due process. On its face, such action is improper and subject to internal discipline ranging from financial penalties and demotion to outright dismissal.

But there are times when the public might support the actions of a whistleblower: when the information involves illegal activities, gross waste and mismanagement, or direct threats to public health and safety, or attempts by senior officials to prevent the information from being made public. Many people will turn a blind eye to a breach of official procedure because of the public good it serves. In this sense the disclosure is judged on highly utilitarian grounds. Any would-be whistleblower must take careful measure of how the revelation will be assessed by the public before deciding to go ahead.

In short, illegal disclosure of information is an inherently political act: it hangs in the balance between the severity of the procedural irregularity and the importance of the substantive information obtained. The issue underscores the difficulty of establishing clear procedures to govern such cases, and this particular feature of bureaucratic life is unlikely to be afforded special protections. Public opinion will ultimately determine the merits and ethics of each case—or lack of them.

The seemingly simple concept of accountability, referred to in the media and political debate almost daily, is far from straightforward. This chapter has proposed a multifaceted, synthetic approach. Accountability has political, legal, and social dimensions; it includes ministerial responsibility, a chain of command and discipline, the responsiveness of public policies to societal needs, and due respect for the procedural and substantive rules of administrative law.

Accountability, then, encompasses a broad range of issues. We brush up against it when we question

- whether ministers have properly fulfilled their responsibilities
- whether public servants are subject to an appropriate system of command and discipline
- whether the actions of public servants are wise and fair
- whether government decision making has been undertaken within the rule of law and the dictates of natural justice
- whether government decisions are sound ways to deal with socio-economic concerns
- whether the actions of governments are ethical
- whether the greater good outweighs the procedural harm of an action that is illegal but beneficial to society, such as leaking confidential information

Simply put, though accountability is central to the theory and practice of government and public sector management, it is inherently political and thus subject to continuous interpretation. Debates about accountability, in turn, become food for thought when we assess the merits of government action—and that discourse is part of the accountability process itself.

REFERENCES AND SUGGESTED READING

Bennis, Warren. 1994. *On Becoming a Leader*. Reading, MA: Addison-Wesley.

Boyd, Neil. 2006. *Canadian Law: An Introduction*. Toronto: Nelson College Indigenous.

Canada, Commission of Inquiry into the Sponsorship Program and Advertising Activities. 2005. *Who Is Responsible? Summary*. (The Gomery Report). Ottawa: Public Works and Government Services.

———. 2006. *Restoring Accountability: Research Studies*. (The Gomery Report). Ottawa: Public Works and Government Services.

Canada, Department of Justice. 2010. *Access to Information Act*. http://laws-lois.justice.gc.ca/eng/acts/a-1/.

Canada, Office of the Auditor General. 2000. "Values and Ethics in the Federal Public Sector." In *2000 October Report of the Auditor General of Canada*, chap. 12. www.oag-bvg.gc.ca/internet/English/parl_oag_200010_12_e_11199.html.

———. 2001. *Report of the Minister of Public Works and Government Services on Three Contracts Awarded to Groupaction*. May 2002. www.oag-bvg.gc.ca/internet/docs/02sprepe.pdf.

———. 2003. *Report of the Auditor General of Canada to the House of Commons*. November 2003. Chapter 3.

Canada, Office of the Chief Human Resources Officer. 2015. "Values and Ethics." www.tbs-sct.gc.ca/chro-dprh/ve-eng.asp.

Canada, Royal Commission on Financial Management and Accountability. 1979. Chaired by Allen Thomas Lambert. *Final Report*. Ottawa: Supply and Services.

CBC. 2005. "Gomery Report: Major Findings." www.cbc.ca/news/background/groupaction/gomeryreport_findings.html.

———. 2006. "Federal Sponsorship Scandal." www.cbc.ca/news2/background/groupaction.

———. 2010. "Integrity Commissioner's Actions 'Unacceptable': Fraser." www.cbc.ca/news/politics/integrity-commissioner-s-actions.-unacceptable-fraser-10932803.

———. 2011. "Never Told of Allegations against Me: Ouimet." www.cbc.ca/news/politics/never-told-of-allegations-against-me-ouimet-11101370.

———. 2012. "Bev Oda Quitting as MP and Cabinet Minister." www.cbc.ca/news/politics/bev-oda-quitting-as-mp-and-cabinet-minister-1.1161211.

Denton, T.M. 1979. "Ministerial Responsibility: A Contemporary Perspective." In *The Canadian Political Process*, 3rd ed., edited by R. Schultz et al., 344–62. Toronto: Holt, Rinehart and Winston.

Dixon, Norman. 1979. *On the Psychology of Military Incompetence*. London: Futura.

Dyck, Rand. 1996. *Provincial Politics in Canada: Towards the Turn of the Century*. 3rd ed. Scarborough, ON: Prentice Hall Canada.

———. 2008. *Canadian Politics: Critical Approaches*. 5th ed. Toronto: Nelson.

Finer, Herman. 1941. "Administrative Responsibility in Democratic Government." *Public Administration Review* 1: 335–50.

Friedrich, Carl J. 1940. "Public Policy and the Nature of Administrative Responsibility." In *Public Policy*, edited by Carl J. Friedrich and Edward S. Mason, 3–24. Cambridge, MA: Harvard University Press.

Gall, Gerald. 2004. *The Canadian Legal System*. 5th ed. Toronto: Carswell.

Greene, Ian, and David P. Shugarman. 1997. *Honest Politics: Seeking Integrity in Canadian Public Life*. Toronto: James Lorimer.

Ingstrup, Ole, and Paul Crookall. 1998. *The Three Pillars of Public Management: Secrets of Sustained Success*. Montreal: McGill-Queen's University Press.

Inwood, Gregory J. 2012. *Understanding Canadian Public Administration: An Introduction to Theory and Practice*. 4th ed. Toronto: Pearson Canada.

Jackson, Robert, and Doreen Jackson. 2009. *Politics in Canada: Culture, Institutions, Behaviour and Public Policy*. 7th ed. Toronto: Prentice Hall Canada.

Johnson, David. 1993. "The Canadian Regulatory System and Corporatism: Empirical Findings and Analytical Implications." *Canadian Journal of Law and Society* 8: 95–120.

Kernaghan, Kenneth, and David Siegel. 1999. *Public Administration in Canada: A Text*. 4th ed. Toronto: Nelson.

Leblanc, Daniel, and Campbell Clark. 2002. "Ottawa Can't Find $550,000 Report." *Globe and Mail*, March 11.

Mancuso, Maureen, Michael M. Atkinson, André Blais, Ian Greene, and Neil Nevitte. 1998. *A Question of Ethics: Canadians Speak Out*. Toronto: Oxford University Press.

Mosher, Frederick. 1968. *Democracy and the Public Service*. New York: Oxford University Press.

Mowen, John C. 1993. *Judgment Calls: High Stakes Decisions in a Risky World*. New York: Simon and Schuster.

Office of the Public Sector Integrity Commission. 2013. *2012–13 Annual Report: Tell Us. You Are Protected*. Ottawa: Queen's Printer.

———. 2015. *2014–15 Annual Report: Tell Us. You Are Protected*. Ottawa: Queen's Printer.

Osborne, David, and Ted Gaebler. 1993. *Reinventing Government: How the Entrepreneurial Spirit Is Transforming the Public Sector*. New York: Plume Books.

Page, Kevin, with Vern Stenlund. 2015. *Unaccountable: Truth and Lies on Parliament Hill*. Toronto: Viking.

Parliamentary Budget Officer. 2010. *Assessment of the Budget 2010 Economic and Fiscal Outlook*. March 11. www.parl.gc.ca/pbo-dpb/documents/Budget_2010_Outlook.pdf.

———. 2011. *An Estimate of the Fiscal Impact of Canada's Proposed Acquisition of the F-35 Lightning II Joint Strike Fighter*. March 10. www.parl.gc.ca/pbo-dpb/documents/F-35_Cost_Estimate_EN.pdf.

———. 2015a. *2014–15 Report on Activities of the Office of the Parliamentary Budget Office*. Ottawa: Queen's Printer.

———. 2015b. *An Assessment of the Government's Fiscal Outlook*. December 1. www.pbo-dpb.gc.ca/en/blog/news/EFOU_Dec2015.

Rynard, Paul, and David Shugarman, eds. 2000. *Cruelty and Deception: The Controversy over Dirty Hands in Politics*. Toronto: University of Toronto Press.

Simpson, Jeffrey. 2013. "Public Servants Aren't Feeling the Love." *Globe and Mail*, June 14, p. 12.

Sossin, Lorne. 2010. "Bureaucratic Independence." In *The Handbook of Canadian Public Administration*, 2nd ed., edited by Christopher Dunn, 364–80. Toronto: Oxford University Press.

Spears, Larry C., ed. 1995. *Reflections on Leadership*. New York: John Wiley and Sons.

Sutherland, Sharon. 1991. "Responsible Government and Ministerial Responsibility." *Canadian Journal of Political Science* 24: 91–120.

Treasury Board of Canada Secretariat. 2003. *Values and Ethics Code for the Public Service*. Ottawa: Public Works and Government Services.

———. 2006. *Federal Accountability Action Plan*. April. www.tbs-sct.gc.ca/faa-lfi/docs/ap-pa/ap-patb-eng.asp.

Wills, Garry. 1994. *Certain Trumpets: The Nature of Leadership*. New York: Simon and Schuster.

Yukl, Gary. 1998. *Leadership in Organizations*. 4th ed. Upper Saddle River, NJ: Prentice Hall.

RELATED WEBSITES

Forum of Canadian Ombudsman. www.ombudsmanforum.ca

Office of the Conflict of Interest and Ethics Commissioner. http://ciec-ccie.parl.gc.ca/en/Pages/default.aspx.

Office of the Public Sector Integrity Commissioner of Canada. www.psic-ispc.gc.ca

Parliamentary Budget Officer. www.pbo-dpb.gc.ca

Privy Council Office. www.pco-bcp.gc.ca/premier.asp

Treasury Board of Canada Secretariat. www.tbs-sct.gc.ca

CHAPTER 10

The Challenges of Leadership

Divorced from ethics, leadership is reduced to management and politics to mere technique.
–James MacGregor Burns, 1978

After reading this final chapter and its related web pages you will be able to

- critically assess the paradox of Canadian public administration;
- identify and discuss 10 key factors of leadership failure; and
- discuss the key factors of successful political and governmental leadership.

10 The Challenges of Leadership

This book began with a paradox. On the one hand, Canadians tend to have a very sceptical, even hostile, attitude toward government. They find its bureaucracies confusing and bloated, staffed by overpaid, underworked, and generally self-serving people. They also question whether governments actually deliver on their promises, and whether political leaders and public servants really care about and understand ordinary Canadians. On the other hand, most also hold deeply felt beliefs that are ultimately very favourable to the role of government. We are proud of our general quality of life, even in comparison to that of our wealthy southern neighbour. Most of us value our health care and public education and our system of social welfare. And we tend to support the other building blocks of Canadian social life: gun control, human rights legislation, multiculturalism policy, environmental regulation, health and safety regulation, regional equalization and development policy, and financial backing for national arts and culture.

But of course all these are matters of public policy and public administration. They are features of the Canadian state, created and maintained for all of us through the work of the public sector. Why then do we hold such contradictory attitudes? We take up this question again as an epilogue to our study.

MAKING SENSE OF A PARADOX

The seemingly contradictory parts of the puzzle can be resolved if we weigh first the particulars and then the principle of societal scepticism about government. One is quite simple to address, the other much more profound.

WEIGHING THE FACTS

From our study of government, we recognize that some aspects of public antipathy toward the public service rest on quite weak foundations. As we saw in Chapter 7, for example, although we often think of public employees as overpaid, most earn relatively modest salaries, and public sector managers would typically earn much more in the private sector. Indeed, relative wage rates have become a significant issue as the federal government tries to retain employees and renew the public service. Better salaries and working conditions are key priorities in this effort.

The assertion that the public sector is inherently inefficient or the quality of its services consistently inferior compared to the private sector doesn't pass muster either. As we saw in Chapter 8, comparing service standards in public and private organizations can yield surprising results: public bureaucracies not infrequently outrank private enterprises.

Accusations of government incompetence, unresponsiveness, and lack of accountability are similarly unsustainable. Of course, one's point of view is conditioned by ideological predisposition, as we saw in Chapters 1 and 2, but it is unjust to generalize. Substantial, widespread public support for the central policies and programs of this country demonstrates that most governments, most of the time, are fulfilling their essential responsibilities and responding to the wishes of the citizenry.

In certain respects, then, criticism of the state—at least in the form of blanket condemnation—simply does not withstand scrutiny. Yet even if our scepticism is overdrawn, the paradox standing at the heart of public sector management in this country is real and deserves serious consideration.

WEIGHING THE FEELINGS

On a deeper level, the profound misgivings we express about our government and public service must be cause for concern. Most people do have serious reservations about the quality of Canadian governance. We wonder whether our bureaucratic organizations are effective, efficient, and economical, and whether they are fully accountable and responsive to the public and the public interest.

Yet criticism of the state and support for its work are opposite sides of the same coin. Most of us rightly view government policies and programs as cornerstones of Canadian society. But we are also rightly critical of how government and public bureaucracies perform their work. We want government to be more accountable to us, to do its work better, and to squarely earn the public trust. In other words, the relationship between society and government is rather like a traditional marriage: society has said "I do," but the government must still honour and obey every day—and the devil is in the details. Or perhaps not quite as traditional as all that: divorce is an option at every election.

RESOLVING THE CONUNDRUM

At this level of analysis the paradox ceases to exist because the broad goals of society are also those of government. All governments in this society recognize that

- public respect and support are contingent on accountability and the perception of accountability;
- government action must be economical, efficient, and effective, as well as responsible and prudent;
- policy and program decisions must be well designed and implemented and consistent with the legal obligations of the state; and
- government must be responsive to the needs of society and the various interest groups within it.

Government is pledged to these ends, in the name of service to the public, and the most important way to achieve them is through the exercise of leadership.

PUBLIC SECTOR MANAGEMENT AND LEADERSHIP

"If there is anything that puzzles me in this game, it is that the longer that you are in the job of prime minister, the harder you have to work to do your job. With anything else ... you get to know the ropes pretty well and it becomes easy. I feel the more you know, the more you have to know and the more problems come at you." Pierre Trudeau was perhaps our most intellectual prime minister, yet his slightly wistful description of the top job in government tells us just how hard leadership can be. Leadership has always been at the heart of effective organizational management, and in recent years interest in the topic has been one of the most important issues in both private and public sector reform.

There is a vast and growing literature on organizational leadership. Baumer and Van Horn (2014), Bernier, Brownsey, and Howlett (2005), Chaleff (2009), Champy (1995), Drucker (2003), Hillier (2010), Ingstrup and Crookall (1998), Kellerman (2004), Kouzes and Posner (2012), Lang (2012), Morse, Buss, and Kinghorn (2007), Newall, Reeher, and Ronayne (2012), Thomas (2008), Wills (1994), Wren (1995), Yukl (1998), and Zenger and Folkman (2002) are just a few of the more notable ones. These works reveal several common elements of good leadership, whether in the private or the public sector, but it is instructive to look first at the characteristics of poor leadership and bureaucratic incompetence before determining the traits of successful leadership.

WHY THINGS GO WRONG

As we saw in Chapter 8, the federal government is committed to improving the leadership calibre of the federal public service, and provincial governments echo this concern. As the clerk of the Privy Council has asserted, effective leadership is vital to policy and program administration, as well as to the development of needed new initiatives. Leadership thus stands at the heart of governance and accountability. And the effects of bad leadership are profound.

Quite interesting work on failures of leadership has been advanced by English psychologist Norman Dixon (1979). Although his work focuses on the military, it offers fruitful insights into

OFFICE OF THE CHIEF HUMAN RESOURCES OFFICER

The Office of the Chief Human Resources Officer is a sub-unit of the Treasury Board Secretariat that develops policies and programs to promote best practices in human resource management within the federal public service.

The CHRO has a wide mandate:

- promoting diversity and employment equity
- strengthening values and ethics within the public service
- promoting management accountability with respect to human resource policy
- enhancing manager and employee performance

- developing indicators to measure staff performance
- establishing and measuring managerial leadership competencies
- furthering managerial leadership development
- devising staff training and development programs
- encouraging the development of staff/manager social networks
- promoting pride in the work of the public service
- recognizing the contribution of public servants through awards, citations, and special events

THINKING ABOUT HUMAN RESOURCE MANAGEMENT

1 The CHRO does not prioritize these items. Would you? How? Why?

2 Would you add new responsibilities to the list?

3 Would you omit any items as unimportant? Why?

WHITE PAPER

government. Dixon lists several forms of organizational incompetence and failed leadership—bureaucratic pathologies—adapted here to a Canadian context.

WASTING RESOURCES

Sometimes government or bureaucratic leaders show little interest in making efficient use of public resources—people, money, and material—because the money doesn't come directly out of their own pockets and it is assumed that resources can always be replenished. The official may feel that spending demonstrates significance and power: the more you have, the more you can use, and thus the more important you look.

Critics of the Harper government's administration of the 2010 G8/G20 summits in Muskoka and Toronto, for example, argued that senior officials in the federal government, including the prime minister, showed wanton disregard for sound financial management. As the cost of these joint summits headed toward $1 billion, many questioned whether the value gained from the meetings could justify the expense to the Canadian taxpayer. And when people became aware that public money had been spent on creating a decorative "fake lake" for the international media centre in Toronto, scorn was replaced with ridicule.

CLINGING TO OUTWORN TRADITIONS

It is always dangerous, Dixon (1979) asserts, for leaders to be fixated on "the way we have always done it." As times change, new problems may very well require new ways of thinking.

As discussed earlier, in 2010 the Harper government announced plans to spend up to $17.6 billion on new jet fighters to replace the fleet of aging CF-18s. In response, the Parliamentary Budget Officer calculated that the cost would likely be around $30 billion at that time. Since then these costs would have increased. These new strike fighters would be state of the art. But are they needed? Such planes are of questionable value in dealing with counter-insurgency campaigns such as those experienced by Canada and its Western allies in Afghanistan, Iraq, and Syria. If bombing ISIS targets is a priority, unmanned drones could do this work far more cheaply and safely from a Canadian viewpoint. And do Russia or China any longer pose a military threat to us? If not, do we really need such aircraft?

Defence planners and their political supporters might simply be caught up in old ways of thinking, developing old-fashioned solutions to current issues. Perhaps money going to the military would be better spent on preparing the Canadian Forces for future counter-insurgency initiatives, for which other types of military equipment are needed, such as armoured personnel carriers and transport helicopters. And perhaps very expensive jet fighters will and should be rendered extinct by unmanned aerial vehicles—drones.

THINKING NARROWLY

We are all shaped by upbringing, education, and experience. If leaders base their policy and administrative decisions on personal preconceptions marked by arrogance, ignorance, intolerance, or prejudice, trouble will ensue. Those leaders either fail to learn or clash with those who hold different views.

Think of the history of governmental policies and actions respecting the residential school system affecting Indigenous Canadians and the issue of missing and murdered Indigenous women. In both cases racism reared its ugly head. With respect to the origins of the residential school system, Canadian governments for too long sought to "beat the Indian" out of Indigenous children by removing them from their families and communities and seeking to assimilate these kids into a "mainstream," English-speaking, white Canadian world. Such policy orientations reveal an antipathy to Indigenous cultures and an ignorance and arrogance that will take generations to heal.

The scandalous reality that, according to the RCMP, some 1,200 Indigenous girls and women have gone missing or been murdered between 1980 and 2012, and the fact that this did not register on the political radar in Canada until the middle of this decade, again suggests that a racist attitude toward Indigenous Canadians may have been at work. Would a Canadian prime minister have said that such an issue was not high on his priority list if the missing and murdered girls and women were white? Note that on December 8, 2015, the newly elected Liberal government of Justin Trudeau launched a national inquiry into this issue.

UNDERESTIMATING PROBLEMS AND OVERESTIMATING SOLUTIONS

Political and bureaucratic leaders can become so immersed in their own environment, and so convinced of their own intelligence, that they begin to operate in a bubble of their own making. They fail to see the nuances of an issue or the strength of those opposed to their point of view, ignoring or dismissing unpalatable information because it conflicts with their own ideas of good policy and management.

Think of the decisions of both Liberal and Conservative governments to begin military operations in Afghanistan as of 2001 and to fight there for 13 years. This mission was justified with a variety of changing messages: that Canadians were helping to defeat the Taliban; that we were helping to build a liberal democracy in this part of the world; that we were working to ensure that Afghan girls could go to school; and, finally, that we were there to help maintain stability and prevent the Taliban from coming back into power. By the time the Canadian combat mission in Afghanistan ended in 2014, that country was still in turmoil, its authoritarian and corrupt government was far from democratic, the concept of female equality was still a foreign ideal, and the Taliban was resurgent. In the meantime, 159 Canadian soldiers had died. Canadian policy makers had failed to understand the complexities of the place they were sending troops into, while believing that through sheer force of effort we could change the political culture of a society far different from ours. It's arguable that Canadians and their federal government have still not fully learned this lesson.

BELIEVING IN SIMPLE SOLUTIONS TO COMPLEX PROBLEMS

Leaders can be overwhelmed by their responsibilities. Their personal, intellectual, and professional background may be insufficient to enable them to cope. Complex problems demand complex solutions, and leaders must comprehend the nature of a multifaceted problem and devise sophisticated ways to resolve it. Leaders show that they are in over their heads when they latch on to simple answers that they can understand and easily advocate—but which have little chance of success.

"Tough on crime" policies often fall into this category. Governments such as Stephen Harper's in Canada and those in the US states of California, Texas, and Florida have asserted that strengthening criminal sanctions—lengthening prison sentences, applying maximum penalties more often, and ensuring the sentences are fully served—will reduce crime. Numerous criminology studies of these issues, however, suggest that the causes of crime are quite complex, often buried deep in the personal history of offenders (Centre for Criminology 2010). Simply toughening criminal penalties does not reduce crime on its own. If so, Texas would be the safest state in the United States with the lowest murder rate. Sadly, Texas aligns far more to the other end of these scales.

PERSISTING DESPITE EVIDENCE

Leaders sometimes become committed to a course of action despite strong evidence that it is undesirable. Such obstinacy might reflect a passionate belief in the rightness of a policy, but more often it stems from a combination of ignorance and arrogance: a lack of awareness of broader dynamics and a refusal to admit a mistake.

Consider an example at the micro-bureaucratic level. As late as the mid-1980s, a public sector office manager in one of the smaller provinces steadfastly refused to support the computerization of her office on the grounds that computers were "confusing" and a "passing fad." She wanted to keep electronic typewriters, quite probably because she feared the unfamiliar new technology rather than from any considered assessment of it. Moreover,

once she had staked out her position she refused to retract it, fearing loss of face.

Of course, she did eventually have to back down as computer technology came to reshape the practice of office work, but in the meantime money had been spent on machinery already obsolete.

DISCOURAGING CRITICAL THINKING

Leaders may also feel threatened by critical thinking because it can confront them with evidence of their own weakness and incompetence. We all know stories of leaders who surround themselves with people who will tell them what they want to hear. Such behaviour perpetuates established organizational practices even though they may need reform. Encouraging critical thinking is one of the most important features of leadership, but it is a challenging position to take.

Very early on in his prime ministership, Stephen Harper was accused by his political opponents of running an overly centralized administration within which dissenting voices were not welcome. By 2010 the mainstream media had reported on a long line of senior public servants who had either been fired or not rehired after questioning government decisions in their fields of expertise. On the list were the former head of Statistics Canada, the former Veterans Ombudsman, the former head of the Canadian Nuclear Safety Commission, and the former Military Police Complaints Commissioner. Between 2011 and 2015 Harper was increasingly criticized for being authoritarian, for showing dictatorial tendencies, and, in the words of critical biographer Michael Harris, for being a "Party of One" (Harris 2014).

SUPPRESSING OR DISTORTING BAD NEWS

It is an all-too-common phenomenon within organizations marked by poor leadership to deny the existence of a problem or, if this proves impossible, to cover it up. The leader hopes that the problem will go away or be forgotten, but of course it may only be exacerbated, leaving a bigger mess for authorities to deal with later.

This characterizes in a nutshell the response of senior Defence officials to the Somalia affair in the early 1990s and the Afghan detainee issue in early years of the Afghan mission. In the first instance, Canadian soldiers were found to have tortured and murdered Somali detainees, while in the latter issue, Canadian troops were accused of knowingly handing over Afghan detainees to face torture at the hands of others. Rather than admit to serious breaches of discipline and ascribe a failure of training and command to Canadian troops and their officers, officials sought to suppress the issue through none-too-effective deception manoeuvres that ultimately made for even worse scandals for the military.

ALTERNATING BETWEEN INDECISION AND FRENZY

Many officials who are otherwise competent fail the acid test of leadership in times of crisis. When experience and knowledge offer no clear direction, officials are thrust into a very difficult environment. Those accustomed to going by the book suddenly find that the book is useless. With intelligent innovation quite beyond them, they postpone making decisions or vacillate between options as events evolve around them. Then, aware that indecision in a time of crisis is wrong, they make weak and frenzied decisions that lack objectivity or a sense of the whole picture. Often, they simply make matters worse.

A recent example highlighting these difficulties was the scandal that rocked Dalhousie University and its dentistry school in the winter of 2015. In December 2014, the media reported that female students in the dentistry program had complained to university officials about a male-only Facebook group that was posting sexist, misogynistic, racist, and homophobic materials online, at times directed against female students in the program. The media soon reported that senior administrators, including the president of the university, had been alerted to other complaints of sexist and racist behaviour of some students and faculty within the dentistry program as early as the summer of 2014 but that disciplinary action was not forthcoming because the female complainants would not lodge formal complaints with their names attached. The women feared retaliation if they went public in this fashion, stressing that there was a poisoned environment within the dentistry school.

Once the story became public in December, however, the Dalhousie administration launched a flurry of activity. Final exams were postponed, students involved in the Facebook group were suspended from certain clinical classes, and an independent investigation into systemic harassment in the dentistry program was launched. The university also established a restorative justice process that was to bring together all the actors in this drama, so that the men and the women could come together as equals, talk about what had happened, share their feelings, and learn from these events and the fury they had elicited. While most of the people involved in these events participated in this process, not all did. And many feminist critics both within and outside of Dalhousie complained that the restorative justice process was inadequate, amounting to a slap on the wrist, while the appropriate penalty for such academic and professional misbehaviour should have been expulsion from the university. These critics noted that if the hatred directed at women had been directed at blacks or Jews, the university's response likely would have been very different. While all the men in this story did eventually graduate, many women and others continued to wonder about the type of culture existing beneath the surface at this university, and the quality of its leadership (CBC News 2015).

LOOKING FOR SCAPEGOATS AND CONSPIRACIES

When poor leaders are confronted with the objective evidence of failure—lost elections, discredited policies, programs that either collapse or persist with no real effect—they often respond by denying personal responsibility. Instead, they search for people or circumstances to blame, thereby absolving themselves.

This dynamic of shifting responsibility can also involve conspiracy theories. Weak leaders suspect either internal or external enemies intent on bringing them down through some devious plot. They were stabbed in the back by malicious forces intolerant of their superiority and unappreciative of their wisdom. Many Americans still believe that the 9/11 terrorists entered their country through the Canadian border. As late as 2009, then Secretary of State Hillary Clinton reiterated this contention even though the US government's commission on 9/11 established that all 19 terrorists had entered

through American airports. Too many Americans still like to deflect attention from that vulnerability and place blame elsewhere.

HOW THINGS GO RIGHT

A review of bureaucratic pathologies is useful on two counts. First, it helps us to better understand why some policies, programs, and other endeavours fail or suffer grave difficulties. Inquiries into the problems associated with the acquisition of jet fighters; the wars in Afghanistan Iraq, Syria and Libya; the residential school system; missing and murdered Indigenous women; and the federal sponsorship program are noteworthy examples of the importance of analyzing government malfunctions.

Second, by isolating the behaviour that was problematic, we develop consensus and insight about the opposite—the attributes of sound leadership. By reversing the hallmarks of failure, we learn about political and managerial competence.

THE QUALITIES OF LEADERSHIP

What are the requirements of sound leadership? What traits should the Canada School of Public Service teach to public servants? Good public sector leadership entails

- forethought
- a clear vision of short- and long-range goals that will benefit society
- the ability to articulate this vision to others
- the ability to engage in complex thought
- the ability to motivate others
- broad-mindedness

- the ability to recognize and reject prejudice and stereotypical thinking
- deep interest in the problems to be confronted
- an understanding of the positions and strengths of adversaries
- flexibility coupled with the courage to persist with sound plans even if others waver
- concern for human, financial, and material resources
- a willingness to embrace new ideas, even when they cast one's own thinking or practice into doubt
- a willingness to be self-critical and to encourage others to be so

LEADERSHIP COMPETENCIES

The Office of the Chief Human Resources Officer has developed an elaborate list of leadership skills for all ranks within the federal public service: deputy ministers, middle managers, and other employees. The complete list, entitled "Effective Behaviours," is on the TBS website. The key points for managers look like this:

• Values and Ethics

- Demonstrate values and ethics in personal behaviour and workplace practices.
- Build and promote a safe, healthy, respectful workplace, free of harassment and discrimination.

• Strategic Thinking

- Develop unit direction based on a thorough understanding of the functional area.
- Coordinate information from multiple projects to form a comprehensive perspective.
- Encourage and incorporate diverse and creative initiatives and perspectives.

• Engagement

- Share information vertically and horizontally.
- Promote collaboration among supervisors on related projects.
- Manage group dynamics in a diverse workforce across projects.
- Communicate with clarity and commitment.

• Management Excellence

- Establish workplace targets for quality and productivity.
- Identify financial and human resources requirements.
- Manage unit workload through negotiating timelines, prudent resource planning, and prioritization.
- Provide regular feedback, and acknowledge success and the need for improvement.
- Monitor and address workplace well-being.

THINKING ABOUT LEADERSHIP

1 Do you think the list embodies necessary precision or unnecessary verbosity?

2 Would you add other items?

3 Would a shorter list be more effective? What omissions would you make?

4 What would your top-ten list consist of?

WHITE PAPER

- a willingness to analyze ideas, policies, plans, programs, and activities critically
- a willingness to learn from others and from bad news and poor decisions
- a willingness to admit mistakes
- wisdom and decisiveness in times of crisis
- a strong theoretical and practical foundation from which to judge proper action

THE THREE PILLARS OF MANAGEMENT

Ingstrup and Crookall (1998) provide an interesting schema of leadership in public sector management. They contend that there are "three pillars" to effective management: aim, character, and execution.

Management Aim

By *aim* they mean that the best public sector organizations have a coherent vision informing all their actions. That sense of mission provides the foundation for all mechanisms of accountability and the framework within which to decide whether the organization is achieving its ends in acceptable ways.

Management Character

By *character* they mean that successful public sector leaders make effective use of people, communication, and trust. They train, direct, inspire, and learn from their employees. To do so, they employ numerous channels of communication—both formal and informal—with employees, partner organizations, and the citizens the organization serves.

Such responsive communication patterns are integral to building trust in an organization. Effective public sector management requires employees to trust their leaders just as these leaders must trust their staff. Trust binds an organization together, as everyone feels like part of a greater whole, working together for important ends.

Management Execution

Finally, Ingstrup and Crookall speak of *execution*. This refers to the tactics used to achieve organizational goals. Good execution is centred on

- effective use of a variety of management tools
- teamwork
- management of change

Good managers are willing to adopt and adapt a variety of management approaches and tools, such as state-of-the-art communications technologies, flex time, work–life balance policies, and on-the-job opportunities for professionalization and skills training. Execution involves constantly fine-tuning procedures to facilitate better policy and program delivery. Teamwork is a related vital feature of organizational life: working cooperatively and strategically to meet goals intelligently. Promoting teamwork is therefore a core aspect of execution.

And finally, good leaders have their finger on the pulse of the institution. Organizational environments evolve, and policy and program orientations do too. Public sector managers handle change by remaining open and responsive to it.

KEEPING THE BAR HIGH

Admittedly, the traits just described set very high standards, but good leadership is integral to government accountability because it means that state power will be exercised in politically, legally, and socially responsive ways. It is informative,

CANADA SCHOOL OF PUBLIC SERVICE

The Canada School of Public Service is devoted to professional training and leadership development for public servants. The school was launched on April 1, 2004, through the enactment of the Canada School of Public Service Act, under provisions of the Public Service Modernization Act, 2004. The Canada School replaced the Canadian Centre for Management Development.

To fulfill its legislative mandate to build individual and organizational capacity and management excellence, the Canada School offers courses in four program areas:

- Orientation and certification: specialized courses for all new employees introducing them to the public service, and professional courses in financial and human resources regulations
- Management and professional development: specialized courses in finance, procurement, human resources, classification, remuneration, staffing, information technology, auditing, communication, policy, service delivery, security, and corporate planning
- Leadership development: specialized training in strengthening leadership competencies,

responding to priority issues, building communities, and strengthening networks of leaders within organizations
- Second-language acquisition and maintenance: specialized French- and English-language training for the public service

The School has its critics, such as Donald Savoie (2015, 153–63), but his criticism goes not to the purpose of the School but to how well it meets its goals. It's also important to distinguish between the School and any university. The latter ideally promotes independent critical thought and research. The former is an internal governmental organization designed to offer professional training directly geared to the needs of federal public servants.

If this School did not exist, would we want the federal government to do without it? Would we want universities and colleges to provide this training? Could they? Or could this training be privatized to independent learning centres?

If this School did not exist, what is the likelihood that the federal government would reinvent it?

---

then, to measure our current and past leaders by these criteria. While each Canadian's list of successful and failed leaders will be slightly different, depending on our personal, ideological, pragmatic, or sentimental impressions, many of us would view few of them favourably. We are not easy taskmasters.

Here the paradox comes into play once again. By demanding a high standard of accountability from

our governments, we encourage the conditions for good leadership; by holding our leaders to difficult standards, we foster accountability. Elected political leaders and public servants have a vested interest in keeping the bar high as well. Good leadership ensures that their work is efficacious and worthy of public support. If a government loses public respect, its days will be numbered. And a new government may well undo its accomplishments.

GOOD FOLLOWERSHIP

We citizens are followers and we need leaders, but equally, leaders need followers. As Garry Wills (1994) has long argued, one cannot speak of leadership without also speaking of followership. The relationship is symbiotic.

Those who follow a leader can range from a few people to an entire nation. Leaders must inspire their followers, bind them to their strategic vision, allay their fears and give them hope, and motivate them to work for a greater good. Successful leaders can forge deep bonds with their followers, building power and purpose through which important goals can be realized for the benefit of both the leader and the led.

What makes a good follower? Whether public servants or citizens, effective followers are intelligent and knowledgeable about the state, the demands of policy and program development and what can be expected in their implementation, the limitations of and trade-offs in government decision making, and the nature of accountability. At the deepest level, ignorant citizens are poor followers, and they get the leaders they deserve.

Well-informed citizens, conversely, are a vital part of the system of accountability. They will be more likely to elect good women and men to office and to demand good men and women to staff and manage the public service. Good leadership depends on good citizens.

We have a civic duty to be interested in our government. We have a duty to be well informed about, sensitive to, and critical of how government functions and the quality of public sector management we receive. We have a duty, in short, to promote good government in our society, and the first and last element of this duty is to be aware.

The host of public policy concerns that have shaped political debate and government action in this country are still with us. Canadian–American relations and free trade, globalization, and the regulatory capacity of the state remain central concerns, as do the policy issues of social cohesion, environmental protection, sustainable development, and viable systems of Indigenous self-government. And heightened concern for national defence, security, and intelligence remains a key focus in light of ongoing fears of the terrorist threat at home and abroad.

We also face concerns about how best to promote economic growth during times of international economic uncertainty. Calls for government interventions to stimulate the national and provincial economies via deficit spending are balanced with concerns for growing governmental deficits and debts, all of which have to be repaid at some point in time. Yet we are also aware that governing is always more than just managing the economy. We also worry about the state of health, education, and social assistance policy; regional development and industrial policy; human rights promotion; culture and heritage protection; agricultural support; infrastructure redevelopment; and a host of other policy fields. We want governments to reinvest in public services to promote the public good. Demands that government reclaim its place in the development of Canadian society and the protection of a liberal social welfare state remain strong, as evidenced by the Liberal electoral victory in 2015. How well the Trudeau government manages all of these challenges and expectations will very much determine whether they deserve re-election in 2019.

Regardless of the course that Canadian governments take over the decades ahead, they will still be expected to lead the public sector and more to the most professional degree possible. Managers and staff will be required to deliver sound and accountable public service, in accordance with ministerial responsibility, legal responsibility, and social responsiveness.

The concept of ministerial responsibility will remain a foundational principle of Canadian government, but the operational influence of senior public servants is likely to remain pronounced, highlighting a sharp division of labour between elected and unelected officials in the decision-making process. Both the command mode of executive decision making and criticism of it have not yet run their course. Whether such a concentration of power is desirable must be a topic of intense political debate in this country until it is resolved.

With respect to the law, judicial review of administrative actions will continue to exert significant control over state action, and government institutions seem set to increase the practice of legal rule making to structure and formalize their exercise of discretion. These activities allow the socio-economic interests concerned greater participation by bringing the state and societal groups together in a dialogue over policy and procedural developments.

With respect to social responsiveness, government will of course continue to be expected to serve the public interest by developing policies and programs that answer the needs and interests of social groups and to tailor those services in response to societal feedback. As society evolves, government responds, but some aspects of governance remain the same. Governments come and go, developing new policies and programs or reaffirming existing ones. Their specific methods and practices fluctuate, as does their ideological focus. But accountability is a constant thread, and our task of evaluating it is never finished. Good leadership is therefore also an unchanging need, inextricably linked to accountable governance. And the fundamentals of effective leadership are unvarying—only the context changes.

I hope that through this text you've deepened your understanding of government. Critical public awareness of government action, management, and leadership is a fundamental part of accountability. Any government serving an informed and constructively analytical citizenry will be the better for it: more conscious of its public duties and more socially responsive. Being alert to the nature and function of government is a vital component of good citizenship, benefiting all those affected by state action: politicians, public servants, governments, interest groups—and you.

REFERENCES AND SUGGESTED READING

Baumer, Donald C., and Carl E. Van Horn. 2014. *Strategic Actors and Policy Domains*. 4th ed. Los Angeles: Sage.

Bass, Bernard M. 2008. *The Bass Handbook of Leadership: Theory, Research and Managerial Applications*. 4th ed. New York: Free Press.

Bennis, Warren. 1994. *On Becoming a Leader*. Reading, MA: Addison-Wesley.

——, and Robert Townsend. 1995. *Reinventing Leadership: Strategies to Empower the Organization*. New York: William Morrow and Co.

Bernier, Luc, Keith Brownsey, and Michael Howlett, eds. 2005. *Executive Styles in Canada: Cabinet Structures and Leadership Practices in Canadian Government*. Toronto: University of Toronto Press.

Canada, Office of the Chief Human Resources Officer. 2010. "A Leadership Development Framework for the Public Service of Canada." www.tbs-sct.gc.ca/psm-fpfm/learning-apprentissage/ptm-grt/ldf-cpl-eng.asp.

CBC News. 2015. "Dalhousie Dentistry Report: University Had Culture of 'Misogyny, Homophobia and Racism.'" June 29. www.cbc.ca/news/canada/nova-scotia/dalhousie-dentistry-report-university-had-culture-of-misogyny-homophobia-and-racism-1.3131522

Centre for Criminology. 2010. *Criminological Highlights*. Newsletter 11:1. Toronto: University of Toronto Centre for Criminology.

Chaleff, Ira. 2009. *The Courageous Follower*. San Francisco: Berrett-Koehler Publishers.

Champy, James. 1995. *Reengineering Management: The Mandate for New Leadership*. New York: Harper Business.

Dixon, Norman. 1979. *On the Psychology of Military Incompetence*. London: Futura.

Drucker, Peter F. 2003. *The Essential Drucker*. New York: Regan Books.

Harris, Michael. 2014. *Party of One: Stephen Harper and Canada's Radical Makeover*. Toronto: Viking Press.

Hillier, Rick. 2010. *Leadership: 50 Points of Wisdom for Today's Leaders*. Toronto: HarperCollins Canada.

Ingstrup, Ole, and Paul Crookall. 1998. *The Three Pillars of Public Management: Secrets of Sustained Success*. Montreal: McGill-Queen's University Press.

Kellerman, Barbara. 2004. *Bad Leadership: What It Is, How It Happens, Why It Matters*. Boston: Harvard Business Press.

Kouzes, James M., and Barry Z. Posner. 2012. *The Leadership Challenge: How to Keep Getting Extraordinary Things Done in Organizations*. 5th ed. San Francisco: Jossey-Bass.

Lang, Amanda. 2012. *The Power of Why*. Toronto: Harper Collins.

Laschinger, John, and Geoffrey Stevens. 1992. *Leaders and Lesser Mortals: Backroom Politics in Canada*. Toronto: Key Porter Books.

Mancuso, Maureen, Richard G. Price, and Ronald Wagenberg, eds. 1994. *Leaders and Leadership in Canada*. Toronto: Oxford University Press.

Morse, Ricardo S., Terry F. Buss, and C. Mo Kinghorn, eds. 2007. *Transforming Public Leadership for the 21st Century*. Armonk, NY: M.E. Sharpe.

Mowen, John C. 1993. *Judgment Calls: High-Stakes Decisions in a Risky World*. New York: Simon and Schuster.

Newall, Terry, Grant Reeher, and Peter Ronayne, eds. 2012. *The Trusted Leader: Building the Relationships that Make Government Work*. New York: CQ Press.

Paquet, Gilles. 1999. *Governance through Social Learning*. Ottawa: University of Ottawa Press.

Savoie, Donald J. 2015. *What Is Government Good at? A Canadian Answer*. Montreal: McGill-Queen's University Press.

Spears, Larry C., ed. 1995. *Reflections on Leadership*. New York: John Wiley and Sons.

Thomas, Robert J. 2008. *Crucibles of Leadership: How to Learn from Experience to Become a Great Leader*. Boston: Harvard Business Press.

Webster, Cheryl Marie, and Anthony Doob. 2012. "Searching for Sasquatch: Deterrence of Crime through Sentence Severity." In *Oxford Handbook on Sentencing and Corrections*, edited by Joan Petersilia and Kevin Reitz, 173–95. New York: Oxford University Press.

Wills, Garry. 1994. *Certain Trumpets: The Nature of Leadership*. New York: Simon and Schuster.

Wren, J. Thomas. 1995. *The Leader's Companion: Insights on Leadership through the Ages*. New York: Free Press.

Yukl, Gary. 1998. *Leadership in Organizations*. 4th ed. Upper Saddle River, NJ: Prentice Hall.

Zenger, John, and Joseph Folkman. 2002. *The Extraordinary Leader: Turning Good Managers into Great Leaders*. New York: McGraw Hill.

RELATED WEBSITES

Canada School of Public Service. www.csps-efpc.gc.ca/index-eng.aspx

Office of the Chief Human Resources Officer. www.tbs-sct.gc.ca/ip-pi/mandate-mandat/chro-dprh-eng.asp

GovLeaders.org. http://govleaders.org

Public Sector Leadership Council. www.conferenceboard.ca/networks/pslc/default.aspx

Key Terms

Aboriginal title. The constitutional concept that First Nations retain an inherent relationship of care, concern, and responsibility for protecting and preserving their lands for future Indigenous generations. While Canadian law recognizes that title can be extinguished by clear and explicit treaty provisions, this point remains debatable in constitutional discourse.

accountability. The duty owed by elected politicians and public servants who are responsible for the procedural and substantive merit of their decision making and are called upon to abide by the concepts of ministerial responsibility, the rule of law, and social responsiveness.

allophone. A resident of Quebec whose mother tongue is neither French nor English.

assistant deputy minister. One of the most senior executive officials responsible for providing administrative leadership of a department, such as ADM Finance or ADM Human Resources. Assistant deputy ministers are ranked below associate deputy ministers (also referred to as ADMs) and are usually responsible for a particular functional portfolio within the department. See also **portfolio.**

associate deputy minister. One of the most senior executive officials responsible for providing administrative leadership of a department. Associate deputy ministers rank immediately below the deputy minister, to whom they are responsible for providing system-wide support and assistance.

attest and compliance auditing. A traditional form of audit that provides a narrow accounting of monies spent in a department or agency, the legal authority for spending, a comparison of planned and actual expenditure, and any irregularities. See also **comprehensive auditing.**

auditing. The management process by which expenses incurred are measured and evaluated in light of pre-established criteria.

auditor general of Canada. An officer of parliament appointed to a 10-year term and given responsibility for conducting comprehensive audits of all federal departments and agencies, many Crown corporations, and the territorial governments. The auditor general's reports usually find that most government programs are implemented appropriately, and a critical report can become a major political headache for the government of the day.

backbencher. A member of parliament (MP) who is either a member of the governing party but not in cabinet or a member of an opposition party but not an official critic for a given portfolio.

bilingualism and biculturalism. The policy, based on the idea that French and English Canada are two of the founding nations of the country, of representing the languages and cultures of these founding nations within the framework of the federal parliament, government, and public service.

Blueprint 2020. The most recent federal public service renewal initiative, launched by the Harper government in 2012 and designed to prepare the way for the better, stronger, and more capable public service that will exist in 2020. This blueprint for reform emphasizes the importance of openness, transparency, innovation, creativity, the use of new technologies, improved communications, collaboration in decision making, and enhanced employee training and development.

bounded rationalism. A theory of management in the middle ground between incrementalism and rationalism. As advanced by Herbert Simon, it suggests that policy makers should strive for the most rationalistic means to achieve desired ends within the constraints of pre-existing systems of organization and the limitations of time and knowledge. See also **incrementalism; rationalism**.

budgetary rationalism. A system of budgeting in which program spending is systematically linked to program planning, prioritization, development, and evaluation. Rational systems of budgeting attempt to base all expenditures on comprehensive plans under which programs are subjected to critical cost–benefit analysis and priority setting. Budgetary rationalism emerged in Canada in the 1960s and has remained a potent force in financial management thinking ever since. See also **planning-programming-budgeting system; policy and expenditure management system**.

bureaucracy. Government as exercised through the power of office holders. Bureaucracy in the classic, Weberian sense is founded on hierarchy, unity of command, specialization of labour, merit, permanent employment, rules, written records, and professionalism. See also **hierarchy**.

bureaucratic politics theory. A theory of management in which actions undertaken in the process of policy making and program administration are understood as being conditioned by the interests, traditions, and values of the organization in which any given actor works.

bureaucratization. The dynamic that occurs as social and economic affairs become subject to the influence and/or control of the state and its institutions.

cabinet. The collection of ministers selected by the prime minister to provide leadership to government departments and agencies and to advise the prime minister on the development of policies and programs.

cabinet committee. One of the functional groups into which a prime minister will divide cabinet ministers to assist in the conduct and development of policy and program decision making. As of September 2016, the Trudeau cabinet included 11 full cabinet committees: Agenda; Results and Communications; Treasury Board; Open

Transparent Government and Parliament; Growing the Middle Class; Diversity and Inclusion; Canada in the World and Public Security; Canada-United States Relations; Intelligence and Emergency Management; Environment, Climate Change and Energy; Defence Procurement; and Litigation Management.

cabinet minister. A person selected by the prime minister to be the political head of a government department and participate in the decision making of the government overall. Usually MPs of the governing party, ministers must exercise their duties in accordance with the rules of individual and collective ministerial responsibility. See also **cabinet; ministerial responsibility.**

cabinet selection. The process by which a prime minister constructs a cabinet. The formal appointment to cabinet is given by the governor general. See also **cabinet.**

Canada School of Public Service. The centralized educational agency of the federal public service that provides employee training and management development courses for public servants. Formerly known as the Canadian Centre for Management Development, the CSPS plays an important role in management renewal policy.

caucus. All the members of parliament representing a given party. With respect to the governing party, members of cabinet remain caucus members and are expected to keep their caucus colleagues updated on the work of their portfolios.

central agency. A specialized support agency that provides expert policy advice and program assistance to the cabinet and prime minister in an institutionalized cabinet system. The key central agencies of the Canadian government are the Prime Minister's Office, the Privy Council Office, the Department of Finance, and the Treasury Board of Canada Secretariat. See also **institutionalized cabinet system.**

Charlottetown Accord. A constitutional amendment proposal supported by the federal government and all provincial governments of the time. It was designed to recognize Quebec as a distinct society, decentralize federal powers, create an elected Senate, and recognize Aboriginal self-government. The accord was defeated in a national referendum in 1992.

Charter of Rights and Freedoms. The constitutional declaration of fundamental rights and freedoms possessed by all Canadians that must be respected by all Canadian governments and their officials. The Charter was brought into force as part of the Constitution Act, 1982.

citizen. For the purpose of public sector management, a person with a right to public services. Government institutions bear a legal obligation to provide citizens with high-calibre services without any cash transaction.

clerk of the Privy Council. The highest ranking public servant in the federal public service. The clerk is also the secretary to cabinet and, as such, acts as the deputy minister to the prime minister. The clerk is the official head of the public service of Canada and has the non-partisan function of giving expert advice to the prime minister and cabinet with respect to the operational dynamics of policy making and program implementation within the federal public service. The clerk supervises departmental deputy ministers and advises the prime minister on matters respecting deputy minister promotions, transfers, and removals.

collective bargaining. The legal process under which unionized employees engage in formal negotiations with the representatives of their employer over pay and benefits, terms and conditions of work, and grievance procedures. Collective bargaining in the federal public service is extensive compared to the Canadian private sector but limited by the merit principle and the role of the Public Service Commission of Canada.

command mode. The centralization of decision-making power and authority in the hands of the prime minister and key advisers with respect to policy and program matters. Also referred to as the command and control mode. See **strategic prime ministership**.

comprehensive auditing. A form of auditing that assesses government programs for economy, efficiency, effectiveness, and accountability. See also **auditing**.

conservatism. An ideology that ascribes importance to individualism, liberty, freedom, equality of opportunity, private property, capitalism, free enterprise, and business interests. Conservatives believe that the state should take a generally circumscribed role in the life of society.

Constitution Act, 1982. Legislation resulting from an agreement signed by the federal government and all provincial governments, with the exception of Quebec, to patriate the constitution, establish a constitutional amending formula, and create the Charter of Rights and Freedoms.

consumer/client. The recipient of government service(s) through a cash transaction. Consumers/clients, in contrast to citizens, do not necessarily possess a right to public services. A citizen, for example, has the right to publicly provided health care services as mandated through the Canada Health Act. In contrast, Canada Post has consumers who can make use of the mail system, provided they pay the fees set by this Crown corporation.

Crown agency. Any Crown corporation or regulatory agency, as distinct from a government department.

Crown corporation. A commercial enterprise established and owned by either the federal or the provincial state but possessing relative operational autonomy from the government. A Crown corporation is not a department and thus is not headed by a minister but by a board of directors appointed by the government.

Crow's Nest Pass Agreement. Federal railway freight policy designed in the late nineteenth century, and formalized in an agreement between the Canadian Pacific Railway and the federal government, to promote the industrial development of central Canada by artificially lowering the costs of transporting manufactured goods from east to west across the country while artificially raising the costs of transporting manufactured goods from west to east.

deficit. The budgetary dynamic in which expenditures and other financial liabilities exceed revenues, resulting in the need to borrow money to meet financial obligations. Such borrowing results in an accumulating debt.

democratic socialist. A socialist who believes that socialist political parties should be radical and forthright in demanding fundamental reform to the nature of national socio-economic life. Democratic socialists call for a greater state presence in the regulation of society and the economy and state ownership of leading national industries. They also tend to view the New Democratic Party more as a social movement than as a competitive political party, with the responsibility to advocate for socialist principles and values.

department. The chief form of institution through which a government organizes its policy and program activities and delivers services either to the public or to other governmental institutions. Every department is headed by a cabinet minister who is the political leader of the institution, the link between the department and the cabinet and parliament. See also **service department; support department**.

Department of Finance. One of the key support departments in the federal government and also a central agency of great power and authority. Finance is responsible for setting the annual federal budget and providing the prime minister and cabinet with advice on macro-economic policy, trade, and taxation. See also **central agency**.

departmentalization. In organizational theory the concept that departments can be organized in various ways depending on function, location, clientele, and span of control. See **span of control**.

departmentalized cabinet system. A system of cabinet organization dominant in Ottawa prior to the 1960s and noted for its lack of central agencies and cabinet committees. Policy making was largely decentralized to each department, working under the leadership of the minister and prime minister. Deputy ministers possessed great power in this system. See also **institutionalized cabinet system**.

deputy minister. The administrative head of a department. Deputy ministers are appointed by the prime minister and serve as the most senior public servant in charge of a department. The deputy's role is to be the chief executive officer of the department, responsible for its routine administrative functioning, while also working with the responsible minister on policy and program development. See also **assistant deputy minister; associate deputy minister**.

deregulation. The process of reducing or eliminating outright the legal rules that control and direct the behaviour of firms in the private sector.

Deregulation is typically seen as a conservative policy to free enterprise from excessive, unnecessary, and costly state intervention in private behaviour.

employment equity. The policy that certain socio-demographic groups that have historically suffered discrimination—notably women, Indigenous peoples, people from a visible minority group, and people with disabilities—should be afforded special recognition as the government strives to alleviate discrimination by ensuring that they are represented in the federal public service to the same extent as their proportion of the general population.

equalization policy. Federal policy now enshrined in section 35 of the Constitution Act, 1982, to provide funding to have-not provinces that brings their revenues up to the national provincial average required to provide public services of a quality comparable to the national average. See also **have-not jurisdiction**.

ethics. The concept of appropriate forms of political and bureaucratic decision making within government. The basic principles of government ethics stress that politicians and public servants are to undertake their duties in light of serving the public interest, maintaining fidelity to law, and avoiding having their private interests interfere with their public duties.

expenditure budget. The portion of the general federal budget dealing with government expenditure on policies and programs. The expenditure budget highlights how, where, and toward what desired goals the federal government will expend public monies. See also **revenue budget**.

expenditure management information system. A rationalist financial management system adopted by the Harper government in 2007, closely based on the expenditure management system (EMS) that preceded it. EMIS seeks to integrate planning, programming, and budgeting into a seamless whole but differs from EMS in placing more emphasis on using modern information technologies to do so. See also **expenditure management system; managing for results**.

expenditure management system. A rationalist financial management system adopted by the Chrétien government in 1995 as a successor to the policy and expenditure management system (PEMS). While EMS was very similar to PEMS, it differed in that it was designed to reduce government spending by helping ministers and deputy ministers review ongoing programs and identify areas for spending reduction. Central to EMS was the system of managing for results. See also **expenditure management information system; managing for results**.

Fabian socialism. The British parliamentary tradition of socialism as distinct from Marxism. The term originates in the Fabian Society, founded in London in 1884 by British socialists including playwright George Bernard Shaw. Fabian socialists believe in achieving socialist ends through democratic means centred on winning parliamentary power. The Fabians were early supporters of the British Labour Party.

First Nation. A self-determined organization comprising the descendants of people who formed a society and a system of government prior to the arrival of European settlers in what is now Canada.

Foreign Investment Review Agency. A federal regulatory agency established in 1974 to screen, analyze, and potentially prohibit foreign, especially American, direct investment in Canada in order to promote the Canadianization of the national economy. FIRA was renamed Investment Canada in 1985 and its mandate severely restricted.

government restraint. The policy of restricting or reducing social and economic spending initiatives and promoting privatization and deregulation as ways to cut government spending and deficits and limit the scope of government involvement in the social and economic life of a country.

governor-in-council appointee. A partisan political appointee hired by the prime minister or a minister to a term contract. Appointees are not officially members of the public service per se because they do not hold permanent positions and do not have to be hired through the rules of the Public Service Commission.

guardian. An official in a central agency such as Finance or the Treasury Board of Canada Secretariat whose responsibility is to ensure that all departmental budgets are as prudent as possible and that all spending is subject to strict control and scrutiny. See also **spender.**

have-not jurisdiction. A province in which the ability to levy taxes to fund basic public services falls below the average provincial revenue-generating capacity across the country.

hierarchy. The concept that an organization should be constructed and managed in a pyramid structure, with managerial authority concentrated at the apex of the organization and with power flowing from the top down.

human resources planning. The aspect of management devoted to the recruitment, training, retention, mobilization, and promotion of personnel.

ideology of the centre. The idea that most Canadians are moderate in their political thinking, desiring a blend of conservative, socialist, and liberal policies and a mixed economy in which the state takes a leading part in national socio-economic development but respects the important role of the private sector. In this view, the party that can dominate the middle ground in Canadian politics will reap the most votes and thus win power.

incremental budgeting. A system of budgeting based on incremental changes to the previous year's budget, also known as line-item budgeting. Managers constructing such a budget simply take the one from the previous year as a reference point and alter it to take account of marginal changes in the costs of running its programs. This very simple form of budgeting was officially transcended by rational budgeting but has great staying power as a way of thinking and acting. See also **budgetary rationalism; performance budgeting.**

incrementalism. A theory of management contending that decision making is best done through small, measured steps, rooted in past actions, with the goal of making improvements to existing systems of organization.

institutionalized cabinet system. The system of cabinet organization prevalent in Ottawa from the 1960s on and noted for often intricate systems of cabinet committees supported by an array of central agencies. Institutionalized cabinet systems are designed to facilitate more rational and systematic policy making by requiring it to arise from a decision-making system involving planning, prioritization, and programming based on consensus among a plurality of cabinet committees and central agencies. Such a system is intended to heighten the influence of elected ministers in decision making by lessening the political and administrative influence that any senior unelected official can have.

judicial deference. The practice by which judges in superior courts will defer to, or uphold, the ruling of a quasi-judicial administrative tribunal when a case comes before the court on appeal or through an application for judicial review. Deference is based on the principle that it is the specialized tribunal, and not the generalist court, that is expert in its field of policy and law.

La Relève. A human resources reform policy developed in 1997 to address the perceived "quiet crisis" confronting the federal public service following a major program review in the mid-1990s. La Relève sought to rejuvenate the federal public service by attracting younger Canadians into public service while enhancing management training and centralizing senior executive training.

land claim. A claim advanced by a First Nation to better arrangements with the federal government respecting the allocation of land rights between Indigenous and non-Indigenous populations and the compensation owing to the First Nation for lands relinquished or improperly seized in the past.

legal responsiveness. A principle of accountability stipulating that cabinet ministers and public servants must be responsive to the rules of administrative law in the exercise of administrative and executive authority.

liberalism. An ideology that mediates the competing claims of conservatism and socialism. Liberalism places importance on individualism, freedom, equality of opportunity, private property, and the role of the private sector while stressing that these values and their policy offshoots have to be balanced with the collective well-being of society, equality of condition with respect to fundamental matters of social policy, and a substantial state to regulate the economy in the service of broad national or provincial interests.

Main Estimates. The complete list of all government spending, by department and program, for an entire budgetary year and selected future years.

The Main Estimates are presented to the House of Commons following the annual budget presentation by the minister of finance.

managing for results. A component of the expenditure management system (EMS) and expenditure management information system (EMIS) established in 1995. MFR obligates departments to produce annual business plans that articulate departmental policy and program objectives and the resources needed to achieve them. MFR also requires that departments and the Treasury Board of Canada Secretariat measure the degree to which those goals are being met, and whether alternative, less costly means are viable. MFR remains a vital part of current federal financial management policy via EMIS. See also **expenditure management information system; expenditure management system.**

mandarin. A deputy minister in the departmentalized cabinet system. The term invokes the seemingly omnipresent power and authority of deputy ministers in the running of government. See also **departmentalized cabinet system.**

memorandum to cabinet. The formal document setting out a policy proposal arising from a department and requiring discussion and ratification by cabinet in order to become government policy. A memorandum contains three elements: the policy recommendation, analysis of the policy, and a communications plan for the policy.

merit principle. The concept that all decision making about the hiring, training, promotion, demotion, and firing of public servants should be undertaken strictly according to objective assessments of competence, usually related to education and demonstrated successful job experience, rather than to subjective assessments of a person's political affiliations or personal connections. Merit became the dominant organizing principle of public service human resources policy during World War I and continues to the present.

ministerial responsibility. The principle that cabinet ministers, as legal heads of departments, are individually responsible and answerable to parliament for all matters dealing with the running of their departmental portfolios. Collectively, ministers are responsible for all policy and program decisions made by cabinet on behalf of the government. All ministers are expected to participate in setting strategic policy and to support the strategic and tactical initiatives of the government.

ministry. The term given to the collective comprising the prime minister, cabinet ministers, and ministers of state without portfolios.

multiculturalism. Federal and provincial policy to defend and promote acceptance of a pluralist and welcoming appreciation that Canadian culture is composed of multiple linguistic, ethnic, religious, national, and social groups.

National Capital Region. The combined cities of Ottawa and Gatineau. The NCR forms the administrative and executive heart of the federal government. Whereas most federal public servants work outside the NCR, the vast majority of senior managers and executives work within home departments and agencies domiciled therein.

National Energy Policy. A federal policy in the early 1980s designed to encourage the Canadianization of the energy sector by imposing greater federal taxes on oil and gas, largely generated in Western Canada, and enhancing the role of the federal Crown corporation Petro-Canada in the development and sale of oil and gas. The policy was greatly reviled in Western Canada.

National Policy. A national economic development policy designed in the 1870s by the government of John A. Macdonald to support Canadian industrialization. It imposed high tariffs on imported American-manufactured goods in order to protect the national market for Canadian firms.

New Professionalism. A public service reform idea emerging in the first decade of the twenty-first century stressing the important opportunities and capacities that the newest generation of young public servants—the millennials—can bring to the public service. The key professional values of this group are openness, transparency, creativity, innovation, participation, considered risk-taking, dehierarchicalization, and respect for the traditions of the public service.

new public management. An approach to public sector management that emerged in the 1980s to foster greater economy, efficiency, and effectiveness in government. It emphasized that the public sector should adopt some of the techniques and behaviour of the private sector and grant public servants much greater operational freedom, subject to the overall control of elected politicians.

Office of the Chief Human Resources Officer. Established in 2009, this office replaced the Canada Public Service Agency as the lead institution within the federal public service, and it functions within the parameters of the Treasury Board of Canada Secretariat. Its mandate is to make and promote policies and programs centred on human resources management in the Canadian government, focusing on staff training and development, employment equity, official languages, labour relations, values and ethics, public service renewal, and leadership development. See also **Public Service Commission of Canada; Treasury Board of Canada Secretariat.**

Office of the Conflict of Interest and Ethics Commissioner. An office established in 2007 under the provisions of the Federal Accountability Act. The commissioner is an officer of parliament whose duty is to oversee the application of the Conflict of Interest Code for Members of the House of Commons and the Conflict of Interest Act. The office provides counselling on proper compliance for those covered by these laws. When requested to by MPs, the commissioner can also conduct inquiries into the behaviour of officials subject to the laws.

Office of the Public Sector Integrity Commissioner of Canada. An office established in 2007 under the provisions of the Public Servants Disclosure Protection Act. The commissioner is an officer of parliament whose duty is to promote integrity within the federal government by assisting government organizations in preventing workplace wrongdoing and by providing an effective channel for public servants and citizens to raise confidential concerns about wrongdoing without fear of reprisal.

Official Languages Act, 1969. Federal legislation stipulating that both French and English are the official languages of Canada, that the federal public service must function in both official languages, and that Canadians have the right to receive services from the federal public service in the official language of their choice.

organic-humanistic model. A school of thought holding that organizations are analogous to living entities, populated by human beings with multiple and complex motivations. The role of management is to understand the human dynamics of the organization, its people, and their modes of communication and to participate with employees in developing policy and programs.

parliamentary budget officer. A position created in 2006 as part of the Harper government's commitment to greater accountability. The PBO has a mandate to provide independent analysis to parliament on the state of the nation's finances, the government's estimates, and economic trends and, at the request of a parliamentary committee or an MP, to estimate the cost of any proposal over which parliament has jurisdiction.

participatory management. A form of management, seen as desirable in organizational theory, in which managers interact with employees, seeking their input and knowledge in the development and implementation of well-designed policy and programs, and also encourage employees to take a deep interest in the life of the organization.

pay equity. The policy concept that women are to receive the same pay for work of equal value as that received by men. The government must take corrective action wherever there is a demonstrable imbalance in pay rates for women and men.

performance budgeting. A system of budgeting between incremental and rational approaches, in which an incremental budget is embellished with efficiency evaluations that correlate program expenditures to services provided. See also **budgetary rationalism; incremental budgeting.**

planning-programming-budgeting system. A macro-system of financial management employed by the federal government from 1969 to 1979. PPBS was a comprehensive system of rational budgeting marked by extensive planning, prioritization, cost–benefit analysis, multiyear programming and budgeting, and intricate operational measurement systems. It necessitated enormous time and effort in the development of budgets and became an ongoing dynamic in government departments. See also **budgetary rationalism.**

policy and expenditure management system. A macro-system of financial management employed by the federal government from 1979 to 1993. PEMS was based on the earlier PPBS and similarly endorsed rational planning, prioritization, and program management but allowed departments and ministers more control over financial matters. See also **budgetary rationalism.**

policy network theory. A concept of managerial decision making that views every policy field as a network of public and private institutional actors and interest groups, all interacting and competing as each advances its own interests.

political patronage. Decision making with respect to the hiring, training, promotion, demotion, and firing of public servants according to subjective assessments of their political affiliations or personal connections rather than demonstrated competence. The political patronage system dominated federal human resources policy from Confederation to World War I.

political responsiveness. A principle of accountability stipulating that cabinet ministers and public servants must be responsive to the rules of individual and collective ministerial responsibility in the exercise of administrative and executive authority.

portfolio. The field of jurisdiction of a cabinet minister. A portfolio refers to the department for which a minister is constitutionally responsible as well as all agencies, boards, commissions, and policy responsibilities that fall under the purview of that department.

POSDCORB. An acronym developed by Luther Gulick to highlight the key functions of management: **p**lanning, **o**rganizing, **s**taffing, **d**irecting, **co**ordinating, **r**eporting, and **b**udgeting.

prime minister. The leader of the governing party in parliament and thus the head of government. The prime minister possesses the top leadership role in the federal system as the head of the cabinet and is responsible for the strategic policy and program direction of the government.

Prime Minister's Office. A central agency providing direct policy-making support and operational, administrative, and communications support to the prime minister. The PMO is a wholly partisan body, and the prime minister chooses its employees directly. The senior officials of the PMO, all unelected advisers to the prime minister, rank among the most influential people in the government.

Priorities and Planning Committee. The overarching cabinet committee in institutionalized cabinets of the Trudeau and Mulroney eras. P&P was chaired by the prime minister, with the mandate of coordinating all other cabinet committees and setting the strategic policy direction of the government. P&P was disbanded by Chrétien in 1993, and its strategic policy-making role reverted to the full cabinet under the leadership of the prime minister.

privatization. The process by which governments divest themselves of Crown corporations. Privatization can occur through the outright sale of a Crown corporation to a single private buyer or through share offerings to multiple investors on the stock market.

Privy Council. The formal, constitutionally mandated advisory council to the governor general with respect to the exercise of executive power in the federal government. The Privy Council per se is an honorary body with hundreds of members, but its executive cabinet, consisting of the prime minister and his or her ministers, has lead governmental authority.

Privy Council Office. A central agency providing direct policy-making support and operational, administrative support to the prime minister, the cabinet, and its committees. The PCO is a nonpartisan institution staffed by public servants, functioning as an important link between the political executive and the administrative organs of the federal government in terms of policy and program transmission. The head of the PCO is the clerk of the Privy Council Office and the secretary to cabinet. See also **clerk of the Privy Council.**

program administration. The managerial techniques of implementing public policy. Program administration uses the tools of financial, operational, and human resources management to deliver programs to the public that meet policy goals.

program review. An initiative of the Chrétien government established in 1994 to assist the prime minister and cabinet in eliminating the deficit. Program review required all departments, with the exception of Indian and Northern Affairs, to engage in a highly rationalistic assessment of their policy and program fields, distinguishing between core and secondary or tertiary responsibilities and objectives. The latter were to be downsized or transferred to other levels of government or privatized, while the former were to be streamlined.

PS2000. A human resources reform policy launched by the federal government in 1990 to reinvigorate the federal public service by 2000.

PS2000 was a highly rationalistic approach designed to bring human resources planning for the federal public service into line with similar practices found in the private sector.

Public Accounts Committee. A permanent committee of the House of Commons always chaired by a member of the Official Opposition party. The PAC has the duty to oversee the financial management of the federal government by closely reviewing the reports of the auditor general of Canada and conducting investigations when it deems them necessary.

public administration. The study and oversight of all structures, institutions, policies, and programs of the state. See also **public sector management.**

public choice theory. The management theory that the actions of politicians, public servants, and interest groups in the policy-making and program administration process can be understood in terms of economic and material self-interest.

public policy. The broad priorities, goals, and objectives of a government entity with respect to human activity and the interests of the government. Public policy refers to a set of interpretations of the appropriate outcomes of government actions in a given field.

public sector management. The administrative functioning of the state and its officials. The methods by which state officials organize themselves in order to implement public policies, traditionally focused on the mobilization of financial resources (budgeting policy), human resources (personnel policy), and operational and strategic leadership.

public service. The institutions, organizational structures, and staff of governments designed to facilitate the implementation of laws, public policies, and government programs within society.

Public Service Commission of Canada. The agency responsible for all hiring, promotion, lateral transfer, demotion, and dismissal from the federal public service. The PSC, created in 1967, is the successor to the Civil Service Commission, which was established in 1918 with the mandate to promote and protect the merit principle in all human resources decision making within the federal public service.

Public Service Labour Relations Act. A 2005 revision of the Public Service Staff Relations Act of 1967 that recognizes the right of most federal public servants to engage in collective bargaining with their employer, represented by the Treasury Board of Canada Secretariat. The new legislation continues the legal framework of collective bargaining while modifying certain technical rules respecting the application of the merit principle to hiring and promotion processes to make them more flexible but still subject to collective bargaining and grievance procedures.

Public Service Labour Relations Board. A quasi-judicial administrative tribunal responsible for adjudicating collective bargaining disputes between unionized bargaining units and management and resolving grievances respecting the application of contract language. The board also addresses pay equity disputes and engages in compensation analysis and research.

Public Service Modernization Act. Passed in 2003, the PSMA marks the federal government's latest human resources policy initiative. It is designed to facilitate more efficient staffing decision making, to streamline public service labour relations, to improve accountability, and to ensure greater management training and development through the work of the Canada School of Public Service.

public service renewal. A federal policy dating from 2006 representing a commitment by the Privy Council Office to reform the federal public service through renewed emphasis on recruitment, improved planning and priority setting, staff training and development, and better use of communication technologies to facilitate productivity.

rationalism. A theory of management holding that decision making is best undertaken through comprehensive planning, prioritization, ends–means assessments, cost–benefit analysis, and performance measurement. See also **incrementalism.**

rationality. In public sector management the concept that organizational behaviour should be rooted in ends–means relationships whereby the goal is to achieve a desired end by the most economical, efficient, and effective means possible.

Red Toryism. An ideological variation of conservatism that places importance on tradition, the maintenance of Canada's historic link to Britain and the British monarchy, and the Canadian national collective identity, all of which are seen to require the active protection of the state.

regulation. Public mandates and requirements established by either federal or provincial law to control, direct, and influence the actions of individuals, private firms, or related government institutions in order to achieve a public purpose.

regulatory agency. A government institution that operates semi-independently from the government of the day in order to engage in socio-economic regulation. Regulatory agencies apply legal rules of conduct to individuals, corporations, and other institutions of government with respect to a given field of activity.

reinventing government. A concept of government reform widely promoted by American authors David Osborne and Ted Gaebler. The thesis they advocate involves ten major reform initiatives that governments should adopt.

representativeness of the public service. The concept that the membership of the public service should represent the society it serves by reflecting the socio-demographic diversity of the general population in terms of gender, language, race, religion, colour, region, ability, and so forth.

revenue budget. The portion of the general federal budget dealing with the revenues that the government takes in through taxes, duties, tariffs, user fees, sales of goods and properties, and other income-generating measures in a given year. See also **expenditure budget**.

scientific management. An approach to organizational theory championed by Frederick Taylor in which the role of management is to reduce work to clearly defined, objective practices and methods that can be constantly made more economical, efficient, and effective.

service department. A federal government department whose key policy and program responsibilities are to provide services directly to citizens, corporations, interest groups, and other clients. The majority of federal departments are in this category. See also **support department**.

social conservative. A conservative who emphasizes the importance of social policy and moral issues, usually with a grounding in religious beliefs, as opposed to economic policies and matters of business. While most conservatives believe in a limited socio-economic role for the state, social conservatives stress that it has a vital role to play in regulating matters relating to pornography, abortion, same-sex marriage, and lewdness in mass culture and supporting moral issues such as family values, faith-based welfare policies, and school prayer.

social democracy. The belief that socialist political parties should espouse moderate and practical socio-economic policy positions in order to appeal to the broad centre of the political spectrum. Canadian social democrats assert that the New Democratic Party must be willing and able to work with the private sector in matters of economic policy. They also believe that the NDP must see itself as a political party with a credible message for electors rather than as a visionary movement appealing only to democratic socialists.

social responsiveness. A principle of accountability stipulating that cabinet ministers and public servants must be responsive to the broad social needs and interests of the communities they serve in the exercise of administrative and executive authority.

socialism. An ideology of social collectivism that elevates the concept of class consciousness, the socio-economic interests of common working-class and middle-class people, equality of condition and freedom from want, and concern for the gross inequalities in wealth and power found through the working of a capitalist society and economy. Socialists believe that solutions to the profound social and economic problems found in modern capitalist societies can be found only through active and progressive public policies designed by the state, under the leadership of socialist governments, for the benefit of common people.

socio-economic policy. The collective state policies designed to address social (health, education, welfare, environmental, and cultural) concerns and their relationship to economic (trade, business, income, commercial, and tax) concerns.

span of control. In organizational theory the concept that a superior can exercise effective control and direction only if the number of subordinates is limited. Organizations can be structured with a relatively wide or narrow span of control, depending on the functions of the organization.

special agency. A federal government institution that operates semi-independently from the government of the day to provide a unique service to the government or to Canadians generally. Examples of such agencies are the Canada Revenue Agency and the Canada Border Services Agency. This service delivery necessitates such independent status and leadership and is based on a board of directors or commissioner model.

spender. An official in a line department or agency who is primarily interested in increasing the flow of monies into that institution in order to enhance its program of work and, correspondingly, increase the official's own power, prestige, and workforce. See also **guardian**.

state. The portion of society comprising the broad public sector, as opposed to the private sector, and based on the institutions of government. The Canadian state can be understood as comprising all the institutions accounted for and controlled and directed by the federal government, all provincial and municipal governments, and all First Nations governments. One can also refer to the federal state as all the public institutions in the federal realm and to a provincial state as all the public provincial and municipal institutions in that province.

strategic prime ministership. The policy dynamic of a prime minister who sets the strategic direction of government by selecting four to six key policy and program aims to define his or her four- to five-year term in office. The implementation of these aims will be "brought to the centre" for prime ministerial leadership and direction, while all other, more routine matters of policy and administration will be left to ordinary ministers and departments to manage.

structural-mechanistic model. A school of thought holding that organizations are best understood as analogous to machines, with a definite hierarchical structure, in which the task of management is to design and operate the organizational machine to maximize productive output.

support department. A federal government department whose key policy and program responsibilities are to provide organizational and operational support to the government itself, its institutions, and its policy and program capacity. See also **service department**.

surplus. The budgetary dynamic in which revenues exceed expenditures and other liabilities, resulting in excess monies at the end of a fiscal year. Such surplus monies are then available for new spending.

Treasury Board of Canada. The only statutory cabinet committee of the federal government, established pursuant to the Financial Administration Act, 1985. All other cabinet committees exist at the discretion of the prime minister. The Treasury Board is responsible for federal public service human resources policy, oversight, and management. The minister responsible is referred to as the president of the Treasury Board, and the board usually consists of five or six ministers, one of whom is always the minister of finance. The board is assisted by its administrative wing, the Treasury Board Secretariat. See also **Treasury Board of Canada Secretariat**.

Treasury Board of Canada Secretariat. A central agency providing policy and program advice to the prime minister, cabinet, and all government departments and agencies with respect to internal matters of financial management, human resources management, and accountability. The TBS also acts as the official employer of the federal government with respect to collective bargaining and is responsible for administrative support of this function.

treaty right. An entitlement respecting land, social services, or economic rights extended to First Nations and their members by virtue of legal agreements between First Nations and the Crown.

tribunal. A generic term given to agencies, boards, and commissions that possess both policy development and program implementation responsibilities, as well as legal powers to resolve disputes arising from the application of their powers. These bodies are often referred to as quasi-judicial administrative tribunals in that their roles are half administrative and half adjudicative. Classic examples are labour relations boards, workers' compensation boards, and human rights commissions. Tribunals are subject to the rules of administrative law.

Index

audits and auditing, 228–35

budget of 2009, 64

budgets of 2015 and 2016, 225, 234, 317

deficits and surplus in, 209, 211–12, 224, 225, 234, 236, 317

and Department of Finance, 138

in election of 2015, 206

expenditure budgeting, 214–20, 225–28

Expenditure Management System (EMS), 219–25

expenditures and revenues in, 207, 209–11

incrementalism in, 215, 216–18, 224, 225, 236

main officials and institutions, 214, 215, 223, 226, 230

and national debt, 209, 211, 212, 236

parliamentary budget officer (PBO), 208, 349–51

performance budgeting, 218–19

planning-programming-budgeting system, 219

program budgeting, 219

program reviews of government, 311, 317

purposes and ideal elements of, 215

rationalism in, 215, 219–20, 225, 236

revenue budget, 214

spenders *vs.* guardians, 226–28

systems appraisal, 224–25

tactics used in, 225–28

taxation in, 211, 212–13

See also financial management

bureaucracy

concept and principles of, 171–74

employment in, 172–73, 174

hierarchy of, 124, 172

and management, 161

negative aspects of, 175–76

and organization, 174–75

purpose, 175–76

rules in, 173

and span of control, 177–78

tension in, 123, 130

Weber's view, 171–76

and written records, 173–74, 175

bureaucratic politics theory, 195, 196

Bush, George W., and administration, 24

C

cabinet

citizens in, 84–85

decision making in, 77, 81, 92, 93–94, 130, 131

departmentalized cabinet, 130, 144

discussions and secrecy in, 92–93

formation and selection, 79–80, 83–90

in Harper and Trudeau governments, 87, 91, 93

and ideology, 85

institutionalized cabinets (*See* institutionalized cabinets)

ministerial responsibilities, 92, 95

ministers in, 83–84, 85–90, 92–93, 94, 145

members of parliament (MPs) in, 83–84

as political executive, 77–78, 79–80

and prime minister, 80, 81, 83, 84, 85–86, 87, 88, 92, 93–94

provinces and regions, 85–87

size and structure, 88, 90

cabinet committees, 132–33

Canada Customs and Revenue Agency (CCRA), 248

Canada Health Act, success of, 167–68

Canada Post, 109

Canada Revenue Agency, 101

Canada School of Public Service, 263, 383

Canada–United States Free Trade Agreement (1989), 23

Canadian–American relations, 13, 21–25

Canadian Centre for Management Development, 322, 383

Canadian Environmental Assessment Agency, 112

school for, 263, 383

senior political appointments, 264–65

service delivery, 322

size of, 245–49, 256

strikes, 286–88

and unionization, 283–88

women in, 249–52, 253–54, 255, 277, 280–82

Public Service Commission of Canada (PSC)

employment equity, 280

jurisdiction and role, 64, 66

professionalization, 61–62

and unionization, 284, 286

Public Service Employment Act (PSSRA), 283–84

Public Service Labour Relations Act (PSLRA)
(2005), 284, 286

Public Service Labour Relations Board (PSLRB),
284, 286–87

Public Service Modernization Act (2003), 266, 313,
315

Public Service 2000/PS2000, 265, 310

Purchase, Bryne, 307

Q

Quebec

constitutional aspects, 14–15

as distinct province, 13

French speakers in federal public service, 276

linguistic and cultural policy, 15, 17

as ongoing challenge of federal government, 13–17

as part of Canada, 13–15

referendum of 1995, 14, 16

and regionalism, 17

sponsorship scandal, 354–55

the Queen, executive power, 78

R

rationalism

bounded rationalism, 193, 194, 195, 196

in budgets and budgeting, 215, 219–20, 225, 236

in management decision making, 191–94, 195, 196

political views of, 42

reality *vs.* perception paradox, xxii, 5–6, 30, 373–74

recession of 2008–10, 12, 205–6, 316–17

Red Toryism, 52, 53

reform in management

Blueprint 2020, 266, 267–70, 318–20

changes in Canada, 321–22

evaluation, 323–25, 326

incremental pace, 308–9, 310, 321, 326

initiatives, 310, 311–20

integrated planning, 313–14

new public management (NPM) (*See* new public
management [NPM])

in recruitment and training, 313, 314, 315–16

and reinvention of government (*See* reinvention
of government)

theory in Canada, 306–7

regional development, and audits, 231, 232

regionalism and regional disparities, 13, 17–20

regions, and cabinet, 85–87

regulation, 11, 110–12

regulatory agencies, 110–14

reinvention of government

changes in Canada, 321–22

and Chrétien government, 310–12

criticisms of, 307–10

and Harper government, 312–18

incrementalist approach, 308–9, 310, 321, 326

and J. Trudeau government, 318–20

principles and manifesto, 301–7, 321

public service renewal and initiatives, 312–20

theory in Canada, 306–7

See also new public management (NPM)

La Relève program, 266, 311–12

election promises, 66–67, 149, 206, 234

environment and greenhouse gas policy, 25

expectations of, xviii

financial management, 206, 225, 234

openness, 149–50

and previous government policy and programs, 97, 325

reinvention of government, 318–20

role of government, 7

taxation, 206, 213

and terrorism, 22, 24

U

unionization and unions

collective bargaining, 283, 284–88

federal system, 284–86

history in Canada, 283–84

and labour strikes, 286–88

legislative actions by government, 288

United States, relations with, 13, 21–25

unity, national, 14–15, 17

Urwick, Lyndall, on organization, 177–80, 184, 187

V

Values and Ethics Code for the Public Service, 358, 359–60

values for public service, 358, 359–60

VIA Rail, 109

visible minorities, 87, 281, 282

W

Wall, Brad, 18

War on Terror, 23–24

Weber, Max

on bureaucracy, 171–76

on management, 187

welfare system, 5–6

Western provinces, and regionalism, 17

women, public service and employment equity, 249–52, 253–54, 255, 277, 280–82

Wouters, Wayne, 267, 313–14

Wright, Nigel, 103, 357

written records, in bureaucracy, 173–74, 175

Z

Zussman, David, 316